GRAVE AND GOSPEL

BEIHEFTE DER ZEITSCHRIFT FÜR RELIGIONS- UND GEISTESGESCHICHTE

IN VERBINDUNG MIT F. W. KANTZENBACH UND H.-J. SCHOEPS
HERAUSGEGEBEN VON
HANS - JOACHIM KLIMKEIT

XXX

J.-M. BERENTSEN

GRAVE AND GOSPEL

E. J. BRILL — LEIDEN — 1985

GRAVE AND GOSPEL

BY

J.-M. BERENTSEN

E. J. BRILL — LEIDEN — 1985

ISBN 90 04 07851 7

PRINTED IN THE NETHERLANDS

To Åse
– who shouldered the burdens
and shared the joy.

CONTENTS

ACKNOWLEDGEMENTS

I wish to express my deep gratitude to several persons and institutions for their support in the completion of this study. First of all to co-workers and friends in Kinki Evangelical Lutheran Church, Japan, who received this foreigner with an open heart and an open mind. In their fellowship I was introduced to the fascinating world of Japan and to the problems which I later on got the opportunity to struggle with full time for years.

The possibility of a serious and scholarly approach to the problem of ancestor worship and Christian faith in Japan – the result of which is published in this book – was given when the Norwegian Missionary Society in 1974 called me to a position of research at the School of Mission and Theology, Stavanger. I express my gratitude both to the NMS and to the school and its staff for providing everything needed for effective and rewarding research.

Although I set out on the study after several years of service in Japan the work could not have been carried through without a new visit with the purpose of collecting material and discussing the p. oject with specialists in the field, Japanese and expatriates. This materialized thanks to a scholarship grant from the Norwegian Research Council for Science and the Humanities in 1976. The same institution has provided economic support both for the linguistic check and proof-reading of the final manuscript as well as for its publication. For all I express my deepest gratitude. The same is extended to those institutions and individuals who contributed to make my stay in Japan in 1976 most rewarding. Japan Lutheran Theological College, Tokyo, offered dormitory and library facilities through Professor Ishida Yoshiro; International Christian University, Tokyo, Oriens Institute for Religious Research, Tokyo, and the former International Institute for the Study of Religions, Tokyo, all put their libraries at my disposal and offered opportunities for fruitful exchange of ideas with well known scholars. Especially to be mentioned is Professor Morioka Kiyomi, in 1976 teaching at Tokyo University of Education. The fact that a scholar of Professor Morioka's fame and capacity took of his precious time to guide the young Norwegian in the jungle of relevant Japanese literature and even made it possible to benefit from the kind service of others in his staff, was to me a source of inspiration for which the deepest gratitude is conveyed. For the useful contacts in the Kyoto area my thankfulness is especially expressed to the NCC Center for the Study of Japanese Religions, Kyoto, and to Professor Matsuzawa Kazuko, National Museum of Ethnology, Senri.

From the very outset my work was followed with interest and continuous encouragement by two scholars who more than any one else acted as my advisers. I thank Dr. Nils Egede Bloch-Hoell, Professor at the University of Oslo and director of the Egede Institute, Oslo, and Dr. Aksel Valen-Sendstad, Professor at the School of Mission and Theology, Stavanger, for the kind of constructive critique that makes a researcher press on through problems and difficulties. I also express my gratitude to the University of Oslo for accepting my dissertation as partial requirement for the Degree of Doctor Theologiae, to my opponents Professor Olof Lidin, Copenhagen, and Professor Ludvig Munthe, Oslo, for pertinent critique when the dissertation was defended in September 1982, and to the publisher E.J.Brill, Leiden, for including my work in its series *Beihefte zur Zeitschrift für Religions- und Geistesgeschichte* under the general editorship of Professor Hans-Joachim Klimkeit, Bonn. None of the names mentioned, however, are meant to serve as alibi for what is presented in my study. The author alone carries all responsibility for whatever shortcomings and inconsistencies that may be found.

The present book is a somewhat adjusted and shortened edition of the doctoral dissertation. Reductions have been made mainly in the footnotes. In this connection thanks is expressed to Pastor David A. Roschke, who took upon himself to correct my use of the English language, and to my mother, Mrs. Gudrun Berentsen, who typed the final manuscript. This she did in the long and lonely evenings following the death of my father. In fact, the passing away of both my father and my father-in-law during the years of research in this particular topic made the various problems close and personal in a way that definitely brought my labour beyond the level of academic exercise.

Finally my sincere gratitude is expressed to my wife, Åse, and our three children who all took their share in the hardships that made this work possible. Without their unfailing support the undertaking would have been shelved long since.

Stavanger, May 1985

Jan-Martin Berentsen

0 INTRODUCTION

0.1 *Stating the Problem*

The purpose of the following study is to work with a systematic analysis of basic religious and ethical premises underlying Japanese ancestor worship in order to present the problems this phenomenon creates for Christian faith and attempt a relevant discussion of the theological issues at stake.

This definition of our problem implies that the purpose of our study does not primarily lie within the field of science of religion. In this field as well as in anthropology and sociology, not to mention folklore, studies have been undertaken – although perhaps not yet in abundance – to describe and analyse ancestor worship. We are not, however, primarily interested in ancestor worship from historical, anthropological, and phenomenological points of view. Neither is the purpose of our study to attempt an inquiry into the dissemination of basic ideas underlying ancestor worship in modern Japanese society, i.e., the degree to which these ideas are actually accepted as valid and consciously believed in today.

Our basic presupposition is that the socio-religious phenomenon of ancestor worship is an integral and important element in the cultural heritage that has molded, and still molds the Japanese mind. We want to ask what kind of religious and ethical premises form the basis of this phenomenon, with the subsequent question what problems arise in the meeting between these fundamental suppositions and Christian faith. In other words: What beliefs and concerns about the relationship between individual and collective, life and death, god and man, sustain the ancestral rites, and how are these beliefs and concerns to be viewed and responded to from a Christian point of view?

Our primary task is, accordingly, a confrontation and conversation between Christian faith and the fundamental issues underlying ancestor worship, i.e., a theological conversation centered around theological concerns as these present themselves in the meeting between this socio-religious phenomenon and Christian faith in the Japanese context. More precisely defined in theological terms our study will be in the field of missiology, as a systematic and thorough analysis of such a meeting between Christianity and the religious life of people is an important undertaking for Christian world mission.[1] In our view theology of mission has tended to concentrate its interest on the major, so-called «higher», religions to a degree that has saved little interest and energy for a serious grappling with the more vaguely defined and diverse practices of local folk-religion. In the following study we intend to attempt a contribution to an improvement of this situation.[2]

The confrontation and conversation we are aiming at in this study is something every Christian in Japan, Japanese in the first place but also missionaries, sooner or later have to face. The encounter with ancestral rites presents the church with a complex set of problems which has not yet been made the object of a systematic and comprehensive analysis.

The author's personal interest in the problem was kindled through his meeting with ancestor worship during years of missionary work with Kinki Evangelical Lutheran Church in Japan. At the very outset of our missionary service an evening meal with friends in a prominent, traditional household in old Nara city took place in front of the big and beautifully decorated family altar, leaving strong impressions on our mind. Later on we often made a stop on our way to the railway station in the early morning, watching a neighboring grandmother paying respect to the ancestors in front of the *butsudan* with doors wide open to the garden. What really put us on the trail to a more thorough investigation into these problems, however, was the conversation with a recently-baptized, young mother, who – in her narrow apartment flat – had lit candles and incense sticks below a picture of her newly-departed father placed on the book-shelf, and the late-at-night talk with the young man who withdrew his request for baptism because he was about to take over the responsibilities for his family's *butsudan*. With experiences like these the author met people who said: «Ancestor worship is idolatry.» If so, on what basis is this judgment made? Others contended: «Ancestor worship is nothing but the Japanese version of the Christian's fourth commandment.» If so, how can such a judgment be justified? The main thesis of our study is that ancestor worship as a socio-religious phenomenon cannot be adequately considered along either the one or the other of these two lines of thought. It has to be dealt with in a more complex way which calls for both rejection and acceptance on the part of the Christian.[3]

0.2 *Method and Progression*

Following a presentation of the ancestral rites' place in life in historical and actual perspectives, an important part of our task will be a limited systematic analysis of ancestor worship from the point of view of its religious and ethical significance and implications.

The phenomenon of ancestor worship in Japan is an extremely complicated one involving ancestors on household, clan, and national levels. Furthermore, it is found within different religious contexts, i.e., in Buddhism, Shinto, and the New Religions.[4] We will, however, for the purposes of our study limit ourselves to the household level, and as the historical process of religious development in Japan made Buddhism the primary vehicle for traditional ancestor worship on folk-level, we will focus on ancestor worship in the context of traditional Japanese Buddhism.

These two limitations are made, however, more out of the need for a methodologically responsible way of handling a vast material than on the basis of clear-cut distinctions in actual life. Such distinctions do not exist. Clan and national ancestors, and ancestor worship in contexts other than that of traditional Buddhism may therefore be taken into consideration in so far as they shed light on important issues in our discussion.

In addition to the limitations just stated, our study is limited also in the sense that we will base our systematic analysis on printed sources and research done in the fields of science of religion, folklore, anthropology, and sociology. We do not pretend to do primary research in these fields, even though a systematic analysis of the main motives sustaining the ancestral rites like the one we will undertake may be of significance also from the point of view of the science of religion's question: What is ancestor worship?

Basic research, by outstanding Japanese scholars such as Yanagida Kunio, Ariga Kizaemon, Hori Ichiro, Takeda Choshu, et al., has contributed vastly to the understanding of Japanese ancestor worship. Their writings are available mainly in the Japanese language, in books and numerous articles. Mention should also be made of Maeda Takashi's *Sosen suhai no kenkyu* (*A Study in Ancestor Worship*), 1965, which is a basic and comprehensive sociological analysis, and Tamamuro Taijo's *Soshiki Bukkyo* (*Funeral Buddhism*), 1963/1974, which is a study in folk-Buddhism with special reference to its forms of ancestor worship.[5] Modern Japanese research in this field is of fairly young date as it has flourished only after the Second World War with the following end to the taboo on thought and scholarship since the Meiji era.[6]

It would be an impossible task for our purpose to go through all Japanese-language material on ancestor worship. We base our analysis on what we have found to be a fairly representative selection for a responsible interpretation of the phenomenon. As may be inferred from the listing of the above-mentioned scholars and from our bibliography, relevant material for our study has been found mainly in the research done in Japanese folk-religion and popular Buddhism.

In Western languages, especially in English, ancestor worship has been dealt with in several publications since the end of the war. Compared with works dealing with Japanese religion in general and particular religions such as Buddhism and Shinto, however, publications dealing especially with ancestor worship are not numerous. In our view scholarly interest in this phenomenon has been out of proportion to its actual significance in the religious life of the people. The sources we have used will be referred to in their proper place in our text below. Here should be mentioned only R.J. Smith's *Ancestor Worship in Contemporary Japan*, 1974, which is the first comprehensive study to appear on the topic in a Western language.

We collect our information to the basic question «What is Japanese ancestor worship?» on an important premise. We start with the presupposition that ancestor worship has a cognitive content expressed through symbols like prayer and sacrifice, which makes it possible to interpret the phenomenon and draw information from literary sources as to what religious and ethical ideas are involved. This is important even if it may be impossible to arrange this «content» into anything like a «systematic theology» of ancestor worship, which we think it is. To work, then, on an interpretation of ancestor worship based on printed sources forms the methodological basis for our systematic analysis.

To which extent a person engaged in ancestor worship is aware of this «content», accepts it as valid, and consciously believes in it, is a question which cannot be answered through a study like this. There may well be a gap between a reasonable interpretation of the symbols in their religious context and the subjective explanation given by a particular individual when it comes to personal involvement in the rites.[7] Some may take part in ancestor worship simply out of custom and/or social pressure. Some may perform the rites out of a deep conviction of the validity of the spiritual realities expressed through the symbols. Some may be ambivalent in their attitude, half believing, half ignoring or rejecting its spiritual basis.

A research into this problem – as important it may be – is not what we are aiming at, although reference in due time will be made to existing data on this aspect of the problem of ancestor worship in modern Japan.

A second premise for our study – already hinted at – has to be stated plainly. We do not consider ancestor worship in Japanese context to be treated as an isolated religious practice. It is rather to be seen as a socio-religious substratum underlying and integrated into various religious contexts. This is well documented through research already done. Hori Ichiro, for example, sees ancestor worship as a significant element in what he calls «Japanese folk religion». His rationale for treating this «folk religion» as an entity is not that it operates as a distinct religious body but the fact that there are several significant, common tendencies running through the variety of Japanese religions. These common elements are what constitutes Japanese folk religion, in itself again a conglomerate of intermingled religious beliefs and practices.[8]

Our decision to limit ourselves to ancestor worship in traditional Buddhism is not contradictory to what we are now saying. Although ancestral rites are found – in one form or another – in almost every religious context, the contextual garment most familiar to the average Japanese is without comparison the traditional Buddhist one. As is well documented by Takeda Choshu, Buddhism on folk level in Japan was understood and absorbed in terms of ancestor worship, and ancestor worship was carried out in terms of Buddhism.

Such a limitation of our study to popular Buddhist context may obscure interesting peculiarities of ancestor worship in other surroundings. Nevertheless, it assures – in our view – an interpretation congenial with the basic issues of ancestor worship as a folk religious practice. This is supported by the fact that except for one point, to which we shall return below, there seem to be only minor variations of ancestor worship within the different schools of traditional Buddhism in Japan.

Following the systematic analysis of basic motives involved in a proper interpretation of ancestor worship we shall proceed to a discussion of these issues in the light of the Christian faith. Questions to the problem of individual-collective, life-death, human-divine raised and answered in the context of traditional ancestor worship have to be taken seriously on part of the church. They are all concerns of central importance also in Christianity. The Christian, therefore, has to address himself in earnest to these questions from the standpoint of his faith in order to be able to communicate the gospel in a relevant and adequate way to a mind molded in the spiritual milieu of ancestor worship.

We will try to proceed in this discussion referring to attitudes, interpretations, and conclusions drawn in various quarters of Christianity in Japan. Although we have not as yet seen any comprehensive theological treatment of this subject the various problems have been dealt with in articles in church periodicals, in handbooks for Christians, in catechetical material, and in pamphlets. In accordance with our main objective, however, no systematic analysis of the different denominations' attitudes to ancestor worship will be undertaken. Material from different churches will be used only to shed light upon the theological issues at stake, whereas our conversation itself will be a systematic-theological approach to the basic problems that emerge from Christianity's encounter with ancestor worship. No doubt any evaluation of these problems, and consequently one's whole approach to ancestor worship, may differ according to one's personal position within the Christian tradition, as we shall have ample opportunity to see. It should therefore be stated that our own stand is the Evangelical Lutheran confession, which will be reflected in our approach to and discussion of the various problems.

Ancestor worship has presented a problem all through the history of Christianity in Japan. The problem came into focus already in the history of the *Kirishitans* in the seventeenth century. Aspects of the same phenomenon created tensions between church and state as well as within the churches by the rise and reign of State Shinto and nationalism with its emperor worship leading up to the Second World War. Again we see aspects of the same problem in the never ending discussion on the Yasukuni shrine for the war-dead.[10] Since ours is not a historical study, however, we will draw upon such material only in so far as it may contribute to our systematic-theological discussion.

Abbreviations

The following abbreviations will be found in the text and/or notes:

CA: Confessio Augustana/The Augsburg Confession IMC: International Missionary Council LWF: Lutheran World Federation RGG: Die Religion in Geschichte und Gegenwart RSV: The Holy Bible, Revised Standard Version WA: Weimar Edition of Luther's works WCC: World Council of Churches

Notes to Introduction

1. Especially since the Tambaram meeting of the International Missionary Council with H. Kraemer's famous book *The Christian Message in a Non-Christian World*, this has been a concern of first priority within the international missionary movement, and subsequently within the modern ecumenical movement. Cf. the study project «The Word of God and the living faiths of men», which was launched in 1955 in cooperation between the World Council of Churches and the IMC and has led to the extensive and ongoing program of dialogue sponsored by the WCC since the latter half of the 1960's. For a brief introduction to the development in this field since the Tambaram meeting see Hallenkreutz 1970. Cf. further Hwang 1967 on the study of ancestor worship in light of the Christian faith as a must for missiologists. A recent Lutheran voice to the problems presented by ancestor worship in the Japanese context is Shibata 1978.
2. Cf. similar concerns articulated by Professor Harry Parkin, Nommesen University, Sumatra, at the All-Asia Lutheran Conference, Singapore, 1976 (Lutheran World Federation 1976, pp. 10–11).
3. The problem of Christian approach to ancestor worship is well known in other contexts both in Asia and other parts of the world. The closest parallel to the Japanese situation would probably be the Chinese. There are differences in the practice of ancestor worship, however, that – among other things – make it advisable for us to limit ourselves to the Japanese scene (cf. Smith 1974, p. VII). That is not to say that the problems discussed in this study are of no interest in the Chinese and other contexts.
4. For our purpose we are not in the need of a strict definition of the term «New Religions», which may be difficult to give. What we are referring to by this term is «religious organizations that have come into being outside the framework of the established Shinto, Buddhist, or Christian bodies and maintain an independent existence» (Agency for Cultural Affairs 1972, p. 92).
5. Japanese names are rendered according to Japanese custom, surname first followed by given name. The spelling system employed in our transcription of Japanese words is the modified Hepburn system most commonly used in Japanese-English dictionaries. However, neither in names nor in other Japanese words used in the text will any difference be made between long and short u and o. Italics are used for transcribed Japanese terms and also for book-titles. As for quotations, however, these are left as they are whether they conform to our own system of italics or not.
6. This is pointed out in Takeda 1957/1975, p.5, and may be one simple reason for the «paucity of information» on the practice of ancestor worship which R.J. Smith finds hard to explain (Smith, op.cit., p. VII).
7. This is a gap pointed out and elaborated on in Ooms 1967, pp. 292 ff., and in Maeda 1965, especially in the chapter «Sosen suhai no suitai» («The Decline of Ancestor Worship»), pp. 157–231. (The chapter is translated and published in extenso in Newell 1976 A, pp. 143 ff.)

8. Cf. Hori 1968, chapter I: «Main Features of Folk Religion in Japan», esp. pp. 10–11.
9. Cf. Takeda op.cit., pp. 214 ff.
10. In order to distinguish between Shinto and Buddhist sanctuaries the term «shrine» will be used for a Shinto sanctuary, while «temple» will be reserved for Buddhist ones.

1 ANCESTOR WORSHIP – ITS «SITZ IM LEBEN»

Before we enter into our analysis of basic religious and ethical premises upon which ancestor worship functions and the subsequent conversation with Christian faith, a presentation of the «sitz im leben» of this socio-religious phenomenon is necessary. By this we mean to include a sketch of the ancestral rites in historical perspective, a presentation and preliminary discussion of central terms, and a brief delineation of the actual functioning of ancestor worship in household and temple setting.

Even though our study is neither a historical nor a semantic or sociological inquiry, such a threefold presentation of ancestor worship's role in actual life is important. Firstly, in order to comprehend the scope and the nature of the problems involved in the confrontation between ancestral rites and Christian faith, it is imperative to have some understanding of the role of the rites in the history of the Japanese people. Is Christian faith at this point encountering a socio-religious phenomenon that has been with the people for ages, or is it encountering a practice that has been brought to the islands in recent centuries? Are we confronted with a problem that has only been of marginal significance, or one that has played a major role?

Secondly, a particular difficulty in a study like ours is the language-problem. This is already apparent when we look at the very concept «ancestor worship» itself. Is this a pertinent rendering of the corresponding Japanese terms? It is further obvious from this example that actual terminology and content matter of the terms are closely interrelated. It is important for us, therefore, to give a presentation of the most important Japanese concepts used in connection with the ancestral rites together with a preliminary discussion of their content matter.

Thirdly, a delineation of the pattern of ancestor worship in household and temple setting is necessary in order to depict as concretely as possible the phenomenon with which we are subsequently going to deal on a theoretic level. This should help us to keep in mind the practical ramifications of our discussion with respect to the actual household and temple community, and it will hopefully prevent our encounter from developing into a purely academic exercise.

Our presentation of the «sitz im leben» of the ancestral rites is, in other words, a threefold look at the garments in which Japanese ancestor worship is dressed.

1.1 *Ancestor Worship in Historical Perspective*

Is ancestor worship an original, indigenous Japanese phenomenon? Is it a practice which was brought to Japan from China together with Buddhism in the seventh century A.D.? Or, as a third possibility, is ancestor worship, as it developed in Japan over the centuries and is to be observed today, an amalgamation of indigenous, and imported Buddhist and Confucian beliefs?

Even a first and superficial acquaintance with the phenomenon shows that Japanologists have been very much in disagreement as to the correct answer to questions like these.[1]

As a typical example of the position which regards Japanese ancestor worship as a purely Chinese import, we may quote an article in *Transactions and Proceedings of the Japan Society, London*, from 1915: «A few words as to Teijo's reverence for his ancestors. This, too, Japan learned from China; and it was only very slowly that the institution of ancestor worship spread amongst the upper classes.... There is not a particle of evidence to show that it was known to or practised by the Japanese people in the early centuries of their history.»[2]

A somewhat more modified and differentiated position, but still in the category which denies genuine ancestor worship any significance in indigenous Japanese beliefs as seen in primitive Shinto, is that of the noted Japanologist W.G. Aston. «If we restrict this term [ancestor worship] to the religious cult of one's ancestors, as in China, this form of religion has hardly any place in Shinto.»[3] Aston concedes to the existence of what he calls «pseudo-ancestor-worship» among the nobility, meaning that some of the nobles «traced their lineage from, and paid a special worship to, personages who never existed as individual human beings.» The common people, however, had «no ancestor worship, pseudo or real.»[4] Michel Revon, accordingly, presents Aston's position by a brief quotation from another of his works: «Shinto, the old native religion of Japan, had no cult of true ancestors.»[5]

Then there are scholars who advocate an opinion on the origin of Japanese ancestor worship almost diametrically opposed to that of Hall and Aston. To these scholars ancestor worship is not only an indigenous Japanese practice but is the very core of original Shinto. Strong advocates of this opinion were found already among the Shinto revivalists of the *kokugaku*-school in the eighteenth and nineteenth century, and their view was to have a significant influence on many Western scholars.[6]

The writer who, perhaps more than anyone else, introduced Japanese ancestor worship to the popular West as the «real religion of Japan», was Lafcadio Hearn.[7] Believing firmly in Spencerian theories on the evolution of religion, he saw «the family cult» as «the first in evolutional order» also on Japan's religious scene.[8] «The real religion of Japan, the religion still professed in one form or other by the entire nation, is that cult which has been the foundation of all civilized religion, and of all civilized society – ancestor worship.»[9]

When Revon, in the article referred to above, sees the truth about ancestor worship and pre-Buddhist Japan as lying somewhere between these two extremes, he seems to be supported in his view by modern Japanology and Japanese folklore. After the first far-reaching impact of Chinese culture in the seventh century, ancestor worship in Japan was dressed in Buddhist clothing and subsequently understood in terms of Buddhist thought. About this there seems to be little doubt. But there can neither be any doubt that when Buddhist ancestor worship spread so rapidly, and finally was almost universally adopted, one important reason was the fact that it proved a well-suited vehicle for basic elements in indigenous Japanese thought. This is well documented by the excellent research of Japanese folklorists after the war.[10] When Buddhism in Japan was absorbed and digested in terms of ancestor worship, and ancestor worship subsequently carried out in Buddhist terms, the reason for this lies both in the basic features of indigenous Japanese thought itself and in the fundamentals of Buddhism. Ancestor worship, as it developed after the introduction of Buddhism, came to represent a Buddhist dress-up of indigenous Japanese thought.[11]

When it comes to the actual content of ancestor worship in the pre-Buddhist age, and whether it is more to the point to speak of a vague and undifferentiated cult of the dead instead of «ancestor worship», opinions vary, mainly because of the scarcity of available material.[12] Ancestor worship is not directly spoken of in the oldest written records to Japanese history, the *Kojiki* (Record of Ancient Matters) of 712 A.D. and the

Nihon-shoki (Chronicles of Japan) of 720 A.D. Takeda Choshu may nevertheless be right when he points out that indirectly it is at its very center. The raison d'être, namely, for the sovereignity of the emperor in the old records is the sovereignity of his ancestor. That the justification of the ruling position of the emperor-family took the form of relating him to the highest possible ancestor (the sun-goddess) shows the strong position of ancestor worship among the people at that time, according to Takeda.[13]

From studies of non-literary sources, however, such as folklore studies and studies of burial practices, inferences have been drawn to the actual content of this early practice.[14] From ancient times the Japanese have thought of the corpse and the spirit as separable entities. After death the spirit separated from the corpse and continued its existence. This spirit of the dead was to be feared, cared for, and worshipped with utmost attention and courteousness. It was believed in some way – through the course of time – to develop into an ancestral spirit, a supra-individual «ancestor» or a *kami*.[15] An important point to note is the belief that these ancestral spirits were not thought to move away from the world of the living. They were believed to remain in close communication and interaction with the living, protecting their descendants and returning home on certain occasions during the year.[16]

Already at this early stage ancestor worship was intimately tied to the institutions of the household (the *ie*) and the clan (the *uji*).[17] It is impossible to speak of the one without the other. According to Hori Ichiro these two concepts, the «ancestor» and the «household», may well be seen as the two essential elements in Japanese religion and consciousness and, according to Takeda, Japan has in no period of its history escaped from the principles of the *ie*-structure, to which ancestor worship belongs.[18] The intimate relationship between ancestor worship and household/clan already in the pre-Buddhist era is clearly observed in the coalescence of ancestral deities and tutelary clan-gods (*ujigami*).[19]

The phenomenon of ancestor worship, which for more than a millenium has been dressed in Buddhist garments, has – in other words – roots down in indigenous pre-Buddhist Japanese folk-beliefs. The belief in the continued existence of the soul, its gradual development into the status of an ancestral spirit, the communication and interaction between the dead and the living, and the intimate relationship between this religious practice and the social milieu in household and clan, were all Japanese essentials for which Buddhism proved a suitable vehicle towards a thorough amalgamation of indigenous and foreign ideas. Thus original Japanese soil seems to have made the basis for popular Buddhist belief to spread in Japan. The Buddhism of memorial rites and ancestor worship was more attractive and understandable to the Japanese than the complicated, lofty and esoteric kind.[20]

The development of ancestor worship in Japan after the introduction of Buddhism is easier to trace, since from now on there is no lack of written sources.

In many respects the great reform of 645 A.D.,the Taika-reform, represents the apex of the early Buddhist and Confucian influence from China upon Japan. With this reform as its basis, «Japanese Buddhism was made a spiritual principle of the empire system, and also the spiritual foundation of the great family system of that time. Ancestor worship became one of its most significant functions.»[21] The Taika-reform made important regulations in burial practices,[22] and Buddhist funeral services and subsequent masses for the dead were introduced on the Japanese scene.[23] Even if Tamamuro Taijo may be right in pointing out that the Pure Land-sect of the early Kamakura era (1185–1333) was the first sect to develop a Buddhist funeral service for the masses,[24] different funeral rites and masses for the dead had by that time been in practice in the early Buddhist sects for centuries. Both in the Tendai and the Shingon sects these ceremonies, with their reading of sutras and recitation of *nembutsu*, were conducted in order to have a salvatory effect on the dead.[25] In this connection it is interesting for us to note that what later developed into a permanent family-altar for the worship of the ancestors – the *butsudan* – took its beginning in this early era as a temporarily-erected altar for the services towards the dead.[26]

Another important aspect of the association of Buddhism with ancestor worship in these early days, is the construction of Buddhist images, erection of temples, copying of sutras etc., with the expressed purpose of serving the well-being of the dead.[27] Takeda gives an interesting example on this dating from 658 A.D.: «This image of Amita-Buddha was constructed by Asemaoko, a widow, in honour of her deceased husband, Sako of Ichi, in a spirit of veneration. May my dead husband, the generations of ancestors and all the beings in the universe attain to eternal religious enlightenment and pleasure by the virtues and the merits of this image.»[28]

More or less powerful clans and families erected their own clan-temple (*ujidera*) for the benefit of their deceased ancestors. This was a custom which proved to be extremely important for the development of Buddhism in Japan, and it became a symbol of the unity between ancestor worship and Japanese Buddhism. The *ujidera* became the Buddhist parallel to the indigenous *ujigami*.[29]

As a third point to the early association of Buddhism with ancestor worship, we note the great mid-summer Bon-festival, or Festival of the Dead, the greatest of Japanese Buddhism's yearly festivals. It is a festival totally focused on ancestor worship, built upon a sutra known in Japanese as the *Urabon-kyo*, which gives the basis for the necessity of caring for the ancestors through prayers and offerings.[30] According to Smith, reference to the Bon-festival is found already in the *Nihon-shoki*, «which reports that in 606 the Empress Suiko (554–628) ordered its observance in all the temples of the country», and which – with regard to the *Urabon-kyo* – states that Empress Saimei (655–661) in 659 ordered the sutra to «be expounded in all the temples of the capital and 'requital made to the ancestors of seven generations'».[31]

The Bon-festival which reached Japan in Buddhist clothing, was already at that time a highly syncretistic observance, containing «Central Asian Buddhist, Hindu, Taoist, and Confucian elements, to which the Japanese were to add many indigenous beliefs and practices».[32] The festival spread among the common people over the years and seems, by the end of the twelfth century, to have been universally observed, replacing the native mid-summer spirit-festival.[33]

The Kamakura era (1185–1333), then, represents the decades when ancestor worship in the form of funeral services and subsequent masses for the dead, intrinsically linked to the clan-temple and the Bon-festival, spread among the common people together with Buddhism. With the Jodo sect of Honen the funeral services and masses for the dead, with their salvatory chanting of the *nembutsu*, spread rapidly. In the first half of the medieval period (1185–1603) the funerals of common people turned out to be mainly of this type.[34] The founders of the True Pure Land (Jodo-shinshu or only Shinshu) sect saw in this development a strong animistic, magic, and non-Buddhist influence on true Buddhist doctrine. With their emphasis on faith in Amida alone as the only way of salvation, they rejected from the very beginning the common practice in all the other sects of offering food and chanting of *nembutsu* for the salvation of the dead. However, the common people did not follow the True Pure Land teaching in this respect.[35] On the contrary, in this first half of the medieval period all the sects of Buddhism flourished to the extent to which they conformed to these basic elements of old popular folk-beliefs, centering around funerals and masses for the dead with their close relationship to ancestor worship.[36]

Tamamuro gives in summary the following four points to remember as to the reason for the rapid spread of Buddhist temples in this period, especially over the years from 1467 to 1665:

1 The most important point of contact with the common people was the funerals and masses.
2 The most elaborated funeral sects, the Jodo and the Zen, spread markedly.
3 The other sects spread to the extent to which they were «funeralized».
4 The relationship between temple and families was strengthened through this centering around funerals and masses.[37]

Having traced the development so far, we are, however, already at the beginning of the Tokugawa era (1603–1868), which presents new, decisive, and interesting aspects.

The decisive trend in the development now became intimately linked to the Tokugawa government's ban on the new and foreign Christian religion. In the process of suppression of Christianity, Tokugawa Ieyasu's edict of January 27, 1614 played an important role. The edict points out that Japan is the land of Shinto gods and of Buddha. «But the Kirishitan band have come to Japan, not only sending their merchant vessels to exchange commodities, but also longing to disseminate an evil law, to overthrow right doctrine, so that they may change the government of this country, and obtain possession of the land. This is the germ of great disaster, and must be crushed».[38]

The best way for the government to crush the *Kirishitan* band was to obtain an effective supervision of the total population to ensure its religious orthodoxy. For this purpose the Tokugawas decided to use the numerous Buddhist temples and priests, and Ieyasu's edict was accompanied by a set of 15 rules to guide the priests in the supervision. It is very interesting – for our purpose – to note that one of the paragraphs explicitly mentioned that persons who failed to attend the various ancestral rites and festivals were to be examined and reported.[39]

In order to ensure an effective system of reporting, every household in the nation was required to register as parishioners and supporters of a certain temple. In this way the Tokugawa government enforced by law a formal and compulsory relationship between household and Buddhist temple, the so-called *danka*-system. This system was to have a profound influence upon the subsequent development of the nation down to our days. A central bureau of registration was established in 1640, followed by local offices in all parts of the country, in order to supervise the enforcement of the system.[40]

The effect of this was twofold. First, the definite tendency to concentrate ancestor worship on funerals and masses for the dead, already prevalent in pre-Tokugawa days with the corresponding tendency on part of the sects to concentrate their life and work on such activities, was greatly reinforced. Second, the dissemination of these activities in the population was eventually completed. «Under this system every member of the nation was regarded as a believer in Buddhism, though not all of them became so of their own accord. Buddhist believers were required to delegate to their temples all acts in regard to their ancestor worship, such as the funeral service for family members, memorial services for the dead and mainte-nance of burial places. Also, the expenses necessary for the upkeep of the temples to which they belonged were shared among the votaries. Disobe-diance to any of these was regarded as an act of political treason.»[41]

From this time on, funerals and masses for the dead became the prime occupation of the Buddhist priests and temples and the cornerstone in the economy of the various sects.

The process, however, did not go on without protest. The *Kirishitans* were effectively silenced, but the misuse of the *danka*-system by political and religious authorities to intimidate the masses, among other things, led eventually to severe critique from Confucianists and scholars of the School of National Learning, many of whom severed their ties with Buddhism altogether.[42]

Out of this protest against Buddhism, Confucian and Shinto funerals were born, Confucian first and then – more or less as a copy – came Shinto rites.[43] The protest was never directed against ancestor worship as such, but against Buddhism monopolizing what these people considered to be pure Confucian and Shinto ideals. With the great scholars of the *koku-gaku*-school, Shinto and Confucian ideas united in a powerful religious and political anti-Buddhist and anti-Tokugawa drive. Coining popular slogans like «Unity of Politics and Religion», «Down with Buddha, Destroy Shaka», this movement eventually led to the downfall of the Tokugawa government and to the famous Meiji-restoration in 1868.

The Meiji-restoration represents the end of the feudalistic era, and both the ban on Christianity and the *danka*-system with its compulsory adhe-rence to Buddhism were legally abolished. A serious attempt was made to replace Buddhism with Shinto as official state religion, and, as a means to disestablish Buddhism, Shinto funerals and masses for the dead were propagated among the masses. In this respect, however, the restoration was not successful. Time was not ripe for the immediate introduction of Shinto as state religion. The hold of Buddhist practices on the people was so strong that the masses by and large remained with the traditional rites and their formal ties with the temples, in spite of the legal fall of the *danka*-system.[44]

Notwithstanding this lack of immediate success, the Shinto-Confucian restoration had a far-reaching influence both upon the actual content of ancestor worship and upon its role in society.

In the *kokugaku*-tradition the so-called *kokutai*-ideology developed, a nationalistic philosophy focusing on the essence and entity of the Japanese nation. In this philosophy ancestor worship played a central role, centering as the ideology did around the idea of the emperor as the descendant of the common, national ancestors of the people, and the head of the Japanese «household».[45] Ancestor worship, thus, provided a cornerstone for the surging emperor-worship and was in this phenomenon eventually expanded to its maximum national apex. These ideas were codified and brought to the people through the Imperial Rescript on Education of 1890.

Just as important was the fact that the old household-institution (the *ie*) was regarded and propagated as the necessary basis for the modern society now to be built, in spite of democratization and Westernization, «and, accordingly, the rule of ancestor worship remained with it».[46] This was the view of the traditionalists in the heated, year-long debate on modernization between this group and more Western-oriented modernists. The traditionalists carried the day in the discussion, and the institution of the household with its ancestor worship was coded in legal terms in the Meiji Civil Code, finally promulgated in 1898. Especially relevant for our purposes is Article 987:

> Ownership of the genealogical record, articles of worship, and tombs is a special right pertaining to succession to a house.[47]

Thus through the Imperial Rescript on Education and the Meiji Civil Code, ancestor worship and filial piety together with emperor worship and loyalty, were legally codified as the pivots around which both the lives of individuals and the life of the nation came to center toward the end of World War II. Ancestor worship was not only preserved in its old forms, it was strengthened and utilized for new and wider purposes.[48]

Japan's defeat by the end of World War II, with the profound reorientation which this triggered off, represents the last step in our delineation of ancestor worship in historical perspective and brings us to the contemporary scene.

A look at the legal changes that took place shows clearly how ancestor worship and the *ie*-institution were at the center of this ideological reorientation. The New Constitution that was promulgated, replacing the old one of Meiji, took a firm stand in modern democratic principles like respect of the individual, equality of the sexes and freedom of belief. This necessitated revision of the old civil code, rooted as it was in the traditional, patriarchal household-structure, with definite legal consequences as to family-status, inheritance, continuation of the house and ancestor worship. Exactly to this point, the revision of the civil code triggered a new and lively discussion between conservatives and liberals both in the revision committees and in the National Assembly. The first party was eager to maintain as far as possible the old principles, the second eager to scrap the old forms altogether.[49]

When the New Civil Code finally came into effect on January 27, 1948, it was a civil code which «provides in most respects for a very different kind of family structure. The household is no longer a legal entity and its head is stripped of its powers».[50] Legally Japan turned away from the old *ie*-structure to that of the Western nuclear family.

At one important point, however, the New Civil Code clearly presents a compromise between the conservative and liberal interests. Article 897 reads:

> The ownership of genealogical records, of utensils of religious rites, and of tombs and burial grounds is succeeded to the person who is, according to custom, to hold as a president the worship of the memory of the ancestors.[51]

Here, in other words, the inheritance of the ancestor cult is exempted expressis verbis from the general rule of division of property, and provisions are made for its inheritance by the person who, «according to custom», should be responsible for its continuance.

Opinions vary considerably among Japanese scholars as to the interpretation and consequences of this article. Some defend it on grounds of pragmatic-practical reasons, saying that the Japanese will hand down their ancestral cult in this manner anyway. Ancestor worship «becomes a matter of concern to the new law only in cases where it gives rise to litigation», and the article is not intended to limit the freedom of belief stated in the constitution.[52] Others have launched a severe attack on the article, saying that in practice it amounts to a solid protection of the *ie*-system and, indirectly, to a support of ancestor worship which flies in the face of the constitution's stipulation of freedom of belief.[53]

However this may be, the very existence of Article 897 is in itself a strong proof of the influence and actual position of ancestor worship in Japan. Stoetzel may be right in drawing the following conclusion: «... it cannot be said that the law encourages the traditional family or ancestor worship; but neither, on the other hand, does it prevent either of these institutions from functioning.»[54]

There is more to be said, however, about ancestor worship in post-war Japan than may be inferred from the country's civil code, although research shows that it is not an easy task to assess its actual significance in the population today.[55]

We referred above to the discussion between conservatives and liberals. Obviously, the new ideas had their ardent supporters among the Japanese, at least among educated people and in the intelligentsia. To say, therefore, that the constitutional and legal changes were completely forced upon the people by foreign forces (i.e., the allied forces), would not be true. When it comes to the broad masses, however, it may well be the case that these changes were not born out of «internal necessity» but out of «external powers» and were received with «a considerable amount of embarass-ment».[56] Neither were the legal changes believed to generate any rapid change in the actual life of the people.[57]

Nevertheless, the years since the war have, in the wake of industrializa-tion and urbanization, brought about great changes to the family, affecting the position of ancestor worship. The large-scale migration from rural areas to the cities caused great numbers of families and individuals to move away from their traditional site of residence and their traditional ties with the temple, and establish themselves as small, nuclear, urban families. The contact with their original temple became more or less sporadic, in many cases severed completely, and as «metropolitan priests were not active in reaching out to these newcomers ... a large population, free from any parish ties, appeared in metropolitan areas.»[58]

When more than 70% of the population now is reported to live in a nuclear-type family consisting of one or two generations, and the rate of nuclear families in urban areas actually keeping a family altar in their home is only 30%, these are statistics which imply that a great proportion of the population today live without immediate contact with traditional, daily ancestor worship.[59] This may be a safe conclusion even though the rate of possession of altars among the 20–30% living in the extended-type families is between 90 and 100%, in rural and urban areas alike.[60]

It is not, on the other hand, to be concluded that the absence of an altar in a modern nuclear family simply proves that the family has turned its back on ancestor worship as such. This is an extremely complicated question with many factors involved. One simple reason for the absence of the altar may be that the nuclear family in question is a branch of a household whose ancestral tablets are taken care of by some other member of the family, for example the husband's older brother. What will be done in the nuclear family, however, when the first of its own members die? This is a problem which the family has yet to face.[61]

Obviously the decline of the *ie*-institution has resulted in a decline of ancestor worship as it was traditionally practiced within the household, with its close ties to the native parish temple. The traditional «process of daily proselytization in the family has nearly disappeared» when it comes to most nuclear families.[62] This is an enormous challenge which many new and old urban temples have taken up. In their attempts to establish new contact with the «religiously floating population», funeral services and masses for the dead are used as an effective pipeline.[63]

The problem of the decline of traditional ancestor worship, however, is not only a problem of change in its traditional, environmental structure. When Maeda Takashi discusses the reasons for the rather low participation in ancestor worship on the part of the young, he points out that it cannot be fully explained by the social position of the young in the family structure, not yet involving any responsibilities for the family altar. There is a great difference in the depth of the «ancestor faith» between today's old and young generation.[64] Maeda observes, namely, the same difference in rate of worship between the old and the young when it comes to worship of the *ujigami* of the Shinto shrine. When the young do not bow in front of the *ujigami*, it has nothing to do with social position and family structures but with their religious faith and devotion. The reason for their attitude towards the ancestors may be the same.[65]

What Maeda here is saying is that the decline of traditional ancestor worship has to do with the much wider problem of secularization over against traditional religion in general. In the midst of this process of secularization, the attitude of the young to ancestor worship may be characterized by doubts and inconsistencies, by external conformity to social pressure, and by internal discrepancy between rational thinking and religious feeling.[66]

Ancestor worship in modern Japan is, in other words, caught in a dual dilemma, that of profound changes in sociological structures, and that óf secularization over against traditional religious values. In this respect, as in many others, the present seems to be a transient situation, puzzling both to the general public and to the temples.

What does this hold for the future? Is ancestor worship simply to vanish? This does not seem to be the case. Apart from the fact that it is still continued in traditional ways by some part of the population, there are significant things to notice.

For one thing, ancestor worship plays an important role in all of the new religious sects flourishing in the midst of modernization and secularization. As typical examples we could mention Rissho Kosei-Kai and Seicho no Ie.[67] There are very interesting things to notice concerning ancestor worship in Rissho Kosei-Kai, for example. In this context deliberate changes seem to have been made in order to make ancestor worship up to date in the new society based upon values like respect of the individual and equality of the sexes. In the traditional *ie*-setting, ancestor worship was and is geared to paternalistic and feudal patterns of the household, centering around ancestors of patrilineal descent and leaving out those of the wife and other outsiders. Rissho Kosei-Kai, however, explicitly states that ancestor worship in their context involves ancestors «in both our paternal and maternal families».[68] Not only this, in the family altar any deceased person may be enshrined: «Posthumous names will be given to any deceased person whom you desire to enshrine in the family altar. You may receive such names for as many persons as possible because such a practice consoles the spirits of the dead and transfers your merit to them for the attainment of Buddha-hood.»[69] Here the old, traditional religious values of ancestor worship are definitely geared to new sociological structures in modern Japan, making them more attractive not least to women and young people.

Secondly, special attention should be paid to the striking activities of a certain temple in Osaka, the Isshinji.[70] The speciality of this temple is to perform masses for deceased persons who did not live in family relationships which assure that these rites are taken care of in the ordinary way. Bones of such persons are turned in to the temple after death. Out of these human bones Buddha-statues are eventually made and erected in the temple and rites performed for these persons.[71]

Although the temple reports of some decline in the number of entrusted bodies after the war, there is nothing to suggest that its peculiar activity is dying. People still bring to the temple the remains of persons whose souls are to be taken care of.[72]

Among other things, Fujii draws the following conclusions from interviews he has made among people making use of the temple: 1. To leave one's bones entrusted with Isshinji serves as a prevention against negligence after death. 2. Isshinji answers a religious need in the massses, especially the masses which do not have other means through which they may be cared for after death.[73]

Isshinji is a peculiar example, having no real parallel in Japan. It may, however, serve to show that even though we may speak of a general decline of the traditional milieu of ancestor worship, a lot of people still take special precautions if they will not in some way be taken care of after death by their own descendants.

It also serves to show that the problem of ancestor worship in contemporary Japan is not only a problem of sociological structures but one of existential, religious significance, touching upon the very fundamentals of human life. Looking towards the future, therefore, we venture to conjecture that no matter how the external structures of society may change, ancestor worship may persist in some form or other, unless these fundamental religious problems are answered in other ways and by other means.

We have attempted to trace very briefly the history of ancestor worship down to our days. Our next task is to give a preliminary presentation of the most significant terms related to ancestor worship.

1.2 *Terms and Concepts: A Preliminary Discussion*

This is not yet the place to enter into a deeper analysis of the cognitive content of significant terminology related to ancestor worship. However, the fact that we have already used some of the terms, e.g., «ancestor», «worship», «household»/*ie*, without any attempt at definition, makes it clear that a preliminary discussion of central and often repeated terminology is due.

We have repeatedly used the term *ie*-structure for the traditional Japanese family system, and we have seen how closely it is related to ancestor worship. Any analysis of the latter has to take its departure in an analysis of the *ie*-structure.

We have partly rendered the term *ie* with the English household, family, and partly used the Japanese term itself. This is done deliberately, because the term *ie* has a particular content for which there is no real English

equivalent. A look at a Japanese dictionary makes this clear. A whole series
of different meanings and nuances may be given to explain the term. For
our purposes the first three points listed in *Kojien* are of importance:

1   house; dwelling place;
2   group of people living in the same house; family; household, espe-
    cially as seen in the traditional extended family;
3   «house» as transmitted from the ancestors and maintained through
    generations, including name, occupation, craft etc.[75]

Of these three meanings (2) points to *ie* in its horizontal dimension,
including family and kin in any actual generation, while (3) points to *ie* in
its vertical dimension, signifying its lineage through the generations.
    There is another Japanese term for «family»: *Kazoku*.According to
Takeda Choshu, however, there is an important difference between these
two concepts. *Kazoku* is a general concept used for the ultimate unit of
social life for which most peoples have their equivalents. *Ie*, on the other
hand, is a peculiar Japanese concept, denoting *kazoku* in a fixed system.
Kazoku is a nuclear family of one generation, established by marriage,
terminating at death, whereas *ie* is a multigeneration, everlasting entity,
established by the ancestors and transmitted through the generations.[76]
Thus *ie* as a fixed system and an everlasting entity is of the greatest
significance in relation to ancestor worship. We shall return below to the
actual structure of the *ie*, its internal relationships, the important distinction between «main house»/ *honke* and «branch house»/*bunke*, and its
relationship to the clan/*dozoku*. At this point, a quotation from George
B. Sansom may suffice to underline the peculiarities of the traditional
Japanese *ie*: «The distinguishing feature of the Japanese family system is
the importance of the house as contrasted with an indeterminate group of
blood relations loosely described as a family.... To be more precise, the
House is composed of the head of the House and of members who are
subject to his authority. Those members may include not only his kindred
by relationship of blood, but also persons, male and female, who are not
his blood relations and who enter the House with his consent. The House
is in fact a name group and not a blood group.»[77]

Closely related to the system of *ie*, then, is the term «ancestor» as a
translation of *sosen* or *senzo*.[78] Who are the «ancestors»? What are the
qualifications needed in order to be counted an «ancestor»? The question
is basic but at the same time extremely complicated to answer. This is well

documented by the fact that there are almost as many definitions as there are scholars.[79] Scholars agree, however, that the term is an elastic one that may be used in a stricter or looser sense, so that in fact «ancestor worship involves more than worship of ancestors.»[80]

A very brief and fairly clear definition of the term is the following given by Hirai Atsuko: «Strictly speaking, an ancestor is the founder of iye; in a looser sense, it means parents to successive generations of iye, especially the parents of the generation here and now».[81]

The interesting thing in this definition is that the distinction between «ancestor» «strictly speaking» and «ancestor» in «a looser sense» is drawn between the founder of the *ie* and the parents of succeeding generations. This reflects a very significant and real distinction in the Japanese use of the term.

We have already in note 4 mentioned Ariga Kizaemon's distinction between «lineal ancestors» («ancestor I») and «ancestors of origin» («ancestor II»).[82] «Ancestor I» includes the founder of the *ie* and those of his descendants who have carried the *ie* from generation to generation. «Ancestor II» denotes the person from whom the founder is thought to have derived.

Now, the significant thing here is that the «ancestor II» served as a basis and a guarantee for the unique position of the founder of the *ie*. If this purpose could be effected, the «ancestor II» did not necessarily have to be genealogically related to «ancestor I». In many cases the «ancestor II» was fictitious or a postulate, serving to enhance the position of the *ie*-founder.[83]

Also according to Takeda Choshu, the importance of the founder of the *ie* can hardly be overemphasized. The basis of ancestor worship lies exactly in this ultimate value of the *ie*-founder. The real meaning of *sosen/senzo* does not lie in the person pointed to but in his status as worthy of worship as an *ie*-founder.[84]

In Hirai's definition quoted above, «ancestor» in a looser sense means «parents to successive generations of iye, especially the parents of the generation here and now». These ancestors may well be termed «ancestors proper».[85] They are the traditional Japanese «ie senzo daidai reii» (the souls of all the ancestors of the house).[86] Concerning the actual counting of ancestors along the line of descent, Smith says: «In every interview I conducted, I found that the ancestors of the house were reckoned from the generation of the founder. That is, each branch house considered its founder to be its senior ancestor.... A man takes care of the ancestors of his own house, not those of the house from which he has branched off or in which he was born but with which he no longer has much contact.»[87]

When it comes to persons actually included in a looser meaning of the term «ancestor», however, the group may even be wider than Hirai's «parents to successive generations». The extensive investigation of ancestral tablets found in family altars which Smith has undertaken, offers interesting facts on this point. According to Smith, the tablets found may be organized in three groups: Lineal tablets, Non-lineal tablets, and Non-kin tablets. The first group include tablets of «all persons related in any way to the descent line», both males and females, adults and children.[89] This group account for by far the greatest number of tablets. The second group are persons «entirely unrelated to the direct line of succession.... the kin of those who either have been adopted in or have married in».[90] The third group «are persons entirely unrelated to any past or present Lineal or Non-lineal member of the household. Tablets in this category might include one for a teacher, a stranger, a lover, etc.»[91]

People interviewed by Smith had no difficulties justifying the presence of the first group of tablets in the family altar. They seemed to deserve their place there according to traditional practice, even without being «parents to successive generations». The second group (and the third), however, «represent an anomaly. There is absolutely nothing – either in the rationale for ancestor worship or in the principles that most people invoke in explaining what tablets one ought to have in the altar and why they should be there – that explains the presence of tablets for Non-lineals.»[92] From this Smith draws the following conclusion: «I suggest that the practice of placing Non-lineal tablets in the household altar may be a fairly recent and increasingly common one.»[93] Deceased persons of all the three groups were, however, referred to as «ancestors», even though not all should be termed «ancestors» of the *ie* according to «the traditional meaning of the term 'ancestor' in Japan.»[94]

We may, in other words, note three meanings of the term «ancestor»:

1   The founder of the *ie* as the senior ancestor or ancestor par excellence.

2   The «ancestors» of the *ie* traditionally meaning «the souls of all the ancestors of the house», counted in a stricter or looser sense.
3   Any deceased person whose tablet may be found in a family altar and who, accordingly, is an object of the rites performed.[95]

Asking the question who the ancestors are, there is, however, one more thing to be mentioned. The term «ancestor» is not to be defined solely on the basis of social structures and relationships. It has also a specifically qualitative implication. The real status of «ancestor» is, namely, ordinarily not attained simply by way of death. It involves a process of growth in three stages, from the status of a «spirit of the dead»/*shirei* to that of an «ancestral spirit»/*sorei*.[96]

The first stage in this process is the 49 days following death. This is a period of uncertainty for the «spirit of the dead»/*shirei*. During this period its tablet is usually placed separately in front of the *butsudan*. On the 49th day the tablet is raised to the family altar itself, symbolizing an elevation in the status of the dead. The soul hereby enters the second stage and may now be called *niisenzo*/«new ancestor».[97] The soul is, however, still subject to change and growth over the years, and the step leading to the final and decisive stage is not reached before the *tomuraiage* at the 33rd anniversary after death. By this time, the spirit looses its individuality and joins the supra-individual, collective, anonymous group of the ancestors of generations. It becomes a full-fledged *sorei*/«ancestral spirit», and is subject to no more growth. It has attained the status of partaking in a supra-individual, ultimate, holy and protective being. Ideally, the individual tablet is now to be removed from the altar, brought to the temple, and replaced at the *butsudan* by a tablet symbolizing the collective group of the household's ancestors through generations.[98]

The term «ancestor» is not, accordingly, a concept that should be used indiscriminately for all the dead. Such an all-embracing term for the dead exists, however, in the word *hotoke*, the Japanese equivalent for buddha. Originating, probably, in popular interpretation or misinterpretation of Buddhist doctrine, the expression «to become *hotoke*» in the minds of the people simply came to mean to die.[99] Thus, in referring to their *hotoke* people include indiscriminately all spirits enshrined in their family altar, regardless of their actual position in the process toward «ancestor-hood».

Using this terminology there is, however, an important distinction to make, the one between *hotoke* and *muen-botoke*, «buddhas without attachment or affiliation».[100] Within this group of *muen-botoke* there may be different categories, but they are all united in the same unhappy fate not to follow the normal course to «ancestor-hood». They are not remembered and cared for by their offspring, either because they do not have any or because they are neglected.[101]

Then, finally, let us turn to the different terms used for the act which is rendered by the English word «worship», and to the distinction between *sosen suhai*/ancestor worship strictly speaking, and *sosen kuyo*/masses for the dead.

Is it adequate to talk about ancestor «worship» in a Japanese context? Or should it rather be termed ancestor «veneration»? Is the translation «ancestor worship» an overstatement of what is actually taking place? On the other hand: Would the translation «ancestor veneration» be an understatement with regard to the descendants' attitude toward their ancestors?

In Christian terminology there is a decisive difference between these two terms. The former – worship – is terminus technicus for the proper human attitude toward God. The latter may be used both in this man-God context, and – just as well – to describe a certain attitude in inter-human relationships. God is the object of worship and veneration. Man may be object of veneration, but never of worship. Is it possible to draw such a line of demarcation among Japanese terminological equivalents for concepts like «worship», «veneration» as these are used in relation to ancestors?[102]

The two Japanese terms most frequently used for «ancestor worship» are *sosen suhai* and *senzo matsuri*.[103] Besides these ancestor worship is often referred to as *sosen sukei* or *senzo saishi*. Using verbs, the expression «to worship the ancestors» may be *sosen o suhai suru, sukei suru, reihai suru, ogamu, matsuru*. In all these verbal expressions both the idea of religious worship and that of veneration/respect are included. In some the one may be more prevalent than the other. The term *matsuri* (verb: *matsuru*, in characters written by both the *sai* and the *shi* in the above-mentioned *saishi*) is the most common expression used for the worship of *kami* in Shinto. The terms *reihai suru* and *ogamu* are terms which Japanese Christians use for the worship of God. The same may to a certain degree be said about *suhai suru*.[104] The one of the above-mentioned terms which may come closest to the English «veneration»/«respect» in interhuman relationships is probably *sukei suru*.[105]

The important thing for us to notice, however, is that Japanese scholars as well as common people seem to use all these terms interchangeably when it comes to ancestor worship, or at least without any decisive distinction as to their content and implications.[106]

The actual usage of these terms in Japanese literature, in other words, does not justify the drawing of any sharp line of demarcation between some terms used for inter-human relationships, including one's relationship with the ancestors, and others used for one's worship of the divine.

When it comes to the implications of the term «*suhai suru*», it seems that to translate «venerate» deliberately in order to tune down religious implications in the direction of «worship» would not do justice to its inherent meaning. According to Maeda, the word *suhai* implies a recognition of supernatural power on the part of the object of «worship», à recognition that the object of *suhai* is superior to man and is in a position to control the life of the «worshipper».[107]

Thus even a preliminary terminological inquiry seems to make clear that a translation of *sosen suhai* like «ancestor veneration», as a conscious rejection of the expression «ancestor worship», might give a wrong impression of Japanese ancestor worship as simple memorialism and nothing more. The actual Japanese terminological usage seems to validate the following conclusion by Smith: «I have no doubt that the family's dead are its gods. Like all gods they are worshipped and petitioned.»[108]

When we use the term «ancestor worship», however, it has to be noted that we do not imply this act of worship/veneration alone. An extremely important element in the *senzo matsuri* is the masses for the benefit of the dead, which in Japanese terminology is spoken of as *sosen kuyo*.[109] The basis for these masses for the dead is the belief in the transfer of merits/*tsui-zen-eko*, from the living to the dead. In *sosen kuyo* the important thing is, in other words, not that the dead are prayed to, as in *sosen suhai*, but that they are prayed for.[110]

Some of the occasions for ancestor worship, then, are dominated by the *kuyo*-aspect, while others are dominated by the *suhai*-aspect. And, likewise, the attitude toward some of the dead enshrined in the altar may be dominated by that of worship and supplication, while the attitude toward others is dominated by that of care and a desire to assist.[111] A consistent and clear-cut distinction between these two aspects is, however, impossible to draw. They are not to be regarded as two separate phenomena, but rather as different aspects of the one phenomenon which is referred to by the overriding term «ancestor worship». Terminologically, therefore, the expression «ancestor worship» is rather unfortunate, since it tends to exclude the *kuyo*-aspect in the mind of the reader. When we continue to use it here, it is simply for a lack of a better, inclusive term.

This should be sufficient as a preliminary discussion. All the concepts we have discussed in this chapter are of the greatest significance for a proper understanding of ancestor worship in the Japanese context, and we will have ample opportunity to return to the actual meaning of these terminological symbols in our analysis below.

As a final step in our delineation of ancestor worship's «sitz im leben», we turn to a sketch of its actual functioning in household and temple setting.

1.3 Ancestor Worship in Household and Temple Setting

The following sketch of the actual functioning of ancestor worship in home and temple setting is drawn with a definite feeling of uneasiness. This is a field, namely, of great variety in actual practices. Practices may vary both according to Buddhist sect and geographical location, and variations may be observed from household to household even when sect and locality are one and the same. It is not our task to try to depict and account for all these varieties, even though we shall report some of them. We shall attempt a synthetic approach focusing on chief elements, admitting a danger in not giving due attention to local and other differences.

1.3.1 Household-Temple: Interwoven in Ancestor Worship

What is said above regarding central terms related to ancestor worship indicates that these rites have their primary «sitz im leben» in the context of the household. As functions of «the religion of the household»[112] ancestral rites are to a large extent performed in the home, by its members, at the family altar and/or the family grave.[113]

The widespread involvement of temples and priests in the performance of ancestral rites is, in other words, not so much seen as a sine-qua-non for the efficacy of these rites, as a practical expediency enhancing their worth. In some of the rites temple and priests are involved; in others they are not. In some of the rites where they are involved, for example the funeral, they may seem more indispensable than in others, for example the subsequent masses. Actual practical cooperation in ancestor worship is carried out, in other words, between the household on the one hand and the family temple on the other.

The invisible link between the living and the dead members of the household is symbolized through the family altar and the grave, where, accordingly, most of the rites for the dead take place.[114]

The butsudan, which usually occupies a central position in the home, may be a modest one or a gorgeous and extremely expensive one, depending on several circumstances. The simplest and most modest kind of family altar consists simply of a tablet (or tablets) of the dead with the necessary utensils placed upon an ordinary shelf, while the expensive butsudan is a large guilded altar of the height of the room itself. The standard of the *butsudan* may often be regarded as a symbol of one's regard for the ancestors, and may therefore at times greatly exceed the economic level of the family.[115]

The most important item to be kept in the *butsudan* is without doubt the small tablets/*ihai* for the dead, with their posthumous name/*kaimyo* inscribed. This *ihai* is simply the constituting element in the family altar, its sine-qua-non.[116] One more significant item which may be kept in the *butsudan* is the «book of the past», the *kakocho*, where the death-days of all the dead who are to be taken care of (at the actual altar) are entered.

A *butsudan* may be appropriated simply by way of inheritance, which is the case with the person traditionally singled out as the successor to the family cult. A newly established family which is not in the position to inherit any altar, a so-called branch-family, will probably not appropriate a *butsudan* before a member of this new family dies. On this occasion tablets and posthumous name will be provided by the temple, and – so far as this is received and put up in the home – a new family altar is per definition appropriated.

The second pivot of the ancestral rites is the grave. Traditionally speaking this is the family grave located in a graveyard attached to the family temple. In this respect, however, industrialization and urbanization have created almost unsolvable problems for political authorities as well as for individual families. Large scale migration to the cities has separated a large bulk of the population from the site of their traditional family grave, and the need for new land for industry and city-building often clashes head on both with the desire of local groups of people to preserve old burial sites and with the desperate need for new ones.[117]

According to Fujii, death in a city-family leaves the bereaved with three choices:

1   To bury the dead after funeral service in – or arranged by – a city temple in the traditional family temple at one's place of birth and thus renew one's ties with that temple.

2   To bury the dead in the city temple where the funeral service is performed and thus enter into a new relationship with a new family temple.

3   To leave the ashes of the dead and the tablet with a public charnel house after the funeral service and severe one's temple relations altogether.[118]

However this may be done, actual graves are marked with gravestones, which are sometimes erected for individuals and sometimes erected to all the ancestors of the house collectively. In the first case, the stone bears the posthumous name of the person if it is a temple graveyard, and the name used during the person's lifetime if it is a secular graveyard. In the second case the stone is marked «... ke no senzo daidai no haka.» («The grave of the ancestors of all generations of the ... family.»)

This grave, the actual place of interment, serves as a place of ritual for some of the succeeding ancestral rites. Visits are made to the grave. It is regularly cleaned. Offerings are brought, and prayers said.

However, a special word should be said about a unique Japanese burial custom often referred to as the «double-grave system». According to this burial system, the place of interment and the subsequent place of ritual are not one and the same, but separated immediately or some time after the burial. The first grave/*umebaka* or *sutebaka* is where the corpse is actually put. This grave is more or less isolated and is not to be visited again for later rituals. For ritual purposes a special grave/*mairibaka* is made. At this second grave the subsequent rites for the dead take place. This is a burial practice that has been fairly widespread and is still in use in certain areas of the country, especially in the Kinki region, although the single-grave system is by far the most common today.[119]

The public correlation to the family altar, the tablet for the dead with its posthumous name, and the grave is the family temple/*bodaiji*.[120] Three components are essential in the functioning of a family temple: The temple, the resident priest or priests, and the supporting families.[121] The traditional reciprocal relationship between these three runs briefly stated as follows: The temple keeps the family grave of its supporters in the temple graveyard. The priests take care of the ceremonies for the repose of the soul of the dead and care for the religious life of the family, while the family provides the financial support for the existence of the temple and the priests. The normal activity of the *bodaiji* concerning the dead members of the supporting families, may be systematized in two groups:

1   Temple festivals at the spring and autumn equinoxes (*higan-e*) and at Bon (*urabon-e*). In connection with these festivals there are rites for the unmourned dead (*segaki-e*) and a week of sutra reading in front of family altars in the homes.

2   Masses for the dead in the homes on monthly, yearly and other fixed occasions, performed upon the request of the families. [122]

The responsibility for the performance of the ancestral rites lies – as stated above – with the household and its members, while it, to a large extent, is carried out in actual cooperation with the family temple. To get a clearer picture of the kind of rites involved, we shall use a distinction between rites – or a set of rites – performed only once, and rites that are to be repeated daily or yearly and perpetuated through the generations. This is a distinction which roughly coincides with a distinction between rites for individuals and rites for the collective ancestors.[123]

1.3.2 *Rites Not to Be Repeated (Rites for Individuals)*

This series of rites starts out with the funeral, which in turn is followed by a limited number of masses for the repose of the soul of the deceased.

The preparations for the funeral are in the cities taken care of by professional undertakers, whereas in rural districts they are still often in the hands of local community groups. Parallel with practical preparations, the recitation of sutras may start, performed either by a priest or by a suitable layman. The first religious ritual of any importance, however, is the reading of the *makura-gyo* (the «pillow-sutra-chanting») at the time of the placing of the dead in the coffin. This is supposed to be read by a priest, and often represents the first visit from the temple.[124] It is followed by the vigil/*tsuya*, and the next day, then, is time for the funeral proper/*sos-hiki*.[125]

Whether held in the home or in the temple, the service is conducted by one or several priests. Of the main elements in the funeral service firstly to be mentioned is the reading of sutras. There are practical differences at this point in different sects, but sutra-recitation as such is always a chief element in the service. In most of the sects it is understood as having a salvatory effect on the dead. Shin-shu, however, denies this and regards the sutra-chanting simply as a kind of «evangelism» over against the mourners present.[126]

A second important element, by Gabriel called «der Glanzpunkt des buddhistischen Begräbnisses»,[127] is the solemn entrusting of the dead into the care of the Buddha, the socalled *indo-watashi*. In connection with the *indo-watashi* there may be a sermon, which again is followed by renewed recitation of sutras.

A third essential element is the offering of incense towards the end of the ceremony. The priest starts the offering and is usually followed by the members of the mourning family and – in turn – by all the people present at the funeral, who offer incense sticks either provided by the organizers of the funeral or taken along by the participants themselves.

Upon the completion of the funeral service, the coffin is brought to the crematory, where the family will gather once again the following morning to collect the bones. These are not immediately buried, however, but the urn is brought home and placed in the temporary altar erected for the coming ceremonies. The ashes are kept in this altar for a certain period of time and subsequently taken to the grave and buried, an occasion which may or may not involve religious ceremonies.[128]

While the burial represents the end of the funeral, the funeral itself is, as we said, only the first in a series of rites for the deceased individual. It is followed by the masses or memorial services/*hoji, hoyo* or *butsuji*-ceremonies, which in many respects may be seen as «essentially periodic repetitions of the funeral ceremonies».[129]

As to the place for the performance of the masses and the actual officiants of the rites, practices vary and there does not seem to exist any obligatory pattern. The rites may be performed at home or at the family temple. Priests may be called upon to perform the rites, or they may be performed by the house head or any other qualified person in the family. The pattern that seems to be most widespread, however, is to have the masses conducted at home and to have the priest come, mainly for the proper reading of the prayers and sutras.[130]

The actual set of rites now to start may well be ordered in two stages, corresponding to important stages in the «growth» of the spirit of the dead: The rites performed up to the *imiake* at the 49th day after death, and those performed from the time of *imiake* until the *tomuraiage* at the 33rd or 50th anniversary. (This last group is also called the *nenki*.) In some areas ceremonies may be performed every day for the first 49 days.[131] Most common, however, is probably the seven seventh-day masses on the 7th, 14th,.... days, culminating in the ceremony on the 49th day, the so-called *7x7 hoji* rites. From then on the frequency of rites is reduced drastically. To the 7x7 pattern are added periodic rites on the 100th day after death, on the 1st, 3rd, 7th, 13th anniversaries, culminating in the *tomuraiage* at the 33rd anniversary. This makes up a set of altogether 13 *hoji*- or *butsuji*-masses for the sake of the deceased individual, often referred to as the «13-masses pattern».

However, this pattern is by no means universally adopted. Smith may be right when he says about the rites following the 49th day: «Practices vary widely, but in general these rites are held on all or some of the following anniversaries of death: the first, third, seventh, thirteenth, seventeenth, twenty-third, twenty-seventh, thirty-third, fiftieth and hundredth.»[133] Which ones of these altogether 18 possible rites are actually observed in any particular case, may vary greatly from family to family.[134]

Whatever the pattern may be, the occasion for such a periodic rite is a rather important event in the family. Usually kin and close friends are invited for the ceremony, which in case of the first 7x7 is performed in front of the temporary altar. Later on the *nenki* may be performed in front of the *butsudan*, or a separate altar may again be set up in the *tokonoma* for the occasion. In the latter case the tablet for the person in question will be brought from the *butsudan* together with food offerings, incense, and other paraphernalia, and placed at the separate altar. Usually the priest of the family temple takes part as the leader of the ceremony, reading the sutras, and, in some cases, delivering a sermon.[135] The ceremony usually ends with a meal prepared for all the relatives and friends present. In many cases it also involves a visit to the cemetary, where sutras are read and offerings left at the grave.[136]

When the series of *nenki* ends at the *tomuraiage*, it marks a new turning point in the process of the individual spirit of the dead. Ideally this should be demonstrated by removing the tablet of the individual from the *butsudan* and having it disposed of in some way or other, a practice that in many cases seems to be neglected.[137]

Parallel with this set of periodic *hoji*-ceremonies there are two other groups of rites that should be mentioned. The one is what is usually called by the term *shotsuki* or *shotsuki-meinichi*, and refers to the annual death-day rite. This is a rite, in other words, that takes place every year on the date of the person's death. The second is called *gakki* or *mai-tsuki-meini-chi*, and refers to the monthly death-day rite. It is a rite that takes place every month on the day at which the person passed away.[138] These monthly and annual rites resemble the periodic ones in the fact that they are rites directed to a certain individual for a certain period of time, and are not to be perpetuated through the generations. They are, however, of a far more modest scale than the periodic *hoji*-masses and are discontinued after a fairly short period of time.

Now, let us turn to the other set of rites and festivals which are in many respects of a somewhat different nature.

1.3.3 *Rites to Be Repeated (Rites for the Collective Ancestors)*

The first and most decisive point on which these rites differ from the *hoji*-ceremonies is that they are not directed towards and performed for the sake of a particular individual but oriented towards the collectivity of the ancestors represented in the family altar.[139] Neither is the period of time for the performance of these rites limited in any way. They are supposed to be carried out daily or yearly infinitely through the generations. Their raison d'être may be found partly in needs on the part of the dead, partly in needs on the part of the living.

First in this category should be mentioned the rites performed daily. These are rites of a purely domestic character with no temple or priest involved. In spite of a danger to oversystematize, we could perhaps make a distinction between the rites that involve offerings and are performed by one member of the family as a representative of the rest, and rites that involve no offerings and may be performed on a purely individual basis by any member of the family.[140]

Daily offerings at the *butsudan* are a common feature.[141] In some families these offerings are made both morning and evening, in others only once a day and then most often in the morning. This usually takes place before the family eats. Incense sticks are lit, and offerings are made of rice and tea or water. Besides these most common items the offering may practically include a share of whatever the family has for its meal. The offering is brought by a representative of the family, often the house head, mostly, however, by his wife or his mother, and does not require «concerted action by the whole family».[142]

Just as these formal offerings may be seen from the viewpoint of sharing with the ancestors, the family will also share – in a more informal way – any particular delicacies or gifts of food they may receive. This may be done either by placing some part of the gift at the altar before the rest is eaten, or by placing the whole thing for a while at the altar.[143]

Together with these daily offerings go praying, talking, reporting, and giving thanks to the ancestors. These elements may not be conspicuous in the formal offertory rite,[144] but they are important parts of what we above systematized as the second group of daily rites. Any member of the family may at any time go before the *butsudan* for such purposes. The most common and simplest form of such an individual partaking in everyday ancestor worship is a brief, formal bow with palms together. The actual situation and the circumstances of the family and the individual will further to a large extent determine the form of the address to the ancestors.

On an ordinary day a prayer may go like this: «Please, keep this house safe through another day.» On the day of the son's or the daughter's entrance examination to the university, a prayer for success may be said. In the case of success then, a joyful report with due thanksgiving will be offered. The ancestors may at any time be held informed on important events in the family, their help may be solicited and grateful thanks offered.

These everyday rites reflect, in other words, partly a need on the part of the ancestors, partly a need on the part of the living, picturing both groups as living in an interdependent relationship that we shall return to in a later chapter.

Secondly, we have rites and festivals taking place on an annual or semi-annual basis, the Bon festival, the New Year festival, and the Higan festivals at the spring and autumn equinoxes. In these festivals we again see domestic rites and temple festivals interwoven in ancestor worship.

Of the four seasonal holidays Bon is definitely the most important seen from the point of view of ancestor worship.[145] Due to the different traditions intermingled in the Bon festival, it is not surprising to find elements of a somewhat conflicting nature. The basic dual nature of Bon is aptly pointed out by Inoguchi when he says that Buddhism made an old Japanese ancestor festival, which was concerned with the joyful rendez-vous of the living with their ancestors, into a festival which primary concern was the salvation of the souls, especially those who were stricken by some kind of misfortune.[146] This double nature is still obvious in the festival, which in most places is celebrated from 13th to 15th of August. Together with New Year, Bon is the main holiday of the year with stores and offices closed and the whole nation on the move for reunion of families.

Prior to the 13th, preparations are carried out making everything ready for the festival. The family grave is cleaned, flowers are left at the grave, and incense burned. Traditionally a path may be cleared and lights or torches put up to guide the ancestors back home. At home the *butsudan* is cleaned and decorated, and special Bon-lanterns may be hung around the altar and at the gate. A special altar/*shorodana* may be set up in the *tokonoma* for the Bon rites, and outside the house another separate altar may be erected for the *muenbotoke*, the wandering spirits who do not have a family with which to unite. On the 13th, flowers, incense, and food offerings are brought before the tablets, which may be placed at the *shorodana*. The Bon-lanterns are lighted, a welcome fire is lit at the entrance, and in many cases the family go to the grave in the afternoon to meet the ancestors. By the evening the united family gather in the home together with the ancestors, who may now be served and spoken of as if they were actually present.[147] This reunion is generally governed by a non-sacred and pleasant mood, aptly expressed in the Bon greeting still in the use by many: «Kirei na obon de o me de to gozaimasu» («congratulation on a beautiful Bon»).

This evening, or at another suitable time during Bon, the priest makes his round to conduct a brief prayer for the repose of the dead or perform a ceremony similar to the *hoji* rites at each house. The priest, however, plays no central role at Bon and may at times not even be invited inside. No priest is necessary to perform most of the rites, with offerings and readings of sutras. This is all done by the family itself through its representative, most often the head of the household.

The 14th marks the climax of Bon. The family may make a new trip to the grave and a visit to the temple. In the evening they once again gather in front of the tablets for offerings and sutra-chanting. The day of return for the ancestors comes with the 15th. In the evening they will be sent off to their resting place, and this farewell is marked in different ways.[148] A farewell fire may be lighted at the entrance, like a welcome fire was at their arrival, and the family may go to the graveyard, to the seaside, or to the river bed for the sending off of the ancestors. The departure may be accompanied by the reading of sutras and by formal farewell greetings like: «Come back next year».

As we have already referred to above, some spirits are distinguished and made the object of special attention at Bon. One group is the spirit(s) of a family member(s) who has passed away since Bon last year, i.e., a spirit who is celebrating its first Bon together with the family.[149] Special rites will be conducted for this *shirei*, in some cases at a special altar, and in these rites the priest may play a more important role than in the rest of Bon. Next year the *shirei* will not be treated separately but will be a part of the group of ancestors celebrated in the ordinary Bon. Niibon is not, in other words, celebrated universally, like Bon itself, but only in families where one or more of its members have passed away since last year's Bon.

A second group is the *muenbotoke*, which by some people are taken care of in a separately erected altar outside the house. These rites are often spoken of as the *segaki*-ceremonies, a term which literally may be translated «feeding of the hungry spirits». The spirits of both these groups deserve special attention because they differ, each in its own way, from the collectivity of ancestors in communion with the living at Bon. The first

group differ from the point of view of growth after death. The second from
the point of view of belonging or relationship.

When it comes to the New Year/*shogatsu* festival it is a much debated
problem whether this is to be seen essentially as an ancestral festival.[150]
However this may be, there are reports to show that the ancestral tablets
come out of the *butsudan* to the *tokonoma* for special ceremonies at New
Year, as at Bon, and, even if one does not go that far, that the ancestors
are included in the New Year celebrations for instance by the way of
offerings.[151] However, generally speaking Inoguchi may be right when he
says that it is forgotten today that *shogatsu* was originally an ancestor
festival, and that it is now widely regarded as a special festival (Year
festival).[152]

The Higan-ceremonies at the equinoxes, however, are still widely
celebrated in a way that leaves no doubt about their ancestral nature. The
term *higan* carries the meaning of leaving the circle of transmigration and
reaching the shore of Nirvana, and as such points to the purpose of the
festival: To effect the birth of the dead in Amida's Western Paradise.[153]
Accounts vary somewhat as to what is actually included in people's
celebration of Higan. According to Ooms, Higan in Nagasawa is primarily
an occasion for the family to reunite and visit the family grave. The grave
is cleaned, but no decorations are made for the family altar and no rites
are performed.[154] Beardsley, on the other hand, reports from Niiike that
also at Higan «the memorial tablets of all the household ancestors come
out from the *butsudan* to the *tokonoma* to be honored in a ceremony
essentially like the *hoji* for a single forbearer just described», food offerings
are made, prayers chanted, and the visit to the grave includes both regular
cleaning and rites of prayers and offerings.[155] Again, the emphasis lies on
Higan as a family ancestral festival, but once more – as we have seen all
through this chapter – the priest and the temple may be involved, as the
family «may also schedule a special memorial service for the dead to be
held at the temple or in the home.»[156]

This brings us to the end of the ancestral rites and festivals that are to be
noted to get a clear picture of ancestor worship in home and temple setting.
Finally, the question could be raised whether there is, or to which extent
there is today, any fixed pattern or set of rites and festivals adhered to by
the people involved in ancestor worship. Do people observe all the
occasions they are supposed to from the point of view of religious
tradition? Or do they observe some of them, and if so which ones? This

is a question to which it is extremely difficult to give a general answer with any reasonable degree of certainty, but there seems to exist in contemporary Japan a great variety in the actual observance of the different occasions for worship.

Maybe we should be content – for our purposes – with the general conclusion that came out of Smith's valuable research into this, namely that «the overall pattern of worship is puzzling in the extreme», when household is compared with household as to actual observance of various occasions.[157] His findings reveal «a degree of variability in what is usually called customary usage on a scale hitherto unsuspected for Japan».[158] «Perhaps the ancestral rites are, above all, an area where individual preference is given free rein. With the weakening influence of institutionalized Buddhism, households no longer need to be so concerned as they once were with the formally prescribed occasions of worship. The household may now worship its ancestors in the ways it seems fitting and most efficacious. This may well represent the ultimate effect of the privatization of worship....»[159]

A brief sketch of ancestor worship in home and temple setting has revealed the former and the latter as very much interwoven in the actual performance of rites pertaining to the household ancestors. The dead are taken care of, worshipped, and remembered in close interaction between the family with its home altar and the family temple with its priests. This interaction is carried out partly through rites for individual spirits, rites which are basically of a one-time nature, and partly through rites and festivals for the collectivity of the dead, rites that are to be repeated and perpetuated ad infinitum.

Together with the historical sketch and the preliminary presentation of terminological implications, this should have given us the necessary understanding of ancestor worship's «sitz im leben».

We are confronted, as we have seen, with a phenomenon which is thoroughly integrated in the life of the Japanese people, both historically and sociologically. Even though its origin and initial shape and content may be obscure, ancestor worship as it has developed over the centuries in close interaction with the wider religious history of the country seems to represent a thorough amalgamation of ancient pre-Buddhist and Buddhist ideas. At folk level Buddhism came to be associated with ancestor worship in the way that the whole nation eventually came to be organized in a religious-political system with the ancestral rites in home and temple as central pivot. In other words, both from the point of view of religion, social life and politics, ancestor worship has been of the greatest significance. Even though things have changed in modern, post-war Japan, no serious missiological encounter with ancestor worship should take place without a keen awareness of these perspectives. We now proceed to an analysis of basic implications of the rites described.

Notes to Part 1

1. See Revon 1917, pp. 455–457.
2. Hall 1915, p. 153.
3. Aston 1905, p. 44.
4. Op.cit., pp. 46–47. Aston's distinction between «real ancestors» and «pseudo-ancestors» seems close to Ariga Kizaemon's distinction between «lineal ancestors» and «ancestors of origin». To this we shall return below, ch. 1.2.
5. Revon op.cit., p. 456.
6. The *kokugaku*-school is the School of National Learning, with its most notable representative Hirata Atsutane (1776–1843). Cf. Revon op.cit., pp. 455–456.
7. Hearn 1904/1917, pp. 27 ff. Lafcadio Hearn may also be referred to as Koizumi Yakumo, which is the name he took on becoming a Japanese citizen.
8. Op.cit., pp. 28–29.
9. Op.cit., p. 27. Even though serious scholars have made references to Hearn, e.g., on ancestor worship (as Anesaki 1930/1966, p. 70), Hearn himself may rather be titled a writer or author than scholar. De Lancy Ferguson expresses doubts whether Hearn ever really understood Japan (Ferguson 1966, p. 35 b). Cf. J. Carey Hall's very critical remarks on Hearn and his interpretation of Japanese ancestor worship in Hall 1915, p. 153.
10. Some of these are already mentioned in our introduction. Yanagida Kunio, the founder of modern Japanese folklore studies, is to be seen in the *kokugaku*-tradition of Hirata Atsutane (see the foreword by Hori Ichiro and Herman Ooms in Yanagida 1970, p.4), and some of his theories have provoked debate and opposition. We list Yanagida in this third category, and not in the second together with Hirata and the *kokugaku*-school, mainly because folklorists in Yanagida's tradition such as Hori Ichiro and Takeda Choshu, have a much more balanced view of Japanese ancestor worship and its relationship to Japanese Buddhism, than the extreme position presented in our second category.
11. This is the position of Takeda Choshu as stated in Takeda 1957/1975, pp. 214–215. The position is shared by such a renown Buddhist scholar as Watanabe Shoko. See Watanabe 1959/1975, pp. 119–120, 124, and Watanabe 1964, pp. 62–63.
12. A good illustration of the caution many Japanese scholars exhibit at this point is the following remark by Matsudaira Narimitsu: «It is difficult to know how the spirits were treated before the coming of Buddhism to Japan. To my great regret, the only thing I can say positively is that the forms of the

memorial service for the dead have not been entirely changed by Buddhism.»
Matsudaira 1963, p. 189. Cf. Smith 1974, p. 6.
13. Takeda 1957/1975, pp. 137–138.
14. As for the study of burial practices in Japan, we may refer to Inoguchi 1965;
    Haga 1974; Tamamuro 1971/1974.
15. See Hori 1962, pp. 132–135; Watanabe 1964, pp. 62–63; Smith 1974, pp. 6–7.
16. Watanabe 1964, p. 63; Hori 1962, p. 136. This is a main point in Yanagida's
    discussion of the origin of the Japanese Bon festival (Festival of the Dead),
    and in his theory that the New Year festival and the Bon festival originally
    were identical or corresponding festivals, centering around this motive of the
    return of the dead. See Yanagida 1970, pp. 50–69. Cf. Hori 1962, pp. 162–163.
17. We return to these concepts in their relation to ancestor worship below, ch.
    1.2 and 2.1.
18. Hori 1962, p. 133; Takeda 1957/1975, pp. 135–136. Cf. Takeda 1965, pp.
    593–594.
19. Re the problem of the relationship between clan-gods and ancestral spirits,
    see Smith 1974, pp. 7–12.
20. Takeda 1957/1975, pp. 145–146.
21. Hori 1968, p. 86.
22. See Tamamuro 1971/1974, pp. 94–95: Graves should not be made unnecessa-
    rily beautiful. One should be buried according to one's status. Corpses
    should be buried on designated burial sites. Self-immolation on the death of
    one's lord was prohibited.
23. Hori 1962, pp. 182–183.
24. Tamamuro 1971/1974, p. 78.
25. As for the different rites observed in these sects, such as the *Hokke-sanmai*,
    the *Joko-sanmai*, see Tamamuro 1971/1974, pp. 105–112. Re the importance
    of the salvatory effect of funeral and memorial rites and re the estimation of
    these by the nobility, government officials, and common people at this time,
    see Hori 1968, pp. 97–99, esp. the example he gives in note 25, p. 99.
26. Takatori/Hashimoto 1968/1975, pp. 150–151.
27. Takeda 1965, pp. 594–595.
28. Op.cit., p. 594.
29. Takeda 1957/1975, pp. 150–154. Such enormous and beautiful temples as the
    Todaiji and the Kofukuji at Nara are examples of *ujidera*, clan temples of the
    imperial family and the noble Fujiwara family respectively. Takeda 1965, p.
    595.
30. We shall return to the content of Bon on several occasions below.
31. Smith 1974, p. 15.
32. Op.cit., p. 17. The problem to which degree the Bon festival, as it came to be
    observed in Japan, is an imported or an indigenous festival, has caused a lot
    of discussion among Japanese scholars and foreign Japanologists. Smith
    presents Suzuki Mitsuo and Yanagida Kunio as representatives of the two
    conflicting stands respectively. It seems to us, however, that the majority of
    Japanese folklorists, with different degrees of modifications, adopt the stand
    of Yanagida that Bon – when it comes to its content – is to be seen as a
    pre-Buddhist, Japanese mid-summer festival related to indigenous ancestor

beliefs. Such peculiar native folk-beliefs formed the basis for the rapid spread of Buddhist Bon in Japan. See, e.g., Takeda 1957/1975, p. 146. Buddhist scholar Watanabe Shoko holds to the same opinion. Watanabe 1959/1975, p. 124.

33. Smith 1974, p. 19.
34. Tamamuro 1971/1974, pp. 113–120. Together with the spread of belief in the salvatory effect of the chanting of *nembutsu* for the dead went a rapid spread in the belief in individual evil spirits of the dead (*goryo*) and *nembutsu* as the most powerful means of protection against these evil spirits. Hori 1968, pp. 112–117.
35. Tamamuro 1971/1974, pp. 119–120; Hori 1968, pp. 127, 133. We shall return to this notable exception below, section 2.2.2.
36. Tamamuro gives in his book a very interesting account of this development. Op.cit., pp. 77–208. He points out that even the Zen sect, both the Rinzai and the Soto schools, developed in the medieval period from a meditation-oriented to a funeral-oriented sect of Buddhism. Op.cit., pp. 128–129.
37. Op.cit., p. 210 (our own translation). In the period 1467 to 1665 more than 90% of the temples of modern Japanese Buddhism was built. Op.cit., p. 260.
38. Quoted from Gubbins 1877/1878, p. 47.
39. § 3: «Such chief parishioners as do not attend on the anniversary of the founder of the sect, on Buddha's death-day, at Bon, Higan, the death-day of their ancestors, must lose their certificates, and notice be given to the Office of Sects. They must certainly be examined.» Cited from Gubbins, op.cit., p. 48.
40. Smith 1974, p. 21. The *danka*-system as such was not invented by the Tokugawas but had its beginning in the preceding Muromachi era. Fujii 1974, p. 71. What the Tokugawas did, was – through this system – to forge the household with its ancestor worship and Buddhism into a rigid, administrative-political system and force it upon the people from above. Takeda Choshu points out that the basis for this system is not to be found in isolated historical events, e.g. in the suppression of Christianity, but in the substratum of Japanese history as such. The suppression of Christianity was only the particular event which generated its practical-political incarnation. Takeda 1957/1975, pp. 194–195. Cf. Tamamuro 1971/1974, pp. 262–270.
41. Takeda 1965, p. 596. Cf. Smith 1974, pp. 22–23. Many Japanese scholars see in this process towards popular «funeral Buddhism» a complete degeneration of original Buddhism in Japan. Cf. Watanabe's statement as quoted by Smith 1974, p. 23.
42. As for this critique, see Tamamuro 1971/1974, pp. 267–274; Smith 1974, pp. 24–25.
43. The first Confucian funeral was conducted in 1651. Shinto funeral is mentioned in writing for the first time in 1687. It does not seem to have been put into practice, however, before 1785. Funerals like these do not seem to have been performed very often, as the necessary official permission was not easily obtained. Tamamuro 1971/1974, pp. 282–283.
44. For a brief sketch of these developments, see Smith 1974, pp. 26–30.
45. Takeda 1957/1975, pp. 201–208. Smith 1974, pp. 31–32. The view of the

nation as a household – a national house/*kokka* – has been of the greatest significance in Japanese political philosophy.

46. Takeda 1965, p. 597. See also Takeda 1957/1975, pp. 201–202, and Steiner 1950, pp. 171–172.

47. Quoted after Smith 1974, p. 33.

48. The government published in 1937 an ideological-ethical textbook for the education of the people, which offers an excellent study in this *kokutai*-philosophy. The governmental circulation of the book was forbidden by the Allied Powers in 1945. The book is available in English translation: Hall/Gauntlett 1949.

    Re the coalescence of Buddhist funeral rites and masses with national ideology in this period, see Takatori/Hashimoto 1968/1975, pp. 195–197. Re the wider problem of ancestor worship and Japanese law, we may refer to the following: Hozumi 1901/1943; Minear 1970; Kawashima 1950, pp. 143–207; Kawashima 1957/1959, pp. 1–215; Maeda 1965, pp. 103–156; Hirai 1968; Steiner 1950; and Wagatsuma 1950.

49. See Steiner 1950, pp. 172–176; Wagatsuma 1950, pp. 406–414; and Stoetzel 1955, pp. 94–98.

50. Smith 1974, pp. 33–34.

51. Quoted after Smith 1974, p. 34. This is the official Japanese translation from 1966. A somewhat better translation of the article appears in Sano 1958, p. 30: «Art. 897 (Succession to the ritual effects, etc.) (1) Rights to keep the book of pedigree, ritual effects, and the gravesites is inherited by the one who is responsible for presiding at the rites and feasts for the ancestors in accordance with the custom (or tradition), regardless of the regulations in the previous article....»

52. Quotation from Stoetzel 1955, p. 95. This is the view of Kawashima Takeyoshi and Wagatsuma Sakae. See Kawashima 1950, pp. 150–157, and Wagatsuma 1950, p. 413.

53. So Maeda 1965, pp. 154–155.

54. Stoetzel 1955, p. 96.

55. For our purpose it will suffice to point to some of the tendencies observed in modern research and ask some questions pointing to the future. As to valuable and detailed studies on these problems we refer to Maeda 1965, pp. 157–231; Koyama 1960/1972, pp. 73–120; Minakawa 1972; Fujii 1974; Morioka 1975, pp. 99–113; Sano 1958, pp. 1–37; Smith 1974.
    Concerning the problem of ancestor worship and the change in family structures, we shall return to this in ch. 2.1.

56. Koyama 1960/1972, p. 74 (our own translation).

57. Kawashima 1950, p. 157.

58. Morioka 1975, p. 105. This segment of the urban population is often referred to as the religiously floating or fluctuating population. Cf. the title of Fujii 1974.
    Research done in the 1950's shows that at that time the hold of the old family system was still quite strong, not only in rural but also in urban areas. See Koyama 1960/1972, pp. 78–81, and Sano 1958, p. 37.
    An inquiry into the attitudes towards ancestor worship among the youth that

may be fairly representative, is found in Baber 1958, pp. 102–103 (note the small figures in the column «Never», «Disapprove»):

Table 38. In Your Home, Are Deceased Parents, Grandparents, and Ancestors Worshipped and Ceremonies Held for Them?

Where respondent grew up	Faithfully		Sometimes		Never	
	Boys	Girls	Boys	Girls	Boys	Girls
Total	60.8	56.0	29.8	31.3	9.4	12.7
City	55.9	50.7	32.0	33.5	12.1	15.8
Town	61.9	58.2	30.3	30.6	7.8	11.2
Village	69.8	64.5	24.9	27.5	5.3	8.0

N = 4,901

Table 39. Do You Approve of Worshipping and Holding Ceremonies for Deceased Parents, Grandparents, and Ancestors?

Where respondent grew up	Approve		I don't care*		Disapprove	
	Boys	Girls	Boys	Girls	Boys	Girls
Total	39.9	40.4	54.6	53.7	5.5	5.9
City	38.1	38.7	55.3	55.0	6.6	6.3
Town	42.6	42.0	51.9	53.8	5.5	4.2
Village	42.0	41.6	54.5	52.3	3.5	7.1

N = 4,946

* As stated in the questionnaire: «I don'ty care one way or the other.»

59. Statistics taken from Fujii 1974, p. 72 and Morioka 1975, p. 106. For more statistic material as to the possession of altars together with necessary analysis of the material, see Smith 1974, pp. 152–160.
60. Morioka 1975, p. 106; Smith 1974, p. 160.
61. Cf. Smith 1974, p. 163; Dore 1958, p. 3l6; and Takahashi 1975, pp. 47–48. The latter study presents material to show that once the male spouse is dead, almost 100% of the investigated families have a *butsudan* – even separately established, nuclear families. For these families the *butsudan* does not serve the traditional worship of the generations of ancestors, but serves the purpose of offering masses for the benefit of the deceased closed relative.
    Cf. further what Maeda says about the change in attitude towards and responsibility for ancestral rites as the young grow older, Maeda 1965, pp.

179–180. As to the rate of people actually taking part in daily ancestor worship before the *butsudan*, Maeda gives in the afterword of his book figures from an extensive investigation carried out jointly by four universities in Kyoto in 1964 (Maeda op.cit., pp. 233 ff.). The interrogated people were of both sexes, included both urban and rural population, and were divided into categories according to age, education, occupation, and Buddhist sect-affiliation. We render a diagram built on Maeda's figures, which presents in percentages the affirmative answer to the question:
«Do you worship daily at the *butsudan*?»
(Note that the question asks about daily worship. The figures, at least for the young, might have been higher if sporadic participation had been included.)

Other categories Age categories	With only Compulsory education	With senior High School	Farming) Forestry) Fishing)	Other occupations	Shin-shu (True-Pure-Land)	Shingon-shu.
Old people (60–)	66.7 % (986 of 1,479)	56.7 % 318 of 561)	65 % (out of 799)	55 % (out of 509)	70.5 % (out of 1,300)	53.5 % (out of 372)
Young people (20–39)	24.6 % (185 of 752)	17.4 % 303 of 1,735)	31 % (out of 419)	16.6 % (out of 1,400)	22.4 % (out of 1,256)	20.3 % (out of 359)
	I Education		II Occupation		III Buddhist sect	

62. Morioka 1975, p. 106.
63. See the very interesting study on this in Fujii 1974, pp. 91–144. Another interesting inquiry into the problem of modern Japanese and the funerals and masses is the study undertaken by Sotoshu Kyoka Kenshujo at Komazawa University. Its overriding title is *Sosai o ba to shita dendo no kenkyu* (A Study in Funerals and Masses as Occasions for Mission), containing three separate reports. In the conclusions of the last report, it is stated that 2/3 of the people interrogated approve of the traditional funerals and masses, while 1/3 want them more simple. Further, that 2/3 have a general Buddhist understanding of the ceremonies. Minakawa 1972, p. 41.
64. Maeda 1965, pp. 186–192.
65. Maeda op.cit., p. 185.
66. Maeda op.cit., pp. 188–189.
67. Re the importance of ancestor worship in these two groups, see Rissho Kosei-Kai 1972, pp. 20–24, and Wimberley 1969 and 1972.
68. Rissho Kosei-Kai 1972, p. 23.
69. Rissho Kosei-Kai 1972, pp. 24–25. We shall below, ch. 2.1, see how far such

a practice has spread also outside this particular group.

70. Fujii Masao has made this temple a special object of study. Fujii 1974, pp. 183–207: «Kotsu-botoke to datsu-shukyo fudojinko-ka» («Human bones as Buddha and defection from Religion»).

71. The temple traces its roots to way back in the medieval age. The first bone-Buddha was made in the latter part of the last century, out of bones from ca. 50 000 bodies. The temple was completely destroyed in 1945, but in 1949 a new statue was made out of pieces from the old one found in the debris, together with the bones of ca. 220 000 war victims. A second statue was erected in 1957, a third in 1967, and a fourth is planned for 1977. Fujii 1974, pp. 184–188.

72. According to Fujii about 50% of the people turning in bones at Isshinji, are seeking the temple for the first time, a fact which shows that it is not an outdying practice functioning only because of custom. Fujii op.cit., p. 198.

73. Fujii op.cit., pp. 198–199.

74. Takeda 1957/1975, p. 13.

75. *Kojien* 1955/1975, p. 91.

76. Takeda 1957/1975, pp. 14–15.

77. Sansom 1951, quoted from Matsumoto 1960, p. 11.

78. *Senzo* consists of the same two characters as *sosen*, in reversed order. Probably there is a distinction between these two terms. They are, however, to a great extent used interchangeably as expressions for ancestor worship. It does not serve our purposes to attempt any analysis of their distinctive meanings.

79. See Ooms 1967, pp. 242–243, where categories of Plath, Hirata, Yanagida and Ariga are given.

80. Op.cit., p. 242.

81. Hirai 1968, p. 43.

82. See Ariga 1969, pp. 357–381. Cf. Smith 1974, pp. 8–9.

83. Ariga gives the traditional interpretation of the descent of the Imperial house as the most outstanding example. The «ancestor I» of the Imperial house is emperor Jimmu Tenno. Its «ancestor II» is the sun-god Amaterasu-Omikami. Ariga 1969, p. 361.

84. Takeda 1957/1975, pp. 21, 87. We shall return to important implications of this in ch. 2.3.

85. Ooms op.cit., p. 254.

86. Ooms op.cit., p. 251.

87. Smith 1974, p. 163. Cf. Ooms op.cit., p. 248.

88. Smith 1974, chapter five: «Who are the Ancestors?», pp. 152–183.

89. Op.cit., p. 169.

90. Op.cit., p. 172.

91. Op.cit., p. 172.

92. Op.cit., p. 173.

93. Op.cit., p. 174. What Smith says about «Non-lineal» tablets in these quotations is, obviously, relevant still more for the «Non-kin» tablets.

94. Op.cit., pp. 174, 183.

95. It is interesting to note that this third group, according to Smith, seems to

make an opening of the old *ie*-centered ancestor worship toward a modern family-centered ancestor worship adapted to the new social structures in contemporary Japan. Op.cit., p. 174. Cf. what we said to the practice of Rissho Kosei-Kai p. 21.

96. This process of growth shall be a main point in our analysis below, ch. 2.2. Here we give only the important traits for the sake of a proper understanding of the term «ancestor».

97. Eder 1956, p. 101; Smith 1974, p. 41.

98. Re this process of growth see Smith 1974, pp. 69–114; Eder 1956; Ooms 1957, pp. 274–282; Takeda 1957/1975, pp. 100–105. The actual timing given here may vary to a certain degree, depending on geographical location and sect. The principle of growth, however, is not altered by such differences. See further below, sections 2.2.1–2.

99. We shall return to this below, sections 2.2.1 and 2.3.1. Re the problem of *hotoke* and *muen-botoke* see Smith 1974, pp. 41–55; Ooms 1967, pp. 251–256; Takeda 1957/1975, pp. 232–235.

100. Op.cit., p. 41.

101. Ooms 1967, p. 254.

102. This is the main question we have in mind in this part of our terminological clarification. Obviously, the question is of the greatest importance for our study and cannot be satisfactorily answered through a terminological inquiry alone. We shall return to this in our systematic analysis below, ch. 2.3. However, a presentation of the terms may give valuable clues to a proper understanding of the problem. Such a noted anthropologist and Japanologist as Edward Norbeck makes this termonological question a problem of the greatest magnitude when he says that ancestor worship «might better be called ancestor care since the Japanese of historic times have not truly worshipped ancestors but instead have given them respectful care and felt close to them....» Norbeck 1970, p. 141. Cf. the following statement by Bernhard Bernier: «The term 'ancestor worship' is not strictly correct, for the dead are not worshipped, but rather ritually honored and respected .... The phrase 'respect for the dead' would be more appropriate....» (Bernier 1970, p. 121.)

103. *Senzo matsuri* may well be a more Japanese expression than *sosen suhai*, which may be a «Japanization» of the English «ancestor worship». This was suggested to the author by Professor Morioka Kiyomi, Tokyo.

104. See Christiaens 1975 A, p. 579.

105. This may be the reason why Japanese Roman Catholics prefer this term for that of *suhai* when they talk about ancestor worship. Christiaens 1975 A, p. 579. Cf. his booklet of 1976: *Katorikku no sosen sukei* (The Catholic Veneration of Ancestors).

106. References to show this interchangeable use of the terms may be given in abundance. The following may serve as examples:

    Matsuri and *ogamu* are used for worship of ancestral spirits without any important distinctions in Fujii 1974, p. 207. Hori gives examples of *senzo matsuri* used as a term for the regular Buddhist masses for the dead, Hori

1975, p. 141, and he uses *suhai suru* for worship of the spirit of the dead, Hori 1962, pp. 135, 176. Takeda uses *matsuru* about ancestors, and *sosen suhai* as equivalent to *senzo matsuri*, Takeda 1957/1975, pp. 67–69, 237, 240. As for the terms *suhai* and *sukei*, these are used interchangeably in Takatori/Hashimoto 1968/1975, p. 163, and *sukei* is used to define *suhai* in *Kojien* 1955/1975, p. 1179. In Takahashi 1975, p. 38, *reihaisha* is used for persons engaged in ancestor worship.

In Kataoka 1974/1975, which is no scholarly work but a popular book, the same interchangeable use of terms is conspicuous. *Ogamu* is used as an act of veneration/ worship toward men, ancestors and *kami*/god, pp. 22, 28. *Matsuru* is used both about *kami* and ancestors, p. 28, and *reihai suru* is used both about god and ancestors, p. 28.

107. Maeda 1965, pp. 56–59. Cf. Hirai Atsuko who sees the worship of ancestors as a correlate to their power to protect and admonish their descendants, Hirai 1968, p. 43. Takeda Choshu's emphasis on the absolute value of the founder of an *ie* as an absolute object of reverence, Takeda 1957/1975, p. 20, points in the same direction.

108. Smith 1974, p. 146.

109. The term *kuyo* carries the meaning of providing for somebody through the bringing of offerings. The two most common forms of *kuyo* among ordinary people are the offering of money, fruit, vegetables, etc., and the reading of sutras. Takeda 1957/1975, p. 239.

110. Smith 1974, p. 128. Re the theory of «transfer of merits» related to ancestor worship, see Takeda, op.cit., pp. 237–239. We shall return to this in ch. 2.2.

111. Smith 1974, pp. 128, 144–145.

112. Cf. the title of H. Ooms's dissertation: «The Religion of the Household: A Case Study of Ancestor Worship in Japan.» Ooms 1967.

113. Cf. Smith 1974, pp. 69–70, 71.

114. To which extent ancestor worship is part of what takes place at the god-shelf/ *kamidana* is a problem we shall not enter into. Neither will we refer to Shinto funerals and rites for the dead. Re this see, e.g., Herbert 1967, pp. 159, 166–167, and Reitz 1939.

115. Maeda 1965, pp. 175–176. Note Smith's remark: «In any household the kind of altar and its cost will depend on such a large number of considerations that it is difficult to generalize about them at all.» Op.cit., p. 89.

116. Takeda 1957/1975, pp. 98–99; Maeda 1965, p. 175. Note that a Buddha-figure, which often is found in a family altar, is no indispensable element. Maeda reports many *butsudans* without such a figure, a fact which goes to prove that the *butsudan* is primarily a symbol of ancestor worship and no regular buddhist altar.

117. Re these problems in modern Japan, see Fujii 1974, especially the chapter «Toshi ni okeru bochi mondai» («Graveyard-problems in the cities»), pp. 145–182.

118. Fujii 1974, p. 92.

119. The «double-grave system» throws considerable light on popular ideas on the relationship between corpse and soul, life and death, etc. The phenomenon is a fairly recent discovery of Japanese folklore studies, receiving the attention

of scholars in 1919. For further information on the «double-grave system», see Hori 1951, pp. 218–221; Hori 1962, pp. 135, 176; Mogami 1963; Takeda 1957/1975, pp. 100–105; and Smith 1974, pp. 74–78.

120. The following points to the understanding of the *bodaiji* are taken mainly from Fujii 1974, pp. 113–114, which is a case study of a typical city temple in Yokohama.

121. Temples often make a distinction between supporting families/*danka* or *danto*, and individual support based on personal faith/*shinto*. In Jodo-shu, e.g., the following definition of the terms is found: *Danto* – one who continually requests the temple's services for the ancestors. *Shinto* – one who believes in and supports the doctrine of the sect and belongs to a certain temple. According to Fujii, however, this distinction is so vague and unprecise that he deliberately uses the term *shinto* for both groups. Op.cit., p. 122.

122. Op.cit., p. 129.

123. Ooms applies a similar distinction when he presents the family rites in Nagasawa. Op.cit., p. 230.

124. Beardsley 1959, p. 339; Gabriel 1938, p. 570. According to Gabriel there will be a second visit from the temple the following morning for more recitation, and even a third and fourth before the funeral proper starts, depending on the amount paid to the temple. Op.cit., p. 570.

125. The funeral service may be held either in the home or in the temple. Beardsley reports the former, Gabriel the latter. In Minakawa's investigation people were asked where they wanted the funeral service conducted. In rural Kanuma 80% wanted the service in the home, quite in accordance with traditional practice, while 11% expressed a desire to have it conducted in the temple. In Tokyo the percentages were 52 and 41 respectively, that is, a far stronger desire to have it conducted in the temple. Minakawa 1972, p. 29.

126. See Gabriel op.cit., p. 571. We shall return to this in section 2.2.2.

127. Op.cit., p. 574. See also Beardsley op.cit., p. 341.

128. Beardsley reports from Niiike that priests and people gather again for the burial seven days later, when the priest will hand the family the posthumous name of the deceased. Gabriel, however, speaks about burial at an unspecified convenient time later on «ohne Sang und Klang». According to Gabriel the *kaimyo* is given already at the *makura-gyo*-ceremony. Beardsley op.cit., p. 342; Gabriel op.cit., p. 575.

129. Dore 1959, p. 429.

130. Cf. what we said to the *bodaiji* on p. 31. As for different practices at this point, see, e.g., Ooms op.cit., p. 235; Beardsley op.cit., pp. 454–455; Gabriel op.cit., pp. 576–577; and Dore op.cit., pp. 314–315. Minakawa has a report on the desire of people to have the *hoji*-ceremonies performed at home or at the temple, parallel to that on the funeral proper reported in note 125. In Kanuma ca. 91% want them conducted at home, while in Tokyo only 45%. Minakawa op.cit., p. 33.

131. Ooms op.cit., p. 233; Gabriel op.cit., p. 576.

132. Tamamuro gives the historical development of this «13 masses-pattern» of rites. The 7x7 pattern traces its origin in ancient India. In China Buddhism added three masses to this (the 100th day, the 1st and 3rd anniversaries) and

got the «10 masses-pattern». Japan took over this Chinese system, but Japanese Buddhism between 1100 and 1400 A.D. added three more anniversaries and got the «13 masses-pattern». The necessary gods/bodhisattvas and the necessary steps in the process of judgment were added to the existing *juo*-theology, and developed into the *jusan shinko*, the «13 faith». Through the middle ages most of the sects adapted themselves to this pattern, and it was to a large extent popularized to fit the need of the people. Tamamuro 1971/1974, pp. 155–192.

133. Smith op.cit., p. 95. The same anniversaries are listed in Minakawa's investigation into which anniversaries are actually observed. Minakawa op.cit., p. 35.

134. This is shown both by Smith op.cit., pp. 104–114, and Minakawa op.cit., p. 35. According to Minakawa, of the 18 possible rites mentioned, the following seem to stand out as more often observed than the rest: The 7th day, the 49th day, the 1st, 3rd, 7th, 13th and 33rd anniversaries. Where the anniversaries (*nenki*) are concerned, this seems to fit in with the «13–masses-pattern».

135. Minakawa presents some interesting figures on sermons in connection with these ceremonies. They may be of different content (a eulogy to the dead, on Buddhism and the Buddha, on the after-life, on human existence, etc.). An average of 44% of the interrogated persons reported having heard such sermons, ca. 58% having not, while almost 80% expressed a desire to have such sermons as part of the ceremony. Minakawa op.cit., pp. 36–37.

136. See Gabriel op.cit., pp. 576–578 and Beardsley op.cit., pp. 454–455 for more details to a typical *hoji*-ceremony.

137. Smith op.cit., pp. 97–98. We shall return to the implications of this in sections 2.2.1 and 2.3.1.

138. Smith op.cit., p. 95 and Tamamuro op.cit., pp. 174–175.

139. This may hold true as a general statement even if prayers at times may be directed to a particular person among the ancestors.

140. This is a distinction applied by Dore op.cit., p. 427. It may be useful for the sake of clarity, even though it may be going too far in systematizing what is not always distinguished in actual life.

141. Dore reports it to be strong in Shitayama-cho, Tokyo, op.cit., p. 316. Maeda reports it to be generally performed in the village of Ueda, Tochigi-ken, op.cit., p. 181. Ooms says that of the houses in rural Nagasawa that had a *butsudan* (only two did not have), all except three made daily offerings, op.cit., p. 241.

142. Dore op.cit., p. 427. Cf. Smith op.cit., pp. 118–119; Maeda op.cit., p. 181.

143. Smith op.cit., pp. 136–137; Ooms op.cit., pp. 240–241; Dore op.cit., p. 427.

144. Cf. Ooms who says that in Nagasawa no prayers go with the daily offering except in such new religions as Rissho Kosei-Kai and Nichiren Sho-shu. Op.cit., p. 241.

145. See above p. 14. Most of the accounts of the Bon-festival, at least in Western languages, are mainly concerned with its essential character as a family festival, but there is an interesting account on Bon as celebrated in a temple in the article of Boyer 1966/1967. The article is, however, in some respects too imprecise, and it does not make the necessary differentiation between

various elements of the ceremonies.

On the different practices at Bon, there are lots of reports. For our presentation we rely on Smith 1974, Ooms 1967, Beardsley 1959, Norbeck 1954, Dore 1958, Yanagida 1970, Inoguchi 1965 and Tamamuro 1971/1974. The brief presentation we give is a highly synthetic one, as there are numerous local variations in the celebration of the festival.

146. Inoguchi 1965, pp. 217–218. He further points to the complex nature of Bon in raising and giving a summary answer to the question: How is it that the ancestors, who have joined or fused into the collective, supra-individual entity *sorei*, visit separately and individually their own families? Op.cit., pp. 222–223.

147. Water maybe set out for them in the garden to wash their feet, e.g., Inoguchi op.cit., pp. 220–221. Many customs related to this return of the ancestors are found: The making of small straw horses to ride on, the welcome fire, the path-making, etc.

148. The author will never forget how this was celebrated every year in the small village at Lake Nojiri in Nagano-ken. Small boats, making up a hundreds-of-meters-long flotilla, were put to sea carrying burning torches, accompanied by a magnificent show of fireworks. A beautiful view in the dark mid-summer night.

149. The family's encounter with this particular spirit is called Niibon or Arabon, a word literally meaning New Bon or First Bon. Re Niibon, see Smith op.cit., pp. 102–103 and Bernier 1970, pp. 103–109. We shall return to the meaning of Niibon in section 2.2.3.

150. Yanagida's position on this is clear. He sees New Year as originally an ancestral festival parallel to Bon. Yanagida op.cit., pp. 50–69. Also Inoguchi regards New Year as an important ancestor festival, with many elements parallel to Bon, although changes over the years have occured and obscured the common elements in Bon and New Year. Op.cit., p. 225.

151. Beardsley op.cit., p. 455; Smith op.cit., pp. 98–99.

152. Op.cit., p. 225. Cf. Smith who says that the ancestors are far less central to the New Year festival than at the equinoxes and at Bon. Smith op.cit., p. 99.

153. Tamamuro op.cit., p. 205.

154. Ooms op.cit., p. 240. Ooms says, however, that the special rice dumplings made for Higan «may also be offered to the ancestors», a statement somewhat in contradiction to the one saying that «no rites are performed». Special food for Higan such as rice dumplings, used both for eating and offering, is a common feature, reported also by Norbeck op.cit., p. 149 and Smith op.cit., p. 99.

155. Beardsley op.cit., p. 455. Higan in Niiike differs from Bon more in scope than in essence, as «Bon comes off with more of a flourish».

156. Smith op.cit., p.99.

157. Op.cit., p. 112. See to this problem Smith's chapter «Patterns of Worship», op.cit., pp. 104–114.

158. Op.cit., p. 106.

159. Op.cit., p. 113. Of special interest is Smith's table 5: «Households Observing Various Rites», which gives the actual observance of rites in descending order

of frequency, from the investigation of 457 households. We render the table as it is found in op.cit., p. 105:

Households Observing Various Rites (N = 457)

Observance of rites, in descending order of frequency	Households	
	Number	Percent
Festival of the Dead (Bon)	287	62.8 %
Daily morning rite (mai-asa)	282	61.7 %
Periodic anniversaries of death (nenki)	275	60.2 %
Monthly deathday (mai–tsuki–meinichi)	255	55.8 %
Equinoxes (higan)	243	53.2 %
Daily evening rite (mai–ban)	204	44.6 %
New Year (shogatsu)	197	43.1 %
Annual deathday (sho–tsuki–meinichi)	191	41.8 %
«When we think of it»	57	12.5 %
«Never»	7	1.5 %

2 ANCESTOR WORSHIP – A SYSTEMATIC ANALYSIS

It is not intended in this chapter to present an analysis of ancestor worship that attempts to organize its religious and ethical premises into a consistent system. As we have already stated in our introduction, we do not think that is possible. Ancestor worship does not function on the basis of a thoroughly reflected, consistent religious system. It is a phenomenon which presents an amalgamation of different traditions and ideas, some of which are difficult to reconcile with each other.

Nevertheless, ancestor worship implies certain basic presuppositions as to the essential nature of human existence. This chapter will contain an attempt to focus on these basic premises and to analyze them in order to prepare for the subsequent presentation of the relevant problems that arise out of the meeting of this phenomenon with Christian faith. It will be systematic only in the sense that we will arrange this analysis around certain themes that seem to stand out as being of special importance for our purposes. These themes may well be interrelated, something that will be clear below, but they do not allow for the construction of a «system». The headline above might, in other words, have been worded: Ancestor Worship – A Thematic Analysis.

A thorough study of ancestor worship seems to support the feeling one gets already through a first and superficial acquaintance with the phenomenon, namely that three main problem areas present themselves as significant. The first is that which is related to ancestor worship as part of the social, inter-human milieu. Ancestor worship is a social phenomenon which functions in a certain social context. As such it has important implications both to the structural relationship between the individual and the social nexus that ancestor worship represents and to the ethical code that governs this relationship.

This leads naturally into the second area, which is concerned with the problems of the relationship between the living and the dead. At this point ancestor worship clearly transcends the realm of the social and ethical and proceeds into that of religious attitudes and values.

Thirdly, an investigation into the relationship between the living and the dead will take us into the area of problems which concerns the nature of the object of ancestor worship, the relationship, so to speak, between the human and the divine.[1]

2.1 *Ancestor Worship and the Social Fabric*

We have made clear in our introduction that we limit ourselves to ancestors on the household level. From our historical survey it should be obvious, however, that ancestor worship has played an important role in a much wider social context. It has been central to the social and religious consciousness of the clan, and it has served as a significant vehicle for the fostering of national unity and morality, especially as interpreted and propagated in the pre-war family-state ideology (*kokutai*-ideology or *kazoku kokka kan*).[2] This indicates that ancestor worhsip has been interwoven, in one way or another, in the social fabric on all levels of society, with implications for moral conduct in all spheres of social intercourse.

When we turn to its role in the household setting, we turn to the traditional *ie* as «an indispensable ingredient in the faith of ancestor worship».[3] This role of the *ie* makes it imperative that our analysis takes off with such a study of the social and ethical aspects of ancestor worship. It is repeatedly pointed out by Japanese scholars that any analysis of ancestor worship will have to depart from here, as «one cannot understand fully the meaning of ancestor worship in Japan, which is the family religion there, without referring to the social and religious significance of the *ie* lineage concept».[4]

2.1.1 *Ancestor Worship and the* Ie

Both in chapter 1.1 and in 1.2 we have spoken repeatedly about the *ie*-institution. The term points to a fixed family system that is carried on infinitely through the generations as an everlasting entity, and to speak of ancestors is impossible without reference to the *ie*.[5] The concept is of tremendous importance for the understanding of Japanese culture in general, although modern times have brought great changes to the social and juridical premises for the institution.[6] It is necessary for us now to get a clearer understanding of the actual structures and implications of the *ie*, and of the consequences of modern change in this respect.[7]

The traditional *ie* is, generally speaking, to be characterized by the rule of four «P-s»: It is patriarchal, patrilineal, primogenitural, and patrilocal.[8] Firstly, it is patriarchal in the sense that it centers around the male head of the house/*kacho*; not, primarily, because of any subjective abilities and charismatic potentialities on the part of this particular individual, but because of the institution of headship that this person represents. This position is to be inherited just as the family property is to be inherited. In the last case, however, property may be divided between several heirs, whereas the rights of headship of the house/*kacho-ken* cannot be divided and are to be inherited by one single person.[9] This institution of the «head of the house» represents in any actual generation the whole collectivity of the *ie*. To be invested with the authority of this position, therefore, involves the inheritance of both rights and responsibilities, among which that of taking care of the family altar and of the family grave is among the most prominent.

Secondly, the *ie* is patrilineal since it is perpetuated along the head of the household's line of descent. The main duty of the *kacho*-designate, therefore, is to marry and produce a male descendant in order to preserve the continuity of the *ie*. The wife of the *kacho* or *kacho*-designate is expected to serve this unity and continuity of her husband's *ie*, not only by giving birth to a male heir, but in a much wider sense as she is expected to conform to and actively carry on the ways of the house/*kafu*. Among these «ways of the house», one of the most important duties would be to take care of the ancestors daily, ancestors who are not, accordingly, those of the wife's own ascent, but those of her husband's.

Thirdly, the structure of the *ie* is primogenitural, which in the context of the above goes to say that the position as head of the household primarily is succeeded to by the oldest son/*chonan*. The rest of the children are supposed to move out at the time of marriage and establish their own household (*bunke*) and then leave the family altar in the custody of the oldest brother and his family. The latter carries on the *ie* as its main representative (*honke*).

In cases where there is no son, there are other accepted ways to carry on the *ie*. The principle of male primogeniture may, however, be deviated from even in cases where there is a *chonan*. We said above that the authority of the household is not primarily founded on subjective abilities on the part of this particular individual, but in the institution of headship. This is not to say, however, that personal qualifications do not count. Since the institution of family headship is of such importance, there may be cases where the *chonan* «may be judged physically too weak, mentally incapable, or otherwise incompetent to assume this position», and where, therefore, another person is preferred.[10] In other words, the principle of male primogeniture is not of such a preponderance that it is allowed to jeopardize the tradition of the *ie* itself.

Fourthly, the *ie* is patrilocal. The son who succeeds to the family headship is supposed to remain in the house. When he marries, his wife will move into the house of her husband's family. In the cases of adoption to headship (see below), the adopted *kacho*-designate will move into the household whose headship he is designated to take on, he will change his own family name for that of his new family, and his ancestors will – in his new position – be the ancestors of the house he has now entered.

These four principles are all subordinate, however, to the overriding principle of preservation and continuation of the *ie* itself. Ideally, the *ie* is an everlasting entity in continuity from the past into the future, and the fundamental principle which the above four are supposed to serve is simply the perpetuation of this entity.[11] Therefore, the adoption system /*yoshi-seido* is universally accepted as a valid means to continue the house where there is no male heir.[12] The procedure for the succession of the house may therefore be found in one of the following four (five) alternatives clearly stated by Smith: «In every generation the house headship is assumed by a single male heir, and there are four ways to insure this succession: Through a son who takes an in-marrying wife; through an adopted son who takes an in-marrying wife; through a daughter who takes an in-marrying adopted husband; through an adopted daughter who takes an in-marrying adopted husband.... There is even a rare fifth alternative available when the succession to a house has lapsed completely: A person will be designated the successor and given the family name, property, and ancestral tablets».[13]

The fact that the break in genetic continuity, which an adoption constitutes, is not considered to create any break in the continuation of the *ie* serves to prove that the relationship within the Japanese *ie* is not, ultimately, a blood relationship, but a social and structural lineage-relationship. The *ie* is, in other words, «a name group and not a blood group», where people not related by blood to the others in the *ie* are accepted in principle as belonging to the same *ie* as soon as they are adopted or integrated to the appointed status.[14]

From the point of view of organization, the *ie* is to be seen as a «complex-structured family, or complex family», that is a family which – in contrast to the nuclear or «simple-structured family» – may include more than two generations living together.[15] There are, as Sano points out, two types of complex families. In the one, all the children are supposed to live with their parents as long as possible even after marriage («pluralistic complex familiy»). In the other, all the children, except the inheriting son or daughter, are supposed to leave the house upon marriage («singularistic complex family»). «The Japanese family in historical times followed the line of *a singularistic complex family*».[16] Thus, the *ie* is to be perpetuated along one single line of descent, for which reason it may also be characterized as a «lineal family».

This single line of descent is represented in any generation by the person who succeeds to the family headship. The complex family centered around this person is the main house/ *honke* referred to above. The younger brothers of the heir will move out upon marriage and establish their own households/*bunke*. At the outset the *bunke* will be a simple family of only one generation, but in principle it is the starting point of a new complex family, a new *ie*, eventually with its own family altar and its own branch-houses. The newly established *bunke* will in many respects be in a subordinate position to the *honke*, something which is reflected in ancestor worship. The family altar is handed down through the *honke* as the main house's right and responsibility, and the members of the *bunke* are supposed to join with the *honke* on some of the special occasions for worship of the common ancestors. Such a group of households would, especially in rural areas, make up a larger unit, a clan, often referred to by the term *dozoku*, which has been of great significance both in social and religious life.[17]

In this analysis we have already touched upon the aspect of *ie* most crucial in our context: The *ie* as an everlasting entity, transcending any actual generation and any actual member of it. The Japanese household is «not merely a temporary union of certain individuals».[18] Nor is it to be defined simply as the collective of a particular individual. The *ie* is an entity which transcends the actual living family, it is an everlasting entity in continuity from the past into the future, including past, present and future generations, that is: including both the dead, the living and the not yet born. In the *ie* these groups are all united in an interdependent community which transcends life and death, and which it is – per definitionem – necessary to perpetuate.[19] «The eternal continuity or eternity of *ie* is a rule or norm for Japanese in general. Once established, an *ie* is supposed to last forever and never to become extinct».[20]

This transcendent or ultimate reality of the *ie* is symbolized in the family grave and the family altar, that is: in ancestor worship. Any *ie* has a founder as its fountain, and, just as this founder is regarded as of absolute, ultimate value, so is the continuation of the *ie* which took its beginning with him.[21] Any attempt therefore to give an exhaustive description of the *ie* in purely sociological terms, would not do justice to the metaphysical and ultimate aspects of the *ie* in its intrinsic relationship with ancestor worship. The *ie* is, in other words, both a social and a religious unit. This is also to say that any attempt to give an exhaustive presentation of ancestor worship in sociological terms would fail to come to terms with the transcendental aspects and the ultimacy of the *ie*-institution. To this all-important inter-relatedness between *ie* and ancestor worship Takeda says: «In every *ie* there is supposed to be an ancestor or one who founded the lineage. The implication of such a concept of the ancestor for each member family of the *ie* and each person is twofold: ethical and religious. Ethically, everyone of an *ie* is obliged to act in a way worthy of a distinguished lineage. In other words he is never to bring disgrace to the great names of his ancestors. Religiously, it is required of everyone in the *ie* to pay tribute to, and show his respect for, the ancestor. It is important to respect and worship the ancestor not only because he is the founder but also because he is ever concerned about the happiness and welfare of his descendants and has already given them enough protection and security».[22]

Finally then, in our analysis of the *ie*, a question has to be asked as to the relationship between the individual member and the household. Kawa-koshi answers this question right to the point when he says that within this institution «the actual members do not exist as individuals, but are born to take part in and serve this everlasting group».[23] Any member of the *ie* is to be seen more in the category of partaker than in that of individual. This may be said about any person of the *ie* regardless of status. Whether he is house head or servant, a person has to look upon himself as partaker and cooperator in the *ie*, supposed to serve this eternal entity according to his actual position within the structure. The overriding authority is that of the *ie*. No individual may assert his individual norm or judgement over against that of the house. Even the house head is, in principle, nothing but the actual representative of this external authority.[24] He is not the lord of the *ie* but rather its custodian. Its property, its name, its traditions and ancestral tablets do not belong to him. Nor do they belong to the collective family of any actual generation in the way that they may dispose of them simply on the basis of general consensus. They all belong to the *ie*.[25] This social nexus, then, ultimately symbolized in the ancestral tablets, is the protector of both the family and the individual and at the same time the moral arbiter of inter-human relationships in the *ie*. Living and dead are linked together in an ethical circle of obligation (*on* and *ho-on*) to which we shall return below.

Life in this traditional *ie*-structure was regulated in detail and enforced by law through the Meiji Civil Code. We have already seen, however, how this was radically changed with the New Civil Code after the war and how modern changes in Japan have brought great changes also to the family system. «Japanese scholars are in agreement that: (1) the *ie* has influenced Japanese society for more than three and a half centuries..., and (2) with the development of modern capitalism in Japan in the 20's the change in the *ie* has been definitely in the direction of the nuclear family, and this transformation has become more pronounced since 1946».[26]

This process of nuclearization of the family has not, it seems to us, been a simple and unambiguous one-way drive. It is fairly easy to measure the changes in law and in external structures. But as far as the traditional roles were deeply rooted in social, ethical, and religious values, the influx of the new and Western attitudes and structural principles came to create a deep-going conflict of values in the area of family life. The result of this is far more difficult to measure. It does not seem, however, to have been a complete relinquishing of the former for a wholesale acceptance of the latter. Rather it seems, even if the dilemma is by no means solved, to be a reciprocal adaptation of the two to each other in a way that «will be consonant with the realities of their traditional culture and the modern industrial world».[27]

Thus anticipating our conclusion, we should look somewhat closer at the changes as they affect ancestor worship. By the New Civil Code the *ie* system was deprived of its legal status. It no longer figures as a legal entity, nor does the institution of «house head» with its supreme authority. All legal consequences of the *ie* structure have been changed for those of a «conjugal-unit-centered married life»[28] based on respect of the individual and equality of the sexes, with respect to the status of husband and wife, to the status of the children, to inheritance, and so forth. Nowhere in the New Civil Code, however, is any obligation laid on anyone to arrange one's family the one way or the other. We have referred above to article 897 which makes it optional to carry on ancestor worship and related practices «according to custom». There is one more article which may be read as a cautious approval of the old system. Article 730 simply states that «immediate blood relations and other kinsfolk living together should help one another».[29] From the point of view of law, Stoetzel's conclusion may be correct: «The extended family system is still possible, while at the same time the option of organization on another basis has been provided».[30] Nevertheless, the significance of the new code is not to be minimized. Most important of its effects may well have been the «liberation of the family members from the authority of the family».[31]

What, then, are the actual changes in family structures? A rapid rise in the rate of nuclear families of couple and children over against complex or extended families, has been obvious. Fujii reports that the rise in the rate of nuclear families was as high in the five-year period 1960–65 as it was in the 40 years from 1920 to 1960. The rate of nuclear families in 1965 was 70.4% of the nation's total number of households.[32]

This information alone, however, is not sufficient to picture the change, since, as Sano points out, there is a natural development over time from a nuclear family into a complex family.[33] The high rate of nuclear families might simply reflect the high rate of young couples, while many of these may over time develop into a singular complex family of traditional type.

The statistics above, therefore, have to be compared to statistics reflecting people's attitudes towards the succession of the *ie*, as Fujii does in his book. He reports answers given to the following question: «In the case of no child, do you think it better to adopt one (even not of blood-relationship) in order to secure the succession of the *ie*?» The result of this investigation shows that the rate of affirmative answers has dropped from 73% in 1953 to 43% in 1968.[34]

Interpreted together, therefore, Fujii sees in these figures a definite change in people's attitude to the vertical relationship of the *ie* with its value system based on obligation, towards adoption of the horizontal relationship of the nuclear family with its values based on emotions. The increasing number of nuclear families, in other words, does correspond to a decreasing importance of the traditional *ie*.

There are many investigations by Japanese scholars to support this conclusion. Edited by Koyama Takashi, the Institute for the Study of Family Problems (Kazoku mondai kenkyu-kai) published in 1960 an extensive investigation into family life in four typical communities: a mountain village (Obata), a community made up partly of farmers, a community made up partly of non-farmers (Komae) and an apartment residental area of Tokyo (Toyama).[35] A main objective of the study was to investigate people's attitude towards the traditional and the new family systems represented by the Meiji and the New Civil Code. This study made clear a definite difference between rural areas and urban, the former still in many respects close to the old system, while in urban areas family life of more than half of the population conformed in many ways to the new system.[36] The study points out, though, that these findings should not be generalized into the rural and the urban type. That one lives in an urban area, in an apartment building, even in a nuclear family structure, does not necessarily equal a conscious support of the new family system.[37] In conclusion, the study states that the old system finds support among (1) people involved in primary occupations (fishing, farming, forestry) and blue-collars, (2) older people, and (3) people with only compulsory education. The new system is supported by (1) white-collars, (2) educated people, and (3) younger people.[38]

Going back to Fujii's figures for the rate of approval of the succession of the *ie*, the radical drop is an indication of the change that has taken place. However, the 43% approval as late as in 1968 may also be interpreted as a strong indication of the persistence of traditional values. Taking into account the huge urban population's estrangement from farmland, to which the *ie* system was closely linked, and the massive propaganda and exhortation in favor of the new system through the mass media and public education since the war, it may be said to be surprising that 43% still have this attitude to the continuation of the *ie*.

This persistence of old values is pointed to by most scholars in their investigation of post-war changes. Without venturing to a general conclusion for the total society, Sano in 1958 made the following conclusion for the particular areas of her research:

1. Complex family system still prevails without obvious signs for percipitated change;
2. The principle of the lineal family also appears to remain intact for the time being;
3. The rule of residence, on the other hand, has been observed more uxorilocal than generally believed or professed, and the degree of deviation from the traditional pattern in this respect is greater in the urban sample than in the rural.[39]

Now, change has accelerated since the time of Sano's research, as we have referred to above. Nevertheless, more recent studies, too, allow for the persistence of *ie* values. Referring to rural areas Ezra Vogel, for example, says: «Even today, when a very large proportion of farmers are entering the industrial labor force, it is common to continue the *ie* on the same plot of land».[40] In city life in industrialized areas the institution has, according to Vogel, little practical meaning, and has grown weaker and weaker. «In the most industrialized sector of society, the *ie* has declined in importance, but there is still no reason for an individual to have divided loyalties. The *ie* is replaced by the large economic firm on the one hand and the small nuclear family on the other.... In those sectors of society where the *ie* continues as an important economic unit (among farmers, independant professionals, and small businessmen), it continues to serve as the basic solidarity group».[41]

In Takahashi's study referred to above, the author points out that in spite of all external changes from old to new structures, the Japanese family consciousness is not yet substituted by an «ideology» based on nuclear family values. In spite of 30 years with the New Civil Code, the Japanese family is still dominated by the parent-child relationship more than by that of husband-wife. The two systems exist in competition, side by side, and the author expresses strong doubts that there will be any complete change to a nuclear-family ideological consciousness in the near future.[42] The fact that the rate of *butsudan* in nuclear families of successive or inherited households/*honke* is much higher than in nuclear families of separately erected households/*bunke* – 94% to 49% – shows that a nuclear family by itself does not necessarily mean that modern family-ideology has substituted that of the traditional linear family. The two may simply overlap.[43]

What we have seen from post-war sociological research should be sufficient to support the view that no simple conclusion as to the position of the traditional *ie* structures and *ie* values in present family life is possible. The changes that have taken place have produced one group – mainly in industrial urban areas – for whom the old *ie* structure is irrelevant. For another segment of the population – particularly in the rural areas – the traditional system is still significant. In between these groups the third – and possibly the largest – is to be found. This group is living with family structures that in some way may be «consonant with the realities of the traditional culture and the modern industrial world», and for many this goes to mean a nuclear family structure containing essential and typical Japanese elements.

Finally, in this section on ancestor worship and the *ie*, we have to ask how the modern changes in family structures have affected ancestor worship.

For the part of the population still living by and large within the *ie* structure, it goes without saying that ancestor worship still functions in the traditional way. By those most radically alienated from the old structures, ancestor worship may be regarded largely irrelevant, outdated and even feudalistic. When it comes to the group in between, several indications serve to show that ancestor worship is adapted to the new realities.

We have already in chapter 1.1 referred to Rissho Kosei-kai as a typical example of ancestor worship adapted to modern values like respect of the individual and equality of the sexes.[44] The practice, however, to adopt «ancestors» not formally to be called so from the point of view of the *ie* structure, may be observed as a trend in families far beyond the limited range of Rissho Kosei-kai.[45] In his extensive research Smith found quite a number of such ancestral tablets of non-lineals and non-kin that were not supposed to be in the altar from an *ie* structural point of view. According to Smith, the indications are that this is a fairly new practice, reflecting a change from the *ie*-centered to modern family-centered ancestor worship.

Along similar lines go some of the points that Takahashi makes in her study. She is of the opinion that two of her hypotheses as to the change of ancestor worship in modern Japan may be seen as verified from the statistic material collected. The first is that the significance of ancestor worship as the number one factor for the continuation of the *ie* is reduced. Nevertheless, ancestor worship as the rite for «spiritual interchange» between ancestors and descendants continues to be a religious act of the common people. The other is that the modern element of companionship between husband and wife is bringing this horizontal relationship into ancestor worship. When separated by death, ancestor worship towards the spouse will be an essential element.[46]

Another indication of ancestor worship geared to modern «individiua-lism» is the practices at the Isshinji-temple referred to above.[47] It is an example of how Buddhism as «funeral Buddhism» in the context of the *ie* has adapted itself to modern circumstances and to the fact that a great bulk of the population are living more as individuals than as *ie* partakers. The change of family structures left unsolved many of the religious needs that were met by traditional ancestor worship, and these, then, are catered to by ancestor worship re-arranged and re-interpreted the way we see it at Isshinji.[48]

The practices at Isshinji, though, may seem grotesque to many modern Japanese who have little sympathy for traditional religion. Thinking of this group, Takatori/Hashimoto have some penetrating remarks that deserve our attention. Ancestor worship may be said to be a worship of the continuity of life. Now, there are indications that traditional ancestor worship's preoccupation with the past, in the modern nuclear family is changed for a preoccupation with the future, a worship of life-continuity with the future, or, in other words, «descendant worship» instead of «ancestor worship». «For the modern Japanese parents who have difficulties in believing in a transcendant god, it seems that the child may play the role of the divine. There is no greater thing than the expectations the parents harbor vis-a-vis the new-born child».[49] Takatori/Hashimoto see this as possibly a precursor to a new era when new communities are created on new criteria and in greater freedom, and where ancestor worship may be given a universal interpretation and serve the well-being of the universal ancestors.

In conclusion, we should once again stress the importance of ancestor worship as an intrinsic element of the traditional household the way we have seen in the first half of this chapter. When it comes to the situation in contemporary Japan, we are confronted with a complicated state of affairs. The traditional unity of household and ancestor worship may be found accepted and conformed to by some, rejected by others, and – maybe by the majority of the common people – considered as part of the traditional culture that in some way or other has to be carried on and transformed into a consonant coexistence with the realities of modern, industrialized Japan. We are probably right when we, with Takahashi Hiroko, view the values represented in ancestor worship not only as objects of change, but as agents leading the changing process as well.

This analysis of ancestor worship and the *ie* has repeatedly made us touch upon the ethical implications involved. We now turn our attention to that part of the problem.

2.1.2 *Ethical Implications of Ancestor Worship*

The general problem of the relationship between religion and ethics in Japanese culture is an extremely complicated question that we shall not attempt to answer. That both Shinto and Buddhist philosophy have had a profound influence on Japanese ethics, should be beyond doubt.[50] It should be just as obvious, however, that it was neither Shinto nor Buddhism but Confucianism that came to provide the ethical system that «was taken over as the ethical code of Japan».[51] In the assimilation of Confucian ethical philosophy and practice in Japan, the indigenous institution of ancestor worship played an important role. Just as we have seen was the case with the adoption of Buddhism, Chinese Confucianism, too, came to be «assimilated by the Japanese in such a way as to fit [it] to their institution of ancestor-worship. In the assimilation of Confucianism it was filial piety which was most stressed».[52] All through its history in Japan, from its early introduction and not least during the Tokugawa era, Confucianism came to interact with ancestor worship, partly with the effect that the latter caused certain aspects of the Confucian moral system to receive particular emphasis, partly with the effect that «the aboriginal institution of ancestor-worship was... further solidified when it acquired from Confucianism a theoretical basis».[53]

Thus, although Ooms may be right when he says that «the ancestor cult does not have its own moral code» and that «its ethical prescriptions are not clearly defined»,[54] it is nevertheless obvious that it has implications for ethics which – over the centuries – have been closely associated with the philosophy that provided the «moral code» and defined the «ethical prescriptions».

Ancestor worship, in other words, provides basic premises for ethics with implications for concrete moral behavior. On the basis of what we have said about ancestor worship and the *ie*, it should not be surprising, however, that these are premises and implications not so much of a universal nature for moral conduct in general, as of a specific nature for behavior within a limited social nexus. Our purpose in this chapter is, accordingly, not to attempt a portrayal of Confucian morality in toto as derived from ancestor worship but to point to these general premises and implications.

In the first place, ancestor worship – as we have seen it in the framework of the household – has important implications with respect to ethical criteria for the evaluation of good and evil. As a basic symbol of the family, ancestor worship is constitutive to the primary social nexus to which an individual belongs, and in which he functions as a partaker and coopera-tor.[55] No one in the family is playing his own game. The overriding principle is the harmony and the peace of the group, disturbance of which constitutes a serious taboo.[56] Positively stated, within this social nexus, the prosperity, unity, harmony, and honor of the group is considered to be the summum bonum. The ultimate ethical criterion, therefore, is not to be found in any universal standard transcending individuals and social groups. Neither is individual happiness and edification to serve as the ultimate criterion for good and evil. Whether the interests of the family, including living and dead, are served or not, is ultimately the standard applied for a proper distinction between moral and unmoral conduct.[57]

This implies that the aspirations and the will of the individual are never to be invoked as justification of a person's acts and behavior. The will of the individual is supposed to be in harmony with the collective will and objectives of the family, and the will of this collective is further supposed to coincide with that of the ancestors.

The idea of the living members of the family carrying out the ancestral will of their forefathers, was elaborated on by many outstanding representatives of the *kokutai* ideology. Writing on ancestor worhsip in Hozumi Yatsuka's thinking, Hirai says: «It almost seems that ancestral will unfolds itself through the history of iye and the family must continue in order to help such an unfolding. Ancestral will can be both explicit, where there exists a House law given by the ancestors, and implicit in other cases. In the case of the latter, room for interpretation by the living is naturally considerable. In any case, it is regarded as the descendants' responsibility to their ancestors to give life to that will».[58]

This is not to say that ancestor worship has to go together with a conservative and past-oriented value-orientation. That this is a strong tendency, there is little reason to doubt.[59] However, Plath makes an important point when he notes that «in the Japanese view the ancestors do not demand that life continue exactly as they knew it. What they expect is not so much specific performance as effective performance – effective meaning whatever will assure the continuity of the household line. Far from hindering change, ancestor worship in Japan at least can be a spur to it».[60] The decisive point is, that the individual and the family at any time should know themselves to be in accordance and in harmony with the will of the forefathers. That will, namely, is the ultimate one.

Together with the ultimate will goes ultimate authority. Within the *ie*, as we have seen above, ancestor worship makes the household itself an absolute, objective authority of any individual integrated in its structure. When this authority is represented in any actual generation by the household head, his authority is final because – and as far as – he acts on behalf of the ancestors and the *ie*. His unique position in the everlasting line of continuity from ancestors to descendants means that he is endowed with «a transcendent, transhuman, mysterious power and holiness which has its origin in a transcendent, transhuman and mysterious being».[61] When he serves as moral guide in the family, it means that he represents the ancestors as the final moral arbiters of the house. «A household head is a servant of higher authority, and the ancestor is the last tribunal».[62] This is the final authority over against which no person is supposed to assert his own individual norm or judgment. On the contrary, each member of the family is supposed to submit to this ultimate authority of the group, rooted as it is in that of the ancestors.

Thus, ancestor worship carries implications that have been decisive in the formation of the basic and most talked-about characteristic of Japanese social intercourse, the loyal submission to a limited social group, first and foremost to the family. In Japanese social life «complete and willing dedication of the self to others in a specific human collective... occupies a dominant position».[63] There have been strong statements both by Japanese and foreign scholars to the effect that the Japanese «has no clear consciousness of his individual self».[64] «An individual is not considered to be an independent entity. Rather, his interest is absorbed in the interest of the collectivity to which he belongs, and the interest of the collectivity is recognized as having primary importance, while the interest of the individual has merely a secondary importance».[65] However, if this is interpreted to mean that the individual is completely neglected within the social nexus, we would probably over-interpret certain data at the expense of others.[66] How ever enigmatic the status of the individual may be, it should be clear, though, that in the context of ancestor worship the individual is related to a collective that is invested with an ultimacy that cannot be transcended, and because it cannot be transcended it cannot be opposed or objected to without isolating the individual from the group. There is a primacy of the collective to which the individual necessarily is secondary.

In the second place, ancestor worship carries implications when it comes to concrete behavior and its motivation.

A main motive in ancestor worship is that of gratefulness.[67] Thanks to the ancestors, both to their labor and accomplishments while alive and their benevolent protection as ancestral spirits after death, the house and the individual are alive and well. This benevolence bestowed upon the house and its members is rendered by the concept of *on*.[68] Just as parents bestow *on* without limit upon their children by giving birth to them and bringing them up, the *on* incurred by a person naturally goes back beyond the actual parents to the ancestors of preceding generations. Being the recipient of such unlimited *on*, the individual knows himself to be in a position of thankfulness, and to be obliged to repay this *on* by and through his own conduct and contribution. Thus the repayment of *on/ho-on* becomes a major motivating force for moral behavior. The ancestors and their descendants are tied together in a circle of obligation.[69] It is important already at this point to note that this is not a circle where the individual is obliged to repay only past favors of the ancestors. The obligation to repay is also motivated by the ancestors' actual protection and benevolent support of the living. Both past and present favors of the ancestors create the foundation, so to speak, upon which the family may successfully function as an integrated community if each individual takes his share in repaying the *on* in this circle of obligation.

Now, the actual repayment of *on* in the family-centered Confucian ethics is carried out through the well-known virtue of filial piety/*ko*.[70] Filial piety is to be considered as a response on the part of the child to the *on* of the parents, and just as the *on* incurred by a person goes back beyond the parents to the ancestors, so is *ko* a duty which is extended beyond the parents to the ancestors as well.[71] The virtue of filial piety is, in other words, closely linked to ancestor worship. Some examples from traditional Japanese ethics make this point clear. According to Hirata Atsutane «the foundation of the 'Way'... is where man is mindful of his ancestors. Why is this? It is because care for the ancestors is filial duty».[72] In Teijo's Family Instruction it says that the «ancestors should be revered and venerated, not treated with remissness or negligence....Such being the case, on the anniversaries of their deaths one should... set out the tables furnished with offerings, do obeisance, and not neglect to make a visit to their graves and worship there».[73] This is a typical expression of ancestor worship as the correct filial attitude to one's forbearers. In the *kokutai*-ideology and pre-war official textbooks this link between filial piety and ancestor worship is again singled out and emphasized: «Loyalty and filial piety is the basic principle of ethics and the foundation of the hundred virtues. The great moral principle of loyalty and filial piety is the expression of ancestor worship, born in the family system and maintained in the family system».[74]

What, then, does filial piety mean in concrete terms? It has different actual implications all according to one's status in the family, and it is not necessary for us to go into details at this point. It should suffice to note that when a family head has a certain power to control and guide the members of the house, it does not permit him to act as a despot. He himself is subject to the authority of the ancestors, and he will be a filial son when he plays his role, faithfully invoking this authority «as the sanction for his headship».[75] The actual proof of his sincerity is his mindful performance of the ancestral rites. Any other member of the family will serve the group according to his/her status as the first and basic requirement of filial piety. This is to be done in such a way that the harmony and the unity of the group is not broken but strengthened and solidified. For everyone, loyalty to the family is fundamental, and to honor the name of the family becomes «an important moral force operating on the individual in all his dealings with the outside world».[76] Whatever brings honor to that name, eo ipso brings honor to the ancestors and is a genuine expression of the piety which is expected within the circle of obligation.

In drawing our conclusions of the ethical implications of ancestor worship, two main characteristics may be said to be significant from our point of view. First, the basis for ethics and morals is found within the social nexus of the family itself. This social nexus is in the context of ancestor worship invested with an ultimacy that makes unnecessary a foundation of ethics in a transcendent reality beyond this group. Through the concept and the reality of the ancestors, the social nexus of the family carries within itself the ultimate reason and the ultimate criterion for ethical behavior.

Second, this ultimacy of the particular group and the corresponding lack of a universal basis for ethics which transcends the human-social nexus, leads to a fundamental ethical distinction between in-group and out-group. Ethics is primarily related to a particular social sphere where it is valid, and where its requirements are known, while there is really no basis which justifies and codifies ethics once one is estranged from this group, or is without such a sphere of belonging.[77]

Keeping in mind the modern changes in the family structure, it is not surprising that one of the main characteristics of post-war Japan is that of a profound moral dilemma.[78] Moral standards and moral behavoir are certainly not the same today as they were in the feudal days of the Tokugawa era. On the other hand, the change that has taken place does not seem so much to be a deep-going, radical change in fundamental principles, as an immediate consequence partly of the narrowing of the family group, partly of the rise and development of new and additional loyalty groups.[79] With ancestor worship partly within changed social structures, it is to be expected that its ethical implications incarnate themselves in actual life in a way which may differ from that of another era.

The complexity and ambiguity of the situation is put into relief if we compare the results of sociological research at this point: On the one hand «large numbers of individuals have become more independent of their families, and the definition of 'the family' with which the individual identifies has narrowed from the wider kinship group conceived as an entity persisting through the generations to the more ephemeral household based on the conjugal family».[80] On the other hand, «whatever the trends may be, familial collectivity orientations remain strong if not dominant in the lives of most contemporary Japanese.... Rather than self-orientations, the average individual in Japan still maintains the family as a frame of reference for many daily decisions»,[81] and «the loyalty of the individual to his group remains the most important attribute of the respected person».[82] This is not to say that ancestor worship is still the most significant factor in the formation of the ethos of the nation. It is to say, however, that its basic ethical implications are still to be clearly recognized in the inter-human relationships of modern Japanese society.

In this analysis of the ethical implications of ancestor worship we have used the term «circle of obligation» to describe the moral relationship between the ancestors and the descendants. The relationship between the living and the dead is not limited, however, to this one of moral character. The study of ancestor worship takes us a step further in our understanding of the intercourse between the living and the dead members of the family.

2.2 Living and Dead – an Interdependent Relationship

When we ask for the implications of ancestor worship to the understanding of the relationship between the living and the dead, i.e., the relationship of this life to afterlife, we are taken to the very core of this phenomenon. At the same time this question takes us from the realm of the social and ethical aspects of ancestor worship to that of the religious.[83]

Asking such a question, we are immediately confronted by a wide variety of beliefs and ideas related to Japanese religion in general. We will strictly limit ourselves, however, to what seems to us to be verifiable inferences from the symbols of the ancestral rites themselves, and bring in material from a wider religious context only as far as it serves an adequate interpretation of these symbols. Even so, we shall have to concentrate on what are the main points for our purposes.

We have repeatedly said that ancestor worship is not a consistent religious system. This becomes eminently clear at this point. The implications it carries for the understanding of death and afterlife present an extremely complex set of ideas, some of which seem to be clearly contradictory to an outsider. And inconsistent they probably are, having their roots in different religious traditions intermingled in ancestor worship, as we have pointed out above. Beliefs originating in indigenous folk religion exist partly in direct opposition to orthodox Buddhist teaching, partly in more or less consistent coalescence.[84]

Bearing in mind and trying to be faithful to this complex nature of our object, we shall first undertake an investigation into the implications of ancestor worhsip for the view of life and death in general. This will make clear to us that parallel to the «circle of obligation» linking the living and the dead members of the family as described in the previous chapter, there is a just as significant «circle of interdependence» between the two. Our second task will be to analyze what this «circle of interdependence» means for the «life» of the dead, and, finally, for that of the living.

2.2.1 *Life-Death from the Perspective of Ancestor Worship*

It has already become clear from our study of ancestor worship and the *ie*, that in the context of ancestor worship death does not constitute an ultimate end to man's existence. Somehow there is a continued existence beyond death which provides the basis for a fundamental community between the living and the dead. This idea of community, then, constitutes a highly significant aspect of the view of life-death. Matthias Eder seems to touch the very nerve in Japanese folk religion when he says that insofar as folk religion is free from Buddhist influence, it is not so much concerned with giving information on the nature of afterlife, as it is with the effort to include the dead in a continued community with the living family.[85] This is also to say that from the perspective of ancestor worship the continued existence in an afterlife is seen as intimately related to one's particular family and not primarily in general and universal categories. The central pivot in Yanagida's delineation of the Japanese view of life-death is to be found right at this point: The ultimate worth – on the one hand – of the future-orientation towards the coming generations, and – on the other hand – of the past-oriented unity with the ancestors.[86] Quite in accordance with this, Ooms found the symbols of ancestor worship to make clear «that the main concern of ancestor worship is the *ie* and afterlife».[87]

This fundamental community between the living and the dead members of the family manifests itself in different ways in the ancestral rites. In our presentation of the rites in section 1.3.2 & 3 we have seen how the ancestors are cared for through offerings and prayers, and how the living share with the dead both in terms of food offerings and in terms of reports to the ancestors of important events of the family. The ancestors are further prayed to for support and protection and they will visit the family for fellowship on certain occasions, the most important of which is the

Bon festival. We have already seen how the idea of reunion with the dead for fellowship in a pleasant mood is a central motif in the festival.

We shall return to some of these points below. In this context we note how these different aspects of the rites reflect the significant feeling of closeness, community, and continuity between the living and the dead. In the words of Hori Ichiro, this unbreakable spiritual bond between the ancestors and the descendants, this closeness and interaction between the living and the dead, provided the Japanese with an answer to the universal quest for permanence and eternity.[88]

The ancestral rites are, in other words, based on «the assumption that some sort of spirit survives the body after death».[89] This is a basic supposition in Japanese religion from its earliest stages. The soul/*tamashii* is an entity in man that after death leaves the corpse and starts its own independent existence. The soul is clearly distinguished from the body, and the two are seen as separable entities.[90] At death this soul enters a period of uncertainty. Polluted by death and potentially dangerous it may wander for several weeks, hovering around the corpse and the family. By death, however, the soul has entered on a path of growth towards purity and safety and ultimate ancestorhood, a goal that will be attained over time through the rites of the living.[91]

The question about the whereabouts of the soul has been answered in equivocal and ambiguous terms. The idea of the spirits of the dead residing in the mountains is old and widespread and is still to be found.[92] At the same time the soul is clearly thought to be closer at hand. It may reside in the temple, in the grave, and in the tablet at the home altar.[93] This ambiguity with respect both to spacial and temporal aspects of the afterlife is well described by Plath: «The world beyond cannot be described in any but equivocal phrases. Spatially it is both here and there, temporally both then and now. The departed and ancestors always are close by; they can be contacted immediately at the household shelf, the graveyard, or elsewhere. Yet when they return 'there' after the midsummer reunion they are seen off as for a great journey. They are perpetually present. Yet they come and go from periodic household foregatherings».[94]

To get a more precise view of the fate of the soul after death, we return to the idea of its process of growth. This is an idea of tremendous importance and closely linked to the set of rites that we above described as «rites not to be repeated». The process of the soul towards mature ancestorhood is generally pictured by Japanese folklorists as correlating to a child's growth into adulthood.[95] As a child passes through stages from birth to adulthood, the soul passes through corresponding stages from *shirei* to mature ancestorhood/*sorei*. Just as the growth of the child is marked by specific rites and occasions, so is that of the soul marked by corresponding rites. In the growth of the child, the rite of marriage marks the decisive turning point between the period of growth towards adulthood and the period of adulthood itself. Correspondingly, the final memorial rite at *tomuraiage* at the 33rd or 50th anniversary marks the decisive turning point between the soul's period of growth towards ancestorhood, and the state of ancestorhood itself. Up to this watershed the soul keeps its individuality, and it is served through individual rites by the living. At the time of *tomuraiage*, however, the soul loses its individuality and sublimates with the supra-individual, collective ancestral being.

But even before this ultimate stage is reached, there are important turning points in the growth process. When the tablet is raised to the family shelf at the 49th day rite, it is done with a sigh of relief, so to speak. The first 49 days are marked by uncertainty and fear. When this day is passed, however, the soul will certainly be subject to further change over the years, but «if everything is done as prescribed, nothing will go wrong from now on».[96]

Without being synchronized with or systematized vis-à-vis the 49th day turning point, the first Bon is also seen as marking a definite change for the *shirei*. At the first Bon after death the *shirei* will be cared for in a special way; later on it will be welcomed back and treated like anyone of the many ancestral souls of the family.

Returning to the watershed at the final memorial rite, we may ask how one conceives of the soul that at this point joins the collective ancestral being. The simple fact that the memorial rites actually take their end at this point, signifies that the dead is no longer conceived of as being in the need of the *kuyo* of the living.[97] In joining the ancestral *sorei* the soul is, in other words, elevated to a state of perfection that transcends ordinary human categories. In the words of Takeda, the holy, protecting, and venerated *sorei* is conceived of in terms of a supra-individual, an unlimited and abstract *kami* or buddha.[98] Even though it may be very difficult to answer the question what kind of *kami* the *sorei* is to be identified with, there is little doubt among Japanese folklorists that after the final memorial rite, the soul is – in its fusion with the collective ancestral spirits of the house – somehow regarded in terms of *kami*.[99]

Now, what we have said earlier about the term *muen-botoke* has already made it clear that there are spirits who fall outside this process of growth towards ancestorhood. The main characteristic of this group is that they are not taken proper care of after death, a fact that leaves them in the unhappy circumstance of being wandering spirits, i.e., spirits who are to be feared and to whom special offerings are to be given, for example, at Bon. These spirits may be comforted in their unhappy circumstances, and their sufferings may be alleviated at least temporarily. It is doubtful, however, that their status can ever be changed into that of a soul following the normal growth towards ancestorhood.[100]

At this point we touch upon a very intricate question. Does the idea of rebirth have any place in this growth process of the soul? It is possibly true when it is stated that «the question of the presence of the concept of reincarnation in Japanese folk religion is a difficult one and possibly one which will never be fully explained».[101] Yanagida lists the possibility of rebirth as the fourth characteristic of the traditional Japanese view of life-death: «... and the fourth would be that the idea that he [the dead] could be reborn again and again to carry on his same work».[102] Now, Doerner quotes Yanagida to the effect that «ancestorhood excludes the possibility of rebirth»: «I cannot guarantee, with my power, that it is true, but by the time they [the souls] have attained the position where they can be worshipped, there is no longer an occasion by which they can be reborn».[103] It seems to us, however, that both Yanagida himself and other folklorists are equivocal on this point. Yanagida speaks of reincarnation of «a distant ancestor» and the possibility that «generations of ancestors come again and again to serve their country» in a way that seems to leave quite an amount of ambiguity.[104] When Tsuboi illustrates the correlative circle of life and death referred to above, he seems to leave room for the idea of rebirth even after the soul has attained the stable staus of *sorei*.[105]

When Ooms, on the other hand, pictures the parallel growth towards adulthood and ancestorhood by the use of a circle-illustration, he does not draw a full circle, but ends the circumference at the point of attained ancestorhood/*tomuraiage*, and adds the following remark to the problem of rebirth: «If the doctrine of rebirth were extant, the end of the second cycle (becoming an ancestor) would mean again the starting point of the first. However, the pattern is not perfect in this point, and it is also difficult to see how an ancestor, once reincarnated, could still keep his character of ancestor».[106] Smith, too, is reluctant to give rebirth any place in the traditional Japanese view of the ancestors: «They are not really thought of as ever being reborn, I think, in part because they need not be».[107]

This presentation of various views shows clearly the complexity of the problem. Maybe we are justified in concluding, however, that the idea of rebirth cannot be said to be entirely alien to the Japanese view of life and death underlying ancestor worship? It may be seen as representing one aspect of the closeness and continuity between this life and afterlife, even though it is impossible to fit it into any perfect, consistent pattern. It seems that other ideas – especially the process towards everlasting ancestral status – have been of greater significance.

There is, however, another way in which the Buddhist idea of rebirth seems to have been adopted to ancestor worship, and which has to do with the general problem of the adaptation of Buddhist ideas to the Japanese view of life-death.[108]

As a point of departure for a brief analysis of the Japanized Buddhist ideas found in ancestor worship in this respect, we go back to the problem of the first 49 days after death mentioned above. Why this change after 49 days? There seems to be little doubt about the strong influence of Buddhism at this point. Its doctrine on the purgatory/*chuin*, where the fate of the soul for its next existence is to be decided, became related to this first period in the course of the soul after death. Buddhism arranged this period into a definite term of mourning for the soul in the purgatory.[109] During its time in the *chuin* the soul has to pass several judges, and the material for judgment is partly made up by the merits of the rites performed by the living on behalf of the soul. The 49th day marks the *man-chuin*, the end of the purgatory period. By this time, the fate of the soul is decided and it may continue its course.[110]

Now, in orthodox Buddhism the *chuin* is a period of transition from the point of death to the point of conception of a new life, and the new life will be a reincarnation into one of the six directions, that of hell, hungry spirit, animal, malevolent nature spirit, human existence, or deva existence.[111] In its junction with Japanese thought and ancestor worship, however, this idea of *chuin* and rebirth was related to the soul of the dead, which came to be regarded as the carrier of the karma in its continued course of transmigration.[112] Thus, the 49 days in the *chuin* became an important period in the process of the soul for the securing of its rebirth in heaven/*gokuraku*.

Together with the ideas of *chuin*, karma and samsara in orthodox Buddhism, goes the idea of Nirvana and the Pure Land. These are not in orthodox Buddhism seen in the categories of afterlife correlating to this life, and have, accordingly, nothing to do with corporal death. They are categories of a completely different dimension as far as they are the absolute negation of both life and death, a dimension transcending both existence and non-existence, correlating, not to this life, but to the whole notion of samsara.[113]

Here again we see a decisive change as these concepts have been related to ancestor worship on folk level. The extremely complex and philosophical nature of these concepts had to give way to a popular «misunderstanding» and a simple identification of Nirvana and the Pure Land with afterlife. Death became the gateway to Nirvana, which was identified with «the other world» of popular belief, where the ancestors rest in peace and from where they protect their descendants.[114]

This seems to be the basis for the peculiar Japanese use of the term *hotoke*. With death as the gateway to Nirvana, and the ancestors traditionally being regarded as worthy of respect and worship, the dead naturally became identified with *hotoke*. In the context of ancestor worship, then, buddhahood was not attained by the way prescribed in orthodox Buddhism but simply by way of death and sublimation with the generations of ancestral spirits.[115]

This coalescence of Buddhist thought with indigenuous beliefs accounts for many of the inconsistencies in the view of life-death from the perspective of ancestor worship. What we just said about death-Nirvana-*hotoke* points to one of the main contradictions. A belief that the soul by death would be put on his way to becoming a *hotoke* by the time of *tomuraiage*, would seem to be fairly consistent with the indigenuous view of the growth process. It would even seem to give place for the possibility of some kind of rebirth of the soul in various directions in the course of the process. However, the dead are identified as *hotoke* long before the time of the sublimation of the *shirei* with the *sorei* at the last memorial rite. They may be so identified and so treated at least after the first 49 days or after the first Bon. The growth process is, in other words, combined with a popular interpretation of Nirvana and attainment of buddhahood/*jobutsu* in a way that ascribes to the dead the status of *hotoke* at the same time as the soul is considered to be on its way to perfect ancestorhood.

Another significant contradiction is seen in the fact that the possibility of being reborn in hell/*jigoku* after the 49 days in the *chuin*, exists side by side with the popular notion of all the dead being *hotoke*. At the same time as the threat of *jigoku* exists as a decisive factor determining the diligence with which the living perform the *hoji* rites, Smith is probably right – from the point of view of traditional Japanese thought – when he says that «there are few things so unlikely to the Japanese as the suggestion that one's own ancestor might be suffering the torments of hell for the misdeeds of life».[116]

Any attempt at synchronizing and harmonizing such inconsistencies into a coherent pattern would probably fail. They are to be accepted as clear evidence of the coalescence of ideas from different traditions. They show that life-death from the perspective of ancestor worship is to be pictured in a way that cannot but disappoint the one who looks for system and coherence.

On the other hand, there are important conclusions to be drawn. One is that of continuity and community. Through the ancestral rites the living and the dead members of the house are linked together in a way that makes both sides interdependent on the other. Together with the view that sees the dead as being in the need of the *kuyo* of the living, however, definitely goes another one, according to which the ancestors are seen in categories that demand respect and worship on the part of the living. This latter aspect is partly seen as a stage which follows subsequently upon the year-long period in which the soul is in need of the *kuyo* of the living, partly it reflects a quality of the dead that coexists with its needs for the ritual concern of the family.

Let us look a little closer, then, at the reciprocal interdependence.

2.2.2 *The Dependence of the Dead upon the Living*

The first half of the «circle of interdependence» is the dependence of the dead upon the living. Especially when we look at the funeral rite and the subsequent *hoji* ceremonies described in section 1.3.2, the dependence of the dead on the rites of the living for salvation is obvious. This point is, accordingly, repeatedly stressed by both foreign and Japanese scholars.[117] The process of growth from *shirei* to *sorei* is, in other words, not to be seen as an automatic process that will go on irrespective of the concern of the living.

At this point there may be some difference between indigenous thought as developed in Shinto, and the interpretation of the growth process in Buddhist context. In his comparative study of life after death in folk Shinto and in Christianity, Doerner states: «It is also incorrect to think of the soul of the deceased as ... depending on the memorial services for attainment of ancestorhood.... After the memory of the deceased has faded ... becoming an ancestor is for all practical purposes an automatic thing».[118] Whether this is correct from the point of view of what Doerner calls «folk Shinto», we are not in a position to judge. Our point is that such a statement cannot be made with reference to ancestor worship in traditional Buddhist context. To use the words of Watanabe Shoko: «For the *borei* [i.e. *shirei*] to become a *sorei*, however, is not only a problem of time. It presupposes the diligent performance of the rites by the bereaved.... If these are neglected, the *borei* will not become a *sorei*; it will not only fall into a miserable existence itself, but bring about all kinds of harms to the living».[119]

This belief is closely connected with such concepts as purgatory/*chuin*, transfer of merits/*eko*, *tsuizen eko*, *tsuizen kuyo*, and others, and has a long history in its relatedness to ancestral rites. Already in early Indian Buddhism the idea that one may confer on another person the merit from one's own good works – which is what is implied in the terms *eko*, *tsuizen eko*, *tsuizen kuyo* – developed on the basis of pre-Buddhist beliefs.[120] In Japan this fundamental idea came to be dominant in the integrated history of Buddhism and ancestor worship from its very beginning. In early Shingon-Buddhism the repeated recitation of the magic *komyo* formula at funerals and subsequent masses was thought to have a strong salvatory effect on the dead.[121] Coming into the Heian era the salvatory effect of the rites was strongly emphasized in both the Jodo and the Zen sects.[122] At the same time, the idea of *chuin* with its corresponding belief in the ten judges, spread rapidly among the masses, and was adopted by all the different sects. This led people to become extremely busy with the masses for the dead, indispensable as they were for the salvation of the soul.

This salvatory effect of the deeds of the living on the dead is also reflected in other ways in early Japanese Buddhism. The main purpose, for example, of the early establishment of clan temples «was to pray for the *bodhi* (enlightenment and salvation) of the ancestors», and the act of building itself was conceived of as a merit for the benefit of the dead, that is *tsuizen kuyo*.[123]

According to Sakyamuni man's fate after death is determined by his deeds in life, and no other person can contribute to it. Nevertheless, the theory of transference of merits came to be one of the characteristic features of Mahayana Buddhism and is to be interpreted in close connection with such fundamental doctrines as the rule of causation and the cosmic oneness of the universe.[124] Even though everything, according to its outward appearance, is veiled in suffering and pain, everything is essentially of the same buddha-nature/*bussho*. The «self» is included in everything and everything is included in the «self» in a way that makes gain for the «self» gain for all, and vice versa. On the basis of such an all-inclusive oneness, the virtuous life of the descendants automatically becomes the deeds of the ancestors. Moreover, since all existence is linked by the rule of causation, the «good religious acts which are performed by the descendants and the merits gained therefrom will produce good results for the ancestors and for the Buddhas as well, which is the significance of merit-transference as expounded by Mahayana Buddhism.... Its real significance lies in the increase of merit for oneself to be transferred to the ancestors in order to expedite the means with which the ancestors can be elevated to Buddhahood».[125]

The transference of merits through ancestral rites is, accordingly, related also to such a fundamental idea as the attainment of buddhahood/*jobutsu*. By their transference of merits the living may promote the buddha-status of the dead. That this is a central motive in the Buddhist interpretation of the masses for the dead is seen, for example, from the inquiry into people's attitude towards funerals and masses undertaken by the Buddhist Komazawa University referred to above. One of the questions raised in the inquiry was that of the meaning of the rites. To this question five leading answers were used, of which two were especially coined to find out to which extent people held a traditional Buddhist view of the rites. One of these two leading answers was whether the interrogated person regarded the masses as being «for the sake of the *jobutsu* of the dead».[126]

This is, briefly stated, the theoretical basis upon which the masses are to be seen as merits promoting the salvation of the dead. Merit, now, may be attained by different means. «The greatest merits can be attained by the dedication of offerings, such as movable and immovable properties, to the Buddha, the recitation of Buddhist sutras and the construction of temples and images of the Buddha».[127] When it comes to the two most common forms of *tsuizen kuyo* among ordinary people, one is – again according to Takeda – the so-called *zaibutsu kuyo*, that is offering of money, fruit, vegetables etc. The other is the *hoho kuyo*, that is recitation of sutras.[128] As we have seen above, both offerings and sutrachanting are central elements in the masses for the dead.

To this should be added some words on the recitation of *nembutsu* as a means for the attainment of merits for the dead. Even though recitation of *nembutsu* originally was conceived of as a means for one's own salvation, it soon turned into a powerful formula as *kuyo* for the dead.[129] Such a salvatory recitation of *nembutsu* for the dead has a long tradition in connecton with funerals and masses. It goes back to the early Tendai sect and is carried on now especially in Jodo-Buddhism.[130] Its importance today is seen both in connection with funerals and masses and with the activities of local so-called Nembutsu fraternities.[131]

Thus, the possibility for the living to enter into the «life» of the dead and actively contribute to the process of salvation – or, negatively stated, to obstruct the process by negligence – is a major motive for the ancestral rites in their traditional Buddhist context.[132] There is, however, one major and very interesting exception to this. Already Gabriel, in his article from 1938, pointed out that Shin-Buddhism (Jodo Shin-shu) differs from other Buddhist sects on this point.[133] This is not surprising, as man's salvation, according to Shin-Buddhist faith, is totally dependent upon Amida's mercy alone. In his *Buddhist Handbook for Shin-shu Followers* Hanayama is keen, therefore, to point out that memorial services in Shin-shu have a different meaning than in the other sects: «By chanting the sutras and having special services on these days, the surviving family expects to send the deceased to a better place by means of the virtues of sutra-chanting. This was the original meaning for having these services. In the Jodo-shin sect, however, these services have a different significance. Namely, they are not for the sake of sending the deceased to a better place, since his destination to be born is already decided by the power of the Amida Buddha's Vow, but for the expression of thankfulness to the Amida Buddha and in memory of the deceased».[134]

At least in theory Shin-shu is clear at this point. It is a question, however, whether its followers are as convinced and unequivocal when it comes to actual practice. According to Tamamuro the popular ideas of the *chuin*, the judges, and the transference of merits, were so dominant in the popularization of all the sects among the masses in the medieval age, that even Shi-shu had to adopt them for its spread among the masses.[135] Over the centuries, then, these ideas seem to have become so intimately associated with the masses for the dead, that even though Shin-shu theoretically rejects the salvatory effect of the rites, Smith may be reflecting the actual state of affairs when he reports that «in my interviews with families belonging to the Jodo-shin sect I found only marginal appreciation of this point».[136]

Finally, we could ask the question whether the process of salvation is thought of as fulfilled once the dead has reached the status of ancestor-hood/*sorei*? That the individual memorial rites take their end at *tomu-raiage*, is a decisive fact that justifies an affirmative answer to the question. By the final memorial rite the soul transcends the period and the stage where it was in the need of the *kuyo*-rites of the living. Whether primarily thought of in the categories of *jobutsu* or in that of *sorei*, the spirit has in any case reached its final destination, and there is no need for a continued transference of merits.

However, if the question is meant to imply the idea that the ancestral soul can now be left alone as a once-and-for-all «saved» spirit independent of the living, the question is raised on assumptions that seem to us completely alien to the suppositions of ancestor worship itself. In this context, namely, salvation is not seen in the categories of a perfect state for the individual soul, but rather in categories of a perfect community of the living with this soul which is now successfully brought to its final ancestral status. Independence, therefore, is not an ideal pertaining to salvation. On the contrary, as we have seen above, there is continued, everlasting community and interdependence. Therefore, even after having attained ancestorhood the dead is not to be neglected. If so, even the *sorei* may develop into an evil spirit and take revenge on the living.[137]

This community is perpetually to be upheld by the concern of the family. In this way they will for ever continue to enter into the «life» of the ancestors through daily care and through the annual festivals when they invite their ancestral spirits to join the living for the annual rendezvous. With the spirit successfully brought to its *sorei* status, however, the interdependent relationship has developed from a stage where the spirit was primarily to be prayed for, to a stage where it is primarily prayed to. This, however, takes us to the second half of the «circle of interdependence»: The dependence of the living upon the dead.

2.2.3 *The Dependence of the Living upon the Dead*

The ancestral rites do not only symbolize the intervention of the living in the «life» of the dead. They reflect also the belief in the intervention of the dead in the life of the living. We have repeatedly touched upon this above. Now it deserves a closer scrutiny.

In our discussion of the term *suhai*/worship in chapter 1.2, we referred to Maeda's statement that the term implies a recognition of supernatural power on the part of the object of worship to enter into and to control the life of the worshipper.[138] For our purposes this is a very significant feature of ancestor worship. A question for further inquiry is, however, whether this is an intervention for good or for evil. Are the ancestors conceived of as malevolent and dangerous, or are they benevolent, protective and benign? Again we are faced with a problem that may escape any attempt at a comprehensive and systematic explanation. We probably will have to be content with some basic features.

It seems that this question cannot be satisfactorily dealt with without once again taking into consideration the post mortem process of growth. The newly dead/*shirei* and the established ancestor/*sorei* have to be distinguished if we are to get an adequate understanding of their actual relationship to their descendants.

As several scholars have pointed out, many of the old customs related to the funeral – some of which still exist – cannot be explained as originating from affection and love towards the dead, but seem to point to the fact that the spirit of the dead is to be feared as a possible source of harm.[139] When, for exemple, the coffin is carried around in a circle and the temporary funeral gate is burned after the funeral, the purpose seems to be to prevent the spirit from finding its way back home and causing harm to the living. This seems to be so even in the case of a normal death – we shall return to the abnormal case in a moment – although opinions may be somewhat ambivalent on this point. According to Matsudaira whether the *shirei* will become a dangerous or a calm spirit depends «on the psychological state of the man at the moment of death».[140] However, later on, when it comes to the attitude of the living towards the *shirei* at the first Bon following its death, Matsudaira states without reference to such a distinction, that «this change in attitude means that the spirit has ceased to be dangerous to human society».[141] Even though such a fear towards the dead may be caused by a fear of pollution from the dead corpse, a fear well known from Shinto, Ooms nevertheless found it – at least partly – to be directed towards the spirit of the dead, i.e., that the spirit may be malicious.[142] The same conclusion is drawn by Smith: «The spirit of the newly dead remains something of a threat to the living, at least until the first bon following death.» «Until it [the *shirei*] severs its ties with the world of the living and becomes an ancestral spirit at the end of its first bon, it is a source of potential harm».[143] Because of this disposition of the *shirei* precautionary steps have to be taken and the spirit has to be given its proper care and attention. This particular concern for the *shirei* is obvious at the Bon-festival, when special attention – often at specially erected altars – is given to the spirit of any family member who may have passed away since last year's festival. Why should this be so? «Certainly they are considered to be dangerous, unlike the ancestral spirits».[144] The spirits of the newly dead – the *shirei* – should therefore under no circumstances be neglected. Their possible harmful intervention is to be warded off through ritual attention and precautionary steps, without which their malice will strike their descendants as *tatari*/curse, revenge.

There is no doubt, however, that this fear of *tatari* is stronger in the case of an abnormal death than in that of a normal.[146] By «abnormal death» we mean both the case when one dies without leaving anybody to care for one's soul, and the case of a violent and unexpected death that may have caused the person to leave the world most reluctantly with wishes and desires unfulfilled.[147] Such unhappy «wandering spirits» have been given various names, such as *muenbotoke, jarei, akurei,* – the latter two particularly pointing to the malevolent nature of these spirits. Whatever their fate, whether unable to join the *sorei* and attain buddhahood since nobody cares for their *kuyo*, or revengeful because they had to leave the world in adverse circumstances, they are dangerous and haunt the life of the living in many ways. They may try to return to life by occupying the corpse of a newly dead person, a cat, etc., and are troublesome both to the living and to the dead.

These are ideas that were strong among the common people especially in the Medieval era, and various means were invented to pacify these harmful spirits. The most important was – and still is – the performance of *sekagi-e*, literally meaning «feeding of the hungry ghosts».[148] This is a Buddhist mass involving priests chanting sutras and offering incense, and performed particularly for the purpose of avoiding the *tatari* of wandering spirits. *Sekagi-e* may be performed both in private homes at separately erected altars and in temples, both on specific, individual occasions, as well as in connection with Bon.

Returning to the normal death, we have already seen that the dead are treated in another way once they have passed their first Bon. The feeling of fear, which is a characteristic sentiment in the attitude towards *shirei*, is – parallel with progress in the growth process – successively overtaken by a feeling of gratitude, which is the dominant sentiment in the attitude towards the *sorei*. This change in sentiment reflects a definite change in the rôle played by the dead which is believed to take place as it moves towards final ancestorhood. If the newly dead may be feared as dangerous and possibly malevolent, the ancestors are primarily seen as protective benefactors watching over the life of their offspring. As this final ancestral status is attained first by *tomuraiage*, the rôle of the soul on its way between these two turning-points may be somewhat ambivalent, as Ooms aptly points out: «It is hard to define the role played at this stage by the soul. It might be a mixture of anticipated protection, a role eminently played by the ancestors, and of a lingering threat of *tataru* (sending a curse), as was the soul's dominant characteristic before the 49th day when there was no connotation whatsoever of a protective role».[149]

The full-fledged ancestors as a source of protection and benevolent support for the family, however, seems to be one of the strongest motifs in Japanese ancestor worship. It is reflected in the daily rituals before the *butsudan*, as we shall see, as well as in Shinto rituals for the dead and in references to the ancestors in, for example, the School of National Learning referred to above. It is, in other words, a fundamental idea in harmony with indigenous sentiments towards the ancestral spirits.[150]

In the daily worship before the *butsudan* this basic rôle of the ancestors is revealed in the worshipper's simple prayer for protection and guidance.[151] Very often these are prayers of a general nature, said by a representative of the family on behalf of the house, showing that the living expect a general and overall protection by the ancestors may be more than any direct intervention in specific matters. This does not mean, however, that the worshipper is barred from asking for direct and specific support. Just as any member of the family is free to pray before the family altar, any member may also present before the ancestors particular concerns for which ancestral support is solicited, be that an entrance examination to a university, abundant harvest, protection on a trip abroad, etc. Such prayers are not very different in nature from prayers that may be said at any shrine or temple. The fundamental presupposition is, as already stated, the belief that the ancestors are in a position to intervene and control the life of their descendants.

Although this idea of benign protection, reciprocated by gratitude and thankfulness on the part of the living, may be the dominant feature in the relationship ancestors-descendants, it should probably not be concluded that the ancestors are invariably beneficent and protective.[152] Most scholars today agree that even the collective ancestors may turn in anger towards their descendants, sending warnings and/or curses/ *tatari*. If such a thing occurs, however, the cause is not to be sought in malign disposition of the ancestors but in the descendants' neglect of their ancestors' right to be worshipped and served within the household. «The ancestor in Japan represents protectiveness and benevolence indeed. And yet he has the right to be worshipped in the household cult for ancestors.... As long as he receives the ritual services due to him, he will be content to preside as the benign protector for his living descendants. If his rights are denied, they lead him to cause misfortune or sickness to his descendants. He will punish them if he is offended by any form of behaviour or neglect that affects him».[153]

Benign protection if properly served, and punitive warning if neglected are, after all, nothing but two faces of the coin that we in section 2.2.1 called the community between the living and the dead. Being a highly significant aspect of the relationship between the two, this community naturally requires the parts involved to play their rôles properly if it is going to serve their well-being.

The fear of ancestral *tatari* was strong in earlier days. To which extent it still exerts its influence on the practice of ancestor worship is hard to decide. In his study of Shitayama-cho, Tokyo, Dore found that «the extent and importance of these beliefs concerning the possible malignancy of the dead should not ... be exaggerated. They seem to form merely an undercurrent activated only in the nervous and exitable».[154] In Minakawa's study of people's attitude towards funerals and subsequent masses referred to earlier, it is interesting to note that neither in rural Kamakura nor in Tokyo did anybody see the meaning of the funerals and the *hoji* rites as lying in the warding off of *tatari*. The inquiry draws the conclusion that the old idea of *tatari* has – unexpectedly, it is said – almost vanished.[155] That the belief in malevolent intervention by ancestral spirits is still to be found, is – on the other side – asserted by other scholars, and Yonemura, for example, gives several examples in his study from 1976.[156] Compared to the idea of the ancestors' positive and protective intervention, Dore may be right, however, when he terms the negative idea of *tatari* as an «undercurrent». Rather than being a conscious driving force in ancestor worship, it may be a more or less subconscious motive for not permitting its neglect.[157]

Finally in this chapter on the intervention of the dead in the life of the living, a word has to be said about shamanism.[158] As pointed out by all students of Japanese shamanism, one of its primary functions has been to serve as a mediation between the living and the dead. It has, accordingly, through the centuries been closely related to ancestor worship. The overall group of «spiritualist shamanesses»[159] (*kuchiyose miko* or only *kuchiyose*) consists of three minor groups, the *kami kuchi*, the *iki kuchi*, and the *shi kuchi* or *shini kuchi*. Of these three the last – *shi kuchi/shini kuchi* – is particularly interesting to us, as this is the medium exclusively concerned with the spirits of the dead. Even though their importance today may be far less than in earlier days, so that Yanagida even says that the *miko* «bring smiles today», they are still active in connection with ancestral rites in parts of the country.[160] They may be called upon partly in connection with the funeral or soon after,[161] partly in connection with festivals like Bon.[162] Their main function on such occasions is to conjure up the spirits of the dead for the sake of communication with the descendants. It may be the spirit of a newly dead, as is most often the case in connection with a funeral, or older ancestors, as in connection with Bon.

Briefly stated, the purpose of this intervention by the dead may be said to be twofold. First, it is a way to get to know the will and the unfulfilled wishes of the dead. As the spirit speaks through the *miko*, the relatives listen to its desires in order afterwards to be able to fulfil them on his behalf. To fulfil these wishes, namely, is regarded as an important part of the *kuyo* for the dead, having a salvatory effect on the soul in *chuin*. In other words, the intervention serves the well-being of the spirit itself.[163]

Second, the message of the spirit is listened to for the sake of the living, or simply for the sake of community between the two. The dead may give valuable advice to the living concerning the future of the household, or it may be asked to reveal the reason why misfortune and unhappiness have befallen the family.[164]

We see, in other words, that shamanism in its association with ancestor worship points to an intervention of the dead which perfectly fits in with the basic features in the relationship between the living and the dead that a study of ancestral rites has already revealed. It points to community and communication as a fundamental characteristic in the relationship of this life to afterlife, and to the mutual interdependence existing between the living and the dead members of the household. As we have seen through all three sub-sections of this chapter, the living and the dead are linked together in a way that makes the ancestral rites a vehicle for the living to intervene in the «life» of the dead in order to further their salvation. Just the same rites point to the possibility that the dead may intervene in the life of the living. To the «circle of obligation» we pictured in chapter 2.1, has come the «circle of interdependence».

In this section we have repeatedly stressed as an important presupposi-ton the belief that the ancestors are in a position that enables them to enter into and control the life of the living. Now, this supernatural position of the ancestors deserves further attention, and we are thereby taken to the last chapter in our systematic analysis.

2.3 Human-Divine from the Perspective of Ancestor Worship

If we were to end our systematic analysis of ancestor worship upon the completion of the two preceding chapters, we obviously would leave a very significant aspect of the phenomenon without proper attention. We therefore have to take a last step and focus primarily upon the nature of the object of the ancestral rites vis-à-vis their subject, i.e., the position of the ancestral spirits vis-à-vis the person who performs their rites.

We have already noticed that the object of the rites in certain ways is seen in categories transcending those of human beings on this side of death. It is pictured in categories which may be equivalent to those of *kami* and/or buddha, i.e., in categories which put the ancestors in a supernatural and suprahuman position which seems to deserve the epithet divine.[165]

In our terminological inquiry we met the problem in connection with the absoluteness of the *ie*-founder and in connection with the term *suhai*/worship. In our systematic analysis we have referred to the same point in connection with the importance and implications of the last individual memorial rite at *tomuraiage*, in connection with ancestral spirits as objects of worship in shrines and temples, and in connection with *on*/*ho-on* as referring also to the ancestors' actual protection and beneficient support.

As this is a highly important point for a missiological approach to ancestor worship, we want to go back to the problem thus already reflected in several contexts. What, really, is the basis for, and what are the implications of a term like «worship» as translation of *suhai* and its equivalents? What are the implications of the fundamental point of view that the ancestral *ie*-founder is endowed with ultimacy and absoluteness?

For a scrutiny of these and related questions we focus once again primarily on the rites themselves. Since exactly at this point, however, the rites may be misinterpreted and give rise to misunderstandings if they are studied isolated from their wider context, we shall in a last and final section proceed to an interpretation of the rites in the perspective of the wider religious framework to which they belong.

2.3.1 The Smaller Context: The Ancestral Rites

The central point in our previous section (2.2.3) was the fundamental assumption that the ancestral spirits are in a position which enable them to enter into and to control the life of their descendants. The ancestral rites do not only involve prayer for the dead, but prayer to them as well. Our investigation has already made clear, in other words, that it is necessary to take issue with statements to the effect that the ancestral rites do not reveal anything more than care for the dead and feeling of closeness.[166] Such statements do not account for the simple fact that the ancestors are petitioned in the way we have already seen. The fact that they are petitioned, however, is in complete accordance with the belief that the ancestors are in possession of power going beyond that of ordinary human potentialities.

This protective power of the ancestors gives them a status within the household which in many ways is parallel to that of the *kami* worshipped at the *kamidana*/godshelf. The latter are worshipped as tutelary gods of the house, and exactly the same tutelary function is one of the essential rôles played by the ancestors. They have the same protective function as the *kami* of the *kamidana*, but are worshipped at a different place and in different ways.[167]

This fundamental point is an essential implication of the term *suhai*/ worship, as we have seen above. The term is not adequately explained by defining it as a mundane reverence towards superiors in general. It implies that its object is of a sacred character, endowed with a supernatural power which makes it superior to man. The ancestors are objects of *suhai* exactly because they are believed to be in such a position. Their suprahuman quality together with their closeness to their offspring make them the guardians of the descendants' fortune, the tutelary spirits of the house.[168]

The ancestors are, in other words, in command of potentialities that in the wider religious milieu are ascribed deities conceptualized as *kami* or buddha. Such being the case, there is no need for a decisive distinction between terms used for man's reverent attitude to the gods and his reverent attitude towards the ancestors.[169] Both are superior to himself in the way that they transcend his own limited possibilities vis-à-vis life and death. Therefore, both may be petitioned for beneficient intervention and support and, accordingly, be given corresponding and proper attention in homage and worship.

This is reflected in the rites in several ways. Again the idea of growth towards mature ancestorhood with its watershed at the last memorial rite is of special significance. The important aspect when we approach the growth process from the point of view relevant in this chapter is the old and widespread belief that the spirits of the dead grow eventually to become *kami* by *tomuraiage*.[170] «The idea has spread widely that the spirits of the dead become tutelary deities when the series of Buddhist-style memorial services is completed in the thirty-third or fiftieth year after death. In many places these are considered to be the particular deities of the household and are enshrined not far from the house».[171] When the prescribed course is walked to its end, the man who died in normal circumstances and has been taken proper care of by his descendants, is eventually to be worshipped as *kami*.

This identification between ancestral spirit and *kami* is symbolized in several ways. The individual tablet may at *tomuraiage* be transferred from the *butsudan* to the shrine of the tutelary *kami/ujigami* or *chigami*, or the posthumous name inscribed in the tablet may be erased and the tablet moved from the *butsudan* to the *kamidana* of the house.[172] Inoguchi reports of a very illustrative symbolization of this belief, taken from Aichi prefecture. It is said that after the thirty-third annual rite, the *hotoke* washes his body and becomes a *kami*. Symbolizing this, a stone is taken from the river and placed by the side of the *ujigami*/tutelary god. At the *ujigami* festival, then, this stone is worshipped as part of the deity by the shinto priest/*kannushi*.[173]

The growth of the dead into an equal in the world of *kami*, has its parallel in reverse, so to speak, in the old practice which Ariga points to of postulating a *kami* as the ultimate ancestral spirit of the house, the «ancestor of origin».[174] In both cases the ancestral spirits of the house are viewed in a perspective which includes continuity with the *kami*. From the one point of view, *kami* is seen in terms of origin, from the other, in terms of destination.[175]

What is said above is in harmony with the absoluteness and ultimacy of the *ie* founder which Takeda repeatedly points out as a fundamental aspect of the rites: «The ancestor exists as a postulate or his existence is presupposed. It is deemed not necessary to have biological data for all the forbears now dead including the one who is supposed to have founded the *ie* .... The important thing is to conceptualize the existence of some being who may be regarded as the founder».[176] Such an *ie* founder, whether conceived of as historical or postulated, is of ultimate value and therefore to be the object of absolute reverence and worship. «The implication of such a concept of the ancestor for each member family of the *ie* and each person is twofold: ethical and religious .... Religiously, it is required of everyone in the *ie* to pay tribute to, and show his respect for, the ancestor».[177]

As we have already had ample opportunity to see, however, such an identification of the ancestors as *kami* is not to imply that the ancestor concept is linked with that of *kami* to the exclusion of a Buddhist conceptualization of the divine. It is linked to the idea of buddha as well. Even though it may be out of place to try to systematize this dual identification, for example, into some kind of consistent spiritual development from the one realm into the other, the identification of the soul as *kami* seems nevertheless to be applied mostly to the *sorei* after *tomuraiage*, while its staus as buddha/ *hotoke* is affirmed already from the time of death, or at least from the time of *imiake* at the 49th day after death.[178]

From the popular parallelism of physical death with Nirvana, the consequence followed of naming those who had entered Nirvana, i.e., the dead, as *hotoke*. This implied further, according to Buddhist teaching, that since these spirits – as *hotoke* – were freed from the wheel of transmigration, they should be regarded as worthy of worship. We have referred to the deep inconsistency pointed out by Takeda between the view which regards the *shirei* as being on its way to full-fledged ancestral status/*sorei*, and that of regarding all the dead as being *hotoke*. The significant point for our purpose, however, is that in naming the dead *hotoke* there is an implicit recognition that these spirits are elevated to a position that transcends ordinary human categories, either as buddhas or as bodhisattvas destined for buddhahood. Simply stated, they are entitled to worship. How ever unsystematically and inconsistently this fundamental Buddhist teaching is adapted to native Japanese thinking, it nevertheless corresponds to the indigenous views according to which the ancestors are entitled to reverent homage by their descendants. Being an object of reverence and worship, the ancestors had in Buddhist categories simply to be identified as *hotoke*.

The designaton of all the dead as *hotoke* is a fact that has puzzled many foreign students of Japanese religion and society. Does it mean that the Japanese do not distinguish between their own family dead and the pantheon of Buddhism? Even though this question seems to us more likely to occur in a Western mind than in that of a Japanese, we should pay some attention to it. In his study of the family rites in Shitayama-cho, Dore says: «In ordinary speech no distinction is made between the spirits of the dead and the Buddhas and Bodhisattvas of the Buddhist faith. They are both called *hotoke* (-*sama*). There is evidence, though, that the two are differently conceptualized, and it will be convenient to distinguish the two as *hotoke* and *Hotoke* respectively».[179] When Dore interrogated his informants as to whether they felt that such a distinction did exist, he found that 40% answered no to such a question, while 51% answered in the affirmative. When the latter group, then, was asked to comment further on the distinction, «the differences pointed out ... fall into two main categories. Firstly, the *hotoke* are much more 'intimate' and more important to the worshipper than the *Hotoke*. Secondly, the *Hotoke* are of a higher rank than the *hotoke* in some supposed hierarchical scale».[180] Now, it is significant for us to notice that even for those who did talk of a distinction between *hotoke* and *Hotoke*, this difference was felt to be one of intimacy and degree, not a difference in principle, as if the one (*hotoke*) should be of human character and the other (*Hotoke*) of divine. Any attempt to make such a distinction would, it seems to us, be an unwarranted imposition of Western conceptualization upon this phenomenon that cannot be justified on the basis of evidence presented by the rites themselves. Even though the term *hotoke* for the dead does not mean that the dead are simply identified with the deities of the Buddhist pantheon, there is no evidence to suggest a fundamental distinction between *Hotoke* who are object of worship and *hotoke* who should not be such an object. As we have pointed out above with reference to Takeda's excellent study at this point, we may come closer to actual facts if we express ourselves the other way around: When the term *hotoke* has been applied to the dead at all, it is a Buddhist way of expressing the basic idea that the ancestral spirit is an ultimate being worthy of his descendants' worship.

This identification of the dead as *hotoke* irrespective of whether they have yet attained mature ancestorhood, throws some light on the practice that not only the distant ancestral spirits are petitioned for support, but even those who have passed away more recently, for example, a father or a mother. Even those, namely, are among the *hotoke* of the family, even those have the supernatural power that enables them to enter into the life of the living for support and protection. When Smith, therefore, makes a distinction between ancestors who are prayed for and ancestors who are prayed to, saying, «in the most general case, prayers are said *for* all the household dead but *to* the senior dead alone»,[181] this should not be interpreted to mean that only a certain group of the dead is in a position that makes such a supplication meaningful. As far as all the spirits enshrined in the family altar are the *hotoke* of the house, it seems to us to be out of place to draw a sharp and consistent line of demarcation between senior dead from whom help may be expected, and others who are not in a position to render such support and therefore should only be prayed for.[182] As far as the supra-individual, collective spirit of all the dead who have passed *tomuraiage* is concerned, this spirit is beyond the need to be prayed for. When it comes to the individual spirits who have not yet arrived at that stage, prayer for and prayer to the spirits accompany each other in a way that, after all, seems to evade any attempt at systematic explanation and arrangement. This, again, amounts to saying that it is just as impossible to distinguish sharply between ancestors who are entitled to worship, and spirits who are not. Even though the sentiment of *kuyo/* transfer of merits for the sake of the dead may be the prevalent sentiment in specific rites and towards specific spirits, the fact that the spirit is enshrined in the family altar and elevated to the status of *hotoke* implies that an attitude of reverent worship should in no case be judged improper.

Thus, a closer study of the actual rites and symbols supports the conclusions that were tentatively drawn already from our terminological inquiry. In front of the *butsudan* the partaker in the family rites is confronted with a ritual object in clear continuity with his own position as an actual member of the house, an object, or better a reality which he himself eventually will join and become part of when his own prescribed course is walked to its end. At the same time it is an ultimate reality that here and now exceeds his own categories and potentialities, a ritual object from whom may be expected help and protection, and to whom, accordingly, corresponding and proper homage is due. A deliberate avoidance of the term «worship» because of its religious implications will not do justice to this aspect of ancestor worship. Just as a Western, fundamental distinction between human and divine cannot possibly be applied to the relationship between the subject and the object of ancestral rites, any disregard of the aspect of religious worship in the rites will fail to come to terms with their innermost meaning.[183]

This, however, is to say that the ancestral rites have to be seen and interpreted within their own religious framework, where the basic continuity between the human and the divine is of paramount importance. We believe, therefore, that some concluding words on this point in the wider religious setting of the ancestral rites will contribute to a better understanding of their implications.

2.3.2 *The Wider Context: A Cosmic-Monistic Setting*

The basic continuity between the human and the divine is a familiar aspect to every student of Japanese religions. It is one of the most important issues when we are in search of an adequate understanding of their essential character, and at the same time one of their most intricate problem areas. «The most noted experts in Japanese religions have several times attempted to explain the concept of divinity. Not only foreign scholars but Japanese as well have found it impossible to clear up this problem».[184] What we have in mind in this section is not to make another attempt «to clear up this problem», but to bring some well-known, significant aspects into focus because they shed some light on the relationship between human and divine in the ancestral rites.

All through our dealing with ancestor worship we have limited ourselves to the traditional Buddhist context. We have noticed, however, a deep-running – sometimes inconsistent – amalgamation of Buddhist ideas with indigenous folk-religious beliefs. As to the relationship between human and divine, it has been made clear both by Japanese and foreign scholars that there are at this point some basic assumptions underlying the major religions as well as Japanese folk beliefs which – together with other things – make it valid to speak of Japanese religion as an entity.[185] This is the reason why we in this section will take into consideration basic aspects in both Shinto, Buddhism and Confucianism.

Where these basic assumptions are concerned, that of continuity man-god is of particular interest to us. When Hori Ichiro points out some of the «common tendencies manifested in the major Japanese religions as well as in the folk-beliefs», he lists as the fourth characteristic «continuity between man and deity, or ease in deification of human beings».[186] The same fundamental assumption is pointed to by the noted Christian scholar on Japanese religion Anzai Shin: «Japanese religions in general think *kami*, *hotoke*, and human beings on the same level, and think that a great human being is considered as a living god, or a living *hotoke*, and that the universe itself results from chaos. Japanese religions, thus, emphasize an unitary notion of the whole».[187]

This is not to say that the Japanese understanding of divinity may be regarded as pantheistic or animistic in a simplistic way. The problem is whether such occidental philosophical terminology is applicable to Japanese concepts without excluding important aspects. It has been pointed out with reference both to Japanese Buddhism and to Japanese religion in general, that the concept of divinity which might be called pantheistic is coexistent with one of an apparantly personal or theistic nature.[188] We think Bellah is correct, however, when he says that «the two conceptions of the divine should not be thought of as competing» and not felt «mutually exclusive».[189] Exactly at this point lies the intricacy of the Japanese understanding of divinity. «Man is the humble recipient of endless blessings from divinity, nature, his superiors, and quite helpless without these blessings. At the same time he is both 'natural' and 'divine'. He is a microcosm of which divinity and nature are the macrocosms. He is a 'small heaven and earth', he contains within himself the Buddhanature, or the *tao*, or *li*, or his true heart (*honshin, ryoshin*) is the same as *li*».[190]

In spite of these two conceptions of the divine there is, in other words, basis for conceiving of the relationship human-divine as essentially one of continuity and fundamental oneness. A clear-cut distinction between nature, man, and divinity is conspicuously lacking. Accordingly, the relationship between god and man cannot be one of confrontation but rather of affinity, harmony, and unity. Man and god are intimately linked to each other since the divine is not conceived of as separate from the world of man.[191]

These are ideas that may not be very articulate in the mind of the average Japanese. They are nevertheless significant for a phenomenological inter- pretation of the ancestral rites, and we shall therefore take a step further and see how this cosmic oneness, with special regard to ancestor worship, may be recognized in Shinto, Buddhist and Confucian contexts.

There may be no concept in the whole range of Japanese religious termino- logy that has been the object of such a thorough scrutiny as the Shinto term for the divine, *kami*. Even though one generation has elapsed since his study was published, Holtom's great monograph «The Meaning of Kami» is still an indispensable and very valuable source in this respect.[192] Supported by Japanese Shinto scholars, Holtom sees as obsolete the widespread etymological explanation of the term as a derivation from *kami* meaning above or superior. It should rather be interpreted as a derivation «from original terms connected with the ideas of mystery, awe, or intangibility».[193] Thus, Holtom finds etymological support for his conclusive understanding of the term's essential meaning: «On the basis of what we have just seen we can state that *kami* in its characteristic content is a religious term through and through. It is not what some would have us believe it is, a 'secular' expression or one that connotes a non-religious or an extra-religious background and meaning».[194] Even though Holtom is well aware of the term's unique content, and of the difficulties in using terms like divine for its translation, he nevertheless comes to the important conclusion that «*kami* is a word which in origin and development is saturated with the atmosphere of the Divine, the Sacred, and the Holy. It calls forth emotions of awe and mystery, or restraint and dedication, of dependence and obligation, that are characteristically religious».[195] This is a significant conclusion for our purposes and should be kept in mind when we observe the different aspects of the continuity man-divine which the term implies.

It is obvious, namely, that the Shinto *kami* idea is closely linked to that of the ancestral spirits. When the noted Shinto scholar Ono Sokyo summarizes the different major types of *kami*, he lists as the third category «kami who are deifications of human spirits. Included are: Imperial ancestors, ... clan ancestors, ... spirits of the dead where the tradition of ancestor worship exists».[196] This is clearly pointed out also by Holtom who, with reference to Saeki Ariyoshi's article in the *Shinto Daijiten* and «the majority of the Shinto writers of today», sees «ancestor worship as the major element in the Shinto god-idea».[197] Thorough study of the *kami* worshipped in Shinto shrines has revealed that two main groups of *kami* emerged and developed over the centuries – on the one hand, those associated with ancestor worship, and, on the other, those associated with nature worship. If the different *kami* are grouped in classes, we find that «individual ancestors who are worshipped as *kami* are most numerous».[198] Whether Saeki is correct as to the comparative size of the group of *kami* originating in ancestor worship is not of particular interest to us. The decisive point is that such a clear connection between ancestral spirits and the *kami* idea does exist.

When it comes to identification of ancestral spirits with various particular *kami*, we touch upon a problem of an extremely complex nature, and we have earlier mentioned the discussion going on between Shinto scholars at this point. It is beyond doubt, however, that certain of the *kami* have a more obvious connection with ancestral spirits than others, for example, the *ujigami* and the *yashikigami* and their equivalents. Where the former is concerned, it implies both *kami* whom the ancestor of the clan/*uji* worshipped, and ancestors worshipped as *kami*. Regarding the latter, many concrete examples may be given of ancestors who after *tomuraiage* have been identified as *yashikigami*.[199]

This has, accordingly, been interpreted by many as one clear sign of the continuity god-man in Shinto. It implies that there is between man and kami a «'spiritual coalescence', *shinjin goitsu*» which accounts for the fact that the former under certain conditions may «be treated as Gods, since they have the same origin and nature as the highest Gods and are therefore potentially entitled to worship».[200]

Such an integrated view of man and *kami* is not only to be observed from a somewhat obscure development of ancestral spirits into *kami*, but is even still more clear in the frequent apotheosis of historical human beings after death. Examples of this might be given in great numbers. One of the older ones – and it may be the most famous – is that of Sugawara Michizane, who is still worshipped all over Japan as Tenjin. A more modern example is that of Emperor Meiji, who is enshrined in the magnificent Meiji Shrine in the center of Tokyo.[201] Even while still alive, a person may be regarded as in possession of miraculous power and thus holding position as *kami*, a case which is described by the specific and characteristic term *hitogami*/mangod.[202]

This practice of apotheosizing human beings has its correlate in the widespread custom of regarding certain persons as representing *kami* in words and conduct, examples of which are both the shamanesses/*miko* and the Shinto priests/ *kannushi* according to their original function.[203] Such phenomena are certainly not limited to Japanese history of religion, but they have nevertheless played an important role in Japan, and, according to Hori, continue to appear: «The practice of paying reverence to a person as a kami continues in Japanese folk religion to the pesent day. There are even people ... who are apotheosized while still alive, people venerated as 'living shrines' .... Such persons are by no means rare and continue to appear today».[204]

All this goes to show that how ever difficult it may be to give an adequate presentation of the relationship between the human and the divine in Shinto – and a simple identification of the two may well invite serious misunderstanding, as has been pointed out by competent scholars[205] – there is an interaction between the two that makes a clearcut distinction between them out of place. To the extent that there is a distincton, it is one of degree and nuance rather than of principle. Both are seen within the cosmic oneness which encompasses all of reality. It should also have become clear from the intimate relationship between the concepts of ancestral spirits and *kami*, that insofar as a corresponding basic continuity may be found also in Buddhist context, it is not only valid but obligatory to interpret traditional ancestor worship in this light. How, then, does this fundamental continuity appear in Japanese Buddhism?[206]

We have already made reference to what Bellah calls «the second basic conception of the divine» in Japan, and which he describes as «the ground of being or the inner essence of reality».[207] Bellah gives as an example the «Buddhist concept of the Buddhanature».[208] By this concept we are at the very heart of Japanese Buddhism. Ever since the new faith was introduced in Japan it has been a fundamental assumption that the absolute should not be sought for in a transcendental sphere but in the midst of all changing phenomena «which are in reality contained in the store of the Perfect One or Buddha».[209] «When the essence of Buddha is concealed, it is called the Perfect-One-Store (*tathāgata-garbha*). When it is manifested, it is called the noumenal body (*dharmakāya*). Being concealed and being manifested are different in fact, but in their true unity, they are not different in essence».[210]

It may well be true as it has been pointed out that the early quasi-Mahayanistic Hosso-school did not admit that all things have Buddhanature and therefore taught that there is a «species of men» who cannot attain Buddhahood.[211] This idea, however, did not get much support in the development of Buddhism in Japan. Both in Kukai and Saicho, founders of the Shingon and Tendai sects respectively, as well as in the later development of these schools, we find clearly expressed the idea of innate buddhanature/*bussho* as the essential nature of all things. When the idea of immediate attainment of buddhahood/*sokushin jobutsu* in one's own body came to play such a dominant role in these sects, the basic implication was – and still is – «that mankind and Buddhas are identical in their essence».[212] Concerning Saicho's and Kukai's teaching on this point, Hori Ichiro says that «his [Saicho's] idealistic theories on the equality of human nature and *buddhahood* penetrated and dominated Japanese intellectuals. Among Kukai's doctrines, the idea and practice of becoming a *buddha* in one's own *body (sokushin jobutsu)* enjoyed great esteem and acceptance, not only by Buddhist priests, but also by many of the intelligentsia and common people».[213] According to Hori, there is a clear link between this Buddhist interpretation of human nature and the native idea of basic continuity between man and *kami*. With particular reference to this point in their teaching he says of Saicho and Kukai that they «are presupposed to have been the theoretical pioneers of the amalgamation between Shinto and Buddhism»,[214] and as to the way these sects were received by the common people «it is evident that behind [this] there lay ... also the idea – and related ascetic practices – that kami and men could actually exchange places».[215]

This assumption of essential cosmic oneness was taken over by medieval Buddhism. In Zen's meditation «the innate Buddhanature is the *a priori* basis».[216] The development of the Amida-faith in Shin Buddhism with its personal and theistic tendencies, however, poses a special problem. According to Masutani Fumio, in the Pure Land sect the essential unity between man and buddha is radically broken. Whereas in «basal Buddhism» «Buddha and man stand on the same ground» and there is «no insurmountable barrier between Buddha and man», «in the Pure Land Sect, the relation between Buddha and man is entirely different.... Buddha has now become an Absolute Being and the Whole Other to man».[217] We are not convinced, however, that Masutani's interpretation of Shin Buddhist doctrine at this point is correct. However much Shinran's teaching on the sinfulness of man and of the impossibility of salvation by one's own power may differ from other Buddhist sects, Masutani seems to draw far-reaching consequences which many Japanese scholars do not share. Both Hori and Nakamura stress that Shinran and Pure Land Buddhism share the basic Mahayanistic asssumption of essential cosmic unity. «Japanese Pure Land leaders never used the term 'slave' [for man overagainst god, as the Hindus did].... They called Amida Buddha 'parent' (singular). It implies all the believers are his children. As parents want to bring up their children to the same state as themselves, Amida makes all sinners Buddhas like Amida. There is no discrimination. If there should be any discrimination, Amida's compassion would not be complete».[218]

The fundamental continuity between the human and the divine that we have seen in Shinto has, in other words, its parallel in Buddhism's basic idea of essential innate buddhanature/*bussho* in man.[219] On this basis, then, the whole idea of *jobutsu* has to be interpreted. The term literally means «to become buddha», «becoming buddha», and has the definite implication of growth and development.[220] As we have already seen, in the context of Japanese ancestor worship this idea was applied to the growth process of the soul after death. The process from *shirei* to *sorei* became interpreted and identified as the process of *jobutsu*.[221] We have seen before how difficult it is to systematize the timing in this process and its coexistence with the growth towards *kami* status. The significant thing to us, however, is not the timing of the process, but the fundamental fact that such an idea of development towards ultimate merger with the buddha exists. Thus, also from the Buddhist point of view the ancestral rites get their significant meaning on the background of essential cosmic oneness.

Finally, some words should be added on Japanese Confucianism. We are not going into any extensive investigation at this point, but since ancestor worship is closely associated with Confucian morality, it is important to notice that even here it is rooted in similar basic assumptions. Authorities within Japanese Confucianism carried further ideas in this respect that were clearly present in its Chinese origin. «The whole Confucian practice of moral self-cultivation ... is to be seen as ... the attempt to attain unity with the universe through moral action. Already with Mencius we get the idea that the mind (*hsin*) within man is in its true form identical with essential nature.... It was the Neo-Confucians of the Sung Period that developed this idea, incorporated aspects of Buddhism and Taoism in it, and made it one of the most important religious influences in the Far East ever since».[222]

Nakae Toju (1608-1648) may be taken as representative of the great Japanese Confucian scholars. Although he may use terminology for the divine which seems to reveal theistic tendencies, such as «'Heaven' ... 'Divine Sovereign' ... 'Only Great Revered Divinity in Highest Heaven'»,[223] he nevertheless blurs the distinction between man and the divine and interprets the various appellations in pantheistic-monistic categories: «Man is heaven in miniature: Heaven is man magnified».[224]

In the somewhat obscure but very interesting work *Warongo*,[225] which is a syncretistic amalgamation of Shinto, Buddhist, and, not least, Confucian ideas from the 17th century, the common cosmic-monistic presupposition is clearly expressed in the oracle of Ube Daimyojin: «The heart of man is the abode of God; think not that God is something distant. He that is honest, is himself a God (Kami), and if merciful, he is himself a Buddha (Hotoke). Know that man in his essential nature is one and the same with God or Buddha».[226]

This review of the wider religious framework in which ancestor worship is found, goes to show how thoroughly it is embedded in what we called a cosmic-monistic setting. The continuity between the human and the divine with its implicit possibility of a gradual growth from the one to the other, which we found to be an essential assumption of the ancestral rites, is not a minor peculiarity pertaining to the symbols of ancestor worship alone. It is one of its major pillars, founded on the idea of cosmic oneness essential in the wider religious context. To the «circle of obligation» between the living and their ancestors (chapter 2.1) and the «circle of interdependence» (chapter 2.2) has come what might be called the overriding «circle of cosmic continuity», within which we find both the subject of the rites and their object. This «circle of cosmic continuity» accounts, as far as we can see, for the fact that the ancestors are eventually entitled to worship as anything else which in this context is to be characterized by divine appellation. We cannot, accordingly, deny the element of religious homage to the ancestors without neglecting one of the major assumptions of ancestor worship. However complicated and manifold our systematic analysis has proved the actual meaning of the rites to be, to assert that they involve this element of religious worship is after all only to assert that this aspect is present in man's attitude towards *kami* and buddha in general.

2.4 *Conclusions*

The purpose of our systematic analysis has been to focus on basic premises underlying ancestor worship in order to prepare for a subsequent inquiry into the problems that arise in the encounter between this phenomenon and Christian faith.

Even though our analysis has revealed that the ancestral rites contain ideas and beliefs which at times are hard to reconcile to each other, we have nevertheless found three problem areas of special significance from a missiological point of view.

We have used the expressions «the circle of obligation», «the circle of interdependence», and «the circle of cosmic continuity» to picture the relationship between the living and the dead in the context of ancestor worship. In spite of a certain danger of oversimplification we shall illustrate the basic issues by way of three corresponding concentric circles, all having a common center in the ancestral rites. We use the circle as a model mainly because of its suitability to symbolize the idea of continuity. Hence the three circles may just as well be termed «community of obligation», «community of interdependence», «community of cosmic continuity».

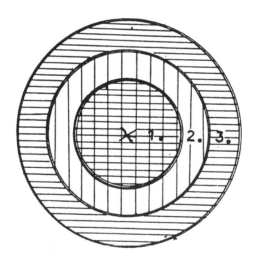

1. The circle/community of obligation
2. The circle/community of interdependence
3. The circle/community of cosmic continuity

The inner circle symbolizes the ethical implications of ancestor worship as a socio-religious phenomenon. Linked together through reciprocal obligations of *on* and *ho-on* living and dead members of a household together form a social nexus, an in-group, which is in itself invested with ultimacy and final authority. This implies that the basis for ethics and final motivation for moral conduct is ultimately found within the social nexus of the family itself. Whatever moral action actual circumstances might demand from the individual, its aim is in the end to serve and strengthen the harmony, unity, and solidarity of the group. Loyalty and service to the household is the final concern for both the living and the ancestors within this circle of obligation.

This community of moral obligation functions within the wider circle of interdependence. Death does not constitute a final barrier between the living and the dead members of the family. Between the two there is both community and communication for which the ancestral rites serve as the most important vehicle. The dead are dependent upon the living on their way to ancestral status, and the living are dependent upon the benign protection and support of the ancestral spirits for their well-being and progress. This interdependent community cannot be neglected without negative consequences for both the living and the dead.

Finally, these circles of obligation and interdependence function within the ultimate circle of continuity and oneness, symbolized through the ancestral rites. There is continuity between the person performing the rites and the object for whom they are performed. The subject will in due time be part of the object. This is not to say, however, that the two are conceived of as being on the same level. The ancestors are endowed with potentialities and power which transcend that of human categories and make them a ritual object from whom help and protection may be expected across the border of death. Accordingly, corresponding homage and worship is due. Whether conceived of in terms of growth into an equal in the world of *kami*, or in terms of becoming a buddha/*jobutsu*, the salvatory process after death is a gradual process from the human towards the divine which makes the ancestors entitled to worship like anything else which is conceptualized as divine – *kami* or buddha/*hotoke* – within this overriding circle of cosmic continuity.

The phenomenon of ancestor worship with all its various rites and festivals contains, in other words, significant consequences for ethics as well as vital presuppositions to the understanding of the relationship between the living and the dead and between the human and the divine. In the encounter with Japanese ancestor worship Christianity seems to us to be confronted with vital issues and problems which call for renewed and contextualized reflection upon basic aspects of Christian faith. To these issues and concerns we will now address ourselves, aiming at a relevant interpretation of Christian faith to a mind molded in the context of these traditional rites.

Notes to Part 2

1. The expression «the human and the divine» is dubious as far as it sounds Western and Christian, presupposing a fundamental distinction between the two. It is not to be understood in this way. «Divine» is here meant to include any object that man considers worthy of worship, whether it is conceived of in the categories of *kami*, buddha, or God in Christian terms. We shall return to this in ch. 2.3.
2. Above, pp. 12, 17. This distinction between three groups of ancestors, ordered according to their social role and position, is clearly seen, e.g., in Hozumi Nobushige's famous book *Ancestor Worship and Japanese Law* (first published in English in 1901, later translated and published in Japanese, 1917). Hozumi speaks in separate paragraphs of «imperial ancestors», «clan-ancestors» and «family-ancestors». Hozumi 1901/1943, pp. 15–33.

   To ancestor worship in the pre-war family-state ideology (as, e.g., in Hozumi Nobushige's thinking) see Morioka 1977. Morioka gives an interesting presentation of what Hozumi Yatsuka called the «ancestor religion», and points to the great problems involved in the attempt to construe a continuity between household and imperial ancestors.
3. Hirai 1968, p.43.
4. Takeda 1976, p. 126. Cf. Takeda 1957/1975, p.13: «To make clear the structure of ancestor worship, one has first to make clear the structure of its premise: the ie.» (Our own translation.)
5. Above, pp. 22–25.
6. Above, pp. 17–19.
7. To these problems there is an almost unlimited amount of material, especially in the Japanese language, where only a few themes have been the object of such a scrutiny by social and other sciences in Japan as the indigenous family system. If we should venture to point out specific items among this material, it might be two renowned books by law-professor Kawashima Takeyoshi from 1950 and 1957: *Nihon shakai no kazokuteki kosei* (*The Familistic Structure of Japanese Society*) and *Ideorogi to shite no kazoku-seido* (*The Family System as Ideology*).
8. See Matsumoto 1960, p. 11; Befu 1962, p. 34; Kawakoshi 1957, pp. 98–100; and Takeda 1957/1975, pp. 13–20.
9. Cf. the Meiji Civil Code article 987, and the New Civil Code article 897, quoted above pp. 17–18.

   Concerning succession to the family headship and inheritance in general, Befu says: «Succession to the family headship... is far more important in the traditional Japanese family system than inheritance of family property; the Japanese family may exist without any property to speak of, but it cannot exist without a head.» (Befu 1962, p. 35, note 3.)

10. Quotation from Befu 1962, p. 35. This is strongly pointed out by Ariga Kizaemon. See Ariga 1969, p. 386.

11. Kawakoshi 1957, pp. 98–99; Matsumoto 1960, p. 11.

12. This may be done in three ways: (1) A son/*yoshi* may be adopted who takes the family name of his new father. (2) A husband may be adopted for a daughter of the house, that is an adopted son-in-law/*muko-yoshi*. The adopted husband takes the family name of his wife, and succeeds eventually to the headship of the house. His wife's father will simply be termed «father» and not father-in-law, and the ancestors of the house will be regarded as his own ancestors. (3) A daughter/ *yojo* may be adopted, for whom a husband will be found later. This husband will succeed to the headship of the family and, from the point of view of the social structure of the *ie*, he will regard his wife's foster-father as his own father.

13. Op.cit., p. 164.

14. Quotation from Sansom 1951, see above, p. 23. This is Ariga's main point in his article from 1954: «Ie no keifu» («The Genealogy of the Ie»). Here he concludes that the *ie* is not, ultimately, to be defined according to genetic blood-relation principles. The blood-related family may even die out and the *ie* be taken care of by outsiders for a while and then at a suitable occasion be re-established by a suitable person stepping into the vacancy. Ariga 1969, pp. 392–394.

15. The technical terminology in quotation marks in this pericope is taken from Sano 1958, pp. 20–21.

16. Op.cit., p. 21. Sano gives the ancient Hebrews and the Chinese as examples of the «pluralistic complex family».

17. We will not consider the *dozoku* any further, as this takes us from the household to the clan level. Modern changes in social life have had even greater consequences for the functions of the *dozoku* than for the *ie*. For the *dozoku* both as social and religious unit, see Kitano 1962/1963; Brown 1964; Takeda 1957/1975, pp. 10–99.

The general way in which we have used the terms *honke* and *bunke* above is common in most of the literature we have referred to and is acceptable for our purpose. We are aware of, however, the complicated sociological and juridical problems involved in the *honke – bunke* distinction. Cf. Kawashima 1950, pp. 61–66.

18. Sano op.cit., p. 33.

19. See Dore 1958, p. 99; Ariga 1969, p. 392; and Kawakoshi 1957, pp. 98–99.

20. Takeda 1976, p. 121. This is clearly demonstrated in the case referred to above, where all the blood relatives of an *ie* may die out, and the *ie* temporarily be «placed under the custody of some trustworthy person who is expected to find a suitable heir.» Op.cit., p.121.

Re this transcendent and ultimate reality of the *ie*, cf. Hori 1962, pp. 136–137. Hori sees the unbreakable, spiritual bond between ancestors and descendants in the *ie* – upheld through the yearly rituals and the masses for the dead – as a solution for the Japanese in the universal and fundamental quest for permanence.

21. Takeda 1957/1975, p. 21. Whether the ultimate worth of the *ie* has its basis in the ultimate worth of its founder, or vice versa, is a problem that we shall not enter into. The important point for us is that both are seen in ultimate and transcendent categories.

22. Takeda 1976, p. 121. Cf. the same author 1957/1975, p. 22, where he points to the ancestor faith as a sine qua non for members of the *ie*, and disbelief as equivalent to treason. Both places, however, Takeda points out that this religious belief differs from other religious faiths in that it is not up to the individual to adopt it or reject it. It simply is there as a fundamental premise for life in the framework of the *ie*.

   The aspect of ultimacy and transcendence in the *ie* to which we have pointed here, was strongly emphasized and elaborated on in the *kokutai*-ideology and the «ancestor religion» mentioned above. Cf. Hirai 1968, p. 43.

23. Kawakoshi op.cit., p. 99. (Our own translation.)

24. Kawashima 1950, pp. 12–13.

25. Ariga 1969, pp. 392–393. Cf. Dore 1958, pp. 98–100.

26. Masuoka/Masuoka/Kawamura 1962, p. 1.

27. Matsumoto 1960, p. 66. Such a reciprocal adaptation of conflicting values in this dilemma is also pointed to by Takahashi Hiroko in her study from 1975. She concludes by stating that essential elements in the traditional family system, e.g., ancestor worship, is not only to be seen as objects of change by the nuclearization process, but as themselves important factors actively leading this process in Japan towards a nuclear family structure containing essential and typical Japanese elements. Takahashi 1975, pp. 51–52.

28. Koyama 1962/1963, p. 51.

29. Quoted from Stoetzel 1955, p. 97.

30. Op.cit., p. 97.

31. So Sano 1958, p. 30.

32. Fujii 1974, pp. 71–73.

33. Sano op.cit., pp. 17–19.

34. Fujii op.cit., p. 73.

35. Koyama 1960, 6th edition published 1972. Some of the findings are published in English in Koyama 1962/1963.

36. Op.cit., pp. 79–80.

37. Op.cit., p. 81.

38. Op.cit., p. 81. Cf. Koyama 1962/1963, pp. 49, 53.

39. Sano op.cit., p. 37.

40. Vogel 1967, p. 105. This study of Vogel is very interesting as it shows how the *ie*-institution in Japan has been a positive, regulating force in the modern migration process.

41. Op.cit., pp. 109, 110.

42. Takahashi op.cit., pp. 38–39.

43. Op.cit., pp. 48–49.

44. See p. 21.

45. Cf. Chapter 1.2, where we registered Non-lineal and Non-kin ancestors as

included in a looser meaning of the term «ancestor». Above, pp. 24–25. Se Smith 1974, pp. 172–174.

46. Takahashi op.cit., pp. 41, 51. The verification of these hypotheses is based partly on the fact that of investigated families where a widowed grandmother lived together with a married child and his/her family, almost 100% had a *butsudan* for the tablet of the grandfather, no matter whether it was a successive or a separately erected household, pp. 47–48.

47. See pp. 21–22.

48. This is an interpretation of the practices at Isshinji found in Takatori/Hashimoto 1968/1975, pp. 197–198.

49. Op.cit., p. 170. (Our own translation.)

50. Cf. Professor of Ethics at Tokyo University Furukawa Tesshi: «Shinto was the essence of traditional Japanese ethics, although Buddhism has also played an important part in Japanese ethics, of course». Furukawa 1967/1973, p. 242.

51. Kishimoto 1967/1973, p. 116. This renowned scholar goes far to point out what he calls «dualism of religion and ethics in Japanese culture» (p. 116). In Kishimoto's view, «Christianity is new to Japanese culture, not only in its monotheistic structure, but in its tight integration of religious principles with its ethical principles» (p. 117).

52. Nakamura Hajime in Nakamura/Wiener 1964, p. 418. Nakamura's treatise on Japan in this renowned work has been of particular value for our study, especially chapter 35: «The tendency to emphasize a limited social nexus», pp. 407–530.

53. Op.cit., p. 418.

54. Ooms, op.cit., pp. 267–268.

55. Regarding the problem of individual and collective in Japanese ethics we may refer to the above mentioned work by Nakamura, and further to Kawashima 1950, Matsumoto 1960, and Moore 1967/1973 which contains several articles on this problem.

56. See Kawashima op.cit., p. 15.

57. There are examples from the history of Japanese Confucianism to show that an attempt has been made to postulate and apply an ultimate ethical criterion above or beyond the parents/ancestors. Nakae Toju, e.g., made a distinction between «the small filial duty» towards parents, and «the great filial duty» towards the «greater fathers and mothers, who gave birth to the world... (the Lord of Heaven)». See Kosaka 1967/1973, pp. 254–55. This tendency to the base ethics on an ultimate reality beyond parents and ancestors seems, however, to have been only exceptional to the dominant trend of investing the household itself and its fountain with ultimacy.

58. Hirai 1968, p. 43. This same point is expressed in *Kokutai no hongi* pp. 87–88. Even if these examples reflect ancestor worship in the framework of the *kokutai* ideology, this point is not at all alien to ancestor worship in general in Japan.

   Re the relationship of ancestor worship and ethics in textbooks of the *kokutai* ideology, see Morioka 1977, pp. 188 ff.

59. Cf. Kawashima who, in connection with ancestor worship and the family system, says that in order to change Japanese society nothing less than a

spiritual revolution is necessary. Op.cit., p. 25.
60. Plath 1964, p. 312.
61. Kawashima op.cit., p. 32. (Our own translation.)
62. Yonemura 1976, p. 183. Cf. Smith 1974, p. 147 and Plath 1964, p. 312.
63. Nakamura op.cit., p. 414.
64. Furukawa op.cit., p. 235. Cf. the same author: «In Japan the full establishment of the individual is yet to come». Ibid., p. 240.
65. Kawashima 1967/1973, p. 264.
66. This will be seen below in our dealing with the concepts of *on* – *ho-on* and filial piety/*ko*.

    Regarding the status of the individual, Kosaka Masaaki aims at refuting the almost universal interpretation that «in Japanese social thought and practice or culture the individual does not have significant status, but only group status, chiefly family» and attempts to provide a different point of view. Kosaka op.cit., p. 258. Re the complexity of the problem and the «widely varying interpretations available», see Moore's concluding remarks in «Editor's Supplement», Moore op.cit., pp. 298–300.
67. Cf. Ooms op.cit., p. 301: «In general we can say that the people we meet, really do not expect either blessings or punishments from their ancestors. The main *leitmotiv* in their attitude is thankfulness and a feeling of obligation.»
68. The key-concept of *on* was introduced to the West in Benedict 1946/1974. Her presentation of this and related concepts has met with some opposition among Japanese scholars, e.g., from Kawashima Hideo. His view on *on* and filial piety is presented in the chapter «Ko ni tsuite» («On Filial Piety») in Kawashima 1950, pp. 77–142. Re his arguments with Benedict see Nagai/Bennett 1953. It is not necessary for us to go into that discussion.

    Because of the difficulty in finding a single English term that covers the content of the Japanese *on*, we prefer not to translate the term. In translating «indebtedness» Benedict is criticized by Kawashima for confusing «*on* with the consequence of receiving *on*. Indebtedness is the consequence of having received *on*.» Tsurumi 1970, p. 93. «*On* is not a gift exchanged between equals, but it is a 'benevolence' bestowed by a superior on an inferior as a *special favor*, for which the recipient must feel an indebtedness *unfathomably deep*.... Thus, since the quantity of *on* is immeasurable and infinite, the obligaton to repay it is also infinite». Kawashima, quoted from Tsurumi op.cit., p. 94.
69. This term is almost identical with what Benedict calls the «circle of giri». Benedict op.cit., p. 134 ff. Re the importance of the fulfilment of obligations as a requital for the favors of the ancestors in the value-orientation of pre-industrial Japan, see Bellah 1957/1969, pp. 123–124, 194.
70. In the words of Furukawa «the most important virtue in family-system-centered Confucianism is piety to one's parents and ancestors». Furukawa op.cit., p. 238.
71. See Kawashima 1950, pp. 84–85, 94. *Ko* presupposes *on* and is to be seen as repayment of *on*/*ho-on* (p. 97). At this point Kawashima sees an important difference between Chinese Confucian *ko*, which is absolute, and the Japanese type where *ko* is conditioned by *on*. In Japan the absolute concept of *ko* was

known in the samurai class, while the conditioned concept was found among the common people (pp. 5–6). See also Nagai/Bennett op.cit., pp. 242 ff.

72. Quoted from Kirby 1910, p. 240.
73. Quoted from Hall 1915, p. 137. Teijo's Family Instruction is a typical Confucian document from the 18th century.
74. Hozumi Yatsuka, quoted from Minear 1970, p. 74.
75. Yonemura op.cit., p. 182. Cf. Dore 1958, p. 102.
76. Dore op.cit., p. 100.
77. Re our two-fold conclusion concerning ethical implications of ancestor worship, see Sumiya 1954, pp. 50–51, 62.
78. «Many parents are concerned that their children are not being taught moral principles, and some openly support the movement to reintroduce traditional moral teaching into the school system.» Vogel 1963, pp. 144–145. What Vogel wrote in 1963 seems no less true today.
79. See Dore op.cit., pp. 374–393; Matsumoto 1960; Vogel 1963, pp. 142–156; and Nakane 1970/73.
80. Dore, op.cit., p. 388.
81. Matsumoto op.cit., p. 35.
82. Vogel op.cit., p. 147. These quotations are not to prove any disagreement between these authors. They seem, basically, to agree on this togetherness of new structures and basic values.
83. Cf. Ooms 1967, pp. 268–269: «Ancestor worship, however, has other functions besides the one of social integration: It has also a religious function. For the villagers, ancestor worship is one of the main modes of contact with the supernatural.... Ancestor worship provides a means of meeting the problem of death, an eminent function in every religion.»
84. Hori Ichiro says that what has been the Japanese idea of the soul and the corresponding view of man and religion is still not clear. Both Shinto and Buddhism are vague and ambiguous on this and give no systematized dogmatic teaching. Hori 1962, p. 179. This is no less true when it comes to the soul, man, and afterlife from the point of view of ancestor worship.
85. Eder 1956, p. 108, note 15.
86. From Tsuboi 1970, p. 13. Cf. also Yanagida 1970, p. 69: «According to Japanese feeling, even if the flesh decays and the body disappears, the tie to the native land is not cut, and each year the spirit returns on a fixed day to the home of its descendants and wants to see how the children are growing.... and contrary to this sentiment of our people, Buddhist priests persuaded them to aim at attaining Buddhahood,... and to be helped off to a distant place. No matter how they explained it, their teaching has not been thoroughly accepted.»
87. Ooms op.cit., p. 286. This idea of an afterlife in close correspondence with the family is reflected in most different sources. See, e.g., Teijo's Family Instruction from 1763: «Man has two souls – the (Kon) animal soul, and the (Haku) spiritual soul. When he dies the animal soul goes out, it is dissipated and lost; the spiritual soul abides in the family (or the house) and exists always.... There is no doubt about it: they do exist, and remain in the families (or houses).» Hall 1915, pp. 137–138. See also Tsurumi 1970, pp. 163–164,

where the same basic idea is found among war-criminals after World War II.

88. Hori 1962, p. 136. The significance of community is also stressed by Smith when he says that wherever the dead may be thought to reside, one of the chief concerns of the survivors is «to see to it that no spirit is cut off from normal intercourse with the living members of his household.» Smith op.cit., p. 66.

89. Dore 1958,p. 325.

90. See Matsudaira 1963 and Hori 1962, pp. 134–135, 176, 181–183. Together with this basic belief have gone different folk-religious practices in connection, e.g., with the funeral. See Maeda 1965, pp. 16 ff; Inoguchi 1965, pp. 18 ff; and Hori op.cit., pp. 183 ff.

91. We shall turn to this process below.

92. This idea gives the basis for the location of a lot of shrines and temples in the mountains, cult-places which have often served as meeting-places for the living with the dead. Many customs related to Bon are clearly based on this idea of the dead residing in the mountains. See Hori 1951, pp. 203–213; Eder op.cit., pp. 106 ff.

93. Smith op.cit., pp. 63 ff. Cf. Inoguchi who sees three distinct stages in the development of the idea of the whereabouts of the soul, the oldest being that of the mountains, while that of the temple and the grave are later developments. Inoguchi op.cit., pp. 188–190.

94. Plath op.cit., p. 308. This ambiguity or inconsistency is pointed out by many scholars. See, e.g., Maeda op. cit., pp. 39 ff.

95. A very useful and clear presentation of this circle of correlating lives is given in Tsuboi 1970, pp. 13–20. See also Ooms op.cit., pp. 290–291.

96. Ooms op.cit., p. 279. See Smith op.cit., p. 95.

97. Inoguchi op.cit., p. 170.

98. Takeda 1957/1975, p. 105.

99. See Tsuboi op.cit., pp. 14–18; Inoguchi op.cit., p. 170; Matsudaira op.cit.; and Smith op.cit., pp. 56, 96. Cf. the practice, e.g., of symbolizing the *sorei* at the grave with the same kind of ever-green branch that is used to symbolize the *kami*. Takeda op.cit., p. 104. This has implications to which we shall return in section 2.3.1.

100. Ooms op.cit., p. 283; Smith op.cit., p. 48.

101. Doerner 1977, p. 168.

102. Yanagida op.cit., p. 146. Note that according to Yanagida «a third feature of the idea of rebirth in our country was that of believing that one would surely be reborn to the same kin group and to the same blood line.» Op.cit., p. 174.

103. Doerner op.cit., p. 170. Quotation from Yanagida op. cit., p. 171.

104. Yanagida op.cit., pp. 176, 177.

105. See Tsuboi op.cit., p. 20, figure 3, where birth and rebirth mark the same point of the circle. The same idea of rebirth even after *kami* status is attained, is expressed by Matsudaira when he talks about the cyclical movement of the soul between human and *kami* existence: «Under favorable conditions, the spirit that has fully matured within a body will ascend to heaven after the death of the body and eventually become a kami. When these spirits prosper and overflow heaven, they descend to earth, enter bodies of new-born babies,

and repeat the life of this world as tamashii.» Matsudaira op.cit., p. 184.

106. Ooms op.cit., pp. 290–291.

107. Smith op.cit., p. 54.

108. This is again an extremely complicated problem. The best presentation of its main aspects that we have touched upon, is found in Takeda 1957/1975, pp. 213–244, a postscript under the title «Bukkyo shizo no nipponka to sosen suhai» («Ancestor Worship and the Japanization of Buddhist Thought»).

109. See Tamamuro op.cit., pp. 82, 155 ff. Cf. also the popular presentation of this in Mock Joya: *Things Japanese* pp. 353–354.

We shall not enter into the problem of the soul in Buddhism. It is pointed out by many scholars that the idea of a substantial soul is not reconcilable with orthodox Buddhist teaching, and, accordingly, nor is the idea of a «life after death». See, e.g., Takakusu 1947, pp. 35, 195; Masutani Fumio in Spae 1965, p. 169; and Miyagi 1969. For the fact that Buddhism in Japan, at least on popular folk-level, nevertheless, came to adapt itself to the idea of a soul and an afterlife, its preoccupation with funeral and ancestral rites is the very best proof.

110. We shall return to the idea of *chuin* and the transfer of merits/*eko* in our next section.

111. See Takeda 1957/1975, p. 221, and Ashikaga 1950, p. 221.

112. Takeda op.cit., pp. 230–231.

113. Op.cit., pp. 231–232.

114. Takeda 1965, pp. 598–599. Cf. Smith op.cit., pp. 50–51.

115. Takeda 1957/1975, pp. 231–236; Takeda 1965, p. 598. That this is not a view particular to Takeda, is shown by the following quotation from Watanabe Shoko: «The three aspects of biological death, birth in the Pure Land, and becoming Buddha were confused. This goal was to be realized by rites carried out by Buddhist priests. Japanese Buddhism degenerated to the point where the dead person was called *Hotoke* (Buddha), and they prayed to Buddha for the happiness of the dead by sutra recitation or the *Nembutsu*.... This was accepted without question. The fundamental ideal of Buddhism in pursuing the realization of human ideals was changed to rites for dead spirits.» Watanabe 1964/70, pp. 28–29.

116. Smith op.cit., p. 54.

117. In his study of Shitayama-cho, Tokyo, Dore found a variety of attitudes and assumptions concerning ancestor worship, the first of which was that the act is «primarily undertaken for the benefit of the spirits of the dead» (Dore op.cit., p. 317). In their study of the village of Niiike, Okayama, Beardsley et al. found a main motive for the ancestral rites to be «to assist the soul to its ultimate destination: mergence or identification with the Buddha» (Beardsley op.cit., p. 449). Cf. Smith who sees the dead as being more dependent upon the living than the other way around: «The dependency of the ancestors on their descendants is total, and it is generally believed that only through the ministrations of the members of his own household can the spirit of the dead at last find peace.» (Smith op.cit., p. 127.)

118. Doerner 1977, p. 161.

119. Watanabe 1959/1975, p. 119. (Our own translation.) That there is a certain

gap in Japanese thinking at this point between Shinto and Buddhist contexts is pointed out in Takatori/Hashimoto op.cit., p. 195.

120. See Watanabe 1964/1970, p. 64 and Malalasekera 1965, pp. 592–593.
121. Tamamuro op.cit., p. 108.
122. Ibid., pp. 113 ff, 121 ff; Hori 1953, pp. 446 ff.
123. Quotation from Takeda 1965, p. 596. Cf. Hori op.cit., p. 442.
124. See Takeda 1965, p. 599 and Takeda 1957/1975, pp. 227–228, 238.
125. Takeda 1965, p. 599.
126. Minakawa 1972, pp. 21, 31. (Translation ours.) The other leading answer, supposed to reflect a typical Buddhist attitude, was: «For the sake of the mourning of the dead.» These two leading answers correspond to the two points in this statement by Takeda: «Ancestor worship in Japanese Buddhism usually takes the form of commemoration and merit-transference for the dead.»(Takeda 1965, p. 599.)
    According to Minakawa's inquiry the idea of merit-transference for the sake of *jobutsu* is not, however, by far so dominant in the popular conscious-ness as that of mourning the dead. It accounts for about 20% of the answers, while the latter accounts for about 45% (ibid., pp. 21, 31). Re the importance of the rites for the sake of *jobutsu* of the dead see also Dore op.cit., pp. 317–318, and Ooms op.cit., p. 281.
127. Takeda 1965, p. 599.
128. Takeda 1957/1975, p. 239.
129. Hori 1962, p. 211.
130. Tamamuro op.cit., pp. 101 ff., 113 ff.
131. Boyer has a vivid report of the former from her participation in a mass for a young boy in a Jodo school (Boyer op.cit., pp. 49–50). Ooms reports on the latter from the Nembutsu-fraternity in Nagasawa (Ooms op.cit., pp. 229–230, 259).
132. That such a soteriological effect of ancestral rites is also significant in ancestor worship outside of this traditional context, is a fact that we shall not consider any further. Transference of merits for the sake of attainment of buddhahood for the ancestors is dominant in Rissho Kosei-kai (Rissho Kosei-kai 1972, pp. 21–25), and in Tensho Kotai Jingu-kyo the idea of redeeming the ancestors plays an important role (Thomsen 1963, pp. 213–214). That the idea of transference of merits may remain even if ancestor worship takes a new form, is seen from the practices at Isshinji, which we introduced in chapter 1.1 (Fujii op.cit., p. 206).
133. Gabriel op.cit., p. 571.
134. Hanayama 1969, p. 41.
135. Tamamuro op.cit., p. 183.
136. Smith op.cit., p. 128.
137. See Tsuboi op.cit., pp. 20–21, where this danger even after *tomuraiage* is said to be – by and large – accepted in Japanese folklore.
138. See above, p. 28, and p. 48 note 107.
139. See, e.g., Tamamuro op.cit., pp. 83–86; Inoguchi op.cit., pp. 128–129; Ooms op.cit., pp. 231–232, 278–279.
140. Matsudaira op.cit., p. 185.

141. Ibid., p. 190. A similar ambivalence is found in Inoguchi 1965. On the one hand he states that the normal *shirei* is not to be feared. It is not malevolent. What is to be feared is the abnormal death, the *muenbotoke* which is malevolent (p. 88). On the other hand, however, he explains the burning of the temporary funeral gate as a means to obstruct the *shirei* from returning home (pp. 128–129).
142. Ooms op.cit., pp. 278–279.
143. Smith op.cit., pp. 41, 102.
144. Ibid., p. 103. Cf. Matsudaira op.cit., p. 109: «This change in attitude means that the spirit has ceased to be dangerous to human society after the service held during the first summer festival following death. From that time on it is a member of the group of *so-rei* (the spirits of ancestors) which cherish offspring and protect them.»
145. We shall return to the idea of *tatari* below, as it is important both in relation to the *shirei*, the *muenbotoke* and the *sorei*. It has played an important role in Japanese religious history. The best example may be the so-called Tenmangu faith, centering on the revengeful spirit of Sugawara Michizane (845–903). It is a faith that made the curse/*tatari* of the spirits of the dead its very center. (See Tamamuro op.cit., pp. 71–72.)
146. Tamamuro op.cit., p. 86. Cf. the reference to Inoguchi in note 141 above.
147. See the chapter «Wandering Spirits» in Smith op.cit., pp. 41–50, and Inoguchi op.cit., pp. 43–44.
148. See Tamamuro op.cit., pp. 194–198, and Smith op.cit., pp. 42–43.
149. Ooms op.cit., pp. 281–282.
150. As an example from Shinto rituals for the dead, we quote Reitz 1939 when he comments upon the sacrifice offered in the Reizen-rite, usually at the third day after death: «Der Zweck des Opfers is Verehrung des Geistes des Verstorbenen, zugleich aber auch stillschweigende Bitte um einen Gunsterweis vom Verstorbenen, der ja inzwischen kami geworden ist» (p. 72).

    As an example from the School of National Learning we might render Hirata Atsutane's form of daily prayer to the ancestors: «To the honourable souls of (far off) honourable ancestors, to the generations of ancestors, to all the honourable souls of relations and to all of the souls worshipped at this soul shrine. I reverence and adore before you honourable souls, and pray you let there be no harm happen to my house or body. Guard me night and day. Hear this my prayer and guard me. Increasingly prosper my great-grandchildren's descendants, give them long life and success to abundantly worship the souls of you their ancestors. I pray you to peacefully hear my prayer and to guard me with good fortune. In fear and trembling I pray and worship you!» (Quoted from Kirby 1910, p. 234.)
151. Smith op.cit., pp. 123–127; Dore op.cit., p. 320; Maeda op.cit., p. 59.
152. Cf. W.H. Newell: «Yanagita Kunio, among others, has also asserted that ancestors in Japan are invariably beneficient to their direct descendants (Yanagita 1926). Since these articles were written, further fieldwork has substantially modified these earlier statements» (Newell 1976, p. 24). Cf. Yonemura 1976, p. 183.
153. Yonemura op.cit., p. 183. Cf. Takeda 1976: «The ancestor is... to be revered;

otherwise divine retribution is sure to follow» (p. 122). The same point is stressed both by Tsuboi, who asserts that – according to folklore – even the mature *sorei* may develop into an evil spirit/*akurei* if neglected (Tsuboi op.cit., p. 20), and Watanabe, who states that the ancestors bestow prosperity and peace upon the house as long as they are not forgotten (Watanabe 1959/1975, pp. 118–119).

154. Dore op.cit., p. 320. Dore does not validate, however, what he says about the «nervous and exitable».

155. Minakawa op.cit., pp. 21, 31–32, 41. Cf. Tamamuro who says that in our days the idea of the curse of the dead has become weak (Tamamuro, op.,cit., p. 135).

156. Yonemura op.cit., pp. 183–186. Cf. Smith op.cit., pp. 123–125 who also gives examples of the belief in ancestral *tatari*, although he concedes that they are rare. Maeda says that it is still strong in rural areas (Maeda op.cit., pp. 61–62).

157. It should be noticed as an interesting fact that the idea of harmful intervention by ancestral spirits is of great importance in such new religious movements as Reiyukai, Tensho Kotai Jingu-kyo, and others. See Dore op.cit., p. 319; Thomsen op.cit., p. 112; Kerner 1976, esp. pp. 210–216.

158. For an introduction to Japanese shamanism, see Eder 1958; Fairchild 1962; and Hori 1975. See also an unpublished dissertation at the Department of Social Anthropology, University of Bergen: Røkkum 1975.

159. Hori op.cit., p. 232.

160. Quotation from Yanagida op.cit., p. 166. Shamanistic activity today is particularly strong in the Tohoku region in Northern Japan. References, e.g., to the shamanesses who gather on Mt. Osore every summer from the 20th to the 24th of July to bring messages from the dead, are found in many studies. See Eder op.cit., p. 376; Fairchild op.cit., p. 62; Hori 1975, p. 237; Hori 1962, pp. 174–175, 192; and Takatori/Hashimoto op.cit., p. 90.

161. Takatori/Hashimoto op.cit., p. 90; Eder op.cit., pp. 368, 371; Hori 1975, p. 243.

162. Hori 1975, p. 237; Hori 1962, pp. 174–175; Eder op.cit., p. 369.

163. Takatori/Hashimoto op.cit., p. 90; Yanagida, op.cit., pp. 166–168; Hori 1962, p. 192. Cf. Fairchild op.cit., p. 62: «The Itako [the medium] relates the conditions of the soul in the other world and makes certain requests of the living, such as to make a stone memorial, otherwise the evil spirits will cause trouble for the soul of the deceased.»

164. Takatori/Hashimoto op.cit., pp. 91–92; Eder op.cit., pp. 369, 376.

165. Note what we said in note 1, p. 102 to the use of the term divine. The same has to be said of terms like supernatural and suprahuman. They should not be understood here as denoting that which on principle – or per definition – lies beyond and is incompatible with man and nature. It is exactly the point we are going to make in this and the following chapters that the ancestral spirits have to be interpreted within the wider religious framework of what we shall call «cosmic oneness», to which Japanese ancestor worship belongs. Concepts such as supernatural and suprahuman nevertheless have to be employed in order to signify the definite transcendence of ordinary human categories that we may observe on the part of the object of the ancestral rites.

166. See, e.g., our reference to E. Norbeck, note 102, p. 47.
167. See Ariga 1969, pp. 375–377.
168. This interpretaton of *suhai* is taken from Maeda op. cit. See note 107 on page 48. According to Maeda, this point is the very core of ancestor worship in its central religious meaning also in Japan. Maeda op.cit., pp. 57, 59.
169. To such an interchangeable use of terms, see above pp. 26–28.
170. Japanese scholars – especially Shinto scholars – are not in agreement when it comes to the understanding of the actual relationship between ancestral spirits and the concept of *kami*. A major problem in this discussion is how it came to be that death – an ultimate source of defilement according to Shinto – could be regarded as an alley to the status of *kami*. When Yanagida seems to regard the ancestor-idea as the origin of the whole aspect of *kami*, he is opposed by many scholars who see such a position as an oversimplificaton of actual facts. It is not necessary for us, however, to go into this discussion. It is referred to both in Tsuboi 1970, pp. 16–17, and in Takatori/Hashimoto 1968/1975, pp. 166–168. When it comes to the basic aspects important for our study, we don't find much disagreement. We shall come back to this in our next section.
171. Mogami op.cit., p. 177. Cf. also Tsuboi op.cit., pp. 16–17; Inoguchi op.cit., p. 43 and especially his chapter «Kamisama ni naru» («Becoming a Kami»), pp. 169–178.
172. Smith op.cit., pp. 97–98.
173. Inoguchi op.cit., p. 177. Cf. his example from Nagasaki prefecture, where the last memorial rite is called *oiwai*/celebration; congratulation, which shows that it is not really a part of the funeral but a congratulatory commemoration of the soul's arrival as an equal in the world of the *kami*, p. 178. Cf. also Yonemura op.cit., pp. 179–180.
174. See above, p. 24.
175. It is not surprising, therefore, that the Shinto funeral contains many elements pointing to the *kami* nature of the dead. It may both be addressed as a *kami* and offered sacrifices that ordinarily are used for the *kami*. See Reitz op.cit., pp. 65, 69, 72–73.
176. Takeda 1976, p. 122.
177. Ibid., p. 121. Cf. Takeda 1957/1975, pp. 20–22.
178. See above, pp. 76–77. Re the identification of ancestral spirits as *hotoke*, see again Takeda's illustrative explanation in Takeda 1957/1975, pp. 231–236, to which we have referred in note 115 on p. 109. Cf. Gabriel 1938 who reports that the 49th day after death – the *manchuin* – is also called *hotoke-okuri*, the meaning of which is to tell that the dead is elevated to the status of *hotoke*: «Erhebung zum *hotoke* = Gott», p. 577.
179. Dore op.cit., p. 213.
180. Ibid., p. 457, note 257.
181. Smith op.cit., p. 145.
182. Infant children may constitute a special case, and Smith may be right when he says that «a couple whose altar contains only the tablets of their infant children will never pray *to* their children's spirits but will only pray *for* them» (op.cit., p. 145), although I am not convinced that it would be impossible to

find exceptions even to this.

183. An indirect support of this view that the traditional ancestral rites as practiced on the folk-religious level involve a definite aspect of worship, the author found in Soka Gakkai. It may be difficult to find official statements to Soka Gakkai's interpretation of and attitude towards ancestor worship, and its actual practice seems to have been somewhat ambivalent. (Cf. Bernier op.cit., p. 163.) In an interview the author was granted with deputy-director Arikawa Satoshi of the International Bureau at Soka Gakkai's headquarter in May 1976, the position was clearly stated that Soka Gakkai rejects the element of worship in the traditional rites as superstitious and mythological and in accordance neither with original Buddhist teaching nor with modern philosophy and science. The *gohonzon* is recognized as the sole object of worship. Soka Gakkai wholeheartedly accepts, on the other hand, the need for ancestor *kuyo*.

184. Basabe 1968, p. 38.

185. See, e.g., Bellah op.cit., p. 59.

186. Hori 1967/1973, p. 214. Cf. what he says earlier in the same article: «In this context, the superiors, including human beings and ancestors, were believed to be semi-*kami* (demi-gods) or even low-ranking *kami* or *buddhas*. Being linked with ancestor worship and dependence upon superiors, the belief in spirits of the dead and also the idea of the intimate connections between men and *kami* (in other words, ease in deification of human beings) were and even today are quite widespread and important» (p. 203).

187. Anzai 1968, p. 51, note 1.

188. Cf. Offner 1963, who in connection with the Buddhist concept of deity talks about two aspects «which became important in Japanese thought.... The first of these is its pantheistic emphasis.... There is a great, absolute, spiritual reality underlying the universe which encompasses all things» (p. 139). «The other element which, strangely enough, was also a part of Mahayana teaching was the concept of Amida as a personal, merciful being much like the God of theistic religions» (p. 140). The same distinction is pointed to in Bellah, op.cit., with particular reference to Japanese religions in the Tokugawa era: «The first of these [basic conceptions of the divine] is that of a superordinate entity who dispenses nurturance, care and love. Examples include the Confucian Heaven and Earth, Amida and other Buddhas, the Shinto deities, as well as local tutelary deities and ancestors. This category shades off imperceptibly into political superiors and parents, both of whom are treated as in part, at least, sacred.... The second.... is more difficult to explain. It might be described as the ground of being or the inner essence of reality» (p. 61). As examples of the two Bellah mentions Zen for the second type and Pure Land Buddhism for the first.

189. Bellah op.cit. p. 61.

190. Ibid., op.cit. p. 62.

191. Cf. Takatori/Hashimoto's interpretation of the *kami*, Takatori/Hashimoto op.cit., pp. 50, 65.
    When we use the term «cosmic-monistic» in the headline of this section, this continuity or cosmic oneness is what we have in mind. The term

«monistic» is used by several scholars. See, e.g., Basabe's very interseting discussion on «The Religious Sentiment of the Japanese» (Basabe op.cit., pp. 109–121), where he questions the applicability of Western concepts, but nevertheless talks of «the monist conception of the Japanese» (p. 112) and calls the basic continuity «absolute monism, in which any man can be God» (p. 113).

192. Holtom's three articles were published in three numbers of *Monumenta Nipponica*: Monumenta Nipponica Vol. III, Tokyo 1940, No. 1, pp. 1–27 («Japanese Derivations»); Vol. III, No. 2, pp. 392–413 («Interpretation by Japanese Writers»); Vol. IV, Tokyo 1941, No. 2, pp. 351–394 («Kami Considered as Mana»).

In his book *Folk Religion in Japan* from 1968, Hori refers to Holtom's work as a good explanation of the concept of *kami* (Hori 1968, p. 57).

193. Ibid., p. 26.
194. Ibid., p. 413.
195. Ibid., p. 413. Cf. p. 401 where Holtom renders and explains Kato Genchi's statement that *kami* is an object that possesses «superior divine nature».
196. Ono 1968, p. 12.
197. Holtom op.cit., p. 392.
198. Saeki 1937, quoted from Holtom op.cit., p. 394. Cf. Holtom op.cit., p. 398.
199. It is not necessary for us to go further at this point. A lot has been written on the identity between particular *kami* and ancestral spirits. In the Japanese language see, e.g., Takeda 1957/1975, pp. 62–99; Inoguchi op.cit., pp. 169–192; Hori 1951, pp. 143–168; and Ariga 1969, pp. 357–381. In Western languages see, e.g., Yanagida 1970, pp. 50–59, 126 ff; Herbert 1967, pp. 461–462; Naoe 1963; and Eder 1956 and 1957.
200. Herbert 1967, pp. 21, 23.
201. For further examples, see Herbert op.cit., pp. 441–459. A special case is the Yasukuni shrine in downtown Tokyo, where all the war-dead are enshrined. It says in the introduction to the shrine on the wall in the adjacent museum that 2 400 000 souls are presently enshrined, and these are repeatedly described as *kami*.
202. Hori 1953, pp. 716–717.
203. Ibid., pp. 716–717.
204. Hori 1975, p. 275.
205. See Proceedings 1968, p. 32.
206. In the development of Japanese religion there has obviously been interaction between Shinto and Buddhism at this point. Sometimes Shinto monism is pictured as having influenced Buddhist thought in the direction of identifying man and buddha (so Mason 1935, pp. 177–183), sometimes Buddhism is emphasized as the influencing force (e.g., Brown 1968, pp. 179–181). The truth probably is that this has not been a one-way drive in either direction but a mutual interaction on the basis of common assumptions (cf. Offner op.cit., p. 138).
207. See above, note 188.
208. Bellah op.cit., p. 61.
209. Nakamura 1967, Vol. I, p. 21. Especially Vol. I in this work by Nakamura is

of interest to the understanding of the monistic basis of the different sects of Japanese Buddhism.

210. Prince Shotoku, quoted from Nakamura op.cit., p. 20.
211. Takakusu 1947, p. 91. Already the Mahayanistic Kegon school criticized Hosso at this point, stating that buddha-nature pervades all things. Ibid., p. 114.
212. Nakamura op.cit., p. 51.
213. Hori 1967/1973, p. 215.
214. Hori 1967/1973, p. 215.
215. Hori 1975, p. 261.
216. Nakamura 1967, p. 90. This is said with reference to Dogen's practice of meditation, *zazen*.
217. Masutani 1957, pp. 124–125.
218. Nakamura op.cit., p. 83. Cf. Hori who quotes the following poem by Shinran to make clear his position on this point:

> One who, without doubting, joyfully
> believes [in the power of the Original Vow]
> Is the equal of the Tathagatha Buddha.
> The great bodhisattva-mind and the great
> faith it arouses are identical with the
> buddha-nature.
> The buddha-nature is the Buddha.
>
> (Hori 1975, p. 264, note 47)

219. We cannot go into further elaboration on this in philosophical Buddhism. For a fairly short and illustrative introduction to this, see Takakusu 1947 and Suzuki 1948/1973.
220. The character used for *jo* means becoming; growing, and is the same character which in the word *seijin*/coming of age; becoming an adult, is pronounced *sei*.
221. Watanabe 1959/1975, pp. 119–120; Hori 1962, p. 180; Takeda 1957/1975, p. 233; and Tsuboi 1970, pp. 22–23.
222. Bellah op.cit., pp. 75–76. «Fung Yu-lan summarizes the views of one of the greatest of the Neo-Confucians, Ch'eng Hao (1032–85) as follows: 'According to Ch'eng Hao, man's original state is that of union with the universe which, however, becomes lost through the assertion of the individual ego. Hence the aim of spiritual cultivation is to destroy the barriers created by the ego, and return to the state of universal oneness'» (ibid., p. 76).
223. Fisher 1908, p. 51 note 21.
224. Ibid., p. 51. Cf. Dening 1908, pp. 113–114 where Nakae Toju is seen as the Spinoza of Japan. According to Dening, even though Nakae's god «has personality», his philosophy is «decidedly pantheistic» (p. 114).
225. The title, which may be translated «Japanese Analects», alludes obviously to the «Analects of Confucius» (Kato 1918, p. 1).
226. Ibid., p. 12. In the same *Warongo* this idea can be used to support the moral ideal of filial piety by the way of identifying the parents with the gods: «It is

essential that you first show filial piety by obeying your parents, for in them you can find all the Gods of both Within and Without.... For your parents are the most reverend among the gods, even the highest of the gods» (ibid., pp. 50, 51).

3 ANCESTOR WORSHIP AND CHRISTIAN FAITH

In the book *Japanese Religion*, published in 1972 by the Agency for Cultural Affairs of the Ministry of Education, Tokyo, there is an interesting remark concerning Christianity in Japan: «One of the reasons Christianity is not more generally accepted may be that to the Japanese religious consciousness, with its orientation toward family and household religion as opposed to a religion of individual choice and commitment and with its almost instinctive inclination to affirm an essential continuity between the divine and the human, Christianity simply seems utterly alien.»[1]

This is no surprising and revolutionary statement. From our point of view it is nevertheless significant that it is found in an official textbook on religion. Compared with the results of our systematic analysis in part 2, it is obvious, namely, that this statement points to some of the basic assumptions behind the ancestral rites that make Christianity seem «utterly alien» to the Japanese. This further underscores what we said in our introducton to the must of a thorough study of ancestor worship from the perspective of mission.

The question whether, or to which extent, it is correct to speak of Christianity as alien to basic presuppositions of ancestor worship, remains to be answered in this part of our study. Before embarking on a search for such an answer, however, we want to put the question the other way around, and – borrowing a rather provocative statement from a student of ancestor worship in Vietnam – ask whether ancestor worship does not contain elements of a «world view» that «is much closer to that in the Bible than the highly secularized one of many missionaries?»[2] However this may be, there should at least be little doubt that Roman Catholic professor Bernhard Hwang is right in saying that «there are a few points of doctrine that ought to be explored and developed on account of their relation to ancestor worship.»[3] A contribution to such an exploration is what we now want to present.

Such a study has to be seen within the wider framework of the general problem of Christianity's relationship to religion and culture, i.e., the problem of accomodation and indigenization. As an eminent feature of the traditional religious culture ancestor worship presents a continuous challenge to Christianity in the latter's struggle for roots and life in the Japanese context.

3.0 *On the Problem of Accomodation and Indigenization*

The problem of accomodation and indigenization of Christianity belongs to the center of any presentation of the theology of mission. It is not our task to give a general introduction to the problem. However, since our grappling with the particular phenomenon of ancestor worship necessarily will be guided by our thinking on this wider and deeper issue, some underlying principles have to be made clear.

3.0.1 *Principles in the Light of the History of Theology*

Firstly, the church is sent to the world to proclaim a definite message. This is a simple but all-important fact that comes out all through the New Testament. In the Synoptic gospels the message may be called «the gospel of the Kingdom» (Mt. 24, 14).[4] By Paul it may be called «the word of the Cross» (1 Cor. 1, 18), and he knows that what he proclaims to the Corinthians is what he himself received, the Gospel «in which you stand» (1 Cor. 15, 1,3). Jude, again, finds it necessary to exhort his readers «to contend for the faith which was once for all delivered to the saints» (Jude 3). What the church in mission is sent to proclaim is, in other words, a given message which nobody is free to change according to time and place. It is constant, to any person in any culture at any time through the ages.

   In principle this is agreed upon by missiologists in various quarters of the church. Roman Catholics are keen – in their discussion on the principle of adaptation – to stress that none of Catholicism's modifications and accomodations in the course of history ever entered «into the inner sanctuary of Catholicism.... Catholicism ... remained what it had always been: Catholicism pure and undiluted.»[5] This obligation of the church to abide by the witness to Christ given in the Scriptures is again vigorously and persistently presented by the Dutch Reformed missiologist H. Kraemer in his various writings. «Missions spring from what is considered to be an inescapable divine commision to preach the gospel to all peoples, heralding the news of God's redemptive acts.... Missions therefore, at least if they are true to their nature, cannot conceive in their programme of a synthesis of religious apperceptions and ideas. If they did so, missions would become a movement for cultural and religious intercourse or chemistry, and not the sustained, determined act of announcing the Good News.»[6]

The same concern for the universal and constant nature of the message is expressed in Lutheran context by – for instance – the Norwegian scholar O.G. Myklebust. In his approach to the problem of missionary proclamation and indigenous milieu he talks about «konstans», «because the Gospel according to its nature is something given and therefore unchangeable».[7] This is interpreted by the author himself to mean that «the Christian faith is universal. It is a faith that is destined for everybody and may be adopted by everybody. The Christian message is according to its very nature an 'alien' message. Its characteristic lies exactly in this that it originates in and is determined by a reality other than the indigenous.»[8]

Secondly, it is clear already in the New Testament that this God-given message is proclaimed in different ways in order to be relevantly conveyed to the messenger's audience. Peter's sermon in Jerusalem at the first Pentecost does not substantially convey another message than Paul's missionary sermon at Lystra and Areopagus. But the way in which it is delivered is obviously determined by a conscious attempt to proclaim a message of Christ that the audience will understand as important and relevant to them. At the same time as Paul is constantly ready to fight for the faithful deliverance of the Gospel (Gal. 1, 8–9), he is in all his missionary endeavors guided by the principle to be a Jew to the Jews, to be «as one outside the law» to «those outside the law», «all for the sake of the gospel» (1 Cor. 9, 20–23). Such is the Pauline wording of what in later missionary theory and practice has been called accomodation or adaptation.

On this point, too, missiologists from various quarters have no difficulties in agreeing in principle. This is well proved by comparing the above-mentioned three scholars. G. Voss is a typical Roman Catholic representative when he advocates «accomodation as a most important missionary technique», and «a missiological necessity» in order to strip Christianity of all its «accidental elements».[9] Although Kraemer's approach leads to fundamental disagreement with Roman Catholic theology of accomodation, he nevertheless has a sharp eye for what he calls «the inescapable issue of adaptation».[10] In the same paragraph where he talks of the «inescapable divine commision to preach the gospel to all peoples», he says that «*de facto*, the spiritual climate and orientation of this environment will code-termine the devolopment of the peculiar nature of the Christian communi-ty.... This is ... a certain kind of coalescence, of symbiosis without loosing identity.»[11] He even expresses himself in a way which brings him comple-tely alongside the above statements by Voss, when he says that «adaptation is not only unavoidable, but ... is necessary and imperative.»[12] Again we find Myklebust sharing the same basic position. In his approach to the problem of proclamation and milieu he is not guided only by the principle of «konstans» but at the same time by what he calls «relevans». «Because», as he says, «it is only in the various countries and among the various peoples that it becomes meaningful». The missionary task of conveying the Gospel is therefore «not only to make it *known*, but also to make it *understandable.*»[13]

Thirdly, having on the one hand the message to be faithfully proclaimed and on the other the audience to whom it is to be relevantly delivered, the question arises how this actually may be done. The audience does not comprise people living in a spiritual vacuum but people moulded in religious beliefs and cultural traditions. What, then, should be a proper attitude to these beliefs and traditions in order to attain a right and fruitful interaction between «konstans» and «relevans»? To use the words of B. Hwang: «No knowledgeable person will argue against the principles of accomodation. But the application of these principles to concrete situa-tions, doctrines and practices is not as simple as it sounds.»[14]

At this point there is no longer unanimity in theology of mission. The problem how to interpret man's religious consciousness and his actual religions has been on the agenda for theological discussion in the church not only since the start of modern world mission and the foundation of modern science of religion but since the days of the early church.[15]

One of the main models in this debate is the traditional Roman Catholic view of basic continuity between nature and grace, between the natural and the supernatural. The innate abilities and faculties of man, although hurt and weakened by sin and its consequences, are nevertheless in their innermost essence uncorrupted. Although man is deprived of his original supernatural gifts (donum superadditum) and his supernatural relationship with God, Roman Catholic teaching positively asserts that original sin has not had a destructive consequence for man's essential nature. It is uncor-rupted with the result that it may be taken into the service of the supernatural and used by the latter as «building material» (gratia perfecit naturam).[16]

The consequences with regard to our problem are obvious. Just as man in his innermost nature is uncorrupted, so are man's culture and man's religion vehicles of pure and uncorrupted elements. Therefore, the church cannot «set up a barrier against any culture, against any legitimate custom or practice» that has «grown up from the native soil». She is «convinced 'that every genuine value, everything that comes from pure and uncorrupted nature, belongs to God and has citizen rights in His kingdom.'»[17] To be sure, the «various historical cultures and civilizations», according to Voss, must be «purged, when necessary, of their pagan degeneracy», and «all that is idolatrous, immoral, and profane, in their creed» must be opposed.[18] Nevertheless, the basic continuity between creation and redemption, rooted in the belief that the God of creation is no other than the God of redemption, assures the missionary that there is something «wise and good and truly human» to be «redeemed and sanctified», there are «seeds that the divine Logos planted in the pagan soil» which «the missionary must cultivate.»[19] To the continuity creation-redemption belongs the continuity religion-Christianity. In the dictum gratia perfecit naturam is implicit a corresponding gratia perfecit religionem.

This belongs to the theological groundwork for the theology of accomodation as developed by Voss. It is, says Hwang, «approved, sanctioned, upheld, endorsed, and encouraged by the highest teaching authority of the Church», and he goes on to quote from Vatican II's «Declaration on the Relation of the Church to Non-Christian Religions», paragraph 2, where it says: «The Catholic Church rejects nothing that is true and holy in these religions. She regards with sincere reverence those ways of conduct and life, those precepts and teachings which, though differing in many aspects from the one she holds and sets forth, nonetheless often reflect a ray of that Truth which enlightens all men.»[20]

Hwang himself is somewhat reluctant to use the word continuity for this basic Roman Catholic approach. He emphasizes the need for uncompromising struggle with «polytheism, supersition, or magic» and says plainly that «Christianity is not just an extension of paganism; it does not lie in the same continuum. It is on a different level of progression in that it comes from God.» Then, however, he goes on immediately to state that Christianity «does not destroy but fulfills all religions and their aspirations», even though «it cannot simply fuse with them.»[21] It seems to us, therefore, that Hwang's position is not really different from that of orthodox Roman Catholicism presented above, where it is appropriate to talk about continuum inasmuch as grace fulfills nature and Christianity fulfills religion.[22]

This Roman Catholic approach has its roots, as we pointed out, in classic Roman theology, especially as it was developed in medieval scholastic anthropology. It is well known from the history of the Reformation that this was one of the fundamental aspects in the reformers' critique of Rome. When *Confessio Augustana* in Article II talks about original sin, the purpose is – at least on the one hand – to do away with what the reformers considered to be philosophical speculations on the nature of man in scholastic theology. The decisive point for the reformers was, however, not to arrive at a new and better anthropology and to present another avenue for insights into anthropological and psychological differences in the nature of man before and after the fall. Their main concern was – in all their dealings with man – to be guided by the overriding perspective of his relationship to God. As far as they were concerned with natural man – and this they were – they radically wanted to abide by the fundamental scriptural doctrine that man's relationship with God is broken, that man over against God is essentially a sinner and a rebel who has turned his back on God and «kein wahre Gottesfurcht, keinen wahren Glauben an Gott von Natur haben können.»[23] Therefore, the correlate to grace in Reformation theology is never nature but sin.

By this the reformers did not say that man through the fall degenerated into a demon or a devil. They affirmed, however, that natural man, not only in his obvious immoral and godless appearance but even in his highest moral, cultural, and religious achievements, remains essentially a sinner who can neither deserve the grace of God nor attain to «wahre Gottesfurcht» and «wahren Glauben». This is neither an anthropological, nor a psychological, nor a sociological judgment but eminently a theological one, with obvious consequences for the view of man's culture and religion. There is in man an inherent «sensus divinitatis». But far from being an uncorrupted core of man's essential nature, it is distorted, disoriented, and causes man subsequently to distort God's own manifestations in his works.[24]

In our view this fundamental critique of the reformers is still highly relevant vis-à-vis a modern Roman Catholic approach to the problem of accomodation. It is impossible to adopt its talk about «legitimate custom and practice», «genuine value», something «that is true and and holy in these religions», as long as these expressions are made in the context of a basic belief in «pure and uncorrupted nature». This approach to accomodation is dominated by a perfecit in its view of creation and redemption that does not do justice to the radical scriptural assertions of sin in actual man, and – consequently – of judgment as an intrinsic aspect in the perspective of creation and redemption.

In the centuries following the Reformation, however, this radical approach of the reformers receded into the background to the advantage of more or less new kinds of fulfilment theories in theological attempts to deal with the problem of religion. During the period of enlightenment the overriding viewpoint became that of religio naturalis, the content of which was directly available to man through reason. The content of Christian theology and Christian talk of revelation had to legitimize itself over against man's natural religion and was supposed not to be in any way contrary to or exceeding the latter.

An important change in this was brought about by Schleiermacher's reaction against the enlightenment's overemphasis on reason. When Schleiermacher defined religion as «das schlechthinige Abhängigkeitsgefühl», he opened the way for a whole new trend in theology that became decisive for the so-called «religionsgeschichtliche Schule» and for the origin and development of psychology of religion. Of special interest to us is the fact that even though Schleiermacher tried to liberate religion from the suffocating grip of reason and relate it in a radical new way to man's consciousness and feelings, he talks all the way of religion as a general category of which Christianity is a part. At this important point there is no real break with the religio naturalis of rationalism.

This basic attitude towards religion and Christianity, then, is obvious in outstanding representatives of Protestant theology in our own century. When E. Troeltsch lays down the principles for his approach to religion and theology, he takes a firm stand in the assumptions of the science of religion in his own days. According to these, the only thing that is objectively and empirically at hand, and therefore the only thing that can be the object of a science of religion, is «das subjektive religiöse Bewusstsein selbst».[25] The presupposition of this approach is the conviction of «die Gegenwart des göttlichen Lebens in der Seele.»[26] The soul of man is, namely, «ein komplexes Ineinander von Menschlichem und Göttlichem», the consequence of which is that the various religions have to be regarded as «stärkere oder schwächere, engere oder umfassendere, persönlichere oder unpersönlichere Erschliessung des Göttlichen.»[27] On this basis is Troeltsch writing his *Glaubenslehre*. Christianity is only one of many concrete manifestations of «diese Gegenwart Gottes in der menschlichen Seele», although it is the top of religious evolution and «die höchste Offenbarung.»[28]

A similar basic approach is obvious in R. Otto's famous book *Das Heilige*. When Otto defines the divine as «das ganz Andere», this is a general characteristic which is experienced and expressed in the world of religions on different levels.[29] The same is the case with the experience of the various aspects of the mysterious, for example, of mysterium fascinosum, i.e., the experience of «der 'Gnade', der 'Bekehrung', der 'Wiedergeburt'».[30] This again is a general religious experience, with one particular expression in Christianity.[31] When Otto, therefore, speaks of «der 'natürliche' Mensch», this is a general characteristic of man as long as he has not had this meeting with the mysterious «ganz Andere». Without such a meeting natural man cannot have the feeling of sin/guilt («Sünde»), nor the experience of atonement («Sühne»). These feelings and experiences may be had in any religious context, but in Christianity they reach their highest level. Christianity is «vollkommener *Religion* und *vollkommenere* Religion als andere, sofern das, was in Religion überhaupt angelegt ist, in ihm 'actus purus' geworden ist.»[32]

Even though the theological background and context of these theologians is very different from that of the Roman Catholic perfecit-theology, their approach to our problem is nevertheless dominated by a similar perspective of fulfilment as far as man's experience of the reality of God is concerned. At the same time these two theologians seem to us to serve as important stepping stones to a vast amount of the Protestant contributions to theology of religion in recent years, although their typical evolutionistic conception of religious development as well as other aspects in their theology are discarded. K. Cragg, for example, contends in his book *Christianity in World Perspective* for what he calls «the open faith» by saying: «We allow the relative value of natural reason, natural law, religious aspiration, the instinct of worship, and whatever else it be, so long as it is clear that these are broken lights, or streams feeling their way towards the tidal estuary where the waters of revelation flow powerfully in to make the river of truth. The faiths find such validity as they possess in their conformability to Christ or their preparability for the Gospel.»[33] The central concern of the «open faith», according to Cragg, «is to relate itself to the 'intention' of other religions.»[34] In doing so, effectively pulling down all «misunderstandings», one will discover that «there are, in the traditional hostility or scepticism of all these [various religions] about Christ crucified, elements of meaning that are in positive alliance with what the Gospel truly itself 'intends' and achieves.»[35] Now, when the various religious aspirations even as «broken lights» nevertheless have more or less «conformability to Christ», and are streams flowing towards the tidal estuary where the revelation flows powerfully in to make the truth, Cragg seems to us – after all – to be saying almost what Troeltsch said about the religions as «stärkere oder schwächere, engere oder umfassendere ... Erschliessung des Göttlichen.» Again, when arriving at the «intention» of other religions one finds «elements ... in positive alliance with what the Gospel truly 'intends'», Cragg seems to be articulating what Otto called «das, was im Religion überhaupt angelegt ist», and which «in ihm [Christianity] 'actus purus' geworden ist». We find, in other words, also in Cragg's approach a similar basic theory of complementary fulfilment.[36]

However much these representatives of Protestant theology of religion have gained from the vast amount of factual information offered by the science of religion, we do not see how they really come to terms with the radical scriptural witness to the fall and its consequences for man so decisive for Protestant theology in its origin. This was the case with pre-Barthian Protestantism, and it is still the case with dominant trends of today. The undeniable merit and far-reaching significance of K. Barth is that he radically called into question this whole theological approach to religion and posed anew the basic biblical assertion of the fallen-ness of man as a fundamental presupposition for any theology of religion that wants to take seriously the scriptural witness. The decisive point of reference for Barth's own theology in this respect is penetratingly expressed in his well-known sentence: «Wir beginnen mit dem Satz: Religion ist *Unglaube*; Religion ist eine Angelegenheit, man muss geradezu sagen: *die* Angelegenheit des gottlosen Menschen.»[37] Exactly because man through his apostasy has become «gottlos», there is, according to Barth, no possibility whatsoever for any kind of natural theology. Even though, as one of Barth's critics has pointed out, he is not altogether without reference to a general revelation,[38] such an «Offenbarung» does not really come to play any role in his theological approach to religion.[39] The all-important concern of Barth is God's self-disclosure in Christ and his grace through justification of the sinner by faith. This is God's sovereign and merciful answer to all man's idolatry and «Werkgerechtigkeit». Thus, Barth became the outstanding representative of another main model to the theological interpretation of the religions of man, according to which the only significant thing to be said is that religion is «die Angelegenheit des gottlosen Menschen».

In his just concern, however, for the uniqueness of the Gospel and in his radical emphasis on the fall as barring any attempt to deal with Christianity and the faiths of man under an overriding general concept of religion, Barth came to overemphasize these important elements in the Protestant heritage at the expense of other elements as well in the Scriptures as in Reformation theology. His battle against natural theology left «no real room for the deeper question: has this whole business of religion anything to do with God, or has God anything to do with it?»[40] Barth did not really come to terms with the problem of man's innate God-consciousness. He did not take at face value what is actually stated in Romans 1 and 2 about the manifestations of God in nature and conscience, and about man's inexcusable position overagainst God even before he hears the Gospel – inexcusable because of his rejection of what he should actually know and his opposition to what he ought to do. In the words of P.Althaus: «Auch K. Barth ... lässt Röm. 1 und 2 nicht sagen, was da gesagt ist, sondern deutet die Sätze künstlich um.»[41]

In our view, then, the right approach to a theological interpretation of the religions is not to embark on a search for uncorrupted and pure seeds, or elements more or less conformable to Christ, in order for them to be extracted and subsequently fulfilled in the context of Christianity. Neither is it to regard the religions as unrelated to God whatsoever, simply as witnesses to man's godlessness. Even though man is to the very essence of his nature a sinner, and his relationship with God is broken, his relatedness to God is not thereby simply nullified. As God's creature man still has to do with him. Exactly this gives the true and solemn theological perspective to the status of fallen man: In midst of his rebellion man cannot escape but is without excuse kept responsible over against God who constantly confronts him with the question, «Where are you?» (Gn. 3, 9).[42] Now, the truth in all religion is that «even in its most degraded form religion is evidence that man is haunted by God. He cannot get rid of Him.»[43] At the same time as man – in spite of all his religious concern – is not seeking God (Rom. 3, 11), he is kept «in bondage to beings that by nature are no gods» (Gal. 4, 8), and cannot but build altars to the «unknown god» (Acts 17, 23) whom he is constantly fleeing. Not only this, but the Scriptures testify to the fact that God, through the order of creation and through his manifestation in man's conscience, which makes man «do by nature what the law requires» (Rom. 2, 14), keeps even fallen man within certain limits to serve God's purpose for the sustenance and development of the world. God is the God of fallen man, and even in his corrupted state man is made to serve God in personal edification and in interpersonal relationships in family and society. The history of man's world as well as that of his religion therefore witness in a complex and often contradictory way both to man's sin and corruption and to his mediation of God's sustaining activity in the world. The relative good and true and righteous that we find in all religious contexts is neither a proof of an uncorrupted core in man's nature nor of any basic knowledge of God that after all is not twisted. It is a witness, however, to the fact that God uses corrupted man to serve his purposes.

In the New Testament this sustaining work of God through human mediation is seen in the perspective of God's forbearance with man's sin for the ultimate purpose of his salvation through Christ (Rom. 3, 25; Acts 17, 30). The New Testament also proclaims Christ as God's eternal mediator in creation and sustenance: «In him all things were created ... and in him all things hold together.» (Col. 1, 16–17) But the New Testament never draws the conclusion that because man everywhere has this relatedness to Christ as God's eternal mediator in creation, then man is, already apart from the Gospel of Christ's death and resurrection, somehow mysteriously included in his redemptive action. To the contrary, God's overlooking «the times of ignorance» and his «divine forbearance» in passing over former sins motivate the apostolic call to repentence and acceptance of the Gospel, because God «has a fixed day on which he will judge the world in righteousness» (Acts 17, 31). The New Testament proclamation of forgiveness, salvation, and redemption is portrayed as a reality into which entrance is given only through a turning around in repentence, a reality of light over against darkness, of life over against death. In other words, there is a profound duality in the God-man relationship, according to the Scriptures: The alternative is not to be related to God and his mercy and grace or not to be related to him at all. The alternative is to be related to God on the basis of one's sin and rebellion or to be related to him on the basis of forgiveness and justification through faith in Christ.

In our approach to the manifold religious life of man, we will therefore have to proceed along this dialectical path. There is continuity between religion and Christianity inasmuch as man can never be «gottlos», i.e., without being related to God. There is radical discontinuity inasmuch as man's inevitable «Gottgebundenheit» is turned into redemptive «Gottverbundenheit» only through the sovereign and gracious act of God in Christ crucified.

This is decisive for our thinking on the problem of accomodation and indigenization. The «inescapable issue of adaptation» has to be faced on the same dialectical basis. We are not to regard man's religion and culture as partly good, partly bad, partly true, partly false, in the sense that the Christian – equipped with the Gospel as detector of adoptable elements –

should be given the task of assorting the pure elements that may be exploited and the polluted ones that may not. Such a compartmentalization simply does not work if the relationship of man to God delineated above is correct. Rather the confrontation with religion and culture will prove itself to be characterized totally by the simultaneity of adoption and rejection. The various religious and cultural elements will more or less carry the mark of man's «Gottgebundenheit», and witness to the fact that even man in his fallen state, under the judgment of God, is subject to serve God's purposes. On the basis of the continuity in creation and redemption man's world of religion and culture carries the mark of adoptability. Simultaneously, all these various elements carry the mark of man's rebellion, and his submission to satanic temptations and forces. Because there is no continuity in creation and redemption without in radical tension with divine judgment, man's world of religion and culture carries the directive: to be discarded.

Seen in this perspective, the whole process of accomodation and indigenization is something very much deeper than adopting some rites and customs and rejecting others, even though this is part of the problem. It is ultimately a creative process, where God in the context of the Gospel and through this tension between adoption and rejection, continuity and discontinuity, draws man's culture into the realm of the new creation in Christ. The various practical problems of accomodation cannot be tackled in a correct way unless one realizes that ultimately it is a task which is not to be fulfilled before the divine consummation of all things. It is eminently a task of an eschatological nature. It is only possible, therefore, to talk of an indigenous church in relative terms. Any church anywhere and at any time is constantly – although in different ways and to different degrees – confronted with fallen man, his culture and religion, and is therefore challenged to relate itself and its message to these.

When we, upon this presentation of the wider problem of the relationship of Christianity to religion and culture, turn again to the particular phenomenon of ancestor worship, it will have become clear that we do not envisage any easy accomodation or adaptation, nor do we advocate a simple rejection of everything involved. Rather the simultaneity and dialectic of adoption and rejection has to be applied to the various aspects of ancestor worsip. In so doing, its main concerns are to be reinterpreted into a new whole in the light of the Gospel.

3.0.2 *Ancestor Worship as Problem Past and Present*

It is well known that ancestor worship is no peculiar problem to Christianity in Japan. From the early beginnings of the Christian church concerns for the dead on folk-level have confronted her in all parts of the world. In order to put our Japanese encounter into perspective we shall attempt a brief historical and actual survey.

3.0.2.1 *A Historical Sketch*

The first encounter took place in the early church from the first century onwards, both at the time of her birth among the Jewish people as well as in her first headway among the Gentiles.[44] Veneration of holy graves of the Jewish forefathers and other Old Testament figures was, as it seems, of great importance in Jewish folk-religion at the time of Jesus.[45] Its purpose was apparently twofold. Partly it served as atonement for sins of previous generations, partly as veneration/worship of the dead.[46] Behind this lay the idea that the dead were continuously partaking in the life of the people, especially in two ways: They worked as thaumaturges, assisting the living through advice and miraculous help, and they acted as intercessors before God on behalf of the living.[47] It is obvious, according to Jeremias, that these ideas and practices created problems already within Judaism. There are clear indications that rabbis officially opposed this popular cult of holy graves and rejected both its element of veneration/ worship and its ideas concerning the thaumaturgical and intercessory activity of the dead. They did not succeed, however, in preventing its development and influence on folk-level.[48] This cult of holy graves among the Jews seems to have been of great importance for the later development of the worship of saints and relics within the Christian church, a fact that, according to Jeremias, has not really been taken into account in the usual delineation of the origin of these practices.[49]

The Christian encounter with traditional cults of the dead quite naturally had its focal point in the funeral. The burial of Christ seems to have served as prototype for the first Christians, who therefore did not adopt the common practice of cremation but buried their dead.[50] Fairly early Christian grave-sites were separated from non-Christian ones, but at this earliest stage there does not seem to have been any further unified rule in this respect. Christians disposed of their dead according to the customs they were used to, either as Jews or as Gentiles.[51]

Over the years, however, a process developed in the direction of a specific Christian funeral. Especially in the West the old practice of family graves had to give way to some kind of church-graveyard, a clear indication of the strong cohesion of the new community in Christ.[52] Of special further interest to us is the development of memorial services at certain intervals after death. Even though there may have been great local varieties in this respect, the third, seventh, ninth, thirtieth, and fortieth day after death, in addition to the yearly death-day, seem to have been widely adopted for memorial services. These were conducted partly at the graves or grave-sites, partly in the churches, and seem to have consisted of hymns, prayers, and the eucharist.[53] Some of these days apparently were adopted on Old Testament precedence. Ambrose, for example, refers to Dt. 34, 8 and Gen. 50,3 as precedence for service on the thirtieth and the fortieth day. Others, especially the ninth, had no biblical precedence but were adopted, according to Augustine, as a result of pagan influence, wherefore he worked for its abolition.[54]

Both Ambrose and Augustine testify to further pagan influence on the memorial gatherings. Excessive eating and drinking took place and old pagan practices even caused Christians to bring forth food- and drink-offerings to their dead. This was strongly and straightforwardly condemned by the two, a condemnation that neither Ambrose nor Augustine nor any other of the church-fathers seem to have uttered concerning other antique influences on the Christian burial practice (as the use of balsam, ointments, incence, and flowers).[55] This is an interesting witness both to the practice of accomodation in the early church and to the consciousness of its problems with regard to the cult of the dead.

Ancestor worship continued to confront the church as a problem of paramount importance when she spread to central, eastern and western Europe, inasmuch as the preoccupation with the dead seems to have been an integral part of the religious outlook of the various peoples all across the continent.[56] E. Birkeli says that just as we see people in China and Japan «today» hold on to rites of their old family religion even long after their conversion to Christianity, we can see from the various regulations of the first church councils in Europe that this was the case also here. Not only was this the case with the laity, even priests and bishops brought offerings to the dead and took part in the old cult.[57] The problem was obviously on the agenda already at the first German Council in 742, which appealed to «the people of God» to «put away the unclean-ness of paganism», to which belonged among other things «offerings to the dead».[58] Again in the 9th century we find a similar admonition issued by Hincmar of Rheims to all the presbyters of the church not to take part in the traditional pagan memorials conducted for the dead at certain intervals after death.[59]

Now, neither Concilium Germanicum nor Hincmar of Rheims were successful in their appeals, and Birkeli says: «Either the difficulties in subduing the old religion have been too great, or the church has been too weak to carry the regulations through and later on adopted a theory of accomodation according to which the northern churches were administered.»[60] This theory of accomodation regarded some of the rites as lying beyond the possibility of missionary exploitation, while others were adopted and used for the purposes of the church. Gifts were received by the church for the benefit of the dead, masses for the souls in purgatory were conducted and prayers said on their behalf. In adopting 30 days as the limit for intercessions for the dead, the church obviously adjusted herself to pagan practices. On the other hand, in her attempts at reinterpreting the traditional pagan meal with the dead and making of it a festival to the benefit of the dead instead, she was apparently without immediate success. It continued on its old premises way into the post-reformation age.[61] In short: «The old cult continued side by side with the catholic practice, which in many ways was well suited to keep the ancestral cult half alive by its own powerful preaching of the intermediate state of the dead and the possibility of coming to their rescue through intercessory prayers.»[62]

3.0.2.2 Contemporary Parallels

These very few strokes of a historical sketch should suffice to place our problem in its due continuity with the past. In other words, the many intriguing questions which confront Christianity in its encounter with ancestor worship, are not problems that were faced by the church for the first time through her ambassadors among far-away peoples in the era of modern world mission. Neither are they peculiar questions which the churches in Africa and Asia in our own age have to face – so to speak – on behalf of the rest of Christianity. They are problems which have been with the church from her very beginning, and which today confront her anew especially among African and Asian peoples.

On the African and Asian scene the missiological implications of ancestor worship have been dealt with in books and articles of great interest as comparative material to our own inquiry into the Japanese context.

Professor John S. Mbiti is a well-known African Protestant theologian who in his writings points to the tremendous significance of the ancestors as part of the spirit world in African thinking. Focusing especially on the Akamba people of Kenya, he discusses both the affinities between traditional beliefs and Christian teaching, and the radical difference in the light of the New Testament eschatological outlook based on the hope of the resurrection.[63] Another African Protestant advocating the need for the church to come to terms with African tradition at this point is the Anglican theologian Edward W. Fasholé-Luke in his essay «Ancestor Veneration and the Communion of Saints».[64] As the title indicates Fasholé-Luke focuses especially on the Christian doctrine of communio sanctorum as a bridge to a genuine Christian appreciation of African ancestor veneration. Yet another African Anglican is Ephraim K. Mosothoane, who is one of the contributors to the South African periodical *Missionalia*'s issue exclusively devoted to Christianity and ancestral cult in 1973.[65] It is interesting to note that Mosothoane's concern runs along the line of Fasholé-Luke's in emphasizing the significance of communio sanctorum in the Christian encounter with ancestor worship. According to Mosothoane «the 'problem' of the ancestor cult seems to have contributed appreciably» to a rediscovery in recent years «of the *Communio Sanctorum* by Christian theologians (both Protestant and Catholic alike).»[66]

Together with Africans, expatriates have also offered valuable contributions to the discussion. When Dutch reformed missionary Gideon Thom sees an open and thorough theological discussion of this phenomenon as a must for Christian churches in Africa today, it is not primarily out of academic and theoretical interests. It is a need for relevant African preaching as well as for African theology.[67] Very informative, both as to the character of the ancestral rites among the Shona people of Rhodesia and the various methods of approach by Protestant, Roman Catholic, and Independent churches, is the study of M.L. Daneel in the above-mentioned issue of *Missionalia*: «The Christian Gospel and the Ancestor Cult». Daneel concludes his article with a few personal remarks concerning the theological problems involved. The overriding principle of his approach is that «there is no element in the traditional religion which is of itself 'pure' or 'good' and can without further ado be incorporated in the Shona church.» For this reason the process of accomodation and indigenization is theologically acceptable «only if it involves a Christianized re-moulding», or – as he prefers to put it – a process of «adaptive re-moulding».[68]

The problem is, of course, felt no less by the Roman Catholics in Africa. Exactly the church among the Shona people which Daneel deals with, presents maybe the best example of the Roman Catholic debate in recent years and of the deep-going differences in the evaluation of this religious phenomenon in different quarters of the church. Fritz Kollbrunner has given a detailed and very interesting account of this debate. According to him, the problem has become acute in the church because neither earlier Christian attempts to do away with ancestor worship nor modern urbanization have succeeded in shattering the position of the cult – and probably never will do.[69] The debate has concentrated on whether and to which extent it is possible for the cult to be «verchristlicht». On the one hand there have been advocates of far-reaching adaptation, exemplified in the African priest J. Kumbirai and his efforts to work out and obtain approval of a burial ceremony very much in line with traditional Shona practices.[70] On the other hand, there are priests who, on the basis of thorough field-studies, contend that «das System der Ahnenverehrung 'taufen' zu wollen» is like «den Teufel selbst zu einem Christen machen zu wollen».[71]

Turning to Asia, useful examples of missiological dealings with our problem are found in several regions. From Indonesia, a missionary voice in 1949 briefly posed some questions on the increasing veneration of the dead in the Dajah-church in Borneo, indicating the need for a thorough examination of the issue.[72] Such an examination of the Indonesian setting is found in L. Schreiner's extensive study of the relationship between indigenous «Lebensordnungen» and Christianity among the Bataks at North-Sumatra.[73] Even though there were periods when ancestor worship seemed to be completely relinquished in the Indonesian folk-churches, the cult has had such a spectacular revival in parts of the country over the past 50 years «dass sie als Phänomen vorchristlicher Übung in christlicher Kirchen verstanden werden kann.»[74] We find in Schreiner's presentation, therefore, a vivid account of the extent to which Christians have adapted themselves to traditional practices and the discussion it has triggered off in the churches, together with Schreiner's own evaluation of the theological issues at stake. Former theological interest in the problem has, according to Schreiner, by and large been the antithetic one of guarding Christian monotheism and faith in salvation through Christ alone against syncretism. «Man hat nicht vermocht, den Vätern und Ahnen, von denen das Heil erwartet und das Gesetz überliefert wurde, einen neuen, spezifisch christlichen Platz im Wirklichkeitsverständnis der Christen zu geben. Die Aufgabe stellt sich darum als Antwort auf die Frage: *Wie können die Christen mit ihren Toten christlich leben?*»[75]

Still closer to the Japanese scene are we taken by Reginald E. Reimer's study of the Vietnamese cult of the ancestors referred to above, inasmuch as the cult in this setting is located in the midst of age-long Buddhist and Confucian influence. In his very few lines on «the Christian approach to ancestor worship», Reimer sees the encounter as a spiritual confrontation, «a power encounter» which implies that «there can be no gentle accomodation, then, between Christianity and ancestor worship.»[76] Although his approach is characterized by terms like «confrontation» and «displacement», he nevertheless sees in the «respect and care for parents» and the concern for «a person's having a 'posterity'», what he calls «truths». These should be «exegeted, developed as theology and shared with the Vietnamese people for whom they will doubtless have a special meaning, and it may well be they can contribute something to our own theological appreciation of what has been in the Bible all along.»[77]

Ancestor worship as a missiological problem in China has been well-known for centuries, mainly due to the famous Rites controversy. When Benedict XIV in 1742 in his apostolic constitution «Ex Quo Singulari» finally put an end to the controversy on the Jesuit accomodation practice he did so by strictly forbidding any participation in rites of this kind because of their religious character. This position was officially held down towards the middle of our own century and applied also to Japan. However, immediately before the last world war Rome officially changed its position for reasons that will be further studied below. Speaking of «usages and customs» of other peoples and cultures, Pope Pius XII said in his encyclical letter «Summi Pontificatus» of 1939: «All that in such usages and customs is not unseparably bound up with religious errors will always be subject to kindly consideration, and, when it is found possible, will be sponsored and developed. Our immediate Predecessor of holy and venerated memory, applying such norms to a particular delicate question, made some generous decisions which are a monument to his insight and to the intensity of his apostolic spirit.»[78] According to G. Voss, this reference to «generous decisions» by Pius XI is nothing else than a reference «to the settlement of one of the most burning missionary problems in the Far East: the permissibility of certain rites and ceremonies that are connected with ancestor 'worship', the cult of Confucius, and State Shintoism.»[79] Thus, in their dealings with ancestor worship as a missiological issue among the Chinese, Roman Catholics have since 1939 had a papal approval of an approach more in line with Matteo Ricci's accomodation practice than with Benedict XIV's later rejection.[80]

Where the Protestants are concerned, one may find references to their dealings with our problem in almost any presentation of Protestant missions in China. Of particular interest in our connection is the fact that the problem was continuously on the agenda of the interdenominational Protestant missionary conferences at the end of the last and the beginning of this century. Before the conference in Shanghai i 1907 a committee had been at work on the problem and a 30-page paper was presented for discussion by the committee's chairman James Jackson.[81] The paper gives both a phenomenological presentation of Chinese ancestor worship, an evaluation of its significant content matter in the light of the Christian faith, and practical advice on how to deal with funerals, memorial days, ancestral tablets etc. The stand of both the committee behind the paper and the conference as a whole is expressed in the first point of the resolution adopted by the conference: «That, while the Worship of Ancestors is incompatible with an enlightened and spiritual conception of the Christian Faith, and so cannot be tolerated as a practice in the Christian church, yet we should be careful to encourage in our Christian converts the feeling of reverence for the memory of the departed which this custom seeks to express and to impress upon the Chinese in general, the fact that Christians attach great importance to filial piety.»[82]

Even though there have been differences in Protestant churches as to attitude and practice, it seems that a heavy emphasis on ancestor worship's religious incompatibility with Christian faith is what more than anything else has characterized their approach. For this reason «it is the common conception of non-Christians that Christians care nothing for their ancestors, and that one has to abandon one's regard for one's ancestors before [Sic] he can join the church and be baptized. This is a very wrong conception and is most unfortunate.»[83] Today it seems that even Chinese Christians who fully share the conviction that the religious implications of ancestor worship are incompatible with Christianity consider this earlier approach as an «undue emphasis» on «the negative side of the change».[84] It is a vital concern for David C.E. Liao, for example, to present an approach to ancestor worship where «side by side with the negative should go the positive....the great process of *installing a much better way of honoring the ancestors.*»[85]

This survey of some interesting parallels in historical and contemporary perspective has now brought us back to the Japanese setting. Before we enter into the exploration of ancestor worship's relationship to Christian doctrine, however, we have to focus briefly on some general aspects of accomodation and indigenization with regard to Christian faith and ancestor worship in Japan.

3.0.2.3 *The Japanese Context*

Some valuable inquiries into the problem of ancestor worship among Japanese Christians have been undertaken. Professor Doi Masatoshi led in the late 1950's a study group brought together at the initiative of the United Church of Christ's Study Center for Mission in order to work at the wider problem of contact between Christianity and religions in Japan. Ancestor worship was purposely included in the investigation because, according to the report, it presents the church with an important problem in Japan. The group raised the question how ancestral rites pertaining to the old family system influence the everyday life of the Christian.[86] Questionnaires were sent to 200 churches of the United Church of Christ all over Japan, rural and urban, and responses were received from 80.[87] Of special interest is the fact that the questionnaire operates with a clear distinction between respect/*keii* towards the ancestors, and worship with supplication/*ogamu, kigan suru*. In accordance with this distinction 57.8% explained their participation in traditional rites/festivals as paying respect to the ancestors, while 3.3% said it was worship and supplication.[88] To these figures the study group adds the comment that «it shows that with respect to the Japanese, even after they have become Christians the mood of ancestor worship remains rather strong. However, through the instruction of the church, worship [*suhai*] is consciously changed to respect [*keii*].»[89] The group concludes the part of their investigation which concerns ancestor worship by saying, firstly, that from the point of view of the family system, one cannot simply destroy the old. One has to show the actual essence of the new, Christian family. In this respect it is imperative to combine the freedom of the individual with the joint responsibility of the family members as a group. Secondly, from the point of view of ancestor worship, it says: «Christianity is based on monotheism and must evade all animistic practices. However, based on its view of the world to come, which – different from Buddhism – is a faith in the resurrection of the dead and the continuation of individual personality, it is both possible and desireable for evangelism in Japan to create – in agreement with Japanese mentality – a pattern for the expression of feelings of love and respect to the dead that may be unique for the Christian Church in Japan.»[90] It is emphasized, however, that this must be based on evangelical faith, not on individual likes and dislikes.

A more recent investigation, and one of another kind is Nishiyama Shigeru's study of the Fukuda Anglican Church in the agricultural Shimo

Fukuda village, Chiba prefecture, published in 1975. The village is a small one, at the time of the field work in 1971 totaling 54 household units of which 21 (38.9%) were Christian.[91] The church was established in 1887, and had in 1971 108 members of which 79 were actually living in the village. These 79 members all belonged to families that for generations had been known in the village as Christian families.[92] Accordingly, when Nishiyama wanted to focus on «the fixation and change of Christianity in a Japanese village», Shimo Fukuda seems to have been a very good choice because of its relatively large proportion of Christians and its having a church of a fairly long tradition.

The author summarizes at the outset the results of his findings in two propositions: «1. Christianity, which in principle is based on personal confession of faith and personal belonging to the church, has difficulties in finding stability unless it becomes a religion belonging to the social unit of the *ie*. 2. Christianity is profoundly influenced by the ancestor-faith, which has its focus in the *butsudan*.»[93]

A study of the Christian families in Shimo Fukuda revealed a definite change over the years in their attitude towards traditional ancestor worship. Most of the families removed or threw away the *butsudan* in the Meiji era, and this «period of no-*butsudan*» lasted until the end of the 1920's. Coming to the 15-year period of war starting with the Manchuria incident in 1931, *butsudan*-substitutes started to increase in order to commemorate the war-dead, although most of these families did not yet set up a regular *butsudan*. The tendency to set up regular Buddhist family altars, however, has become strong after the war and especially in recent years.[94] Through further inquiry Nishiyama attempts an analysis of the motivating forces behind this change, and its implications for the Christian villagers' understanding of Christian life and doctrine. His final conclusions are very interesting from our point of view: «1. Religious adherence to Christianity is in Shimo Fukuda village carried down through the generations by the unit of the household. That is to say, the form of Christian faith has changed. 2. However, change has not come to a halt at the level of shape. Provided by the *butsudan* and/or its substitute, there has been a considerable essential change [*henshin*] in the direction of ancestor-faith. The strength of the various feelings towards ancestor worship is intimately linked to the question of whether one has a *butsudan* or not....3. Accordingly, the dominant factor behind the essential change in Christian faith is the ancestor-faith.»[95]

A third study that should be mentioned is Roman Catholic missionary David L. Doerner's investigation to which we have already referred in section 2.2.1.[96] The main purpose of this study is «to determine to what extent the concepts of ancestor and life after death as found in folk Shinto are retained by a person who embraces the Catholic faith.»[97] For this purpose the author conducted a survey among 100 practicing Catholics of both sexes in Yokohama City, from various age groups and social backgrounds and varying years of experience as Christians. Doerner embarks on his investigation on the basis of a general hypothesis quite in accordance with Roman Catholic view of accomodation: «It is our hypothesis that in Japan it is necessary that any incompatible element in order to be accepted into the culture must be compatible with the already existing indigenous elements.»[98] His findings, then, are interesting on several points, for example, with regard to the believers' ideas of the whereabouts and the function of the dead after death. «To the question, 'Where do you think your ancestors are?' only three people responded 'tengoku' (tengoku is the Catholic term for heaven).... Sixty-one people, thirty-three women and twenty-eight men, responded: 'They are near', 'They are around us', 'They are always guarding and helping us'».[99] From these and other responses to related questions «we see in the Catholics an almost complete unanimity with what Yanagita calls conspicuous Japanese elements about the dead.»[100]

A further interesting point is the actual remembrance and performance of services for the dead. According to Catholic tradition November 2nd is designated «all souls day», on which special services are conducted for the deceased, and the rest of the month is set aside for praying for them. Nevertheless, to the question «When do you especially remember your dead?», «out of the one hundred Catholics only two persons answered 'November 2nd'.... Forty-four people said on 'higan and bon' and twenty-nine people answered: 'When we return to our native countries'».[101] Doerner comments: «Thus we can clearly conclude that the Catholic tradition of remembering the dead on November 2nd has never become a tradition among the Japanese Catholics.... they continue to remember their dead according to the early custom which comes from Shinto and later adopted by Buddhism.»[102] On the basis of his survey, Doerner simply concludes that «the Catholic people have maintained their traditional practices towards their dead», and he sees his original hypothesis as «sufficiently proven».[103] This, to Doerner, has the consequence that he strongly believes «the veneration of one's ancestors is so fundamental to the religious and social structures of Japan that the Catholic Church must make these customs compatible with itself.... A Christian adaptation to Japanese ancestor veneration is very much something possible. It is not too late for the Church in Japan to develop a tract on death and afterlife which incorporates the traditional practices of the people and is compatible with the indigenous beliefs of the Japanese.»[104]

However different these three studies may be in both approach and conclusions, they are unanimous in presenting ancestor worship as a vital point in the whole problem of accomodation and indigenization of Christianity in Japan, and they clearly indicate the complexity of the issue. At this point they necessitate some reflections on two principle issues of far-reaching significance.

Firstly, there is the intricate problem posed by the relationship between the religious and the non-religious nature of the rites. If we in this connection widen our scope for a moment to include not only the domestic ancestral rites in Buddhist clothing, but also Shinto rites for the national ancestors, there seems to be an instructive lesson to learn from the Christian reaction to the official distinction between State-Shinto and Shrine-Shinto around the Second World War.[105] When both Protestants and Roman Catholics in the 1930's changed their stand from opposition to acceptance of State-Shinto, one reason at least was the simple fact that both parties accepted the position officially adopted by the governement, that State-Shinto was to be regarded as purely non-religious rites, only manifesting the feelings of grateful loyalty pertinent to any citizen of the empire.[106] When the Roman Catholics adopted this new attitude and thereby came to what G. Voss calls a «solution» of the old Rites-controversy, the reason was not a change on the part of the church, it was said, but a change in the rites: «The rites and ceremonies in question, though they were of religious origin and had had, perhaps for many centuries, a strictly pagan significance, had been stripped of their religious character.»[107] Optimistic Roman Catholic voices were heard to the effect that this might be a turning-point in the whole missionary development of the Far East.[108] That this was a gross oversimplification of a complicated issue cannot possibly be doubted. Already at the time of the critical debate in the 1930's noted authorities on Japanese religion contended that neither governmental nor private interpretations can change the inner meaning and purpose of Shinto's ancestral rites, which contain genuinely religious aspects.[109] When State-Shinto was abolished after the war and Shinto was reintegrated and again officially defined as religion, the predicament of the churches became obvious.[110]

To us it seems rather obvious that the approach of the churches under the pressure of Shinto natonalism represents no «solution» to the problem posed by the religious and the non-religious nature of ancestral rites. The problem is too complex to allow for a simple alternative – either religious or not – or to justify a compartmentalization of some rites as religious, others as only civil or social.[111] This is the case both with national ancestral rites in the context of Shinto and with the domestic ones with which we are concerned. As we have shown in our systematic analysis, the traditional rites are not partly religious, partly non-religious in a way that should make it possible clearly to separate the two and then abstain from the former and adopt the latter. The complexity of the problem lies in the fact that there is a simultaneity of the two – an interwoven-ness – that makes the rites at the same time both religiously and socially significant. There is a religious dimension to the social nexus, and social implications in the religious aspects. A Christian approach to the rites constantly has to keep this in mind if it wants to be congenial to their comprehensive meaning.

At the same time – and this is the element of truth in the pre-war contention of the Roman Catholics quoted above – the rites are never to be regarded as static entities. In the process of history they may change. They may, for example, more or less loose their traditional religious significance to the benefit of a stronger emphasis on their rôle as socially integrating forces. We are, in other words, facing the problem of secularization.[112] This is also from a missiological point of view a very important issue, and – we must add – an extremely complex one. In popular language the term «secularization» is often understood to mean the process in which people at large are loosing their consciousness of the religious content of traditional rites and religious institutions. One may thus speak of a secularization of people. In order to speak of secularization of religious rites, however, it is not sufficient to look at the consciousness of people at large, how ever important this may be. If the rites are still institutionally functioning on the basis of their traditional religious significance in some part of the population, there is always the possibility of a revival of the religious values in the consciousness of people at large. In order really to speak of secularization of rites, it must be possible to trace significant changes on the institutional level which are draining the rites of their religious content. In other words, secularization occurs as an interaction between the psychological phenomenon of consciousness and the institutional one of the actual nature of the rites. From the point of view of Christianity's meeting with ancestor worship, it is then imperative to ask whether and how and to which extent this phenomenon is affected by secularization and what it implies for a Christian attitude to the rites.

This takes us to the second issue of principle which requires some reflection: The relationship between form and content of religious rites, or – maybe better – the relationship of ritual to faith/dogma. Even though a particular rite of some kind should have lost its traditional religious meaning to people, the problem of its adoptability into a Christian context is not thereby solved. The problem remains whether the ritual form in question is suited to be a conveyer of essentials of Christian faith. When Augustine and Ambrose in the early church rejected the bringing of offerings to the dead, one reason was obviously that such a ritual form could not possibly be filled with Christian doctrine. On the contrary, it blurred an essential point in the message of the church.

In his presentation and interpretation of the Roman Catholic stand vis-à-vis State-Shinto, J. Swyngedouw is keenly aware of this problem. In his own conclusions and suggestions for a proper approach he proceeds on the basis of a clear distinction between doctrine and cultus: «Certainly, we have to distinguish between the accomodation of *doctrine* ... and accomodation of *cultus*....»[113] Whereas the church «cannot accomodate herself in the domain of content of doctrine», in her relationship to State-Shinto «stress was laid ... on the matter of cult».[114] This clear distinction is made on the basis of J. Wach's categories, according to which doctrine is «the theoretical expression of religious experience», and cultus is «its practical expression».[115] It seems to us, however, that a one-sided emphasis on distinction may lead to a schizophrenia between religious form and content that cannot be upheld. Religious rites and cultus are never arbitrary forms. Forms are adopted and employed with the purpose of conveying a content. There is correspondence between the two. This seems to be clear also in Wach's distinction between «theoretical expression» (doctrine) and «practical expression» (cultus), inasmuch as both have a common denominator in the «religious experience». Therefore, even though the distinction between the two is meaningful and necessary from many points of view, it is just as important to be concerned with their correspondence. In order for any religious faith to keep its integrity, there must be congruence between its «theoretical» and «practical expression». From a missiological point of view, therefore, the attitude towards the ritual forms of other religions is not adequately described only by positively presenting the complicated process of adoption. There is also the attitude of negation and rejection when it comes to ritual forms incongruent with the essentials of Christian faith and unfit to convey its message.[116]

When we look at the discussion of this problem in Japanese Protestant circles, there seems to be a wide-ranging common concern for congruence

between ritual form and content of faith, in spite of rather major differences when it comes to particular issues. Of special value to us is the
discussion that has taken place on the problem of the Christian funeral in
Japan.[117] According to Hiyane Antei, the important question to be considered is how a Christian funeral should be in the midst of other-religious
surroundings like in Japan, where there is not only some reason to worry
that elements 'from other religions contrary to Christian thinking may
creep into the rites, but where this actually has happened.[118] The emphasis
in the various responses to Hiyane varies among his co-authors. From the
point of view of mission, Takayanagi Isaburo stresses the need to consider
the use of local, non-Christian Japanese customs at the same time as one
develops forms which emphasize the spiritual essence of the rites.[119]
Several of the respondents agree on the point that forms should not be
absolutized. The Christian funeral in Japan must give birth to a Japanese
form, just as it is meaningful to talk of a Jewish, European, or American
Christian funeral.[120] At the same time these authors clearly state that «not
all Japanese ceremonies can be filled with biblical content»[121] and that
manners and customs belong to the realm of adiaphora «as long as the
Christian confessional motive is kept alive.»[122] There must, in other words,
be congruence between ritual form and theology. «Proper form presupposes clear theological understanding of death.... If the theological understanding of afterlife and the world-to-come is ambiguous, one cannot come to
any conclusion as to what are elements from other religions and what are
not.»[123] This opinion seems to be widely shared by Protestants also outside
of the United Church of Christ. Presbyterian minister and theological
professor Obata Susumu, for example, advocates a «Christian-like funeral
both in spirit and in form»,[124] wherefore «easy adaptation to Buddhist and
Shinto practices ... cannot be permitted.... We should struggle with a
theology of the funeral in order to design one in line with Christian
faith.»[125]

    Although this discussion has focused on the particular issue of the
funeral, its implications of principle pertain to the whole problem of
Christianity's relationship to ancestor worship. As far as respect, love, and
concern for parents and ancestors is to be articulated through forms and
ritual in Christian context, it has to be done in a way in which ritual form
is congruent with content of faith. The relevant question which Christians
should put to the forms of traditional ancestral rites is, therefore, not only
whether they have retained their religious significance or not. To this
comes the question whether they are forms fit to convey the essentials of
Christian faith. By this, then we are heading towards a conclusion in our

general considerations on ancestor worship as a problem for the indigenization of Christianity in Japan.

In our presentation of Doerner's study above, we saw that the author
regarded his hypothesis – «that in Japan it is necessary that any incompatible element in order to be accepted into the culture must be compatible
with the already existing indigenous elements» – as «sufficiently proven»
through his inquiry. Doerner does not verify, however, that the adaptation
to traditional ancestor-faith among Catholic Christians in Yokohama has
taken place without any significant change in Christian doctrine. When he
says that Christianity must make «itself compatible with these beliefs»,[126]
he positively asserts that it is «very much something possible», but he does
not verify whether or how this may be done. Thus he leaves open what is
a major problem from the missiological point of view, a problem well
presented by Nishiyama when he concludes that in the particular village
of Shimo Fukuda, traditional ancestor-faith has over the years brought
about a substantial change in Christian faith among Christian believers.
Although Doerner briefly points to «two pitfalls» of which «the Church
must be aware»,[127] his strong conviction of and emphasis on the possibility
of adaptation is in accordance both with Roman Catholic view of accomodation in general and with major Roman Catholic contributions to the
problem of accomodation in Japan. H. Dumoulin, for example, strongly
emphasizes the positive continuity between the natural values of Japanese
religions and Christianity as a preparatio evangelica. Although he raises
the question of how Christianity can take root in the religious soil of Japan
without loosing its essence, the aspect of confrontation and negation is
significantly absent.[128]
    It seems to be well documented through interesting case studies that this
theory on accomodation has important practical consequences for the
approach of the mission of the Roman Catholic Church in Japan.[129] In the
Catholic village of Saga, Kyoto Prefecture, we find traditional ancestor
worship and Catholic ancestor veneration co-existing side by side. The
church has a special hall for tablets of the departed (ihai-do); Christian
homes have either a regular butsudan or a substitute; hoji rites after the
funeral are performed by the priest according to the traditional Buddhist
pattern. «A difference between the Protestant Tano village and the Catholic Saga is ... that in Saga, acceptance of Christianity does not show any
significant break with established religion».[130] «Just like in Ryujin village,
the Catholic church has taken over the performance of rites for the dead

which Buddhism carried out.... The church seems to have established herself in the village as a new temple.»[131] The pressing problem is, then, whether this kind of accomodation preserves the integrity of Christian faith in Japanese forms, or whether it is a kind of adaptation more suited to bury its essence in traditional religiosity.   There seems to us at this point to be another important lesson to learn from history, namely from the history of the *Kirishitans*. Japanese specialists on their history maintain that at least a large part of the *Kirishitans* had their Christian integrity effectively buried below ideas from other religions, particularly traditional ancestor worship: «During the many years when camouflage was deemed imperative, the faith of these people merged with indigenous folklore to such an extent that it can hardly be recognized as Christian. One of the major metamorphoses ... is the incorporation of ancestor worship into Christianity.»[132]

There seems to us to be both theological and historical reasons for maintaining that there can be no genuine Christian accomodation and indigenization with respect to ancestor worship based simply on the model of continuity. This is clearly said in the conclusions of Doi's study group, when it not only states a concern for «a pattern for the expression of feelings and respect to the dead», but introduces the conclusion by saying that «Christianity is based on monotheism and must evade all animistic practices». As far as we can see on the basis of the first parts of our study, professor Morioka Kiyomi, who is one of the most well-informed specialists on the relationship between Christianity and traditional Japanese values, is right when he contends that there is religious conflict between ancestor worship and Christianity.[133] There is, therefore, according to Morioka, a real danger at this point that in adopting forms from other religions, Christian faith may be buried below ideas from these religions.[134]

Focusing then on the conflict, and being concerned with the preservation of Christian essence and integrity, another approach would be a simple and thorough rejection of ancestor worship with all its forms and concerns. We concluded already in section 3.0.1 that neither approach can be justified on theological grounds. As we saw among the Chinese, there is also among Japanese Christians a legitimate concern that the old and wrong image of Christianity as a religion which destroys the respect to the ancestors be rectified.[135] In his excellent study «The Indigenization of the Gospel», Ito Kyoji says, on the one hand, that tacitly to tolerate accomodation to ancestor worship involves the danger that Christianity elapses into syncretism like Buddhism once did.[136] On the other hand, however, to push strictly in the direction of rejection may take Christianity into closed isolation.[137] It seems to us that Ito points in the right direction when he asks whether there is not another way, a way of «paradoxical encounter», a way of «accomodation through confrontation» and «confrontation through accomodation».[138] Or, to use the wording of Morioka: The way of indigenization must be the difficult road «between isolation and burial».[139] Where our particular encounter with ancestor worship is concerned, this – to us – is tantamount to saying what we already expressed in concluding section 3.0.1, that simultaneity and dialectic of adoption and rejection has to be applied in its various aspects. Also with regard to ancestor worship, accomodation and indigenization of Christianity has to take place through such a process, thereby reinterpreting the motives of the rites into a new whole in the light of the Gospel.

We have attempted to place our problem in its right perspective. We have placed it as part of the wider missiological issue of accomodation and indigenization, and developed some principles in the light of the history of theology. We have further made an attempt at portraying the encounter with ancestral rites as a challenge to the church both in historical and actual perspective. Finally, we have focused on some of the general problems involved when ancestor worship is seen as a vital issue in the problem of the indigenization of Christianity in Japan. We should now be in a position to enter into a meaningful conversation between the central concerns behind the ancestral rites and Christian faith.

3.1 Creator and Creation

In the last chapter of our systematic analysis above, we were concerned with the relationship human-divine as it is to be portrayed in the perspective of the ancestral rites (2.3). We found it to be a significant assumption that the human and the divine are understood in terms of continuity, with the implicit possibility of a process of growth from the former to the latter on the basis of an essential identity. Living and dead, ancestors and descendants are interrelated within a circle – a community – of cosmic continuity, which implies that the ancestors in due time are entitled to homage and worship like anything else that is conceptualized as divine within this comprehensive circle of cosmic oneness. Quite naturally, then, the first point in our conversation will be to focus on the encounter between such an understanding of ancestral spirits and a Christian view of God and man.

We saw above that intimacy and closeness are important characteristics
in the apprehension of the divine in Japanese religion in general and in the
context of ancestor worship in particular. The impressive aspect of Amida's compassion is said to be that he makes all sinners buddhas like himself.
«There is no discrimination.» And in so far as there is a difference in the
conceptualization of the ancestors as *hotoke* and the *Hotoke* in Buddhist
faith, it seems to be that the former are more «intimate» and more
«important» to the worshipper than the latter. The synthetic and integrated
view of the divine and the human which we find behind the ancestral rites
envisages, in other words, the divine as intimate and familiar. To such a
faith the God of Christianity may appear remote and reserved, and in lack
of that indiscriminate love which makes all people divine like God himself.
What is to be said from the point of view of Christian faith in God to this
intimate human-divine relationship within the circle of cosmic continuity?

3.1.1 *God as Man's Creator*

First of all it should be observed that we at this point are touching upon
a very familiar area of conflict between Christianity and Japanese religion.
The Christian doctrine of a Creator God has been felt as problematic and
really unacceptable from the very beginning of missionary proclamation
in the Tokugawa era. Already to Buddhist thinker Suzuki Shosan (1579–
1655) insurmountable philosophical problems arose from the Christian
belief in a «Deus» who was to be understood as the omniscient and
omnipotent Lord and Creator of heaven and earth.[140] According to Shosan
such a faith implied that both God the Creator and the universe created
were deemed to be real and thus made it logically inconceivable for people
to turn to the negative, to the unreal. This represented no less than an
intrinsic incompatibility with Buddhism, and Shosan found it «amazing
that Christians come to this land and compete with the rightful teaching
of Buddha with so inefficient a philosophy».[141] Adding two other examples
from history, we have already mentioned how precisely the Christian
monotheistic conception of God was lost in the case of the *Kirishitans*,
while K.S. Lee contends that a gradual decline of the radical Christian
distinction Creator-creation was one of the reasons for the Church's weak
witness vis-à-vis Shinto nationalism in this century.[142]

That there is an intrinsic incompatibility at this point between Christianity and Japanese religion is observed and asserted by both Japanese and
Western scholars, Christians and non-Christians alike. When Ernst Benz,

for example, says that the basic, essential difference between creation and Creator exists neither in Buddhism nor Shinto and that «the same central importance that the idea of the absolute otherness of Creator and creation has for us, the idea of unity of being has within Buddhist and Shinto thought», it is a statement which seems to be as generally accepted as it is important.[143]

Now, just as we pointed out in our systematic analysis that an adequate understanding of the ancestral spirits has to be based on the understanding of the divine in the rites' wider religious context, the important consequence at this point is to realize that the conflict between a Christian understanding of God and Japanese conceptualizations of the divine in general also pertains to ancestor worship. Although the Christian encounter with ancestral rites may not in the first place appear as a conspicuous encounter between different deities, no Christian consideration on the problem of ancestor worship can be adequate without bringing this vital issue into focus.[144] Also in our encounter, therefore, it is necessary to affirm the main charatceristics of Christian creation-theology over against the fundamental assumptions of ancestor worship. The basic Christian confession of God as man's Creator is, namely, a radical contradiction of the idea that the human and the divine are ultimately to coalesce within a comprehensive cosmic totality. According to Christian faith, cosmic interdependence between the human and the divine as presupposed in ancestor worship does not exist. E. Brunner has called the term «creation» a biblical «Urwort» and thereby given a pertinent expression to the immense significance and far-reaching ramifications of the biblical faith in a God who creates ex nihilo.[145] When this is affirmed in Genesis 1 and 2 as the point of departure for the whole message of the Bible, it is thereby emphatically stated that man has to do with a God who is fundamentally beyond man's own limited and dependent existence. God does not belong to cosmos. His existence is not dependent upon any cosmic law of cause and effect. He is the One who brings it all into being, not in impersonal and philosophical categories as its «cause» or «origin», but personally and freely as «he who spake, and the world was».[146] He is the «only Sovereign, the King of kings and Lord of lords, who alone has immortality and dwells in unapproachable light, whom no man has ever seen or can see» (1.Tim. 6,15–16).

Through the loaded expressions of creation ex nihilo and creation through the spoken word, the Old Testament testifies to God as the transcendent and, at the same time, personal Lord of heaven and earth. Thereby is radically excluded any idea of interfusion of the divine and the

human, also where such an integration is thought of in terms of an *ie* as
somehow derived from an «ancestor of origin» or a *kami*, and in terms of
its members being destined for ultimate coalescence with a supra-individual and supra-human ancestral being. Both aspects represent, as far as we
can see, a faith incompatible with biblical creation-theology. It is important at this point to notice that with all its interest for the ancestors of Israel
and with all the significance attributed to the fathers, the Old Testament
is always clear and unambiguous as to their status as human beings over
against God. Never are the divinity of Yahweh and the humanity of the
ancestors obscured. Yahweh is «the Lord, the God of your fathers, the
god of Abraham, the God of Isaac, and the God of Jacob» (Ex. 3,15).
Yahweh only is God, in whom the fathers trusted, to whom they cried
and were saved to the example of all subsequent generations in Israel
(Psalm 22,4–5). There is no interfusion of the status of the forefathers with
that of their God.

It may well be said that any attempt at a pantheistic-oriented interpretation of the Christian idea of God is a contradiction in terms and will
necessarily involve a radical misinterpretation or reinterpretation of Christianity at all points. A synthesis of God and man is in Christian faith
conceived of solely in terms of personal communication based on God's
word to man, to which we shall return in a moment.[147]

Since these are all well-known thoughts from the discussion on the
concept of God within Japanese religion, we shall move on to further
perspectives in Christian creation-theology with a direct bearing on our
particular problem. What we have said above might serve to reinforce the
misconceived impression of a distant and unconcerned God, if it is not
further developed. Already the very term Creator and the biblical «Urwort» creation imply, however, that God is not to be understood in terms
of a remote divine being. If Christian creation-theology, on the one hand,
rejects any pantheistic portrayal of the divine, it rejects, on the other, any
deistic view of a divinity in solitary aloofness. Just as God is transcendent
to man and the world as pointed out above, he is close at hand as its
Creator. This is testified to all through the Bible – firstly, in its emphasis
on God's continuous activity in and with his creation as its life-giver and
sustainer. Life and existence are not intrinsic qualities implicit in the
cosmic order. Neither are they, where man is concerned, gifts bestowed
upon him by an ultimate ancestral progenitor in the framework of an *ie*,
for which man should direct his primary gratefulness to his ancestral
spirits. Just as God as Creator once freely brought creation into being, he

is the One who freely sustains his creation, without which «all flesh would perish together, and man would return to dust» (Job 34,15).

Secondly, and closely related to the preceding, the faith that God «is not far from each one of us» (Acts 17,27) is contained in the fundamental biblical concept of revelation. When the God of the Bible is proclaimed as the God of Creation, it means that he is the personal God who wills and speaks and hears. Therefore, the Scriptures are not preoccupied with theoretical and philosophical considerations on how God may be in himself. When they reveal to man the nature of God, it is never as the result of human speculation, but always precisely as revelation, i.e., as a knowledge of God rooted in and determined by his own self-presentation to man. The Scriptures' talk of God is never unbinding theorizing on the nature of God for its own sake but a proclamation of God in the context of his revealed will and purpose with man and creation. The God of the Bible, accordingly, is never known abstractly and philosophically as «a god» but consistently as «the King of kings and Lord of lords», to whom belongs both a kingdom and a people. To use the terms of E. Brunner: God is «Gott-zum-Menschen-hin»; man is «Menschen-von-Gott-her».[148]

Thus the transcendence of God is in the Bible always held together with the closeness of God, who is creating, sustaining and revealing himself for fellowship and community. When at times Christian theologians use the expression «God's immanence»[149] to characterize this activity of God in sustenance and revelation, it is obviously an expression which may be used only with very precise qualifications. As H.P. Owen himself puts it, «the very word itself can be misleading. 'Immanence' can easily suggest that God 'dwells in' or 'fills' the world (and especially human souls) as a man may be said to dwell in his house, or water to fill a jar.»[150] The only meaning that possibly can be ascribed to such an expression in Christian context is the continuous dependence of creation upon God's creative power for sustenance. When the Bible speaks of God in terms like «him who fills all in all» (Eph. 1,23), these are expressions that must be interpreted within the basic biblical framework of creation-theology.

Only at one point in the New Testament, says E. Stauffer in the article already referred to, do we seem to have an incursion of immanentist ideas, and that is in Paul's missionary address in Acts 17,22 ff.[151] As one of the very few missionary addresses rendered in the New Testament, it is of particular interest to us and calls for some attention. When Paul, using Hellenistic quotations, says to the Athenians that «'in him we live and move and have our being'; as even some of your poets have said, 'For we are indeed his offspring'» (v. 28), is he not alluding then to an intimacy between the human and the divine more akin to the basic assumptions of ancestor worship than to what we have pictured above as biblical creation-theology?[152]

Especially within the German school of higher criticism, M. Dibelius' essay on the Areopagita in 1939 paved the way for an interpretation of the speech in Hellenistic terms. The effect was that the address was deemed to be – necessarily – either a free composition of the author (Luke), or in some way or other a later interpolation totally alien not only to Pauline theology as found in his epistles but to the rest of the New Testament and to the Old Testament as well.[153] This interpretation of Dibelius and his followers has not, however, won universal acceptance among New Testament scholars. Especially outside Germany, strong objections have been raised to Dibelius' methodology. That Paul here uses Hellenistic words and phrases is obvious. What is not obvious, however, is that these are to be interpreted on the basis of their own original context. Why should they not rather be interpreted primarily in the light of the new context into which they are put, i.e., in the light of the Jewish-Christian belief in God? Or, as W.W. Gasque puts it in his presentation of B. Gärtner's study: «Words and phrases are borrowed from pagan writers inasmuch as they can be understood in a Jewish manner, but the *meaning* given to them is quite different from that of their original context.»[154] Similarly F.F. Bruce contends that the Hellenistic quotations do not imply that the author acquiesces to the realm of ideas to which they originally belong. If it is kept in mind that Paul in Athens speaks as a missionary to pagans, and that we have in Luke's summary a speech which «may in any case have been more *preparatio* than *evangelium*», the quotations «have their place as points of contact with the audience.»[155] Seen in this perspective there is to Bruce no insurmountable difficulties in interpreting the quotations as part of a first missionary presentation of God the author and sustainer of our life.[156]

As far as we can judge, both on the basis of the actual text and from our own experience of a missionary situation, the latter interpretation of the Areopagita seems convincing. Far from contradicting basic Jewish and Christian creation-theology, and therefore being proof of a later theology alien to Paul and the rest of the New Testament, the Hellenistic quotations are simply a part of Paul's missionary homiletical technique. In using this – perhaps daring – homiletical point of contact, Paul's concern has been to take a first step in order to «impress on his hearers the responsibility of all men, as God's creatures into whom he has breathed the breath of life, to give him the honour which is his due.»[157] God is not a remote, reserved and unconcerned God, but close at hand as life-giver and sustainer, asking for the honor which every man was supposed to give him within the fellowship for which man was created.

Now, if this interpretation is correct, we may be permitted for a moment to undertake an experiment of thought. What would have been Paul's approach if his address had not been to Athenians at Areopagus but to a family in front of their *butsudan*, by an apostle not well versed in stoic philosophy but in Japanese religious mentality? He might have said that he understands from their activities at the family altar that they are not only concerned with the memory of their forefathers, but with the intimate fellowship in gratefulness with their ancestral spirits – their *kami* and their *hotoke* – to whom they believe they owe their very existence. He might have said that this gratefulness of theirs should first of all be directed to God «the King of kings and Lord of lords», who «does not live in shrines made by man» but is the maker of heaven and earth, and who – at the same time – is close at hand to every one of them as their life-giver and sustainer, as one of their own sages has said: «The heart of man is the abode of God; think not that God is something distant».[158] Then he might have used this homiletical point of contact to go on to talk of God who dwells «in the high and holy place, and also with him who is of a contrite and humble spirit» (Is. 57, 15), on the closeness of God and the fellowship with him in Christ, and then have ended his address with a serious call to repentance. Would that be an address in spirit and concern very different from the one at Areopagus? Would it not be a relevant approach of Christian missionary preaching to people who are preoccupied with the intimacy of their gods, and who somehow have got a twisted image of the God of the Christians as a remote and unconcerned «Creator»?

3.1.2 *Man as God's Creation*

In this perspective we may further elaborate on the Christian doctrine of man for a meaningful conversation. To the faith in God as man's Creator, namely, belongs the conception of man as God's creation. When it is said in the Scriptures that God created man in his own «image» and «likeness» (Gen. 1,26), and that the ultimate hope and goal of man is to «become partakers of the divine nature» (2 Pet. 1,4), are not these expressions which in a Japanese context of ancestor worship may be interpreted in terms of man's innate buddha-nature/*bussho* and the soul's process towards buddha-status after death/*jobutsu*? Not that we believe that these particular expressions from the Scriptures can drastically undo the basic monotheistic faith of the Bible and open up for general pantheistic notions of a cosmic totality. But when it comes to the Christian view of man, do not expressions like the «image of God», the ultimate sharing in «divine nature», and – we may well add – man being «God's offspring» (or: «God's family», as the Greek *génos* may also be translated) in the Areopagita, do they not all imply that there is – after all – something divine in man? Do they not pave the way for a Christian view of man and his ultimate destination which justifies a real parallelization with the idea of man being on his way to full-fledged ancestral status, with the idea that Amida makes all sinners buddha like himself?

The concept of imago Dei has played an important rôle in the history of theology. There have been – and there still are – widely different theological interpretations, corresponding to the differences in anthropology which we referred to in section 3.0.1. However, among the representative interpretations in Roman Catholic and Protestant theology we find – in spite of deep-going divergences – none who attempt an approach to the concept as if it denotes something divine in man's own nature, and thereby blurs the radical distinction God-man.

The controversial expressions in Genesis 1,26 are found in a context which is marked, on the one hand, by man's distinction from God his Creator, and, on the other, by his distinction from the rest of creation. Although the expressions necessarily contain important implications as to man's nature, their primary purpose seems to be to characterize man in his relationships. Of all God's creatures only man is made in the image of God. This puts man in a unique position in all the rest of creation. This uniqueness is, on the one hand, portrayed in the way that only with man has God entered into a personal relationship of communication, only to man did he direct his word in a personal address to which man should respond exactly as responsible being.[159] On the other hand, it is portrayed in the way that man is commissioned as God's custodian over the rest of creation. This reign of man over creation is no position to which man is entitled – ultimately – because of inherent potentialities, but because he was put into this position on God's creative command with the purpose of exercising his reign under God's blessings, responsible for it in constant response to God's address. The implication with regard to the nature of man is, as far as we can see, that man only is made and destined for such an existence in personal correspondence with God as his counterpart in creation.[160] Therefore, in so far as this createdness for personal and responsible correspondence and community with God within his creation is manifest in actual man's innate god-consciousness and consciousness of moral responsibility in personal intercourse, the image of God may be said to be retained even in actual, sinful man after the fall. However, when the New Testament at the same time envisages imago Dei as something which belongs to the «new nature» put on by man through faith in Christ (Col. 3,10), it is obviously presupposed that the image of God according to its central meaning – the personal correspondence with God on the basis of his word – is radically corrupted and can only be renewed by a new creative act of God.

In our context, then, the concept of imago Dei seems to be significant for two reasons. Firstly for what it does not imply: It is not a concept which refers to an innate divine essence in man. Secondly, it is a concept which underscores what we have said above, that a remote, unconcerned deity is not the Christian alternative to such a continuity in essence between God and man. Exactly in being created as God's counterpart destined for personal correspondence in fellowship, lies man's uniqueness, his greatness and worth. This is a faith which has important consequences both for man as an individual and a social being, to which we shall return below in chapter 3.3.

But what about man's final goal? Even if such a God-relationship is what man was once created for, isn't there still a possibility that in the final consummation of all things God is an indiscriminate God who makes all sinners even with himself? Isn't there still a possibility that man's ultimate destination is to coalesce with the divine in a way which makes any distinction in personal categories between man and God meaningless? Isn't such a view exactly what is implied when in the end man is said to «become partakers of the divine nature» (2 Pet. 1,4) and God shall be «all in all» (1 Cor. 15, 28)?[161]

As far as the Hellenistic sounding expression in 2 Peter 1,4 is concerned, many scholars regard it as one of several indications that this letter cannot possibly be of apostolic origin. According to W.G. Kümmel, who sees this verse in close connection with Acts 17,28, ideas like a natural «Gottferne des Menschen» which can be overcome only through a bestowal upon man of divine nature, are completely alien to what all the rest of the New Testament says about man. 2 Peter in general advocates a timeless, Hellenistic doctrine of redemption which «aus dem Rahmen der geschichtlichen Heilsauffassung des Neuen Testaments herausfällt», and chapter 1, 4 presents an anthropological view «die zum Menschenbild des übrigen Neuen Testaments nicht passen».[162]

We should not jump too hastily to conclusions as to the meaning of this particular expression in 2 Peter. Among some of the church fathers the idea of the «theiosis» of man – man's deification – as the goal of salvation was of particular importance. Already in Irenaeus we find the thought that the image of God is not a predicate of man from the time of creation, but rather the final goal of man towards which he was destined to grow.[163] Of greatest importance, however, became the idea of the «theiosis» of man in Clemens and Origen of Alexandria. In their impressive endeavor to synchronize Greek philosophy and Christian faith the ultimate goal of man's existence came to be the «theiosis» of every individual through unification with the divine Logos.[164] The underlying assumption of far-reaching consequences for their whole theological system was a positive assertion of «the ultimate oneness of God and man», in so far as «the deepest self of all reason-endowed beings is divine.»[165]

The theology of Origen, however, was never accepted in the church as representative Christian doctrine and was finally rejected as heretical at the ecumenical council in Constantinople 553. Thereby the influence of Origin at this point was effectively inhibited in the western church, whereas central points in his theology were advocated and handed down in the eastern tradition. In the Greek Orthodox Church the idea of «theiosis» – or «theopoiesis» – as man's final goal has thus continued to be of central theological significance down to our own days.[166]

According to Greek theology it is important to distinguish between the image of God, in which man was made from the time of creation, and the likeness of God, which man was created eventually to obtain. Already before the fall man was not created perfect. He was set in motion «zur Vollendung hin», created for eventual attainment of «Vollkommenheit, Unsterblichkeit, Ähnlichkeit und Vergottung».[167] The doctrine of the deification of man is, therefore, primarily a part of Greek Orthodox anthropology, although it is more fully expounded in the context of redemption.[168] In Greek theology, namely, the teaching of salvation and redemption has its particular emphasis and focal point in the unification of divine and human nature in the incarnation of Christ: «So vollzug sich in der gottmenschlichen Person des Herrn die hypostatische und ewige Vereinigung der göttlichen und der menschlichen Natur, welche die Grundlage und den Anlass zur Rettung und Vergottung des gesamten Menschengeschlechtes ist.»[169] In and through the human nature in the person of Christ, humankind as a whole is objectively restored, redeemed, and united with God. The consequence of this unity of human and divine nature in Christ, then, is in the end «die Verherrlichung und Vergottung der erretteten Menschen, die 'der göttlichen Natur teilhaftig sind'.»[170]

Greek theologians are aware of the pantheistic flavor such a theological reasoning contains and are eager to maintain that the deification of man should be understood in ethical and not in pantheistic categories.[171] It seems to us, however, that the deification of man as it is presented in their theology is not confined to ethical categories. When the unity of divine and human nature in the person of Christ is seen as basis and prototype for the «theopoiesis» of man, it cannot simultaneously be maintained that «diese Vergottung nur in etischem und nicht in realem ... Sinne gedacht werden muss». Even though we confess that the two natures were not confused in the person of Christ, we still confess that there was a real unity between the human and the divine which makes it impossible to separate the two, and which definitely goes beyond ethical categories. As far as we can see, the New Testament does not justify any assumption that man shall ever become divine as a parallel in reverse to the way in which God became man in Christ. When Greek theology sees the primary significance of the incarnation as an elevation of human nature to unity with the divine, it seems to us to be an approach guided by Hellenistic philosophy which seriously confounds the basic relationship God-man in biblical creation-theology. The locus classicus for the doctrine of the incarnation in John 1, 14, «the Word became flesh», cannot be interpreted in reverse order – «flesh became the Word». The New Testament message of the incarnation is not proclaimed as prototype and objective point of departure for human divinization, a Christian parallel, so to speak, to man's *jobutsu*.[172] It is proclaimed as a unique once-and-for-all event, when God in Christ came «in the likeness of men» (Phil. 2,7) to restore man's personal fellowship with himself through his atoning death and resurrection. All through the Old and New Testaments the categories of God as God and of man as man are retained, also in the consummation. This is particularly evident in the Revelation of John where the very idea in its view of the new heaven and the new earth is the restored, perfect fellowship God-man: «Behold, the dwelling of God is with men. He will dwell with them, and they shall be his people, and God himself will be with them» (21,3). In this perfected personal community there is no confusing of divine and human categories. There is a God to be served and praised and a host of men to serve and praise him: «Therefore are they before the throne of God, and serve him day and night within his temple; and he who sits upon the throne will shelter them with his presence» (7,15).[173]

If, in other words, the incarnation in Christian theology does not represent a parallel to the idea of man's interfusion with the divine as in the process of man's *jobutsu*, or in the ultimate coalescence of the individual soul with the *sorei*, it is nevertheless of the greatest importance as corrective to the misconception of the Christian God as remote and unconcerned. God's closeness and concern for man is not manifest in his dissolving the basic distinction between himself and his creation, making man even with himself, but in the fact that in Christ he took upon himself the nature of man to restore and ensure the fellowship of personal communication. «For in him all the fullness of God was pleased to dwell, and through him to reconcile to Himself all things, whether on earth or in heaven, making peace by the blood of his cross» (Col. 1,19–20).

How, then, are we to understand 2 Peter's talk of participation in «the divine nature»? Is it simply to be discarded as Hellenistic influence alien to biblical thinking, as some scholars do? There can be little doubt that this particular expression is borrowed from Hellenistic philosophical terminology. However, just as we saw in our dealings with Paul's address at Areopagus, this fact is not sufficient reason to maintain that when such an expression is used in a biblical context, it still has to be interpreted on Hellenistic presuppositions. As several scholars have pointed out, the borrowing of Greek expressions may also in this case be interpreted as an effort to present thoughts in line with basic biblical anthropology and eschatology.[174] The eschatological hope of participation in the restored and perfected fellowship with God that is generally found in the New Testament, is here expressed in Hellenistic terminology. The whole New Testament is agreed in the view, however, that this eschatological consummaton of the fellowship God-man is not simply an extension of the fellowship as experienced in this world. It is an eternal fellowship based upon a radical renewal and glorification of man's sinful and mortal nature. This is what the author of 2 Peter boldly expresses through the words «partakers of the divine nature».[175] Other New Testament authors use other modes of expression. Paul elaborates on this in connection with his exposition on the bodily resurrection of Christ. Just as Christ rose from the dead «in glory» so «the dead will be raised imperishable» (1 Cor. 15,52). The perishable shall put on the imperishable and the mortal shall put on immortality (v. 54). «Just as we have born the image of man of dust, we shall also bear the image of the man in heaven» (v. 49). Therefore Paul can also say that «when Christ who is our life appears, then you also will appear with him in glory» (Col. 3,4). The most daring expression in the New Testament for this radical renewal of man for perfect God-fellowship may be that of 1 John 3,2: «Beloved, we are God's children now; it does not yet appear what we shall be, but we know that when he appears we shall be like him....»[176] Neither at this place, however, is the intention to portray man in ultimate coalescence with the divine so that man is no longer man. Echoing the words of Genesis 1, it is a bold expression for the new man in whom the image and likeness is restored for perfect God-fellowship, for complete harmony with the divine will and sharing in the divine glory.

In concluding this section we may say, accordingly, that to Christian faith man is at no point, neither in this life nor in that to come, absolved from regarding himself as God's created human being, and God as his Creator to whom honor and worship are due. Man was as man created and will for ever remain as such. At this point there is inevitable conflict with all attempts to bridge the gap between God and man through any kind of ultimate coalescence. Man was not created, however, for the inhuman humanity of fallen man. Therefore, the closeness and concern of God, which is manifest already through his continuous sustenance of his creation, is most eminently and pregnantly expressed in God's own bridging the gap, coming in «the likeness of men» in Christ for the sake of restoring the community which man has forfeited. The final destination of man, consequently, is not envisaged in terms of an ultimate coalescence with the divine but in the perspective of a restored and recreated new man in perfect correspondence with God, sharing in divine glory.

This Christian view of God as man's Creator and man as God's creation has further consequences for the relationship between the two of particular importance in our context.

3.1.3 *The God-Man Relationship*

The immediate consequence of what we have developed in our two preceding sections is basically and straightforwardly expressed in the first of the Ten Commandments. When God, according to the Exodus narrative, conveyed to Israel his will at Mount Sinai, he set out by introducing himself as «the Lord your God, who brought you out of the land of Egypt» (Ex. 20,2), and continued to command his people: «You shall have no other gods before [or: besides] me» (v. 3). In the following was formulated some further implications of this command with regard to graven images, to the proper use of Yahweh's name and the Sabbath, and finally were given his regulations for human intercourse. This sequence of the Ten Commandments is of the greatest theological significance. The faith in one God, maker of heaven and earth and liberator of Israel from «the house of bondage», necessarily implies that to him belongs a unique position of honor. To no human being, neither living nor dead, neither king nor commoner, shall be attributed a status of honor that may usurp that of God. That would be a simple and radical negation of the very basis of faith itself. Corresponding to this unique position of God as man's ultimate object of honor, is the basic equality of all people as humans, with a common responsibility to give to God the honor due to him.

Thus, biblical monotheistic faith in God from the very beginning faced the problem of idolatry. It occupies a prominent place through the whole Old Testament and has done so down through the history of the Christian church and mission, not least in its meeting with ancestor worship. It is, in other words, an important concept in our context. Since it is also, however, a concept that is apt to be abused and misunderstood both by Christians and non-Christians, we should briefly state what we believe the concept means in a biblical context. Worship of graven images and concrete idols may be implied in the term, as seen in Ex. 20,4–5, but is by no means a sine qua non for a proper use of the concept and a proper understanding of its theological meaning. This Luther made clear in his explanation to the first commandment in his Small and Large Catechisms. The meaning of the commandment, he says, is that we shall above anything fear and love God, and «put our trust in him».[177] He then elaborates on this in his Large Catechism and is obviously concerned to emphasize that idolatry, or «falschen Gottesdienst und Abgötterei»,[178] is not only – not even primarily – related to concrete images and idols: «Sie [Abgötterei] stehet nicht allein darin, dass man ein Bild aufrichtet und anbetet, sondern fürnemlich im Herzen, welchs anderswohin gaffet, Hülfe und Trost suchet bei den Kreaturen ... und sich Gottes nicht annimmpt.»[179] To have a god is for Luther, namely, «etwas haben, darauf das Herz gänzlich trauet.»[180] Seen in this perspective idolatry is not first of all a theoretical problem and a problem of external symbols of religious worship but a very practical one of that in which man puts his ultimate trust and confidence. Understood in this way it seems to be a problem that must be straightforwardly faced also in the encounter with ancestor worship and to which we shall return in a moment.

The sequence of the Ten Commandments is significant, however, not only because it places the worship of God first, with the meaning just stated, but because it puts the regulations for interhuman behavior in a decisive theological perspective. When the commandments are often divided into two groups, the one consisting of those which concern man's relation to God and the other of those concerning interhuman behavior, the meaning is not that the two can be separated and interpreted irrespectively of each other. The first commandment gives rather the decisive frame of reference for man's total moral behavior. In all his interhuman relations man is to behave as God's responsible being, whose ultimate purpose is to honor God by abiding with his will for man. This again is pedagogically well expressed by Luther in his Small Catechism where he introduces his explanations to all the subsequent nine commandments in the same way: «Wir sollen Gott fürchten und lieben, dass wir....» This is of particular significance for the problem with which we deal. The fourth commandment – «Honor your father and your mother» – with which we shall deal extensively in chapter 3.3, is like all the rest of the ten to be understood in the overriding context of the first. This point cannot possibly be overemphasized in our context. By placing the descendants' duty to honor their off-spring – with all its implications – in the perspective of man's worship of and trust in God alone, the Old Testament radically divests parents and ancestors of ultimate authority and of any position that should call for man's ultimate trust and corresponding homage. To the fundamental difference God-man in Christian faith belongs – in other words – a difference in principle between the worship of God and the honor due to parents and ancestors.

Again we are touching upon a point of conflict well known from the history of Christianity in Japan and closely related to the one presented in section 3.1.1. Precisely the first of the Ten Commandments stirred controversy from the very beginning. In his attack on Christianity an apostate Japanese Catholic named Fabian saw no problems with nine of the ten. They were «practically reducible to the Five Commandments of Buddhism. But the first commandment, 'Thou shalt venerate *Deus* alone' (Thou shalt have no other gods before me) was by no means allowable. This teaching advocated rebellion against lords and fathers by its demand for exclusive veneration of *Deus*.»[181] The same fundamental problem occurred again later in the context of the *kokugaku* school. According to R.N. Bellah, although the *kokugaku* scholars were very much influenced by Christian thinking, they «yet made a crucial objection, namely that the Christian position would make the obligation to God absolute, thereby undercutting the obligation to ancestors and parents and the emperor and so on.»[182] Because of this central point Christianity in their view «threatened the basic structure» and «was fatal to loyalty and filial piety as they were traditionally understood.»[183]

On the basis of our systematic analysis in part 2 it seems to us that this is a conflict that still confronts Christianity in its encounter with ancestor worship. The problem of worship and ultimate trust, i.e., the problem of idolatry, cannot be evaded or simply left as non-existent. It deserves rather further attention.

At this place a closer look at the relatonship between ancestral rites and Yahweh-faith as reflected in the Old Testament may benefit our study.[184] However the historical connnection may be between practices reflected in Old Testament texts and ancestral cultic practices among early Semitic peoples, it seems obvious that certain passages in the Old Testament are referring to at least some kind of ritual practices towards the dead. With the Japanese shamanistic conjuring up of spirits of the dead in mind (section 2.2.3), the story told about Saul in 1 Sam. 28 is very interesting. The story says that his friends knew of «a medium at Endor» (v. 7), and Saul in his distress pays the medium a visit with the purpose of consulting the spirit of newly departed Samuel. When the spirit subsequently appears, it is significantly referred to by the medium as «a god [elohim] coming up out of the earth» (v. 13). The story reveals, in other words, both that such a practice was known to exist and that the spirit of the dead could be called by a common appellation for god, «elohim».[185]

Likewise, the references to sacrifices to the dead that we find in a couple of texts are interesting. In Psalm 106,28 the fact that Israelites in Canaan ate sacrifices offered to the dead is presented as part of their sinful acceptance of pagan practices, and according to Dt. 26,14 it belongs to the right handling of the first fruits, that nothing of the tithe shall be «offered ... to the dead». Again scholars disagree as to the actual implications of these references. Eichrodt contends that Dt. 26,14 does not refer to any worship of the dead as powerful beings, but only to a simple and common sharing with them rather motivated by their needs. Charles – on the other hand – sees the sacrifices as part of a proper and well-organized ancestor worship.[186] This difference between the two is further apparent in the way they look at the Old Testament family as a cultic unit (e.g., 1 Sam. 20, 6,29), and in their interpretations of the Levirate Law in Dt. 25,5 ff. To Charles, the very core in both instances is the family's well-structured ancestral cult. The family as a cultic unit has its basis in ancestor worship, and the Levirate Law is seen exactly as a precautionary measure to ensure the continuation of the family cult.[187] Eichrodt, however, although he agrees as to the importance of the family as a cultic community, sees no proof given for the hypothesis that this cultic community in Israel simply developed from ancestor worship.[188] Neither are there, according to Eichrodt, in the instructions of the Levirate Law any traces in the text of a cult to be perpetuated. Its purported significance does not go beyond that of ensuring the remembrance of the name, with all that meant in Israel.[189]

We are not in a position to make a scholarly judgment in this matter. If, to us, some of Charles' exegesis seems to be highly disputable, Eichrodt, on the other hand, seems to be almost too eager in defending his thesis that ancestor worship was no prevalent phenomenon among the pre-Mosaic Hebrew tribes. However this may be, it seems to be beyond doubt that the Israelites did know of a view of the ancestral dead, according to which they were not only «alive» but somehow in a position which made it useful for the living to solicit their advice. Some will say they were believed to be empowered both to benefit and to injure the living, wherefore they were to be offered sacrifices and could even be called «elohim». If so, the similarities with the view of the dead behind the Japanese rites are not insignificant.

Now, if Old Testament scholars disagree on a lot of aspects in this whole area of problems, there is a wide-ranging unanimity exactly on the point most decisive in our context. When we ask, namely, how the Yahweh-faith of Israel reacted to this view of the dead with its various practices, the Old Testament presents us with a clear picture of conflict.[190] The story of Saul's visit to the medium at Endor is told with the definite consciousness that Saul here does what is not permitted in Israel. That such a consultation with the dead was in flagrant opposition to the faith in Yahweh, was repeatedly expressed in the Law: «Do not turn to mediums or wizards; do not seek them out, to be defiled by them: I am the Lord your God» (Lev. 19,31; Cf. 20,6,27; Dt. 18, 10–11). The reason given for the prohibition is significant. It does not say that the practice is useless, for example, but that Yahweh is the God of Israel. The same motive drove the prophets to wage their war against the practice, as witnessed in Is. 8,19. To consult the dead obviously represented a contradiction of the basic faith in Yahweh as the only Lord of life and death, and the only one whom man should «consult». In the same way the practice of bringing sacrifice to the dead is reported as an example of sinful conduct that cannot find a modus vivendi with the exclusive status of Yahweh.[191]

There is one more very interesting example showing that the prophets' war against practices concerning the dead was to safeguard the radical distinction between man and Yahweh. During the years of the monarchy the custom has obviously developed to bury the dead kings in the temple. This practice, however, is vehemently rejected by Yahweh through the mouth of Ezekiel: «And the house of Israel shall no more defile my holy

name ... by the dead bodies of their kings, by setting their threshold by
my threshold ... with only a wall between me and them.... Now, let them
put away their idolatry and the dead bodies of their kings far from me....»
(Ez. 43, 7–9).

There is in the Old Testament, in other words, a consistent awareness
of «the basic incompatibility of ancestor worship or the cult of the dead
with Yahwism.»[192] The consequence of their confession of Yahweh as the
maker of heaven and earth and the liberator from the house of bondage,
was the radical renunciation of any practices towards their dead that might
compromise this faith in Yahweh as the only object of worship and the
only consultant and helper of man in life and death. As far as ancestor
worship in Japan confronts Christian faith with a similar danger, there
seems to us to be an important lesson to learn from the Old Testament.

As we have already seen in our systematic analysis, the practice and
attitude of worship is closely linked to that of prayer to and trust in the
ancestors/the dead on the basis of a belief in their power to benefit or injure
the living. Now, are the dead in general and the ancestors in particular in
such a position? Do they have such a power? Are they to be called upon
and petitioned, and correspondingly worshipped or venerated? Although
the answer given by the Yahweh-faith of the Old Testament seems to be
fairly clear, we cannot leave the questions at this point. An investigation
into the encounter of Christianity with ancestor worship from the point
of view of the relationship God-man has to face the problem of the saints
in Christian theology and piety. Is not the development of the veneration
of saints in the history of theology the best proof that also Christianity
ascribes to human beings a power and position very close to that of the
ancestral dead in Japan? This is not the place to trace the historical
development, but some points of particular interest to us should be
noted.[193]

Firstly, coming from our discussion on Yahweh-faith and the departed
in the Old Testament, we note that E. Lucius, in his comprehensive study
on the beginnings of Christian veneration of saints, says that exactly the
Old Testament concept of God with its distance between God and
creation, obstructed in the beginning of the Christian church the elevation
of the dead «in die Göttliche Sphäre», and did not permit «ihnen irgend
welche religiöse Verehrung zu Teil werden zu lassen».[194] When the door
was eventually opened, it could only be done in close connection with a
wider development of theological ideas, a development which again was
significantly influenced by two factors: Christianity's encounter with the

peculiar cult of the dead in the Roman empire and the occurrence of Christian martyrs during the decades of severe persecution.[195] It has been shown by Lucius and others that in many instances what has been called veneration of «saints», both in the first centuries of the church and later on, was actually nothing but veneration of and prayer to ancestors and family dead.[196] This is of importance for us to notice, since we shall see in a moment how exactly the doctrine on the saints is advocated by Roman Catholics in Japan today as a good missiological meeting ground for conversations on ancestor worship.

The second point to notice is the function and theological significance attributed to the saints through this development. Again Lucius pointedly remarks that at one point the Christians' calling upon their departed from the very beginning differed from that of their contemporaries. Whereas the latter regarded the dead as being able to intervene directly in the life of the living, the Christians were content to call upon them to forward their supplications to God, in whose presence they were.[197] This rôle of the dead and the saints as mediators or intercessors with God on behalf of the living has been central ever since, closely related to such theological doctrines as the superfluous meritorious deeds of the saints proper, their co-reign with Christ, and purgatory. This initial distinction from the contemporary pagan idea of direct intervention of the dead was clearly motivated by the Christians' monotheistic faith in God. It did not inhibit, however, the further development of a belief in the saints as powerful celestial beings, capable of assisting the living in a way going beyond that of intercession. This is well known from the development of the cult of relics and the subsequent system of tutelary saints worked out in the Middle Ages, both phenomena which came to play a prominent rôle in popular piety. Although the excesses and abuses of the Middle Ages went far beyond reflected theological thinking, the belief in a powerful position of the saints that made it meaningful to call upon them for assistance and protection was nevertheless theologically integrated into Catholicism together with their rôle as intercessors, both aspects together motivating their veneration.[198] The conflict with basic monotheistic faith in God and worship of him alone which this seemed to create, was attempted to be solved by the introduction of a theological distincton between latreia (or: adoration) for the worship of God alone and dulia (or: veneration) for the veneration of saints, a distinction still highly relevant in Roman Catholic theology and piety.[199]

If we turn again to our Japanese context, it is not surprising, then, that Roman Catholics on theological grounds see a close affinity between

Christian veneration of saints and ancestor worship. Their basic model of continuity, which we pictured in section 3.0.2.3, seems to have their own view of the saints as one of its main pillars.[200] It is a deplorable fact, according to one of their writers on our problem, that «veneration of the saints has fallen into discredit in recent theological trends.»[201] Whatever the reasons for this may be, the author ventures to say that «although veneration of the saints is not a central theme in our faith, it nonetheless cannot be missed and the liturgy has only lessened but not abandoned it.»[202] Exactly in Catholicism's meeting with ancestor worship in a pantheistic-oriented setting this particular doctrine provides «a very good meeting ground» for dialogue.[203] It is important for us to notice the primary reason the author gives for this statement: «Monotheism, taken in its extreme form, can seem very strict and remote and the Catholic Church has always tempered this by not only teaching the Trinity, but also by putting up a halo of angels and saints around the throne of the Triune God.»[204] Veneration of saints and the doctrine of communio sanctorum are thus theological attempts by the church to temper «monotheism, taken in its extreme form». On this basis, at the same time as Christiaens underlines the traditional distinction between latreia and dulia by using the term *suhai* for the former and *sukei* for the latter, he has no difficulties advocating prayer to the saints, asking not only for their intercession but also for the protection.[205] Although there is very little reference to the saints in the new Japanese catechism, there is nothing to contradict Christiaens' position, and in the introduction to the Holy Mass there are examples both of prayers to Holy Mary and all the saints to intercede with God on behalf of the confessing sinner, and of the merits and prayers of theirs as the basis upon which one asks for God's help and protection.[206]

Now, a second point of the greatest importance in our context is the conscious confusing of saints and ancestors found in Christiaens' approach. When he says that Japanese ancestor worship should be reconciled to Christianity through the teaching on communio sanctorum, this is then attempted by consciously including the ancestors of the Christian believer in his group of saints. Following the exhortation to venerate the saints and ask for their protection referred to above, the author asserts: «This may be said also about the ancestors who are in Heaven».[207] In his answer to one of the questions concerning Catholics and ancestor worship recorded in the booklet, Christiaens goes even further and says that it is an honorable duty for a family member to pray for «and solicit the protection of all the ancestors who have departed in good will, even if they have passed away without receiving baptism.»[208] He includes, in other words, among the saints even some – at least – of the believers' non-Christian ancestors. Thereby the road is effectively opened to theological acceptance of traditional ancestor worship's calling upon the ancestors for protection. And, it should be noted again, this is not done consciously facing a missiological risk of blurring Christian monotheism, but purposely to temper it «in its extreme form».

This approach seems to us to have its liturgical parallel in the Roman Catholic funeral service in Japan. If we look at first at the order of the Holy Mass, there is a comment to the opening rite, where the priest and acolytes enter in front of the altar, make a salutary bow in front of it, and offer incense.[209] In the comment the salutary bow – obviously including the offering of incense when this is simultaneously performed – is explained as «a conduct expressing religious respect» towards the altar.[210] Now, if we turn to the guide to the funeral, it has in its foreword an explanation to the use of incense in the funerary rites which says that it is done «in order to express respect towards the body of the dead as a sanctuary of the Holy Spirit.»[211] This has the liturgical consequence that the entering priest at the opening of the funeral rite offers incense facing both the altar and the coffin.[212] At the closing of the rite a prayer is said that the dead may be added to the saints. This is followed by a moment of silent prayer, while the priest once more offers incense to the coffin. Again the careful comment is reiterated, that the offering of the incense is in honor of the corpse of the dead as a sanctuary of the Holy Spirit.[213] The bow and the offering of incense are, in other words, genuine expressions of religious worship, both when they are performed in front of the altar and in front of the coffin, in both cases motivated by man's encounter with God. This seems to us to be a liturgical practice that may well serve to temper monotheism in a pantheistic-oriented setting, whether it is done for such a purpose or not.

It should have become clear at this point, that Christianity's encounter with ancestor worship in Japan today pregnantly actualizes the old controversy over the position of the saints in a Christian-monotheisitc setting, with its difference in principle between worship of God and veneration of men. The development of veneration of the dead and the calling upon them for protection created opposition from the very beginning, although the amount of critique coming from within the church in the early centuries may have been surprisingly small.[214] First with the fundamentally new theological approach of the Reformation was a thorough critique directed at the veneration of saints, with a lasting effect upon theology and popular

piety in the church.[215] That this point was regarded important by the
Lutheran reformers is seen already from the fact that *Confessio Agustana*'s
Article XXI, «Von Dienst der Heiligen», is placed in the first part of the
confession, dealing with faith and doctrine, and not in the second, dealing
with particular abuses in the church. Two points are important in the
article. Firstly, concerning the right veneration of saints – which in the
Reformation context means all departed Christians – it says only that they
are to be recollected in order to serve as examples for Christians in faith
and conduct.[216] Secondly, concerning the soliciting of their assistance
through prayer, it is content with saying that there is no biblical basis for
such a practice, Jesus Christ being our only mediator to whom we may
bring all our supplications with confidence. Precisely such a prayerful
confidence in him is our «hochste Gottesdienst».[217]

Going further to the corresponding article in the *Apology*, the basic
position of *Augustana* is elaborated on in light of the Roman Catholic
reaction to it. One starts by positively assuring that the reformers do teach
that the saints are to be honored,[218] and presents then a threefold interpretation of such a legitimate veneration in line with the first point we noted
in *Augustana*. Then we notice that the *Apology* concedes to the possibility
of the saints praying – together with the angels – for the living church, just
as living Christians do. This, however, is an assumption for which there
is no clear evidence in the Scriptures, and which therefore does not justify
any calling upon them to solicit their assistance.[219] At this point the
Apology reiterates the reformers' severe critique, not only of the popular
practice and abuses but of its reflected theological basis.[220]

The objections may be briefly summarized in two points. Firstly, the
position ascribed to the saints in the Confutation's reaction to *Augustana*
is tantamount to making them into significant mediators between God and
the living.[221] This again is tantamount to a bestowal upon the saints of an
honor which is due to the only mediator – Christ – alone.[222] Secondly, the
function of the saints has the harmful consequence that Christians put
their confidence in the saints which should be put in Christ alone.[223] For
such a confidence in the saints there is no promise in the Scriptures,
whereas there is an abundance of promises for the prayerful confidence in
Christ.[224] Remembering Luther's definition of an idol as that into which
one puts one's confidence of heart, it is not surprising that the *Apology*
may use the term «Abgötterei» for the various popular practices deriving
from this confidence in the power of the saints.[225]

In our view this basic Protestant critique is solidly based on the essential
presuppositions of the biblical God-man relationship as we have attempted

to portray them above and as such it is highly relevant today to the problem with which we are dealing. There can be no doubt that the doctrine on the communion of saints is of particular significance in Christianity's encounter with ancestor worship. Exactly because of this encounter, communio sanctorum may well come to play a much more prominent rôle in Japanese Protestant theology, preaching and piety, than it has actually done in the West. However, it seems to us to be just as important to state that the significance of this Christian doctrine is not that it can serve as a bridge to dependence upon the dead, confidence in their potentialities and soliciting of their assistance as witnessed in the ancestral rites. Even though the Roman Catholic approach – by repeatedly applying the distinction latreia-dulia in their use of *suhai* and *sukei* – does not advocate any simple acceptance of the traditional deification of the ancestral spirit, the fundamental distinction God-man with its implications in the first commandment seems nevertheless to be blurred by the power and the function ascribed to the dead. A veneration of the saints, or the dead, or the ancestors, that is based upon an assumption of their ability to aid the living across the ultimate border of death, with the consequence that one either directs one's prayers to them or bases one's prayers to God upon such a confidence in their mediatory function, is no longer a legitimate Christian veneration of human beings. No matter what term is used to characterize such a relationship to the dead, its theological basis obscures the fundamental biblical admonition that man shall not «consult the dead on behalf of the living» (Is. 8,18) but in faith and confidence put all his trust in God through the «one mediator between God and men, the man Jesus Christ» (1 Tim. 2,5). At this point is an inherent conflict between Christianity and ancestor worship which the Roman Catholic theology and liturgical and missiological practices do not clearly face and express.[226]

Before we conclude this chapter, however, we ask whether and how this conflict is reflected in Protestant Japanese churches.[227] Once again our problem is put into sharp relief if we focus on the funeral with its liturgy and practices. In Japanese writings on this there is wide-ranging agreement that in the setting of traditional ancestor worship, where any funeral is characterized by various offerings as symbols of religious homage paid to the spirit of the departed, there is a danger that even a Christian funeral may develop into illegitimate worship of the dead, or be understood as such by uninformed non-Christian attendants. It is therefore repeatedly stated clearly and frankly that in the funeral, like in any other Christian worship service, the object of worship is God and not the departed. A very good example of this is the instruction given in the Lutheran handbook for believers. Before going into the various funerary rites, it says that the Christian funeral «is not – as in other religions – to pray for the happiness of the dead and/or to worship the deceased.»[228] The importance the handbook attaches to this point is clearly seen from the fact that a warning, lest the rite or the «atmosphere» develops into «worship towards the dead» or «idolatreous worship», is expressed in connection with all the various elements of the funeral, from «encoffinment» to the subsequent memorial services.[229] The same admonition is formulated in a similar clear-cut way in a corresponding handbook of the United Church of Christ, where the chapter on the funeral starts with the sentence: «The funeral is not worship towards the dead.»[230] Examples on this serious facing of the problem of worship/idolatry are so numerous that it may be said to be generally acknowledged – at least theoretically and in principle – among Protestant Christians.[231]

Agreeing in principle on this important issue, the problem occurs among Protestants when one asks what practical consequences this is going to have for the actual performance of the funeral and its various liturgical elements. The opinions are very much divided. The question is: How is this basic Christian principle, with its inherent conflict with the common Japanese view of the dead, going to be clearly expressed and witnessed to without generating the misunderstanding that the Christians are rude and respectless towards their dead?[232]

As we have seen above, the Buddhist funeral usually ends with the priests and the attendants passing by the coffin, offering incense to the dead. Over the years the custom has developed in many churches to end the Christian funeral by a special farewell ceremony/*kokubetsushiki* similar to the Buddhist one. One passes by the coffin, but, instead of offering incense, one usually places/offers a flower in the coffin or at a table brought in for this purpose.[233] The whole discussion, subsequently, on worship and offerings in the funeral setting has very much focused on this practice. In the book on the Christian funeral service and its other-religious soil edited by Hiyane, it is interesting to note that almost all of the contributors – in their concern for a theologically reflected liturgy – comment on this point. On the one hand, there is the opinion that neither flower- nor incense-offerings are to be seen as worship but simply as courteous greetings towards the dead necessary in a Japanese context. Even the bringing forth of other offerings like meals, fruits, etc. should not be indiscriminately denounced and prohibited but rather regarded as a problem of individual feeling.[234] Most of the contributors, however, are more sceptical and cautious in their approach. Some are content with raising the question whether the offering of incense and/or flowers may not be confusing in the direction of worship, and ask where the limits go for the display of meals, fruits, etc.[235] Others maintain that even if the funeral must be as courteous as possible, the flower-offering ceremony as a substitute for incense is a dubious practice leading in the direction of worship of the dead, and should therefore be abandoned.[236]

This latter opinion is advocated with caution in representative writings of the United Church of Christ again in the 1970's. In its publication on death and the funeral from 1974, Yamamoto Naotaka – in an article that deals with problems confronting the Christian funeral in contemporary Japan – regards the flower-offering farewell ceremony as born out of the Buddhist incense-offering and as a practice which – although not necessarily impossible – should rather be done away with.[237]

Looking towards traditionally more conservative Protestant churches we find a similar but somewhat stronger stand in Obata Susumu's widely circulated articles in the popular evangelical magazine *Hyakumannin no fukuin*. Although the remote origin of the use of incense in the funeral may well have had the purpose of avoiding smell in hot India, its function today in the Buddhist funeral service is to serve as a religiously significant element in the mass for the *hotoke* of the dead. In this perspective and in light of the Old Testament rejection of ancestor worship, Christians should not adopt the Buddhist-style offering of incense nor other traditional offering practices. As to the new, alternative practice of flower-offering, it is dangerous as far as it may be adopted and performed with the same non-Christian intentions, although Obata does not say expressis verbis that it should be abandoned.[238]

Although this review is by no means comprehensive as to various Protestant positions, it should suffice to portray the dilemma. That there is a real danger of lapsing into worship of the dead is no far-fetched theorizing by uninformed expatriates but one felt and stated almost unanimously by Japanese Protestant Christians. At the same time there is not unanimity as to the liturgical consequences to be drawn with regard to the funeral service. For our own part, we shall show some reserve in presenting particular practical solutions, being removed from the actual situation where these have to be worked out. On the basis of our own systematic analysis of ancestor worship, however, we are convinced that the way for the churches to go on this issue is to be sought along the lines presented by the voices critical to the adoption of incense- and/or flower-offerings and other ambiguous practices. The Christian funeral is perhaps the form of missionary «preaching» which draws the widest audience in ordinary Japanese society. There is therefore, to be sure, a definite need for a liturgical framework that may genuinely express the human sentiments of love and respect towards the departed. Confronted, however, with the real possibility that certain liturgical forms may not only be ill-suited to convey the basic motives of a Christian funeral but even obscure the fundamental doctrine of God as man's only object of worship and trust, the gain of abstaining from such ambiguous practices seems greater than that of employing them.

This has brought us to the conclusion of our chapter on the God-man relationship as seen in the light of the Christian encounter with ancestor worship. We believe it to be verified that Christianity in this encounter enters into a conflict that cannot be evaded or solved along a simple line of continuity. The danger for the church to blur the meaning of worship and lapse into some kind of idolatry, which has confronted her often before in history, is a challenge today in her meeting with traditional ancestor worship in the Japanese setting. There is a definite need for the church today to be clear on this issue, frankly testifying to the humanness of man – all his passed-away ancestors included – and the divinity of God, as the Yahweh-faith had to do already in Old Testament times. On the one hand, this may be conceived of as a demand of the law not to worship and serve «the creature rather than the Creator» (Rom. 1,25). On the other, it is a liberating invitation of any human being – the one in a long line of known ancestors as well as the one without any – to place all his trust and confidence in God his Creator, available without discrimination to anybody through his Son and our mediator Jesus Christ. By this, we are taken to the next point in our conversation.

3.2 Death and Salvation

Looking back at our systematic analysis in chapter 2.2 we found that the inquiry into the relationship between the living and the dead members of the family took us to the very core of ancestor worship's religious assumptions. In the context of ancestor worship, death does not constitute a final barrier between the two. The dead and the living are interrelated in a community of total interdependence.

We have further seen in section 3.0.2.3 how Christian voices in Japan have been asking for renewed theological reflection on death as a must in Christianity's encounter with ancestor worship and related practices. Saji Ryozo in 1959 pointed to the ambiguity in Protestant theology on death and regarded the Roman Catholic position as envious: «Right or wrong, the church at least has an established and plainly stated, consistent view of afterlife.»[239] Anglican priest Kochi Tokio in 1969 drew attention to the fact that Christian books on death and afterlife are few in Japan, an indication, according to Kochi, that at least Protestants have tended to overlook the problem or to handle it in an all too simple way.[240] Finallly Fr. Doerner's «Comparative Analysis of Life after Death in Folk Shinto and Christianity» is an indication that Roman Catholics – in spite of Saji's envy – do not feel self-complacent with their effort to relate their view of death to the Japanese scene: «It is not too late for the Church in Japan to develop a tract on death and afterlife which incorporates the traditional practices of the people.»[241]

The problem of death, accordingly, cannot but be a central issue in our encounter between ancestor worship and Christian faith. We have already touched upon it in chapter 3.1, both in our discussion on the eschatological hope of participation in the restored and perfected fellowship with God and in our contention that death is an ultimate border which precludes supplications to the dead for helpful interference in the life of the living. Now we shall concentrate on the issue, see what problems our encounter raises for Christian theology, and see how it may faithfully address itself to these. That real theological problems, not yet settled within the church, are involved at this point, is clearly put into relief if we compare the results of Fr. Doerner's recent study with that of Prof. Doi's study group in the late 1950's. According to Doerner the «otherworldliness of life after death of the Catholic tradition», with its belief in heaven, hell, and purgatory, «is somewhat similar to the Buddhist concept of *gokuraku* ('paradise')», and a tract on death and afterlife which is «compatible with the indigenous beliefs of the Japanese» is «very much something possible».[242] Doi's study group concludes, however, that Christianity, «based on its view of the world to come, which – different from Buddhism – is a faith in the resurrection of the dead and the continuation of individual personality», may create «a pattern for the expression of feelings of love and respect to the dead that may be unique for the Christian Church in Japan.»[243]

3.2.1 *The Meaning of Death and «Afterlife»*[244]

For ancestor worship death and «afterlife» are matters of primary concern in the context of the *ie*. H. Ooms has made an interesting observation when he says that whereas the belief in an «afterlife» by Occidentals is naturally considered to be «a necessary condition for ancestor worship», it is possible that this belief «is only secondary to and highly dependent upon this consciousness of *ie* membership.»[245] However the relationship may be between primary and secondary motives at this point, the close-ness, community, and continuity between the living and the dead members of the family provides the members with an answer to the universal quest for permanence and eternity. Life is not considered only in terms of years between birth and death. On the assumption – however unsystematized and contradictory – that some sort of spirit survives the body, the dead and the living are integrated into a circle of interdependence. The dead are redeemed beyond death through transfer of merits by the living; the living are under the protection of the dead on the condition that they are properly cared for. The living are dependent upon the dead for their well-being in life; the dead are dependent upon the living for their well-being in «afterlife». For both the summum bonum is conceived of in terms of a perfect and harmonious community of interdependence across death. Thus man finds in the framework of ancestor worship and the *ie* a modus vivendi with death which not only makes it tolerable but natural and even deeply meaningful. When Hiyane Antei, therefore, in his discussion on the problems confronting the Christian funeral in Japan points to the lack of any radical distinction between life and death common in both Shinto and Buddhism, he points to a characteristic that nowhere is more conspicuous than in the ancestral rites.[246]

Now, preoccupation with death and rites for the dead eventually produced the not too enthusiastic label «funeral religion» to be attached to Buddhism in Japan. When Christian books on death and «afterlife» have been rare to appear, Kochi Tokio takes it to be an indication not only that Christians have tended to overlook the problem but that Christianity has consciously wanted not to present itself as another «funeral religion» but as a religion of the living.[247] Such a fear may well be justified. What cannot be justified, however, is to jump to the conclusion that since Christianity is a religion of the living, it does not concern itself with death. The two cannot be put up against each other in such a way. All through the Old Testament and the New Testament the Scriptures address themselves to the problem of death in a way that definitely arrests any tendency to belittle and minimize the concern with death apparent in ancestor worship. Concepts like «life everlasting», «heaven», and «kingdom of God» are all basic Christian concepts pointing beyond the border of death. The Scriptures' concern with life is simultaneously a concern with life's ultimate riddle: death. We shall see below that Christianity stands forth as a religion of the living exactly because of its triumphant message of victory over death.

3.2.1.1 *Death in Theological Perspective*

Firstly, the question arises how Christianity is to respond to the naturalistic conception of death delineated above. Is death part of man's existence – so to speak – in the way that man from the very beginning is made a mortal creature? Is man simply to be subjected to death as a natural part of his being with which he has to seek a meaningful modus vivendi? When questions like these confront us in our meeting with ancestor worship, we are confronted with an old and much debated problem in the church.

Under the influence of Greek philosophy – with its dualism body-soul – in the first centuries of her history, the view spread in the church that bodily death as such was to be approached as a positive release of the soul. Adam was from the very beginning made a mortal creature, and death was a natural process which man inevitably had to go through as a human being. Death was part of man's material nature. The problem eventually became part of Augustine's famous battle against Pelagius, and when the Bishops Conference in Cartago in 418 A.D. condemned the latter's teachings, it also had the following to say to the understanding of death: «Condemned is the one who teaches death as an inevitability of nature and not as a consequence of sin.»[248]

Although the discussion today is carried on in a context different from that of Greek dualism in the first centuries A.D. representatives of both exegetes and systematic theologians still maintain that man's death as a biological phenomenon is not to be referred to as a consequence of sin, but belongs to God's order of creation. According to Old Testament scholar L. Wächter, even though the negative aspects of death are prevalent in the Old Testament, and the dominant religious motive of death as God's punishment is generally testified to,[249] the mortal nature of man as such nevertheless belongs «zur göttlichen Schöpfungsordnung».[250] P. Althaus makes a similar approach from a systematic point of view. He distinguishes between what he calls the natural «Sterbeschicksal» of man, which as such is no consequence of and punishment for sin, and «der Tod der Sünder».[251] The intention of Althaus by this distinction is not to reduce the universal scope and the serious nature of judgment of the latter. To no one since the fall of man can death be simply «reines Sterben als natürliche Gottesordnung». It is always «zugleich Tod der Sünder».[252] Where actual man is concerned the distinction is therefore a theoretical one. It is nevertheless of the greatest theological significance that the call «zum Akte des Sterbens» belonged to God's original will for man.[253] While God «alone has immortality» (1 Tim. 6,16), to man mortality is part of his «createdness». To live in trust to him who gives and takes life in freedom – i.e., to live under the call to the act of dying – «ist Gnade der Schöpfung».[254]

Althaus is perfectly aware that this position of his and others departs from what he calls «die ältere kirchliche Theologie und die neuere konservative», which maintains that death as such derives from man's fall.[255] He does not, however, as far as we can see, give substantial scriptural evidence for such a distinction between man's natural «Sterbeschicksal» and «der Tod der Sünder».[256] When the New Testament explicitly says that death entered the world «through sin and spread to all men because all men sinned» (Rom. 5,12), we cannot see that there is any New Testament evidence to the effect that by this statement is meant only death as judgment upon man's existence, not death as his biological «Schicksal».

To apply such a distinction upon the Old Testament seems to be just as artificial. When Wächter in his exegesis of Gn. 3,17 ff. says that only the «Mühsal» of life – with its toil and trouble and sweat – is presented as the wages of sin and not death itself, his arguments are not convincing. One thing is that both in Gn. 2,17 and in Psalm 90,7 bodily death is presented as a consequence of sin and a manifestation of God's wrath and judgment.[257] Another thing is that Wächter's emphasis that in the Old Testament mortality belongs to man from the order of creation, and only the sudden, premature death is an expression of God's judgment, raises the following serious question: Why, then, should the ultimate hope which eventually broke through in the Old Testament be that of resurrection to «everlasting life» (Dan. 12,2) and the swallowing up of death «for ever» (Is. 25,8)? Why should not only the sudden, premature death be abolished instead of death as such? To us, therefore, the scholars seem to be right who conclude that in the Old Testament man's death as such «ist Strafe für die Sünde des Menschen»,[258] and that according to the Yahwist in Genesis death is «Unnatur», alien to man as creature.[259]

Also in the New Testament such a comprehensive view of death in terms of «wages of sin» (Rom. 6,23) – both as biological phenomenon and as judgment – is manifest in various ways, not only where it is stated expressis verbis. So Christ, vicariously carrying the sins of the world, had to die the biological death of man as his «last enemy» (1 Cor. 15,26), and thereby experience the judgment of the Father upon himself. Having atoned for the sins of the world, however, he rose from the dead «because it was not possible for him to be held by it» (Acts 2,24). When the sins and the judgment were carried away so was the power of death.[260] Therefore, whereas sin renders death as its wages, «the free gift of God is eternal life in Christ Jesus our Lord» (Rom. 6,23). When the New Testament, accordingly, sees «eternal life» in terms of a hope that «death shall be no more» (Rev. 21,4), it obviously means simply what it says: Death as such shall be no more, because sin is no more. To us, therefore, when old and recent «kirchliche Theologie» maintains that, to man, death as such is the wages of sin, it seems to be justified in its position.[261] The attempt to operate with a theological distinction between death in its «schöpfungs-mässigen Sinn»[262] and death as «Tod der Sünder», is a derailment from the basic and prevalent trend in the scriptural witness to man's mortality.

By placing death in the context of sin and judgment the Scriptures are saying that no interpretation of death in purely naturalistic categories can come to terms with its real cause and significance. Just as with man himself, his death can be understood only in theological perspective, where man – although created for God-fellowship – leads his life in sin under judgment. When death is not an intrinsic part of man's material, bodily nature, it also implies that man's hope vis-à-vis death is not to be projected in terms of an exclusive spiritual continuity for the released soul in an «afterlife». Release, not from body and material existence but from sin and judgment, is the Christian key to the problem of death.

If this has been a significant part of the Christian message to various conceptions of death that has confronted the church before in her history, it is still highly relevant in her encounter with ancestor worship in contemporary Japan. It is interesting to notice that exactly this point is pertinently emphasized by many Japanese Christian writers on the mea-ning of death. In his study of death and funeral in the Old Testament referred to above, Kashiwai Norio, for example, sees the Yahwist-narrative in Gn. 2–3 decisively picturing death as having become an inevitability for man when he broke out of the trust-relationship to God in the garden, and as the conclusive result of God's curse upon the land because of man's disobediance.[263] Because death is in this way related to sin its problem is in the book of Job, Kashiwai significantly points out, intrinsically bound up with that of the righteousness of God and the justification of man.[264]

The same point is elaborated on from the New Testament point of view by Matsunaga Kikuo in the same book. Precisely the perspective that death means ruin in terms of judgment because of sin makes death a dreadful thing and accounts for the interesting fact that the conception of the heroic death is lacking in the New Testament.[265]

The second point to be emphasized has already been touched upon as far as we have seen that such a theological perspective on death implies that it is closely linked to the christological and eschatological ones. All the New Testament witnesses are unanimous in their proclamation that the death and resurrection of Christ has divested death of its power. Taking upon himself the sins and the death of man Christ «abolished death and brought life and immortality to light through the gospel» (2 Tim. 1,10). This event of Christ, therefore, inaugurated a new era for mankind in which a most surprising light has been shed on the ultimate riddle of man's existence. Any man who through faith and baptism is made one with Christ, is made partaker in Christ's victory over sin and death, and shall after bodily death be raised anew to everlasting life (John 11,25; Rom.6,8). The victoriously risen Christ, namely, is only «the beginning, the first-born from the dead» (Col. 1,18; cf. Rom. 8,29), thus being the guarantee upon which Paul may triumphantly exclaim: «O death, where is thy victory? O death, where is thy sting?» (1 Cor. 15,55), and Peter in thankful adoration says: «Blessed be the God and Father of our Lord Jesus Christ! By his great mercy we have been born anew to a living hope through the resurrection of Jesus Christ from the dead» (1 Peter 1,3).

This proclamation of the resurrection of Christ with its implication in terms of hope for man, is without comparison the dominating theme in the New Testament when we look for its teaching on death. Compared to the New Testament's powerful and frequent presentation of this perspective, its further interest in anthropological and apocalyptic aspects of death is relatively small. This is surprising and significant when we keep in mind the preoccupation with such aspects and the large variety of ideas produced in this respect both in the Jewish and the Greek world at the time.[266]

The fact that the New Testament in this way sees the death and resurrection of the one person Jesus Christ as decisive for death and eternal life of mankind as a whole, shows again how far the New Testament is from general, naturalistic considerations. By being placed in the framework of sin/judgment, on the one hand, and Christ's atoning death and resurrection on the other, death is understood in eschatological terms. Just as it entered into the relationship God-man as an enemy, it has been decisively overcome as an enemy in Christ, and it shall be ultimately destroyed by Christ's second coming and the final consummation of all things.[267] The eschatological framework is, in other words, a linear and teleological framework. There is no attempt to come to terms with death as a natural phenomenon with which man somehow has to find an eternal modus vivendi. Death has its terminus a quo, the fall of man, and its terminus ad quem, the final consummation.

Again we see how Christianity in its encounter with ancestor worship's preoccupation with death and the dead is guided by a very different overall perspective. As far as we can see, no serious and meaningful conversation can be carried out unless this difference is clearly recognized. Looking at Japanese Christian sources from this point of view of teleologically oriented eschatology, the picture is somewhat ambivalent. In Hiyane's book on the Christian funeral Kumano Yoshitaka puts his finger on this point when he says that a clear eschatological understanding of Christian faith – of death, resurrection, judgment, and eternal life – is a prerequisite for a proper funeral. The doubts about proper forms in Japanese churches in this respect originate, he says, in the vagueness of faith and doctrine on this point because the eschatological hope is ordinarily not fully preached.[268] As far as we have surveyed relevant written sources, Kumano's criticism is not wholly unwarranted. We have already seen how Roman Catholic missionary Fr. Doerner talks of Christianity's compatibility with indigenous beliefs at this point on the basis of the «otherworldliness of life after death of the Catholic tradition». In his comparative analysis the eschatological perspective of resurrection and final consummation is left completely out of scope.[269]

Turning to Protestants, a little booklet on the death in Christ and the problem of «afterlife», by a Presbyterian pastor and published by one of the leading evangelical publishers, may be mentioned. Although the resurrection of the body is not completely left out, and an apocalyptic perspective is present in terms of the coming judgment of the world, the picture is nevertheless dominated by a speculative Greek-platonic, dualistic conception of the world and of man at the expense of a genuine biblical view of death in linear-eschatological perspective.[270]

Interesting from our own Lutheran position is Lutheran pastor Yamauchi Rokuro's approach. On the one hand, his proposed prayers for the funeral contain repeated references to the resurrection of Christ and to the hope of our own resurrection on the last day.[271] On the other hand, however, concerning the fate of man in death Yamauchi may express himself in words and concepts that contain quite an amount of ambiguity.

In death man goes «through the hard fight, and the soul, throwing away the curtain of the flesh returns to its heavenly home.... It leaves the shore of darkness and sets out in peace for the glorious home of the Lord across the seas».[272] Therefore Christians should pray: «Heavenly Father, we now entrust the spirit of our beloved...into your hands. Please lead it into your glorious kingdom.»[273] Our question is whether one may express oneself in such a way without seriously obscuring the eschatological faith in the resurrection of the body, and without conveying or reinforcing – inadvertantly perhaps – an idea that man's final destination is to be found in some kind of exclusive, spiritual «afterlife» of the soul beyond death?

When this is said, however, it must immediately be added that this is not the whole picture. Both among Catholics and Protestants we find heavy emphasis on the New Testament eschatological perspective of the resurrection in their presentation of the Christian view of death. On the very first page in the Roman Catholic guide to the funeral it is pregnantly stated that the Christian funeral is to be seen in the perspective of the fulfilment of the kingdom of God, the second coming of Christ, and the resurrection of the dead,[274] and Fr. Nemeshegyi has this to say in his commentary to the new Japanese catechism: «The catechism, by treating universal eschatology (the end of the world) before individual eschatology (private judgment, etc.), is following Holy Scripture, where future, cosmic eschatology is given prominence. Modern theology has fully accepted this point of view. Our individual salvation receives its full meaning only through the glorious end of salvation history.»[275] Similar views are not absent in Protestant churches. When Pastor Murakami Osamu (United Church of Christ) answers questions concerning death and Christianity, the christological and eschatological perspectives are put into focus by reference to the hope of «the morning of resurrection» and the expectations of «the day of the eschatological hope.... In short: Although we enter into everlasting life already while living in this world, we are awaiting the end of time, looking towards the glorious return [of Christ] and the morning of the rersurrection», whereupon he quotes 1 Cor. 15,52–53.[276]

The third and last point of importance in this connection occurs to us when we address ourselves more explicitly to the anthropological perspective on death which the ancestral rites actualize. The concerns in ancestor worship are not least – as we have seen – centered around the question what happens to man in death, i.e., an interest in the fate of the soul/spirit in its process from *shirei* to *sorei*. The perspective is thoroughly anthropologically oriented, whether it is with individaul overtones focusing on the particular soul in question or with a collective emphasis focusing on the social nexus to which it belongs.

Thus, even though we said above that anthropological considerations on death in the New Testament recede into the background to the benefit of its message of victory over death in Christ, our encounter with ancestor worship nevertheless brings the anthropological problem as such into focus. If it is the case that vital concerns behind the ancestral rites are only of minor interest to the New Testament, that in itself is an important observation. The question confronting us is simply the old and familiar problem of body-soul, mortality-immortality.[277]

This, of course, is closely related to what we have said on the preceeding pages of this chapter, and we may return to already quoted references in order to set our problem in relief. Fr. Maruyama, for example, bases his approach to ancestor worship on a clear doctrine of the immortality of the soul, of which he says that «we Catholic believers are firmly convinced».[278] Pastor Yamauchi – as we just saw – explains death in terms of a «curtain of the flesh» which man throws away, while the soul sets out for its «heavenly home...across the seas». Pastor Horikoshi, again, talks in very clear-cut terms of the body and the soul, of which the former is the instrument of the latter. Man's life, however, does not end with the mourning of the body. The important question is what happens to the soul. The soul, namely, is «the chief component of human life»,[279] and the Bible gives quite an exact answer to what happens after death: The body returns to dust and ends, whereas the soul returns to God who gave it and is without end. Unless it is saved through the mercy of God in Christ, it is heading towards eternal condemnation, which is a judgment upon the soul after the annihilation of the body.[280]

We notice the very interesting fact that whereas there is not much of particular Japanese flavor in these ideas as they are here rendered – parallels might easily be found in Western sources – they represent a preoccupation with the fate of the soul in death that in many respects is close to what we find in ancestor worship and seem to open up for the compatibility between the two of which Doerner speaks. Our question is, however, whether such a sharing in a preoccupation with man's immortal soul is not to be seen more in terms of a common denominator in philosophical presuppositions of Western and Japanese folk beliefs than in terms of a significant point of contact between the latter and Christianity. In this respect the modern theological discussion on body-soul, mortality-immortality seems to have produced a wide-ranging and – for our purpose – significant concensus, at least among Protestants: To talk of body and soul in a way that leaves the first to be annihilated in death as the mortal part of man, while the latter in death is set free to some kind of everlasting life as man's immortal component, cannot be maintained as Christian anthropology. The Scriptures do not allow for such a clear-cut and decisive compartmentalization of terms like body, soul, and other anthropological concepts. Man is not partly material body, partly spiritual soul. Man is created an integrated psychosomatic totality. When God «breathed into his nostrils the breath of life», then man was not somehow given an immortal soul in custody; he «became a living being». (Gn. 2,7.) The consequence of his sin and rebellion is not, accordingly, that man's body has to return to dust, whereas his soul because of an inherent immortal quality is exempted from this dreadful «wages of sin». Man simply has to die as man. Nothing in his own nature can provide him with an assurance of some kind of survival in death. In this respect it is said pregnantly and with full weight that God alone has immortality. (1 Tim. 6,16.)[281]

This is a very important point to be made in our conversation. What at first sight may seem like compatible lines of thought in a common, popular conception of the immortality of the soul proves itself at closer scrutiny to open up for radically different anthropological perspectives. The idea of an immortal soul in man which through death is set free for its process of growth towards a *sorei*, and which already, as an innate *bussho* in living man's nature, makes man a potential object of worship, has no parallel in Christianity. In Christianity, just as the concept of man so also the concept of soul is seen in the context of the human being a creature and sinner, which means that man – totally understood – is a being who is living towards death. A Christian response to ancestor worship and its understanding of death, which does not pay due attention to this point but concentrates on anthropological speculations along the lines of an immortality-of-the-soul-idea, does not come to terms with vital aspects in Christian faith.

This, however, is not all that has to be said in this respect. What we have developed above may give reason for the question whether man – body and soul – is simply annihilated in death in a way that is tantamount to equalling death with the end of his existence? Anthropologically speaking this would seem to be the only logical conclusion. At this point, however, it seems to us that exactly the theological perspective in which the Scriptures see man and his death prevents us from falling victim to logical anthropological considerations. It is a fundamental fact in the Scriptures that God is the Lord even over the realm of death. (Psalm 139,8; Amos 9,2; Acts 2,24–28.) Although man has to die, he cannot die away from his

God-relatedness. When we said that death was not part of man as he was originally created, we did not say that man was in himself somehow endowed with immortality. Immortality was granted in his God-fellowship, symbolized in Gn. 2 through man's free admission to the tree-of-life. [282] Nowhere, however, does the Bible draw the conclusion that because man sinned and was banned from admission to the tree-of-life and eternal God-fellowship, he simply has to die a death of total annihilation, escaping away – so to speak – from his responsible being with God for which he was created. Rather the perspective is that man in and through death has to be related to God, in judgment or – by his own grace in Christ – in forgiveness.

When the Scriptures visualize man's hope vis-à-vis death in eschatological perspective in terms of resurrection and final consummation, two things, therefore, are of importance to us at this point. Firstly, the resurrection is a resurrection of all men, not only of those in Christ. (Dan 12,2; John 5, 28–29; Acts 24,15.) Secondly, it is a bodily resurrection of total man, a resurrection «in glory», in what Paul may call «a spiritual body» as far as those who are dead in Christ is concerned. (1 Cor. 15,43–44.) There is, in other words, an upholding of man by God in and through death which is total in a twofold sense: It encompasses all men, «both the just and the unjust» (Acts 24,15), and it encompasses total man, body and soul. Seen in this perspective we are justified in talking of a continuity for man in and through death. So far as ancestor worship testifies to the essential faith that death does not simply mean man's annihilation, we may agree. The continuity, however, is not exclusively referring to man's soul only. It is a continuity for man applying even to his body, notwithstanding the fact that it is abandoned in the tomb for decay. This is a faith which is boldly expressed in the New Testament, obviously and frankly facing the very limits of human reasoning. The body who rises from death on the youngest day is exactly a risen body and not the product of a completely new creatio ex nihilo. There is continuity between the body abandoned for decay and the body raised in glory, pregnantly expressed when Paul says: «For this perishable nature must put on the imperishable, and this mortal nature must put on immortality.» (1 Cor. 15,53.)[283] This is a continuity, however, which does not have its basis in innate human qualities – neither body nor soul – irrespective of man's status as «Mensch-von-Gott-her», but only in the correspondence with God for which he is irrevocably and inescapably created.

Facing the problem of death and «afterlife» a Christian is therefore left in a radical tension. He knows man – body and soul – to be a mortal being in so far as nothing in him escaped the consequence of sin and rebellion. At the same time he knows man – body and soul – to be a «Mensch-von-Gott-her», upheld by God in and through death towards the resurrection. From this point of view of irrevocable God-relatedness man – body and soul – is «immortal».[284]

Thus, in Christian perspective there is a radical absoluteness in death, in light of which the living and the dead are to be sharply distinguished. There is no communication and interaction between the two based on a faith that something in man – i.e., his most vital part, his soul – after all does not die. At the same time there is a continuity in so far as the absoluteness of death does not mean that the dead are simply annihilated from the sight of both men and God. In life and death man is upheld by God towards resurrection. The further consequences of this for our conversation will be seen in the following sections.

Concluding this section we may say that whereas the death of man in the context of the ancestral rites is seen thoroughly in a naturalistic perspective of anthropological and psychological categories, it is in Christianity radically determined by the overriding theological perspective of the Bible. This is the case already with regard to the dreadfulness of death as man's enemy, which may be really understood only on the background of man's broken God-relationship because of sin. Just as man is never encouraged to find a heroic modus vivendi with sin, neither is he exhorted to find a heroic modus vivendi with death. To the contrary, death has been decisively conquered by God in Christ. His bodily resurrection from the dead is the second pivot around which the thinking on death centers in the Scriptures. Through this event is given the guarantee of the ultimate subjugation of death, not in terms of a survival of an immortal soul in man, but in terms of the resurrection of total man in glory. Thereby, instead of viewing death in eternal, cyclical perspective of body-soul, living-dead, this life-«afterlife», Christianity sees death in a linear, eschatological perspective with its cause as well as its conquest clearly defined. Only in this theological perspective may death be understood in Christian terms, both with regard to its radical absoluteness, and with regard to the continuity it contains between the man of the tomb and the man of the resurrection.

Now, at this point the question arises how the death of the individual here and now is to be thought of in relation to the final resurrection.

3.2.1.2. *The Dead and the Intermediate State*

When we ask for the actual state of the dead, we are asking a question which in the New Testament – as we have seen – is of secondary importance compared to its concern with the final resurrection. When this is observed and properly considered in Christian theology on death, however, it must be added that our present question cannot simply be rejected as irrelevant from a New Testmanet point of view. Especially in an encounter with people who are preoccupied with the actual state of their departed and their own present relationship to them, it presents itself as a significant task for the church to clarify how – to use P. Hoffmann's words – «die Zukunftsaussage» and «die Jenseitsaussage» concerning death and the dead in the New Testament are related to each other.[285]

That this problem is actually raised among Japanese Christians may be seen in both Roman Catholic and Protestant writings. Among the 65 questions directed to the church which pastor Murakami attempts to answer in his book, some are concerned with death, and one is formulated as follows: «Does the Christian go to heaven immediately upon death, or does he/she sleep until the return of Christ?»[286] Fr. Christiaens, again, in his approach to ancestor worship from a pastoral point of view, refers to the traditional Roman Catholic doctrine on purgatory – together with that on the saints, as we have seen above – as one of the significant points of contact with indigenous ideas on death and the dead. He admits «that there are many difficulties connected with it», but nevertheless adds that «if we do away with all the later unnecessary additions we still retain a very plausible reason that some souls have to undergo a further period...of purgation and preparation, and that our prayers are really helpful to them. In this way we can easily adopt the practice of *kuyo*....»[287] Once again we see, in other words, that the encounter with ancestor worship actualizes not only important theological concerns but old controversies in Christian thinking.

Looking first at Protestant theology, the war against the immortality-of-the-soul idea and the emphasis on the death of man as total led theologians to the conclusion that any idea of an intermediate state between the death of the individual and the universal resurrection at the end of time had to be rejected. Only to us, from our position in time and history, is such an idea possible; it cannot be real from the eternal position of God beyond time. To the man who in death crosses the border between time and eternity the moment of individual death and that of bodily and corporate resurrection coincide in an integrated simultaneity. Therefore we have to relinquish any attempts «die beiden Momente der Hoffnung, das Jenseits des Todes und den Jüngsten Tag, in ein gegenständliches Nacheinander zu ordnen.... Grenzt und strandet unsere Zeit nicht überall an den Jüngsten Tag? Liegt der Jüngste Tag nicht gleichsam rings um uns herum, so dass unser aller Sterben uns in die Gleichzeitigkeit mit dem Ende der Geschichte, dem Kommen des Reiches, dem Gericht stellt?»[288] In this way Althaus attempts to move away from an unbiblical focusing on the fate of the individual soul beyond death towards the primary New Testament emphasis on the coming of the kingdom of God with the final resurrection. On the basis of such a radical distinction time-eternity the concern with an intermediate state is not only unnecessary, it is meaningless.

Serious and – as far as we can see – well-grounded objections have been raised to this position also from theologians who share Althaus' view of death as encompassing total man. A system based on a radical philosophical distinction time/history-eternity seems to be superimposed upon the New Testament in a way which is not conformed to its own view of death in linear eschatological perspective.[289] Not only an intermediate state, it seems to us, turns out to be meaningless in such a system, but ultimately – in fact – the whole notion of resurrection of the body. If the dead are no longer in time and history but have already passed into a concurring simultaneity with the youngest day, the coming of the kingdom and the final resurrection, then the actual world in which we live – where the resurrection has not yet occured – and the world to come seem to fall apart in a radical discrepancy and discontinuity which cannot be maintained in light of the New Testament.[290] It must be added, however, in this discussion with Althaus – who through the many editions and the wide circulation of his book *Die letzten Dinge* has profoundly influenced Protestant thinking on eschatology – that he seems in later years to have significantly modified his position. At this late stage he may say that Christian theology does not have to fight against «Unsterblichkeit» as such, and that the stumbling-block which modern theological debate at this point has often created has not been that of the gospel. «Das Verständnis des Todes als Ausdruck des Gerichtes Gottes fordert...nicht den Satz, dass der Mensch in Sterben ontisch ganz zugrunde gehe.»[291] By such a statement Althaus seems to open up for a recognition of an intermediate state which to us seems unavoidable.

At this point we may move on to the second radical solution to the problem of the actual state of the dead, the Roman Catholic idea of the purgatory to which we have already referred.[292] Although Christiaens concedes that «not only Protestants, but many Catholics today are reluctant to admit the existence of purgatory»,[293] and modern Catholic dogmatics may say that the thought of purgation after death is stated nowhere in the Scriptures expressly and formally, only presupposed and hinted at,[294] the purgatory in its essential elements is still an integrated part of Roman Catholic theology. Without going into details as to the location and nature of the purgatory, the council of Trent briefly and basically defined it in a twofold sense. Firstly, it said that such a state of purgation does exist. Secondly, it said that the souls in purgatory may be relieved by the living, especially through the offering of the mass.[295] Accordingly, Roman Catholic catechisms still continue to teach that «dem Fegfeuer jene Seelen zur völligen Reinigung überwiesen werden, die zwar in der Gnade Gottes abgeschieden, aber noch nicht frei von lässlichen Sünden oder zeitlichen Sündenstrafen sind».[296] Also the new Japanese catechism expresses itself briefly but significantly in consistence with official doctrine at this point, and Fr. Nemeshegyi gives the following comment: «Death is the final moment of decision. But in order to be able to enter into the full communion of God's love, all falsity has to be purged away from man's existence. In many cases, this happens after death: illuminated by Christ, man returns, through a process of purification, to his true self.... This process of purification is called 'purgatory'».[297]

Leaving aside all medieval abuses and damaging thoughts developed in relation to the purgatory, its basic presuppositions are of prominent importance in the wider Roman Catholic theological framework. The purgatory is intrinsically related to the Catholic conception of justification, according to which the grace of God is not conceived of in terms of an imputation to man of the merits and righteousness of Christ. It is understood in terms of a power for regeneration and recreation in man himself in «a supernatural breakthrough of a new will for the good and the holy» which then works a yearning for holiness that comes to rest only in the ultimate, complete sanctification of man.[298] Now, since without holiness no one shall see the Lord (Hebr. 12,14), only the one who has attained this state of complete sanctification may enter into God's presence. In order to see God man himself must be clean.[299] The road towards this goal is presented under the elaborate doctrine on sin, with the basic distinction between mortal and venial sins, and man's compensation for his sins through active satisfactio and passive satispassio. At this point, then, the purgatory enters as a must in Roman theology. Only a very few, namely, attain complete sanctification and cleanness with complete satisfaction for their sins already in this life. For all the rest «it cannot be otherwise than that after death there must be an opening...for purification of the soul.»[300] Whereas the possibility for active satisfactio – through fulfilment of the penance imposed by the priest – ends with death, the subsequent purgatory presents the possibility – and the necessity – of satispassio as compensation for unfulfilled penance and atonement for venial sins.[301] Only through such a process «all sin and evil inclinations die, all penalties for sins are removed – the soul enters into the joy of its master.»[302]

It is obvious, in other words, that the view of an intermediate state in terms of a process of purification is not an element of superfluous theological ornamentation, but a doctrine closely related to basic tenets in Roman Catholic theology. From the point of view of Catholicism's own presuppositions, therefore, missionaries like Christiaens and Doerner seem to be completely right in advocating their approach to ancestor worship as an accomodation based on the purgatory-idea as a significant point of contact.

Neither is it surprising, however, that already the fathers of the Reformation had to do away with this teaching. This they did partly from the point of view of its lack of scriptural basis,[303] partly from the point of view that this teaching is irreconcilable with the main article of faith, i.e., the belief «dass allein Christus und nicht Menschenwerk den Seelen helfen soll».[304] This basic critique of the purgatory-idea is once again taken up in modern theology by Althaus, who stresses that «die Frage ist nicht peripherisch, sondern weisst noch einmal in den innersten Mittelpunkt des Evangeliums.»[305] We will in our next chapter come back to the content of this critique, since it is concerned with the basic understanding of the justification of man and his hope of salvation vis-à-vis death. Suffice it at this place to say the following: When we today touch upon this old controversy in modern missiological context, just as this particular doctrine cannot simply be absolved by Roman Catholics because of their overall theological structure, an intermediate state in terms of a process of purification from our point of view has to be rejected because of the basic reformatory teaching on justification through faith by grace. We cannot, like Christiaens, use such an idea to «easily adopt the practice of *kuyo*....»

What becomes, then, of the actual state of the dead? In our preceding section we came to the conclusion that even though death is a death of total man, there is nevertheless an upholding of man in death that is total in a twofold sense: It encompasses individual man in his totality, and it encompasses all men. This implies an intermediate state for all men between individual death and the resurrection at the end of time, which to us seems to be clearly based on New Testament evidence. At this point we have some difficulties with Cullmann's position in the book referred to above. On the one hand, he recognized that from the point of view of salvation history the dead «*are* still in time», and he states that he does «not understand why Protestant theologians...are so afraid of the New Testament position» on the intermediate state.[306] On the other hand, he continues immediately to talk of the intermediate state with regard to the dead in Christ and bases the continuity of man in death on the quickening power of the Holy Spirit in a way that necessarily generates the question whether the continuous being in time is a reality to the dead only in so far as «we have received the Holy Spirit».[307] The pneumatological arguments with which Cullmann continues to elaborate on his view of the dead «in time», seem to us to make an affirmative answer to this question the only possible. At this point we therefore agree with the critic who says that «Cullmann seems to imply that the unrighteous dead who do not have the Holy Spirit pass out of existence until the final resurrection.»[308] Such a consequence does not seem to be drawn in the New Testament. Truly enough the «information» is scarce. What is offered indicates nevertheless the upholding also of the «unrighteous». This seems, however cautious one has to be in the interpretation of the parables of Jesus, to be implied in the story of the rich man and Lazarus (Lk. 16,19 ff.). When the apostles again in Acts proclaim Christ who descended into Hades (Acts 2,24–31), and the New Testament speaks of the fallen angels and the unrighteous who are kept «under punishment until the day of judgment» (2 Pet. 2,9), the assumption seems to be that all men in death are kept by God until resurrection and judgment. We may even go one step further and say with Künneth: «Theologisch kann daher vom 'Zwischenzustand' nur so gesprochen werden, dass zugleich zwei Linien gezogen werden, welche die unmittelbar nach dem Tode sich vollziehende vorläufige Scheidung der Menschen deutlich werden lassen. Der Mensch kommt nach Biblischer Aussage in die 'Scheol', in das Totenreich, jeder 'an seinen Ort'.»[309]

The New Testament abstains from further apocalyptic elaborations on this theme. In light of its concentration on the resurrection of Christ with all its radical implications, it can be no surprise, however, that an emphasis of assured confidence is put on the blessedness of «the dead who die in the Lord henceforth» (Rev. 14,13). That death cannot destroy the fellowship with Christ already established is a joyful assurance which Paul expresses in almost doxological terms: «None of us lives to himself, and none of us dies to himself. If we live, we live to the Lord, and if we die, we die to the

Lord; so then, whether we live or whether we die, we are the Lord's» (Rom. 14,7–8). This is a confidence Paul may express not only with his eyes on the future resurrection, but also with the actual state of the dead in mind. Although such a perspective is not frequent in Paul, there seems to us to be little doubt that it is clearly expressed in Phil. 1,23. When death, compared to life, is said to be a «gain», the reason is precisely that such a departure from life as an actual alternative would mean a transition into a being «with Christ...that is far better.»[310] It is, so to speak, the Pauline version of Christ's words to the crucified criminal: «Today you will be with me in Paradise.»[311] In our context this assured emphasis on the preferable being with Christ in death is important for two reasons. Firstly, because it shows that when Paul describes the dead as «those who are asleep» (1 Thess. 4,13. Cf. 1 Cor. 15,18.), the purpose is not to depict the intermediate state as a sleep-like state of unconsciousness that can at most be negatively preferable in terms of what is not felt and not experienced. It is positively preferable because it brings about a being with Christ «that is far better» than what is already experienced in life. Not unconscious «sleep», but conscious Christ-fellowship is the blessed state of those who die in Christ.[312] Secondly, the emphasis on the preferable being with Christ is important because it leaves aside all further speculations and focuses decisively on the Christ-fellowship. This joyful assurance of a «far better» being with Christ already in death leaves no room for doubts and uneasy feelings because of a coming period of necessary purification before the bliss of God-fellowship may be experienced.[313] When it comes to the further implications of this fellowship with Christ in death, we have on the basis of the New Testament to be reserved in our inferences. On the other hand, exactly in a missiological conversation like ours it is of the greatest importance to clearly state what may be maintained in this respect. The being with Christ, then, involves not only a «rest from their labors» (Rev. 14,13). What we have developed above may also imply that we can agree with Künneth when he says that the Christ-fellowship is not seen in purely passive terms, «sondern es besagt trotz allem 'Ruhen von der Arbeid', Aktivität und bewusstes Subjektsein der in Christus entschlafenen Jünger.»[314] The Christ-fellowship constitutes, in other words, a significant continuity and community between the living in Christ and the dead in Christ to which we shall return below. Künneth goes further, however, and explains this «Verbundenheit mit Christus» in the intermediate state in terms of «einem priesterlichen Dienst» which involves also «der 'himmlischen Liturgie'...der Fürbitte und des Segnens».[315] At this point Künneth seems to be moving beyond «die uns gesetzten Grenzen» to which he himself refers in his comment on the Roman Catholic practice of praying to the saints for intercession.[316] When he positively states that the Lutheran confession «gewiss...den priesterlichen Dienst der Fürbitte durch 'die Heiligen im Himmel'...anerkennt»,[317] he does not reflect the definite mood of reserve in which the Lutheran confession expresses itself at this point. Luther in the *Smalcald Articles* inserts a significant «vielleicht» in this respect,[318] and the *Apology* to CA Article XXI says: «Darüber so geben wir ihnen nach, dass die Engel für uns bitten.... Und wiewohl wir nachgeben, dass, gleichwie die lebendigen Heiligen für die ganze Kirche bitten ingemein oder in genere, also müge für die ganze Kirchen die Heiligen im Himmel bitten.... Doch hat solchs kein Zeugnis in der Schrift, denn allein der Traum, der genommen ist aus dem andern Buch Maccabeorum.»[319]

There is at this particular point, in other words, a definite restraint that seems to us appropriate in the light of the Scriptures. Not that such a service in terms of intercession is rejected as an impossibility for the dead in their being with Christ. With a cautious «may be», however, an agnostic position is consciously taken because such a theological inference points beyond «die uns gesetzten Grenzen», and may open up for unsound and unbiblical devotional practices.

The intermediate state pregnantly characterized as a being with Christ, however, also carries the definite mark of being intermediate. As far as the resurrection and final consummation is yet to come, the dead are also still «in time» and waiting. (Cf. Rev. 6,9–10.) Never in the New Testament is the final goal seen as being attained simply by crossing the border of physical death. Seen from the point of view of their Christ-fellowship and their assurance of partaking in the resurrection «in glory», the dead in Christ may well be spoken of as the ecclesia triumphans. Seen from the point of view that both the living and the dead are heading towards the end, the aspect of waiting – of not yet – is one they still in some way or other share with the ecclesia militans. If we ask, however, how such a waiting is experienced in the intermediate state, we again embark on a theological journey which takes us beyond the limits put before us.[320]

In this way the firm conviction of an unbreakable fellowship with Christ in death never causes the New Testament to change its view of the coming resurrection for a preoccupation with «afterlife». What it says to individual salvation after death in an intermediate state is to be seen within its overall eschatological perspective. It is sustained all the way by the New Testament view of the future consummation. Neither, on the other hand, does its view of the final resurrection mean that the actual state of the dead is simply left out of scope. The two are kept together and decisively interrelated. When preoccupation with the problem of «afterlife» is encountered in the framework of ancestor worship, therefore, the church has to reaffirm her basic confession in the «resurrection of the body and the life everlasting». At the same time the question of the actual state of the dead shall not be evaded.[321] Not only does the Christian know that all people are being upheld in death in an irrevocable God-relationship towards resurrection and judgment. He knows that the dead in Christ are taken into a new being with the Lord which means a blessed foretaste in waiting of the glory to come. Even though the Scriptures arrest all intricate speculations on the «how» of the intermediate state, the view of death and «afterlife» that has been presented here holds important implications for our conversation that have to be further developed in our next sections.

3.2.2. *Perspectives on Salvation*

Believing that all people due to their irrevocable God-relationship are being upheld in death in a way which implies an intermediate state as developed above, our encounter with ancestor worship generates further questions as to the actual relationship between the living and the dead. What about the idea of the living assisting the dead? In section 2.2.2 we described in detail the soteriological aspects of the ancestral rites and saw how offerings and masses for the benefit of the dead play a central rôle on the basis of the theory of the transfer of merits/*tsuizen eko*. The problem encountering Christianity at this point is by no means new in the history of the church. A basic and general idea of the living assisting the dead was found already in the immediate Jewish and Hellenistic context of the New Testament,[322] and it has ever since been a recurring issue in the discussions over Christian doctrine and liturgy. When some Christians in Japan today regard this particular aspect of the ancestral rites as a practice which can easily be adopted, this is not surprising on the background of the significant parallels to ancestor *kuyo* which may be found both in ancient and contemporary Christian context. Now, which are these parallels, and how are we to respond to the idea of assistance to the dead as encountered in ancestor *kuyo*?

3.2.2.1 *The Problem of Vicarious Baptism*

Among one particular group of Japanese Christians the desire to assist departed ancestors and relatives has taken a form which caused discussion already in the early Church. Referring to 1 Cor. 15,29, the Spirit of Jesus Church (Iesu no Mitama Kyokai Kyodan) has adopted the practice of vicarious baptism for the dead.[323] There is no written material – as far as we know – to verify our assumption that somehow the adoption of this old practice may be related to the Japanese concern for the well-being of the dead as expressed in the ancestral masses. The connection was made, however, by the leader of the church – Murai Suwa – in an interview she granted in May 1976. When we asked about the church's attitude to the ancestral rites and the *butsudan*, Murai herself made the reference to their practice of vicarious baptism/*migawari senrei*, stating that this practice – where a believer may receive baptism on behalf of any number of departed ancestors and relatives – to a large extent solves the problem they might otherwise have with ancestor worship. Vicarious baptism was obviously seen as a Christian and better way of assisting the departed.[324]

We can immediately see how a practice like this may serve to create a link between traditional *kuyo* and Christian faith as the latter is interpreted in this particular church. The question is, however, whether Paul's reference to those who are «being baptized on behalf of the dead» (*hyper ton nekron*) may be used to justify a practice of so far-reaching theological implications as vicarious baptism? If so, we may well ask whether such a practice should not be adopted by Japanese churches in general?

Paul's reference in 1 Cor. 15,29 confronts us with a well-known crux interpretum to sholars down through the centuries.[325] The most elaborate comment on the verse in the old Church was given by John Chrysostom in his homily on 1 Corinthians. According to the bishop, the custom of vicarious baptism had already existed in certain quarters of the church for a long time, depending, however, on a false understanding of Paul's words in v. 29. In John Chrysostom's view «the dead» was not to be taken literally, but spiritually, as a reference to man's mortal body as counterpart to his eternal soul. Paul, therefore, was not referring to the departed, but to the mortal nature of those who were actually being baptized.[326] Such a spiritual understanding of the text became widespread in the old Church. In Ambrosiaster, however, the view is advocated that Paul – without approving of the practice himself – speaks of vicarious baptism on behalf of Christian believers who passed away before being baptized.[327]

Coming to Thomas, both the spiritual understanding as well as that of a vicarious baptism for believing relatives who died before baptism and who are now in purgatory are presented as possible solutions.[328] Thus, according to Rissi, neither the old nor the medieval Church came to any clear conclusion as to the interpretation of the verse. Nor did the 16th century with the renewed and extensive Bible-study of the Reformation. To the contrary, new explanations further complicated the picture. Luther himself, for example, solved the problem by translating *hyper* like «über», opening up for an understanding of the expression in a local sense: Baptism was carried out literally upon the graves of the dead Christians as a sign of the bodily resurrection. [329]

It seems to us that modern research, almost unanimously rejecting both Luther's interpretation and the spiritual understanding of «the dead» as unacceptable evasions of the problem, has left us with three exegetical options that deserve serious reflection.

Firstly, we have the possibility that Paul simply refers to vicarious baptism on behalf of the dead as a common practice in Corinth of which he himself approves.[330] Scholars of this opinion are driven by the fact that *hyper* meaning «in the interests of» is the normal content of the preposition. Since Paul approves of the practice, however, these scholars feel mostly forced to introduce some limitations in their understanding of «the dead». To some it is supposed to mean dead believers or catechumens who passed away before being baptized; to others the expression implies departed, non-Christian family-members.[331] Already the fact that these scholars are forced to presuppose such a limitation «without any justification from the text itself» has been taken as an indication that this interpretation is not acceptable.[332] Our own main problem with this solution, however, is the basic objection that such an understanding of a salvatory effect upon a third – and, in this case, dead – person cannot be reconciled with the fundamental tenets in Paul's «unmagical» view of baptism.[333]

Secondly, the possibility exists that Paul refers to a practice of vicarious baptism in Corinth of which he himself does not approve.[334] This position is based upon two main observations. First the linguistic one that «...all the evidence is against interpreting *hyper* in v. 29 in another than normal fashion; *hyper ton nekron* must be rendered, 'in the interests of the dead', hence baptism for them must be primarily for the purpose of affecting their status and condition.» [335] In other words, a real vicarious baptism for the benefit of the dead. Second, compared with Paul's teaching on baptism in all the rest of his scriptures, however, such an idea is alien to Paul, and therefore the reference does not reflect «the Apostle's beliefs but those of the Corinthians whom he was addressing».[336] Hence v. 29 betrays a practice in the Corinthian church that was either a «modification of Christian baptism, or an importation alongside it...not of Paul's planting nor of his willing.»[337] The only drawback of this interpretation seems to us to be that there is nothing in the text to indicate that Paul does not approve of what he refers to here. May Paul really use such a practice as an argument for the resurrection of the body if he regards it as a serious twisting of genuine Christian baptism? The question is pertinent, but as far as we can see not of the nature that it necessarily makes the interpretation impossible.

Thirdly, there is an 18th century interpretation that has been taken up again among modern scholars by one of J. Jeremias' disciples and subsequently has been adopted both by Jeremias himself and other scholars.[338] The crucial point in this exegesis is a slightly different understanding of the preposition *hyper* than the one that determines the two solutions above. Documentation is given to verify that *hyper* with genitive does not only mean «in the interests of» but has as well a final meaning denoting purpose.[339] In such a case the purpose in view «must often be inferred from the context», and «in our context there can be scarcely a doubt: v. 29 is speaking of pagans who take baptism upon themselves...with the purpose of becoming united with their deceased Christian relatives at the resurrestion.»[340] Thus, Paul's enigmatic reference to the dead does not imply a practice of vicarious baptism. It is rather an indication that among the Corinthians the consciousness of the fellowship with the dead in Christ has been strong enough to serve also as a motivating force for baptism among new converts, something to which Paul had no reason to object.[341]

Granted the validity of this solution we have in 1 Cor. 15,29 a witness to the early Christian sense of community – of belonging-together – with the dead of the greatest significance to our problem and to which we shall return in section 3.2.3. Even though this particular exegesis is still disputed our exploration of the various interpretations provides us nevertheless with the decisive conclusion that the text cannot be used as a Pauline justification of vicarious baptism for the sake of the dead. Nothing in the New Testament teaching on baptism justifies that the rite be used as a Christian parallel to the living's affecting the condition of the dead in ancestral *kuyo*. The practice of the Spirit of Jesus Church in this respect is to be seen more as a contemporary Japanese edition of the old gnostic misconception of Christian baptism than as a legitimate accomodation to indigenous ideas.

3.2.2.2 *Roman Catholic Masses and Intercessions for the Dead*

A second and far more widespread parallel to ancestor *kuyo* in Japanese Christian context is the Roman Catholic practice of and teaching on the offering of liturgical prayers and Holy Mass for the dead. This is a particular feature of the church that we touch upon whether we approach her from a catechetical, liturgical, or missiological point of view. We notice for example, that to the New Japanese Catechism's chapter on suffering and death is added an appendix on prayer for the well-being of the dead, a point which is said to be «especially important» in Japan «where prayer for the dead has been given such a great importance through the centuries».[342] The appendix says that the church performs her daily mass-offering remembering all the dead, praying that God will receive them in his kingdom, and further that Catholic believers ask especially that Holy Mass be performed for the sake of particular relatives and/or close friends on the anniversary of their death or on any other day.[343] Moving on to the brief and popular introduction to the Holy Mass referred to above, we repeatedly see the same point emphasized. The mass is explicitly said to be a sacrifice/*ikenie*; *sonaemono* for all the dead, wherefore prayers for them are also included.[344]

The close resemblance this Roman Catholic practice may have to traditional ancestor *kuyo* is conspicuous in Fr. Maruyama's little pamphlet on Catholic funeral-practice and ancestor worship. Under the headline «Mourning Mass» the author says: «When it comes to the sacraments of the church, first of all mass for the dead is offered at the funeral. Thereafter it is offered again on the third, seventh and thirtieth day...and then 'Yearly Mourning Mass' is offered every year on the anniversary of the death....»[345] The same striking resemblance is seen in actual life in the Roman Catholic Saga village in Kyoto. Here the priest twice a year (at Bon and at All Souls Day) conducts Holy Mass particularily for the sake of the dead in the *ihai-do* of the church.[346]

We have seen in a preceding section that this practice is dependent upon the old idea of the purgatory. Although the term is not frequently met in connection with Holy Mass and prayers for the dead, the essential content matter is obviously there, for example, in the guide to the funeral. Here prayers are said to the effect that the dead «may be freed from the bonds of sin and rest in the joy and peace of God»,[347] and that «all the burdens be taken away from the dead and he/she be guided to the heavenly dwelling....»[348] In a Roman Catholic theological context this can only be seen as a clear reference to the soul's temporary stay of purification in purgatory, where it may be relieved by help of the living through prayers and offerings of Holy Mass. Although the Buddhist concept of the «intermediate state» (*chuin*) has its place in a different overall religious setting, the basic idea of the living affecting the situation of the dead through prayers and offerings is a significant point of contact with the Roman Catholic concept. In both cases the living intervene in the post-mortem process of salvation of the departed, however differently the idea of salvation is conceptualized.

At this point Japanese Roman Catholics are completely in line with an old accepted tradition in the Roman Church. Intercession for the sake of the dead was a common element already in the oldest known Christian liturgies both in the eastern and western churches, usually as part of the eucharist liturgy, where the eucharistic offer was brought also for the sake of the dead.[349] This practice followed the church in Europe,[350] and – although in Rome itself the commemoration of the dead at the beginning seems to have been «a peculiarity of funeral and requiem masses»[351] – it eventually developed as an integrated element of all masses, preceding the act of consecration.[352]

It is significant from our point of view, however, to notice that this development did not take place without at least some discussion and opposition, as it seems from the very beginning.[353] The issue arose in the Augustine-Arius controversy, inasmuch as Arius rejected the practice as of no use. Augustine, however, distinguishing between the dead who do not need the intercessions of the living, the dead who are too bad to have any use of them, and then the great number of ordinary people who need the prayers, justified the intercessions together with the offering of the eucharist because of its benefit for the departed.[354] In the Middle Ages the practice continued nevertheless to be rejected by various groups within the church, at the same time as the motive of offering the eucharistic elements in the Holy Mass for the sake of the dead eventually produced the specific mass for the dead.[355] Theologically, the basis for this development was given in the teaching on justification and sanctification, implying the intermediate state of the purgatory as we have seen in section 3.2.1. The Japanese Roman Catholic concern to accomodate this teaching to the indigenous idea of a transfer of merits from the living to the dead through prayers and offerings, is therefore not surprising against this background.[356]

In this perspective it can neither be surprising, however, that we ourselves are barred from adopting such an accomodation to the idea of *kuyo* in the ancestral rites. The opposition that had been voiced from different points of view in the course of the centuries culminated in the protest of the Reformation. On basis of the belief in man's justification through faith alone, the whole notion of the living's influence upon the existence of the dead was rejected. Together with the purgatory fell not only the liturgical intercessions and the eucharistic offer for the sake of the dead in the evangelical worship service but the vigils and the private masses for the dead as well.[357] As a consequence of the fundamental theological reorientation, the funeral itself was robbed of its very center. Instead of being a rite from which the dead were thought to benefit, it became a worship of God with particular emphasis on the glorious hope of the resurrection of the body, through which the living were both reminded of their own death and were gathered to remember the departed and share in the sorrow and consolation of the bereaved.[358]

As far as we can see, the contemporary Roman Catholic approach to the ancestral *kuyo* eminently serves to prove that the fundamental issue of justification through faith from the time of the Reformation is actualized anew in the life of the Japanese church through her encounter with the ancestral rites. At this point it is essential from our position to maintain that man's acceptance into the presence and glory of God is not dependent upon any kind of human mediation, except for what the One Mediator once and for all did for the many. Consequently, man's hope of salvation via-à-vis death and the life to come is not to be based upon a process for sanctification which may eventually make man ready for acceptance into the closeness of God, a process that may be advanced by one's own and other people's meritory deeds. The hope is to be built solely upon God's own redemptive acts for man in Christ. Thus is precluded, in other words, any idea of man as the agent of salvation for the world to come, both with respect to his own and as a contributor to that of the departed. In this respect the living and the dead are not interdependent. Both are totally dependent only upon the grace of God in Christ and his creative power to do away with the old and make all things new.

3.2.2.3 *Descensio Christi and the Dead*

What, then, about prayers for the salvation of the departed in Christian context, actualized as the problem is in our encounter with ancestor worship? The question is not yet dealt with exhaustively and is obviously linked to the wider problem of salvation for pre-Christian ancestors and relatives. Before we are in a position to attempt an answer, accordingly, another controversial article of Christian faith – together with yet another exegetical crux interpretum – has to be brought into focus: What are the implications of the confession of Christ's descensus ad inferos? What about the text in 1 Peter 3,18 ff.– and possibly 4,6 – which is one of the most controversial passages in the New Testament and often assumed to be a relevant scriptural reference to the aching missiological problem of the pre-Christian ancestors? Do these texts and the doctrine of descensio Christi provide us with «a key to an understanding of the life of the deceased ancestors» and to the problem of prayers for the departed?[359] These questions cannot be dealt with responsibly, still less can any answers be responsibly applied to a missiological encounter like ours, without a serious consideration of the various exegetical solutions offered for a correct interpretation of the actual texts.[360]

The crucial issues for our purposes are the questions to whom «the spirits in prison» (v. 19) refer, and what is implied in Christ's preaching to the «spirits».[361] Are «the spirits in prison» to be identified with departed human beings, and his preaching to be understood in a way so that the verse may be said to be the Bible's testimony that «Christ is still working on the unsaved souls»?[362] Is the author in 3,19 simply saying what he does in 4,6 –«...the gospel was preached even to the dead» – in both cases having in mind a preaching for the souls of the deceased aimed at their salvation? There is no lack of exegetical contributions to this effect.[363] According to Goppelt, the preaching in v. 19 (*ekeryksen*) refers to a proclamation of «das Evangelium, die Botschaft von Jesu sterben und auferstehen», and even though v. 19 talks only of the contemporaries of Noah, the general statement in 4,6 shows that Peter has a proclamation for the dead in general in mind, «auch den verlorensten unter ihnen (3,19)....»[364] What we find in 3,19 and 4,6 is, in other words, a presentation «mit Hilfe... zeitgebundener Ausdrucksmittel» of «die universale Heilswirkung des Todesleidens Christi....»[365] Not that these verses are simply describing «eine laufende Evangelisation» among the dead or a «Heilsordnung für die Toten.»[366] Their decisive message is nevertheless to be understood as «eine kerygmatische Aussage» with the significant implication that to all – even to the dead – reaches «die Rettung ermöglichende Predigt des Evangeliums....»[367]

The missiological ramifications of this interpretation are obvious from the point of view of our problem. If we, on the basis of clear biblical evidence, can affirm that our departed pre-Christian ancestors and relatives are to be conceived of as in some way exposed to a proclamation of the gospel in death, why should not our prayers for a successful outcome of such a preaching be offered continually both privately and in public liturgical context? The problem is, however, that not only is such an understanding of descensio Christi and of man in death significantly absent in any other part of the New Testament, even the texts in question cannot be interpreted in this way without exegetical objections. The best that may be said about this particular interpretation is that it is one among other exegeticl options and therefore uncertain and disputed. When advocates of this solution take «the spirits in prison» to refer – at least primarily – to the souls of human beings, and interpret 3,19 in conjunction with 4,6 on the presupposition that the two verses are talking about the same thing, they are met with opposition from other scholars. At least since the monograph of B. Reicke it has been widely accepted that Peter's reference to «the spirits in prison» is perhaps no reference to human souls at all but rather to supernatural beings, i.e., the fallen angels who in Jewish apocalyptic writings – and also within the New Testament as in Jude 6 and 2 Peter 2,4 – were associated with Noah and the flood, and were thought to be kept «in prison». Some scholars – like Reicke himself – see these fallen angels as being what Peter chiefly has in mind in 3,19, although this «does not exclude the possibility that it can at the same time refer to the souls of dead people», i.e., those who were led astray by the fallen angels at the time of Noah.[368] Others see the enigmatic expression as a reference exclusively to the fallen angels.[369]

If it is correct – as there seem to us to be convincing reasons to believe – that «the spirits in prison», if not exclusively so at least primarily, refers to supernatural beings, the important consequence to be drawn is that the preaching of Christ cannot be interpreted as a proclamation with the definite purpose of conversion and salvation for the receivers of the message. Nowhere in the New Testament is there any thought of a «Heilspredigt» for fallen angels, as Goppelt pertinently remarks.[370] Even though *keryssein* is commonly used in the New Testament as a terminus technicus for proclaiming the gospel, it cannot a priori be equalled with evangelization for the purpose and with the affect of salvation like in 4,6. It has been pointed out by several scholars that both within the New Testament (Rev. 5,2) and in the Septuagint the term has also a neutral meaning of proclaiming news without any implications as to its effect.[371] In the context of 3,19 this must be the meaning of *keryssein*, as Reicke puts it: «Christ went to the spirits and communicated to them the secret about himself as the humbly suffering, and thereby victorious Messiah. This is actually all we can get from the text.»[372] The conclusion is, then, that an understanding of descensio Christi implying a theologically significant doctrine of a proclamation of the gospel to the dead for a post-mortem opportunity to conversion, cannot be inferred from 1 Peter 3,19 on solid exegetical ground.

But what about 4,6, where it explicitly says that «the gospel was preached even to the dead, that though judged in the flesh like men, they might live in the spirit like God»? In this case there can be no doubt that the author is talking about men and not fallen angels. Neither is there any doubt that the preaching is here aimed at conversion and salvation. But who are «the dead», and when did the preaching take place?

It has been advocated that the dead in this context means the spiritually dead, thus pointing to the antithesis of what is offered through the gospel: to «live in the spirit like God.»[373] We have to agree with Reicke, however, when he repudiates this as an avoidance theory. There is nothing to indicate that «the dead» is not to be understood as physically departed people, as the meaning is in the preceding sentence. According to Reicke, the immediate impression is that the gospel is preached to the dead in Hades.[374] He therefore concludes that even though a preaching of Christ to the dead could not be inferred directly from 3,19, the evangelization in 4,6 is to be identified as «an action performed by Christ – in Hades, at His descent», and therefore «we have good reason to direct the attention again to what we stated regarding 3,19, that this verse implies the principle of a universal mission, a universal evangelization. Verse 4,6 is thus a good illustration of 3,19 as to the underlying principle».[375]

Neither this exegesis of Riecke's, however, can be said really to be convincing. Firstly, it is hard to conceive of such an unequivocal statement about the purpose and the effect of a post-mortem evangelization among the dead without having the same thought expressed anywhere else in the New Testament. If this interpretation is correct, it certainly is a most unique utterance in the context of the Scriptures. Secondly, there are significant exegetical objections, of which the ones related to the aorist passive tense *euengelisthe* seem substantial. Why is the passive form used and not the active – as in 3,19 – if the author again is referring to Christ's preaching in Hades? And if the meaning of this verse really is to show that «die Hadespredigt Christi galt nicht nur, wie 3,19 hervorhob, den Verlorensten, sondern allen Toten»,[376] why then is the verb put in the aorist tense and not in the present? Such and other exegetical considerations have led other scholars to the conclusion that the author is referring neither to spiritual dead nor to a proclamation to the dead in Hades but to a past and ordinary proclamation of the gospel to departed Christians before their death.[377] The meaning of such a reference in the wider context of chapter four is that even to the already departed Christians, who through suffering and death «were judged in the flesh like men» and thereby might have caused ridicule and abuse (v.4) from non-Christians because their faith and hope seemed of no avail, even to these the gospel has been proclaimed in order that «they might live in the spirit like God».

In many ways this interpretation sounds attractive, and it does not seem to involve more exegetical difficulties than does any of the other solutions. Even this, however, is uncertain. To us, therefore, 1 Peter 4,6 seems – in spite of the numerous attempts at a reasonable exegesis – to remain an enigmatic crux interpretum.

What are the consequences to be drawn from this discussion of 1 Peter 3,19 and 4,6 for our purposes? As far as we are able to judge, an interpretation of descensio Christi on the basis of these texts as a clear reference to a preaching of the gospel post-mortem in terms of a last «Rettungsbotschaft ...für die vor- und ausserchristliche Menschenwelt» is not founded upon solid exegetical ground.[378] It may at best be said to be one – and possibly not even the best – among other exegetical possibilities. Moreover, if such an interpretation is chosen, it leads not only into significant theological conclusions about which the Scriptures elsewhere are silent but also into problems as to our understanding of other references in the Scriptures concerning God's judgment upon man. For these reasons we dot not see how we can legitimately develop a theology on God's ways with the «vor- und ausserchristliche Menschenwelt» upon these enigmatic texts. In other words, we do not see that the doctrine on descensio Christi – after all – offers significant help in solving this particular riddle of faith. Standing firm on the scriptural evidence of salvation, on the one hand, through faith in Christ alone, on the other of God's universal judgment of all people according to his mercy and righteousness in Christ, the only option to us is to take an agnostic stand as to God's ways with our pre-Christian ancestors and relatives.[379]

This is not to say, however, that descensio Christi as pictured in 1 Peter 3,18 ff. is without significance in our context. Even though it does not satisfy our curiosity as to God's dealings with the «vor- und ausserchrist-liche Menschenwelt» with respect to the problem of salvation, it is highly relevant with respect to the wider ontological framework in which ancestor worship functions. In our encounter with people preoccupied with a spirit-world in which the spirits of the dead have their natural place, and from which the living may expect the punishing interference of *tatari* if the spirits are not properly cared for, we can never side with those who's only reaction over against such beliefs is a high-handed attempt at showing the idea's absurdity. The New Testament knows of a world of «spirits», of «principalities and powers» (Col. 2,15), although it never does express itself in a way which seems to imply that human spirits of the dead are conceived of as belonging among these.[380] The important point in our context is, however, that it is a central concern all through the New Testament to portray Christ as the victor over all principalities and powers. There is a cosmic dimension to the redemptive work of Christ which is portrayed to reach beyond the actual world of man. Here lies the great significance of the descensio-idea in our context. Not that it is to be interpreted as a victorious fight of Christ in Hades; the triumph of Christ was won on the cross. But through the descensio Christi proclamation of his victorious redemptive acts was taken to the realm of the «spirits», and «angels, authorities, and powers» now are all «subject to him» who is «at the right hand of God» (1 Peter 3,22). This cosmic dimension of Christ's work of salvation has the significance of powerfully liberating man from the fear of being subject to the arbitrary interference of spiritual beings or punishing revenge of neglected ancestors. Possibly this is an aspect of Christian faith which may be dealt with in a more relevant and existential way by theologians from parts of the world where man is not yet deceived into believing that except for man himself there are no spiritual powers under heaven.[381]

3.2.2.4 *Intercessory Prayers for the Dead?*

By this we are taken back to the problem of Christian prayers for the salvation of departed ancestors and relatives. We have seen that notwithstanding the significance of descensio Christi in our context, it does not provide us with the basis for a theology and a liturgy of intercession for the dead. Although we have confined ourselves to a sudy of the two controversial passages in 1 Peter, there is no other scriptural basis for such a theology, neither is there any explicit and certain example of such prayers in the New testament.[382] As for departed Christians, the unequivocal emphasis is all the way on the assurance of salvation through faith in Christ in joyful expectation of the resurrection. In this perspective there is no need for prayers, masses, or offerings of any kind. To resort to intercessions for the well-being of departed Christians, therefore, cannot but obscure the vital doctrine of justification through faith with its corresponding assurance of salvation for Christ's sake alone. These two are to be forcefully maintained as the Christian hallmarks via-à-vis the ancestral *kuyo*.

As for departed pre-Christian and/or non-Christian ancestors and relatives, we will have to be content with entrusting these faithfully into the righteous and merciful hands of God the Almighty. In this case to move into further theological considerations with corresponding liturgical practices takes us beyond the limits of faith given in the Scriptures, and leads into speculation and radical obscuration of the all-important significance of life before death. Even in a missionary encounter like the one with which we are concerned, this seems to be the only position that can be justified and maintained on a solid theological basis. In the name of accomodation, to adopt liturgical intercessions for pre-Christian and non-Christian relatives may give an immediate impression of Christian concern for their ancestors. However, it may in the long run produce a much deeper uneasiness and doubt as to the fate of the departed than is the case when they are simply and faithfully entrusted into God's mercy. How are we then going to avoid the idea that their salvation is – after all – decisively dependent upon our intercessions? And who, then, is going to tell how fervent and frequent our prayers will have to be? In other words, we will be moving effectively in the direction of making man an indispensable agent of salvation for the departed.

When this is said there nevertheless remains what we would call a pastoral «but....» This is obvious already in the attitude of the reformers. Although Calvin and the Reformed churches most consistently rejected intercessory prayers, Calvin nevertheless had to acknowledge «den Wunsch des Herzens für das ewige Heil des Gestorbenen.»[383] Granted the love for the departed person, how and why should such a «Wunsch des Herzens» be avoided? The question then arises whether there is any decisive difference between keeping such a wish in one's heart and making it known to God in a simple, private prayer. Luther permitted such a step and did not object to a private prayer out of love for the departed: «Für die Toten, weil die Schrift nichts davon meldet, halt ich, dass aus freier Andacht nicht Sünde sei, so oder desgleichen zu bitten: 'Lieber Gott, hats mit der Seelen Solche Gestalt, dass ihr zu helfen sei, so sei ihr gnädig usw.' Und wenn solches einmal geschehen ist oder zwier, so lass es genug sein.»[384] On the basis of this position of Luther himself, and in view of the fact that a more specific prayer for the dead did eventually appear later on in certain German Lutheran funeral liturgies, Rietschel says that in spite of her strong opposition to intercessions and masses for the dead in the Roman Catholic Church, «die Lutherische Kirche... hat doch niemals die Fürbitte für die Verstorbenen entschieden abgelehnt, wenn sie als unmittelbarer Ausdruck der Liebe gegen den Verstorbenen dem Herzen entquillt.»[385]

Turning to the Japanese Protestant churches a struggle with the pastoral «but...» resulting in a certain ambivalence is apparent, even in the Reformed camp. In the discussion on the funeral published in Hiyane 1959 we find voices as we expected pointing to the reasons why prayer for the dead should not be included in the funerary rites.[386] Others, however, although not directly advocating their inclusion, at least raise the question, referring, for example, particularly to the problem of those who pass away without hearing the gospel.[387] Judging from the renewed investigation of the funeral-problem published in *Shi to sogi* 1974, there does not appear to be any general trend in the United Church of Christ in the direction of approving and including such prayers. With explicit reference to Luther's position it is said rather that intercessory prayers should not be adopted in a Japanese context due to the fact that they may easily be confused with Buddhist *jobutsu* and *kuyo*,[388] and in the specific prayers proposed for funerary occasions there is no trace of intercessions for the sake of the dead.[389] The more interesting is it to find that long-time pastor Murakami Osamu answers the question what the church does about masses for the ancestor by referring specifically to the intercessions for the dead which take place at the post-funeral memorial gatherings.[390] The attitudes and practices at this point are, in other words, ambivalent in the United Church of Christ.

Looking at the Lutheran Church the situation seems to be somewhat similar, although a slight difference may be seen. In the *Handbook for Believers* it is briefly emphasized that the meaning of the Christian funeral «is not – as in other religions – to pray for the happiness of the dead....»[391] This is, accordingly, the main trend in the funeral liturgy. In all the alternatives given for the special prayer there is no intercession for the dead, except for a short sentence in the case of the death of a child.[392] Likewise the brief liturgies and prayers suggested for the encoffinment and for the ceremony after cremation or burial contain no specific prayer for the dead, nor does the order for subsequent commemoratiave services. The thrust in all these cases is a rejoicing assurance of salvation in the light of the eschatological hope, a thanks to God for the one who has passed away in faith and for the unshakeable community between the living and the dead in Christ, and a prayer that the living may eventually join in the everlasting glory.[393]

However, this rather conspicuous lack of interecessory prayers for the departed person is not a principle that is persistently carried through. In the order for the devotion to be held at the moment of death and on the eve before the funeral we find suggested prayers as follows:

...Now we commit the spirit of our beloved brother (sister/child) into your hands. Please grant that our brother (sister/child), covered by the robe of the righteousness of Jesus Christ, may stand before you without wounds....

Please fulfil your promises according to your merciful wisdom and almighty power, grant to him/her the peace of our Lord and let everlasting glory shine upon him/her....[394]

Again, in other words, we touch upon a similar ambivalence. When we consider the wording of these prayers, however, together with the facts that they do not obscure the motive of assurance of salvation in the liturgical context and are not followed up in subsequent and repeated intercessions, it seems to us that they should rather be regarded as a confident and legitimate committing of the dead into the hands of the Lord, than as theologically untenable and illegitimate intercessions. They seem to us to be justifiable concessions to what we have called the pastoral «but....»[395] Even though we have found in this chapter that Christian faith does not contain any basis for a theology on death and salvation upon which may be founded intercessions for the dead or other practices parallel to the ancestral rites aimed at supporting the soul beyond death, this is not to say that the Christian who is confronted with the pain of death through the passing away of a beloved relative, must simply keep silent over against God with his/her wishes and concerns for the salvation of the dying. A genuine concern and affection to commit the person simply and faithfully into the hands of God the Almighty is both a most natural consequence of Christian love in the encounter with death and an important affirmation of the positive aspects of inter-familial relationships so significant in Japanese society.

Our inquiry into the relationship between the living and the dead from the perspective of salvation for the departed has given the result, then, that the basic premise that God through Christ is the one who saves significantly implies that there is no parallel in Christian faith to the soteriological aspects of the ancestral rites based upon the idea of transfer of merits. Further conclusions of our study in death and salvation, however, are still to be drawn. For this purpose we turn to our last section in this connection.

3.2.3 *Interrelatedness and Communion*

In section 3.1.3 we saw that the idea of making supplications to the ancestors for help and protection is irreconcilable with the Christian view of God. In section 3.2.2 we have now advocated the view that neither does Christian teaching on death and salvation present any basis for intercessory prayers on their behalf. The question then arises whether this negative approach to vital aspects of the ancestral rites does imply that the Christian response to what we called the «circle of interdependence» between the living and the dead is simply an antithetic one. Is this the only way in which Christianity should respond to the basic quest for community across the chasm of death which ancestor worship reveals? Although it has already appeared several times in this chapter that such is not the case, we now have to make this explicit.

Crucial at this point in our conversation is the apostolic confession of the communion of saints (communio sanctorum). The expression itself may well be an «additional clause» as far as the origin of the Apostles' Creed is concerned.[396] It nevertheless refers to a central concern in the New Testament and in both Protestant and Roman Catholic Japanese contexts the idea frequently appears in connection with funerary services as well as in a wider discussion on ancestor worship. The following prayer may serve as an illustrating and typical example of its function in the funeral liturgy:

O God, in your presence the world came about and passes away. You are the strength of those who labour and the rest of the blessed departed. We rejoice within the bond of the blessed departed. We rejoice within the bond of the communion of saints and remember all who live in faith, all who have passed away in peace, and especially all our beloved ones who are now at rest with you. Grant us all in the end to share with you in the everlasting blessing. Together with all the church on earth and in heaven we forever offer all honor and glory unto your name. Amen.[397]

Further Fr. Christiaens explicitly puts communio sanctorum into focus for the Roman Catholic discussion on ancestor worship: «Moreover modern theology itself gives us a new approach to the veneration of the saints by reformulating the doctrine of the Communion of Saints, which is expressed in Japanese by its new translation *shoseito no majiwari...* in which not only the saints, but also the living are involved. This *seito no majiwari* is really Japanese in the sense that it also comprehends a community feeling with the deceased.»[398]

Expressed in this clause of the Apostolic Creed is the fundamental

Christian conviction of a community to which death does not represent an irrevocable end. In the New Testament this is pregnantly expressed as being a communion «in Christ», constituted on the one hand through Christ's death and resurrection, on the other of mortal man's baptism to these redemptive events. The one who is «baptized into Christ Jesus» is «baptized into his death» so that, being «united with him in a death like his», he «shall certainly be united with him in a resurrection like his.» (Rom. 6,3–5) Thus the New Testament is saturated by the rejoicing conviction, as we have seen in section 3.2.1.1, that «whether we live or whether we die, we are the Lord's». (Rom. 14,8.) The community in Christ is, in other words, a death-transcending community. Communio sanctorum is a communion to which belong both the living faithful and the dead in Christ as well. In this perspective to become a Christian with a view to fellowship with already departed believers, as reported in 1 Cor. 15,29, may have a deep and genuine Christian meaning. In this way, namely, human fellowship, to which death comes as a frightening enemy, is drawn significantly into eschatological perspective, i.e., within the range of God's creative power for completion and fulfilment.

Just as important as baptism is in this context, so also is the eucharist. Being established through baptism, the communion «in Christ» and the life within the communion of saints is nurtured and sustained through the eucharistic meal. From the very beginning all through the history of the church, therefore, this meal has been the sign par excellence of community: Community with Christ and community with the faithful. Also in this context the death-transcending perspective is conspicuous. Not only from the point of view that it is communion with the risen Lord, but also from the point of view that the eucharist is an eschatological meal, sustaining an eschatological community which Christ is going to fulfil on the day «when I drink it [the fruit of the vine] new with you in my Father's kingdom» (Mt. 26,29.) The eucharist, accordingly, is not only a community meal with a view backwards in history. It is communion with a view to the fulfilment of communio sanctorum in the resurrection, a meal which is proclaiming «the Lord's death until he comes» (1 Cor. 11,26).

It is no liturgical coincidence, therefore, that in the old Church the practice very soon developed of celebrating the eucharist as part of the funeral.[399] Nor is it surprising that when the intercessory prayer for the dead developed in liturgical setting, it developed exactly as part of the eucharist liturgy. This was and is the place in the Christian worship service where the community between the living in Christ and the dead in Christ is most pregnantly expressed.

Looking closer at the eucharist liturgy from our point of view in this section, and on the background of what we said to the intermediate state in section 3.2.1.2, an interesting problem emerges. The doxology following immediately upon the preface, which – with variations – has been in use ever since the old Church and is still widely used today, contains an expression which in some churches is seen as an explicit reference to the death-transcending communion of saints: «Therefore with angels and archangels, and with all the company of heaven, we laud and magnify thy glorious Name; evermore praising thee and saying:....»[400] To whom does «all the company of heaven» refer? To the dead in Christ, i.e., to the ecclesia triumphans who in these words is thought to be now rejoicing in glory and praise before the heavenly throne of God? Such an interpretation is given expressis verbis in the liturgy of the Lutheran Church of Norway: «Therefore the angels praise your glory, and your congregation in heaven and on earth join to praise your Name. We would also join our voices....»[401] In this case we have a significant expression in the heart of the eucharist liturgy giving vein to the thought of community between the living and the dead in Christ experienced in the sacrament.

It seems doubtful to us, however, whether this interpretation of the preface is really what was originally – and in the course of its history has generally been – intended. «All the company of heaven» is an ambiguous expression, but its connection with «angels and archangels» directs our attention to the host of supernatural heavenly beings in the Scriptures associated with the throne of God. Reindell's study of the history of the preface leads him to the conclusion that at this point in the liturgy «die zum Vollzug des Altarsakraments versammelte Gemeinde der Gläubigen auf Erden vereint mit dem Chor der Engelmächte im Himmel.»[402] Such an understanding is unambiguously expressed in the traditional Roman Mass, where to angels and archangels may be added the cherubim and the seraphim, and so also was the understanding in the Norwegian Lutheran liturgy until the above-mentioned text was introduced with the new order of the eucharist in 1914.[403] In the perspective of the history of liturgy, in other words, the preface of the eucharist seems at this point to be concerned – at least primarily – with the heavenly host of supernatural beings and not with the present state of a heavenly ecclesia triumphans.

The question now is whether also from a dogmatic point of view an understanding like the one expressed in the Norwegian text and in modern editions of the Roman Mass has to be seen as somewhat out of place. Or does it rather pregnantly express the death-transcending nature of the communion of saints in a way which might be deeply meaningful also in a Japanese context, and therefore should be seriously considered for adoption into a Japanese liturgical setting? This seems to us to be a thought that should not be rejected too easily. However, on the basis of what we developed in connection with the intermediate state in section 3.2.1.2, the actual wording of the text seems to us to go one step further in definite conceptualization of the nature of the intermediate state of the dead than is actually possible. It may contribute to the popular misunderstanding that the departed in Christ have already arrived at their final destination and pave the way for the popular idea of a two storied relationship between this world and the kingdom of God. If we speak in terms of such a simultaneity in praise between ecclesia triumphans and ecclesia militans, it should be understood basically in terms of a liturgical anticipation of the world to come in the resurrection.[404] Such a perspective is deeply meaningful and in genuine correspondence with the communion-aspect of the eucharist. To us, therefore, something seems to be lacking if and when the doxology at the end of the preface is worded so as to refer exclusively to the oneness in praise between the actually celebrating church (ecclesia militans) and the angels. There are contemporary examples of liturgies which avoid such an insufficiency by including the death-transcending fellowship of believers and, at the same time, seem to safeguard against popular misunderstandings as mentioned above: «Therefore, together with your faithful in all ages and with all the host of heaven, we will also join our voices....»[405] This is a formulation which allows both for a commemoration of the faithful backwards through the ages and for an anticipation in faith of the communion of the redeemed in the consummation, without compromising the New Testament thought that the dead in Christ in some way share with the living in the waiting for that day to come.

We see from this discussion that in the eucharist not only the idea of continuity from the past into the future but also the present continuity across death is manifest in communio sanctorum as a community in Christ. In other words, there is a oneness and a belonging-together in Christ which implies that even though Christianity cannot talk of a reciprocal interdependence between the living and the dead as is the case in the ancestral rites, it confidently talks of interrelatedness between the two in a way which should enable any christian to understand and sympathize with the quest for community across death prevalent in ancestor worship.

In this perspective we have to see the great significance of commemorial gatherings in Japanese Christian context. This seems to us to be one of the traditional customs which has been most widely and most meaningfully utilized by Japanese churches. Already in the introductory remark to the Roman Catholic order for such gatherings communio sanctorum is seen as the significant frame of reference: «Mourning in the Christian church does not only mean the expression of grief. It is a deepening of faith in the resurrection...and so a strengthening of the unity between the brethren in Christ.»[406] Later on the same motif saturates the prayers as in the following example:

O merciful God, hear this prayer of us who are now gathered here in the rememberance of .... Through the death and the resurrection of Christ your Son you have freed us from everlasting death and given to us eternal life. We pray that this our brother/sister who passed away in the hope of the resurrection, shall together with the saints praise you in your kingdom, and we pray that we who are linked together in the same faith and now are offering this prayer shall be given the blessing of the resurrection and be united in your kingdom with this our brother/sister who has now gone before us.
In the name of Christ the Lord. Amen.[407]

In the Lutheran «Prayer for Commemoration of the Dead» we see the same emphasis on the communion of saints. Instead of actual prayer for the departed person is here repeatedly expressed the assurance of his/her salvation; the motive of communio sanctorum, however, is just as strong as in the Roman Catholic example:

Everlasting and Almighty God our Father. Your holy name is praised alike by those who have already passed away in faith and those who are still living in faith in this world.... God, enlighten your church through the Holy Spirit and uphold her in the hope of the everlasting kingdom. Grant all her members to accomplish their life in faith and then succeed to the inheritance you have promised. Give unto us that we, together with the brother/sister who has ended his/her life and is called into your presence, may accomplish our journey of faith and receive eternal rest in your presence.... Amen.[408]

What we see in the commemorative gatherings is, in other words, a deeply meaningful way of expressing and experiencing the communion of saints as a glorious bridge of hope across the chasm of death. It is further a commemoration of the dead which has a significant function as an impetus in the direction of a genuine imitatio sanctorum. The gatherings serve as a pointer to the «cloud of witnesses» in order to strengthen the living to «run with perseverance the race that is set before us» (Heb. 12,1), considering the outcome of the life of the faithful in order to «imitate their faith» (Heb. 13,7). It seems to us that many churches in the West have a lot to learn from this way in which Japanese churches, through repeated commemorative gatherings, cope with the pastoral problem of grief and mourning and are witnessing to the significance and hope of communio sanctorum. Here is a Christian reinterpretation of the quest for continuity and community dominant in ancestor worship, which seems to us to be meaningful far beyond the Japanese context.

The emphasis on the communion of saints as a community in Christ which we have repeatedly made, and which is evident in the way the New Testament relates communio sanctorum to baptism and the eucharist, holds one further important consequence from our point of view. What we have in mind will become clear when we look at the way the idea of communio sanctorum is used by some in their approach to ancestor worship.

In his introduction to the booklet on ancestor veneration and Roman Catholic faith, Fr. Christiaens starts out with a short chapter on ancestor worship and the communion of saints. Here the author brings into the overriding perspective of communio sanctorum the unity of mankind as God's creation in general, and the ordinary fellowship between ancestors and descendants in particular.[409] This approach to communio sanctorum is evident in several of the subsequent answers to questions concerning ancestor worship. In explaining what Christian reverence to ancestors implies, he says: «Through the Holy Mass every Sunday the believer's communion with all the saints...is deepened. Therefore he/she quite naturally will have a deeper fellowship with the ancestors and with all the departed.»[410] Later on it is explicitly stated that «according to Christian faith, all men are the children of God. Therefore, all the dead are linked together in the mysterious body of Christ.»[411] What we encounter in this approach is, in other words, a basic confounding of the communion of saints with human fellowship in general and the community ancestors-descendants in particular, i.e., a radical blurring of the difference between communio sanctorum and communio familiae.[412]

Moving for a moment outside the Japanese scene and the Roman Catholic setting, we find an African Protestant approach to communio sanctorum in connection with ancestor worship which in its final conclusion seems very close to Christiaens' position. Fasholé-Luke sets out by stating that »we cannot simply say that the African ancestors can be embraced within the framework of the universal Church and included in the Communion of Saints.«[413] Participation in communio sanctorum, namely, cannot be separated from participation in the sacraments, i.e., baptism and the eucharist. However, since »the death of Christ is for the whole world and no one either living or dead is outside the scope of the merits of Christ's death...both Christians and non-Christians receive salvation through Christ's death and are linked with him through the sacrament which he himself instituted.«[414] The author then parallels the African ancestors with the witnesses of faith of the old covenant recorded in Heb. 11, and because Hebrews includes »non-Christians whose faith was not perfect«, »we would equally affirm that the African ancestors could also be included in the Communion of Saints in this way, since they had a faith which was not perfect.«[415] Therefore, in spite of his careful introductory statement, and in spite of his emphasis on the significance of the sacraments in the understanding of communio sanctorum, Fasholé-Luke concludes that »even non-Christians can be embraced within the Communion of Saints.«[416] The difference of communio sanctorum and communio familiae is also here radically blurred.

Although we have wanted to emphasize in this section the idea of communio sanctorum in a Christian encounter with ancestor worship, the way it is done in these cases seems to us to be based on shaky ground. Theologizing on the communion of saints is undertaken here with one decisive key of interpretation, i.e., with one particular view of the universality of the redemptive work of Christ with respect to those who never heard the gospel and faced the sacraments. On the basis of one particular answer to this riddle of faith inferences are drawn to the understanding of communio sanctorum which – as far as we can see – go beyond the way the New Testament talks about this community as the body of Christ. Firstly, there is no basis in the New Testament to obscure the fact that the community of believers is a religious and spiritiual community in Christ, – and neither a human community in general nor a community based on blood-relationships. Secondly, there is no basis to make the inference that because Christ is »the expiation for...the sins of the whole world« (1 John 2,2), and because he is Lord with universal and cosmic implications, therefore communio sanctorum may legitimately be confounded with communio familiae. There is in Christ a new »family«, a fact which Jesus made eminently clear when he – approached by his mother and brothers – pointed to his disciples saying: »Here are my mother and my brothers!« (Mt. 12,49). This is not to say that man's bloodrelated social nexus is of no importance; we shall return to that problem in our last chapter. It is to say, however, that communio familiae is not constitutive for the communion of saints. Into the latter community man is grafted through a new birth in baptism, and he is upheld in it as long as he submits himself in faith to Christ's sustaining presence in the eucharist. As far as we cn see, the New Testament does not allow a theology of mission to exploit the idea of the communion of saints in the direction of an obscurring integration with communio familiae in order to solve the problem of the pre-Christian dead. There is a fundamental difference between the dead in Christ and the pre-Christian dead. Whether the latter are also somehow within the range of Christ's redemptive work, is another matter.

Communion and interrelatedness between the living and the dead are expressed both in the Christian communion of saints and in the communio familiae of the ancestral rites. Inasmuch as both are believed to bridge the chasm of death, there is affinity between the two. Neither at this point, however, can we avoid the conflict. In the death-transcending continuity of the ancestral rites the constitutive factor is the being in the family-line, whereas the constitutive factor in communio sanctorum is the being in Christ.

We have ended our discussion over death and salvation as these topics have come to the fore in our encounter with ancestor worship. Our grappling with the various problems involved has shown both affinity between basic ideas sustaining the ancestral rites and Christian faith and deep-going conflict. It has further shown that our particular encounter also in this respect actualizes within a Japanese framework problems which for centuries have caused controversies within the Christian church, and over which Christians are still very much divided.

In concluding our chapter, we summarize briefly the main results of our inquiry. Firstly, we saw how the fundamental theological frame of reference of Christian faith implies an understanding of death that significantly departs from the anthropological and psychological perspectives within which the ancestral rites function. Whereas in the latter context man seeks a modus vivendi with death as an integrated and natural part of his existence, it is in the former seen in the overriding perspective of God's creation and redemption, where both its cause and its conquest are clearly portrayed. Because of his broken God-relationship death comes to man as an enemy of total destruction; because of his existence in God-relatedness there is nevertheless continuity for man in death as far as he is upheld toward the resurrection. Also to a Christian, therefore, there is a meaningful way in which to talk of community between the living and the dead.

Secondly, God's upholding of the dead in an «intermediate state» towards resurrection does not imply any parallel to ancestral *kuyo*. Neither the idea of vicarious baptism nor the creedal affirmation of Christ's *descensus ad inferos* can be used to establish a theological basis for man somehow to assist in the salvation of the departed. The basic premise that God in Christ is the One who redeems, implies significantly that there is no parallel in Christian faith to the soteriological aspects of the ancestral rites based upon the idea of a transfer of merits. As for the dead in Christ, the bereaved – in the midst of grief and mourning – may rejoice in assurance of salvation. As for the pre-Christian departed, the living may faithfully commit them into God's righteousness and mercy.

Thirdly, even though Christianity does not know of any reciprocal and actual inter-dependence between the living and the dead, it confidently confesses its belief in an interrelatedness between them that bridges the chasm of death. Within communio sanctorum the living and the dead in Christ form a community to which death is not destructive, a community in Christ in which both the living and the dead are heading towards the consummation.

By this we have finally been taken to the third and last area of problems involved in our conversation.

3.3 *Individual and Collective in the Family Context*

In our systematic analysis of ancestor worship in part 2 our first chapter presented an inquiry into the rôle of the ancestral rites in their household setting. We looked into the structural relationship between ancestor worship and the Japanese household and into the ethical implications of this socio-religious phenomenon. The third and last area of problems to which we now have to direct our attention is, therefore, the one which concerns the relationship between individual and collective in the family context.

Recapitulating the results of our previous investigation we saw already in connection with the terminological clarification in chapter 1.2 how ancestor worship and household are closely linked through the interrelationship between the concepts of ancestor/*senzo*; *sosen*, on the one hand, and *ie* on the other. This essential interdependence between ancestral rites and household community accounts for the significant concurrence of social and religious aspects of family life. The household members – each in his particular capacity – partake in the *ie* in a transcendent reality of ultimate character. Whatever structural principles are in operation in the actual formation of the family, they are all subordinate to that of preserving and continuing the household itself. The final criterion for moral behaviour, therefore, must be the harmonious and prosperous continuation of the *ie*. Within this social nexus running from past into future, men – living and dead – are interrelated in a circle of obligation. Existing thanks to the past and present *on* of one's forefathers and parents, the grateful return of this debt – *ho-on* – through a conduct marked by filial piety/*ko*, is the overriding and all-important moral principle. In this way the ultimate criterion for ethics is based in the household itself, and the family forms an in-group whose solidarity and loyalty cannot and should not be seriously questioned. Even though changes have been taking place with respect to the *ie* and the corresponding structural elements of ancestor worship in contemporary Japan, these fundamental aspects nevertheless raise interesting and important problems from our point of view.[417]

Some examples may serve to illustrate how the problems we are facing in this chapter have – through decades – been focused and approached from different points of view in connection with the continuous discussion on the relationship between Christianity and Japanese culture. Writing on «Opportunities of the Japanese Church» in 1928, a prominent Protestant leader commented on the practice of removing the tablets of departed ancestors from Christian homes, saying that in this respect Christians to their non-Christian relatives «seem to be behaving very badly toward the departed members of the family. They have lost interest in and become disloyal to the old religious traditions of the family. For this our Japanese Christians are often criticized and even attacked, not so much in the religious sense as in the moral sense.»[418]

In the first decades of the twentieth century the discussion whether ancestor worship with its moral implications presented Christianity with an unsolvable conflict or not, went on among concerned Japanese far beyond the churches. The conflicting opinions of two famous law-professors – Hozumi Yatsuka and Hozumi Nobushige – is interesting in this respect. According to the former, basic Japanese moral principles like loyalty and filial piety are deeply rooted in ancestor worship, which «is not compatible with Christianity, with democracy, or even with parliamentary government».[419] To the latter, however, «reverence for one's ancestors is simply the 'extension of love and respect to distant forefathers'; hence, it is far from irreconcilable with Christianity».[420]

Among specifically church-oriented studies after the war the writings of Sumiya Mikio and Morioka Kiyomi are especially interesting in this respect. Writing in general terms on Japanese society and Christianity, professor Sumiya is very critical towards the old family-system and its ethical basis. He sees this to be in fundamental conflict with a Christian view of the individual dignity of the person, rooted as the latter is in the belief in a personal God, and he asks for nothing less than a revolution in the value-system underlying the traditional Japanese family-system.[421] Professor Morioka, for his part, through his socio-religious case-studies of the acceptance and rejection of Christianity in rural communities in the Meiji-era, again focuses particularly on the individual-collective problem, highlighting the loyalty-conflict which the new faith created and the ways in which individuals and groups attempted to come to grips with the situation.[422]

Recent investigations and writings within the Lutheran community in Japan have focused on the same area of problems, witnessing to the continuous need to consider these questions from a Christian point of view. When the LWF's Office of Communication in Tokyo carried out its Baptism Motivation Survey in 1973–74, the fifth of six subdivisions of questions in the distributed questionnaire was concerned with the family's reaction to the baptism/confirmation of the person in question.[423] We notice particularly three points of interest in this connection. First, the rationale given for this particular subgroup of guestions: «It is of great interest how these individuals who grew up in Japanese homes...and who finally made the decision to become baptized expressed this to their families, and how the families in turn reacted to this.»[424] Second, in the report of the investigation the findings on the response of the families are deliberately linked with the findings on the religious attitudes of the homes, which show that «a third of the respondents had 'Buddhist family altars' in their homes (33.3 %) and held 'observances for dead ancestors' (38.6 %)».[425] Third, the figures show that «almost one fourth of the individuals were met with vehement opposition or 'opposition followed by acceptance'», a fact which moves the project team to the following conclusion: «This means that even today, when individuals become baptized and are ready to enter the Christian faith, one out of every four persons is met with family opposition. This should be called to our attention, if only for the reason that it indicates the importance of the household's religion.»[426]

In other words, the rôle of the ancestral rites in fostering and maintaining loyalty-ties and solidarity with one's household in-group, still puts before the church the task of reflecting seriously upon the relationship between individual and collective in the family context. This is what Magaki Yosuke pleads for in a brief but penetrating article published in the journal of Japan Lutheran Theological College. The author points to two pitfalls: (1) a Protestant over-individualistic approach which in Japan has pulled the individual out of his/her community and made the strong sense of group-belonging in Japan an object of critique, and (2) the constant danger on the basis of group-solidarity to develop once again into the spirit of *kokka*-ideology and the emperor system. In this tension, according to Magaki, it is necessary for the church in Japan in the context of her missionary outreach to ponder once more the biblical balance between due assertion of the individual and proper consciousness of family-belonging.[427]

This last chapter again brings us in touch with theological and ethical issues that are by no means new, neither to the missiological debate nor to theology in general. Among missiologists the problem of the individual and his collective belonging in natural orders like family, tribe and people vis-à-vis his new belonging to the community of the church has been one of the major issues in the debate. In the German tradition from Gustav Warneck the heavy emphasis on the individual's place in God-given, natural «Ordnungen» accounted for a synthesis of gospel and «Volkstum» which made «Volks- oder Völkerchristianisierung» the very aim of mission.[428] This, in turn, in post-war Europe met with vehement opposition by J.C. Hoekendijk who saw such an approach to the problem of individual and collective as based on a naive-romantic and completely untenable understanding of man's «Ordnungen», and emphasized instead the uniqueness of the church vis-à-vis all natural human communities.[429]

Since this particular controversy the debate has continued. G. Vicedom to a certain extent accepts Hoekendijk's charges and agrees that Warneck goes too far in his «Volk»-interpretation due to his positive emphasis on the individual's place in the given «Ordnungen». At the same time he criticizes Hoekendijk for going too far in the opposite direction in his one-sided concentration on the church, paying all too little attention to man in his actual relationship to his given social nexus.[430] Vicedom concludes that this whole problem «muss auf jeden Fall noch weiter nachgedacht und das Gespräch weitergeführt werden», and he points out how a new incentive in this direction is given through the writings of Donld A. McGavran.[431] By this Vicedom refers to McGavran's little book *Bridges of God*, 1955, where the author – from his particular point of view of church growth – insists upon the importance of viewing and approaching man not simply as an individual, but as a person always related to a social nexus, first and foremost the family.[432] This emphasis on the interdependence between individual and collective in terms of family and people, has ever since been one of the sustaining pillars in McGavran's theory and strategy of mission. His thoughts on «people movements» and «homogenuous units» have renewed the missiological debate on individual and collective.[433] In other words, even though we are not going to deal with this general problem in all its many aspects, the questions with which we are confronted from our particular point of view have obvious connections to a familiar and ongoing discussion within the field of missiology.

Without going into details, some introductory remarks should be made to picture the still wider theological framework within which we find ourselves in this chapter. The problem of individual and collective in the family context has even in the general theologicl debate been one of the most controversial issues. How is the given social nexus of the family to be conceived in Christian terms? What does it mean that man by his very nature finds himself within such a given community? How or to which extent does man by himself realize his commitments and obligations to the family in-group? Does this social nexus in itself imply ethical norms which apply to the individuals in their various rôles within the group? What does the Christian belief in God as he has revealed himself in Christ, and as he is calling man into community with himself in and through the church, mean with respect to man's life in his given family? These are basic questions which have preoccupied especially European theologians and have been thoroughly debated in connection with concepts like «Naturrecht» and «Ordnungen», i.e., «Schöpfungsordnungen» and/or «Erhaltungsordnungen».[434]

It would take us far beyond our task to attempt a comprehensive analysis of and contribution to this general theological debate. We will have to give it the attention necessary within the overall framework of our particular study. Obviously our encounter with ancestor worship once again draws attention to a theological problem of considerable magnitude. What is important to us, then, is to see how this problem is actualized in our perspective, and what kind of reflection is required from a church which is still struggling to settle in Japanese soil. Could it be that European theological thinking might benefit from such a reflection? That is our immediate impression when we see how K. Barth emphatically states that the family – understood in terms of a wider collective than the parent-child relationship – is of no importance within either the Old Testament or the

New Testament.[435] Only «Denkgewohnheiten und praktische Gepflogen-heiten der 'christianisierten' Heidenvölker» made the concept of «Familie» into a basic concept in Christian ethics, Barth says, and he sees no reason why this should be accepted.[436] Might such a thinking be one reason why – as Magaki says – Protestantism has frequently made the strong sense of group-belonging in Japan an object of critique?

3.3.1 *Family in Theological Perspective*

Our point of departure for this discussion is one particular aspect of Christian faith which is of fundamental significance in our context. When we spoke of man as God's creation in section 3.1.2 we spoke of man as both an individual and social being. Already the story of creation in Genesis 2 tells of man's coming into being with reference to God who said: «It is not good that man should be alone; I will make him a helper fit for him» (v. 18). «Therefore a man leaves his father and his mother and cleaves to his wife, and they become one flesh.» (v. 24) To a Christian, accordingly, the question can never be whether man is created for individual or social existence. Such an alternative simply does not exist. Man is not permitted to look upon himself as a mere individual, nor as an individual in God-relationship. Our very starting-point is an affirmation of man as a God-made individual created for social intercourse in community. Even though the further implications of this basic statement are conceptualized differently within Christian theology, as we shall see below, there is widespread unanimity on the fundamental issue we are here pointing out. «Im christlichen Glauben ist der Einzelne so bestimmt, dass er nicht ohne die Gemeinschaft, und die Gemeinschaft so, dass sie nicht ohne den Einzelnen denkbar ist», says E. Brunner, and W. Elert talks of «das Aufeinanderbezogensein der Menschen untereinander» as being «bereits in seiner Naturgegebenheit nomologisch verstanden».[437] The point is pregnantly expressed by K. Barth when he says that «Menschlichkeit» is as such «Mitmenschlichkeit»: «Menschlichkeit, die *nicht* Mitmenschlich-keit wäre, wäre Unmenschlichkeit, Inhumanität».[438] In other words, man does not and cannot exist solo. That is simply a contradiction in terms. By God-individual-community the decisive and inescapable triangle is given for human existence. M. Doi's study-group, which we have introduced in section 3.0.2.3, is therefore making an essential point when it presents as imperative for the new, Christian family to combine the freedom of the individual with the joint responsibility of the family-members as a community.[439] Thus the basic correlation between individual and collective in Christianity provides an important gateway for a fruitful conversation with the concerns for the corporate life of the family inherent in ancestor worship and takes us immediately one step further.

It is possible, namely, to determine theologically and still more closely man's createdness for social intercourse in community, as our quotations from Genesis 2 already indicate. The implication of these texts is that man finds himself inescapably born as a man or a woman, a son or a daughter, in a way which testifies to marriage and family as a basic God-given order without which human existence is impossible. Different terms have been coined to express this theological interpretation of man's existence. Brunner – together with many Lutheran scholars – uses the term «Schöpfungs-ordnung», saying that the most significant example «solcher Schöpfungs-ordnung ist die Zusammenordnung von Mann und Weib».[440] Elert, in his attempt to correct a certain misunderstanding of this term «als sollte diese Ordnung als Quelle der Gotteserkenntnis...gelten», introduced the concept of «Seinsgefüge» in order to express that these orders of man's existence are simply a God-given «Tatbestand» which man cannot escape and within which men cannot simply change places.[441] Along the same line Trillhaas talks of marriage as «Grundordnung» and family as «Urform des Gemeinschaftslebens» in order to emphasize that the two have «einen Vorrang vor allen anderen Gemeinschaftsformen» and are to be seen as «'Stiftung Gottes', von Gott dem Schöpfer 'eingesetzt'....»[442].

Moving on to Barth's *Kirchliche Dogmatik*, however, we find a typical example of resistence to the use of terms like «Schöpfungsordnungen» in this respect. On the one hand, Barth defines the man-woman relationship as «der erste und zugleich exemplarische Bereich der Mitmenschlichkeit» and speaks of «Generationsfolge» as something which belongs «zur Geschöpflichkeit des Menschen in seinem Verhältnis zu anderen Menschen».[443] On the other hand, he consistently avoids using the term «Schöp-fungsordnung» for marriage and family.

At a first glance this may appear to be nothing more than a disagreement over terminology. A closer look proves that the matter is not that simple. The immediate reason Barth gives for renouncing the term seems plausible: The emphasis on marriage and procreation as «Schöpfungsordnung» has, for some theologians, led to the unbiblical idea of a general, God-given duty to marry, with the result that the single position is regarded somehow as second-rate and not fully human.[444] The fact that man is created male and female, however, is no general command to marry in the way that persons who never enter into wedlock are not «*menschliche* Menschen».[445]

In this Barth is right, and it may be appropriate to reaffirm his concern in our Japanese context where traditional household-oriented values may have similar difficulties in accepting the single, unmarried position as equally «human».

Nevertheless, Barth's further reasoning in this connection seems to us more than dubious. In the Old Testament to marry, «be fruitful and multiply» (Gn. 1,28) was still «ein unbedingtes Gebot» to which the unmarried position constituted «einer schrecklichen Ausnahme».[446] The reason was that the very hope of Israel depended upon the proliferation of Abraham's descendants (Gn. 12).[447] With Christ and the new covenant, however, the promise to Abraham is fulfilled by God in a way which puts the whole question of marriage and family in a new light, wherefore Barth says that «die Fortpflanzung des Menschengeschlechts...*post Christum natum* aufgehört hat, ein unbedingtes Gebot zu sein.»[448] To marry and have family as well as to remain unmarried are now simply equal options existing alongside each other so that whether a person decides to marry or to remain single is a matter of «*höchst besonderen göttlichen Berufung.*»[449]

Against this way of thinking two basic objections have to be made. First, even though there is some truth in Barth's emphasis on family and procreation as an indispensable element in the Old Testament's way of visualizing the realization of God's promise to Abraham, his use of ante et post Christum natum as a demarcation line in principle for our understanding of the significance of marriage and procreation in human life is not tenable. It confuses the Christian belief in the creation of God with his redemption in Christ in the way that the latter simply tends to substitute the former. Second – and in clear connection with our first objection – Barth uses Paul and the New Testament to individualize the whole question of marriage/family in a way which effectively dodges the real issue of «Ordnung». In simply presenting marriage/family and unmarried position as equal options for the individual, Barth does not come to terms with the basic fact that humankind as such can never opt out of the «Generationsfolge» and still continue its existence. Against Barth's renunciation of terms like «Ordnung», «Schöpfungsordnung», «Grundordnung», has to be maintained, therefore, that his overall theological approach does not validate that the basic idea which these concepts contain – as we have presented them above – can be dismissed.[450]

It is important that this be emphasized in our context. When our encounter with ancestor worship confronts us with the great concern for the household as man's primary social milieu, we acknowledge a definite need to affirm the basic Christian understanding of marriage and family as God-given orders of creation before we enter into any further discussion on the relationship between the individual and this collective in-group. Such an affirmation is tantamount to saying, namely, that any human being within his/her de facto given household context is leading his/her life within the framework of a fundamental «Schöpfungsordnung» – irrespective of one's actual position vis-à-vis Christian faith. This is briefly but significantly expressed in Japan, both in the Lutheran handbook for believers and in the one published by the United Church of Christ. The former says in general terms that the fellowship of the family is a God-given blessing/*megumi* and the very basis of man's existence. Within a family we are born and raised and lead our lives according to our various positions, even if it may be in an imperfect way.[451] Similarly the latter says: «In order to give birth to us, bring us up and help us, God has given us our parents. For a Christian to be dutiful towards one's parents is not only a general ethical demand, but is part of the faith which gives thanks to God for his providence.»[452] In both handbooks the further introduction to Christian family-life is given upon this basic recognition of marriage and family as God-given institutions.

Having underlined man's life in family as life in a basic order of creation the question immediately arises whether by this we want to point to one particular type of family structure which for all ages and in all societies is to be labelled the actual, God-given «Schöpfungsordnung»? This is not the case, and neither is this what is usually intended by the use of this concept. To this we shall return below. Suffice it at this place to quote H. Begemann when he says that God «übt durch die Familie einen Teil seines Weltregimentes aus, indem er Menschen in der Gemeinschaft von Eltern und Kindern zusammen leben lässt und auf diese Weise die Mitmenschlichen Beziehungen grundlegend regelt». By this dogmatic statement nothing is yet said to which form of family God wants.[453]

What is more important at this point, however, is to make another qualification to our talk of orders of creation. It may be asked, namely, whether our affirmation of this concept does not imply that the actual realization and structural formation of these interhuman relationships somehow lies beyond the consequences of man's fall and, as such is unaffected by sin? An affirmative answer to these questions would obviously have a significant bearing upon our whole conversation. As important as it is to affirm the idea of man's place in «Schöpfungsordnungen», however, it is just as important to state that these are institutions which function in a fallen world. When man designs his life in the basic orders, his design, therefore, carries the trademark of the sinner.[454] The consequence is that in any actual context, in Japan as well as anywhere else, the basic orders of husband-wife/ parents-children are constantly exposed to man's exploitation of the orders for immoral, sinful ends. In theological perspective it has to be said, therefore, that man's life within the institution of the family is a paradoxical existence which puts the individual in a radical tension: At one and the same time he is involved in a God-given «Schöpfungsordnung» which he/she should affirm and serve in gratefulness and in structures actually shaped by sinful human architects and thus «Gegenstand des sittlichen *Kampfes*».[455]

The implication of this in our encounter with the basic understanding of the household in the context of ancestor worship is significant. When both the final criterion for moral behaviour as well as the ultimate moral authority is to be found in the family-collective itself, it represents a kind of «Naturrecht» that cannot be approved. Because of the intricate coexistence of «Schöpfungsordnung» and sin no form of family-structure can ever be of the kind that one can simply deduce from it final moral criteria. Therefore, in order for the abovementioned tension and «sittlichen *Kampfes*» neither to develop into an oppressing «Kollektivegoismus» nor into an opposite, individualistic «Gemeinschaftslosigkeit»,[456] final moral criteria and an ultimate moral authority outside and above both the family-collective and the family-individual, is needed. What that means will be further developed as we are now taken into a closer look at that which to the Christian is the will of this external and overriding authority.

An inquiry into the fourth commandment with an attempt at a proper application is what naturally presents itself as the next task to be undertaken: «Honor your father and your mother, that your days may be long in the land which the Lord your God gives you» (Ex. 20,12). The importance of this command not only as a beautiful piece of ancient Old Testament morality but as part of the abiding will of God, is seen from its renewed emphasis in the New Testament (e.g., Mk. 7,1-15; Eph. 6,1-4). It is also significant, in this respect, to notice as a characteristic feature of Jesus's ministry that he did not pull people out of their family but repeatedly sent them back into it (e.g. Mk. 2,11; 5,19; 8,26 a.o.).[457]

Now, what is the basic teaching of the fourth commandment to be applied to our discussion? First of all attention should be paid to its very location as the first among the seven commandments concerned with interhuman relationships. This particular order is not accidental, as Luther points out in his Large Catechism: «Folgen nun die andern siebene, gegen unserm Nähisten gestellet, unter welchen das erste und hohiste ist: Du sollt Dein Vater und Mutter ehren».[458] Already the sequence of the decalogue, in other words, points to the particular importance of proper ethical conduct in the parent-child relationship. The unique position of the parents is further underlined through the term used for the children's behavior: to honor (Hebrew: «kabad»). This is a verb which in the Old Testament is frequently used with God as object (1 Sam. 2,30; Is. 24,15), and the weight of the term is rightly understood when we observe that the noun commonly used for Yahweh's own glory and honor is a derivative from the same radical: «Kabod» (Ex. 16,10; Is. 6,3). On this background Luther as well as many modern scholars seem to us to be justified in emphasizing that what is demanded in the fourth commandment is not simply to love one's parents just as God commands man to love his neighbor as himself. Parents are in a unique position of honor which is to be reflected in the child's attitude and behavior: Because the parents «einen Abglanz des *kabod* (der Ehre Gottes) an sich tragen» is first and foremost honor and not «gefühlsbetonte Liebe» commanded.[459] That this involves also the love that in actual life serves and helps and cares for one's parents goes without saying and needs no further elaboration here.

The commandment reflects, in other words, the parent-child relationship as a God-given «Ordnung», of which the most daring expression is probably given by Luther when he says that God «Vater und Mutter scheidet und auszeucht fur alle andere Person auf Erden und neben sich setzet».[460] Although this way of saying things may be very «Lutheran», the point that is hereby made is no peculiarity of this particular reformer. In his exposition of the fourth commandment even Barth – in spite of his opposition to the talk of «Ordnungen» – says that what requires respect on behalf of the children is no quality – morally or physically – on the part of the parents, but «der *Entsprechung* ihrer Elternschaft zum Sein und Handeln *Gottes*.»[461] The parents are God's «Repräsentanten» vis-à-vis their children, and they stand – «von den Kindern aus gesehen» – «in der Blickrichtung auf *Gott*....»[462] In short: the person who is concerned with the honor and respect of God cannot bypass the honor and respect due to his parents. This is the first and most obvious lesson from the fourth commandment.

There is, however, another lesson, not so obvious and therefore easily overlooked, but nevertheless important in our context. The commandment implies or, it might rather be said, presupposes, a command also to the parents. This is clearly seen from the wider Old Testament context and is reflected in Paul when he continues his reference to the fourth commandment with an appeal to the fathers to bring their children up «in the discipline and instruction of the Lord» (Eph. 6,4). The Old Testament – as well as Paul and the New Testament – presupposes namely a maturity on the part of the parents which makes the very basis for spiritual upbringing of the younger generation. The parents have the responsibility to pass on the commandments of the Lord and «teach them diligently» to their children (Dt. 6,4–7; 11,19) and to further provide them with the necessary religious and moral insight when they ask for the «meaning of the testimonies and the statutes and the ordinances» of «the Lord our God» (Dt. 6,20. Cf. Ex. 12,26; 13,14).[463]

It is therefore in full accordance with the spirit of the command and its biblical context when Luther towards the end of his explanation draws attention to this aspect and comments on how the parents «sie sich halten sollen gegen denen, so ihn befohlen sind zu regieren.»[464] Parents are not free to behave as they please towards their children. God does not want «Buben noch Tyrannen zu diesem Ampt und Regiment», and the place of honor is not given to the parents «dass sie sich anbeten lassen». They are constantly to remember that they themselves «unter Gottes Gehorsam sind, und fur allen Dingen sich ihres Ampts herzlich und treulich anneh- men, ihre Kinder... nicht allein zu nähren und leiblich zu versorgen, sondern allermeist zu Gottes Lob und Ehre aufzuziehen.»[465]

In other words, if the fourth commandment teaches the children to honor their parents, it also implies that the parents make their best to bring up their children in the «instruction of the Lord». Keeping these two aspects together, there seems to us to emerge a not insignificant affinity to the circle of obligation within the Japanese household. The basic religious setting is different; to that we shall return in a moment. Nevertheless, even the fourth commandment pictures the moral interrelatedness of the per- sons linked together in the family-community – whether in the positon of a parent or a child – in a way that may be described in terms of reciprocal obligations. Neither party can exempt itself from its moral obligation to the other without bringing the community as such in jeopardy. To the children's respect and honor of their parents belongs the parents' mature, spiritual upbringing of the children – and vice versa.

If we look closer at the patriarchal extended family within which this commandment was interpreted and implemented through the centuries of the Old Testament and the New Testament, affinities to Japanese values are still more conspicuous. It is neither necessary nor possible for us to go into details at this point, but some interesting observations should be made.[466]

First, the family is important in its vertical dimension through the generations. This is seen both from the prominent place of the ancestors and the cherished idea of being buried with one's fathers (Gn. 47,30) – an aspect of the Old Testament often referred to in Japanese writings – and from the emphasis on unity in blessing and curse of the present and the future generations (Ex. 20,5). Once the family – the house – is established, it runs through the generations as long as descendants exist, and precautionary steps are made to ensure its continuation in particular cases (Dt. 25,5 ff.).[467]

Second, the family is important in its horizontal dimension as the primary solidarity-group of the living generation. The fact that definite borders cannot easily be drawn as to who fall inside the group does not reduce the fundamental significance of the actual household as a corporate solidarity-group. The most interesting examples in this respect for our purpose are the well known accounts in the New Testament of persons turning Christian with all their household (e.g. Acts 10; 16,30–34). For the most important occasion when he was to receive the representative of the new faith in his house, Cornelius had «called together his kinsmen and close friends» (Acts 10,24), and they were all together finally «baptized in the name of Jesus Christ» (10,48). In a most interesting (but almost forgotten) little study from 1915 to the significance of family-relationships for the spread of the Christian faith in the early Church, a Norwegian New Testament scholar says of Jesus that we find in his life and teaching «a genuine Jewish understanding of the significance of clan- and family-belonging – different from the purely individualistic concept that has guided so many Christian sects.»[468] He goes further on to show how the same «Jewish understanding» permeates the rest of the New Testament as well.[469]

We find in the Scriptures, in other words, a high esteem of the family as man's primary social nexus both with regard to its continuity from past into future, and to its rôle as an actual solidarity-group. The two aspects are significantly combined by Paul when he has the following to say as moral advice in connection with widows in the church: «If a widow has children or grandchildren, let them first learn their religious duty to their own family and make some return to their parents; for this is acceptable in the sight of God» (1 Tim. 5,4). Looking at the Japanese translation of this text we immediately discover that we are faced with a moral advice which once again reveals close affinity to traditional values in the Japanese family. When the young generation is asked to «learn their religious duty to their own family», the Japanese wording makes use of precisely the familiar and technical term for filial piety: «*jibun no ie de koyo o tsukushi*». It is a translation which seems to faithfully convey the very nerve in the Greek original: «*ton idion oikon eusebein*». The same is the case with the latter half of the exhortation: «...and make some return to their parents». Here it says in Japanese: «...*oya no on ni mukuiru...*», which again is exactly the traditional, technical term for repaying one's debt/*ho-on*. Also in this case the Japanese text seems to render effectively the original meaning: «*amoibas apodidonai*», where the noun *amoibe* in plural contains particularly the idea of repayment as a return for what oneself has received.[470] It should be noticed also that by the term *progonos* Paul is not referring to parents only, but inclusively to forefathers in a wider sense. (Cf. 2 Tim. 1,3 where – interestingly from our point of view – the Japanese text translates the same term with *senzo*/ancestors.) The vertical dimension of the household as well as its significance as a solidarity-group of the living generation are clearly in Paul's mind.

The implications of what has been developed here are obvious. Japanese emphases on household-continuity and -solidarity, and on corresponding moral values like gratitude to parents and forefathers expressed through filial conduct and returns for what one has oneself received, are by no means alien to biblical thinking on man in his family context. Similar ideas are part of the Bible's own actualization of the fourth commandment.

When Christianity nevertheless faces a real problem in its encounter with these values in the Japanese household, the reason lies not really with these moral principles as such, but rather with the way they are founded, as we have already pointed out. The rationale for the circle of obligation with its corresponding values is never given in Christianity in any religious interpretation of the household in ultimate categories but in God's will and God's «Ordnung». The fact that the fourth commandment is given in a frame of reference which receives its primary ethical thrust from the first is not only significant as a matter of principle but has far-reaching practical consequences obvious already in the Old Testament. The father of the house, or the parents as the actual representatives of the collective house-hold-group, are not the final authority. The Old Testament knows «dass die Eltern nich oberste Instanz, sondern wie die Kinder dem Wort Gottes unterstellt sind....»[471] Therefore, in the midst of its emphasis on the importance of the household and the duty of children to honor their parents, the Old Testament knows also of «eine Pflicht zum Ungehorsam der söhne gegenüber den Forderungen und Sitten der Väter...»[472], namely, when and where the «statutes» and «ordinances» of the fathers conflict with those of the Lord, as Ezekiel explicitly states (Ez. 20,18–20).[473]

But is not Ezekiel in this respect representative of a much later development and a decisively new approach in the Old Testament? When he says that the son shall not suffer from the iniquity of the father, nor the father from that of the son, but simply that «the soul that sins shall die» (18,20), is he not then championing an individualism which has moved a far distance away from the collective approach of early Israel? Would we find in early Israel a similar theological tolerance towards deviations from the statutes and ordinances of the fathers as Ezekiel exhibits? Attempts have been made to portray such a development from an early stage, i.e., pre-exilic Israel, where the primary unit for morality and religion was not the individual but the group, and a subsequent stage represented by the later prophets, where the individual finally gained its rights.[474] The fourth commandment and the togetherness in blessing and curse as set forth in Ex. 20,5 are – according to this approach – examples of the former, Ezekiel 18–20 of the latter, and the whole conception of such an evolution is obviously seen as a process from a primitive to a higher level of religion and morality: «The recognition of the rights of the individul life was certain to be reached by any real progress in morality and religion, and when it was reached it had important consequences.»[475]

It seems to be widely acknowledged in later Old Testament research, however, that such an understanding of the relationship between individual and collective in the Old Testament represents a grossly oversimplified construction which cannot be upheld.[476] What ever interesting developments and variations in emphases may be traced the decisive key to the understanding of the relationship between individual and collective was through the centuries the Yahweh-faith itself. This faith was a personal faith which from the beginning contained «ein notwendig zum Individualismus hinführendes Moment in sich: ihren Character als *Wahlreligion»*.[477] Challenged by this faith each individual within the covenant had to make up his mind whether to «hate» or to «love » Yahweh. What is expressed in Ex. 20.5 is not a belief in a collective unity in blessing and curse which leaves no room for personal faith on the part of the individual family-member. To the contrary, its emphasis lies in the consequenses for the family when fathers and children share in the attitude of hating Yahweh, or loving him and keeping his commandments.[478]

When this is observed, then Ezekiel's «individualism» cannot appear as something radically new. What he is fighting against in chapters 18–20 is the attempt to move away from personal responsibility – personal decision to love the Lord and keep his commandments – with the pretext that no matter how one personally behaves, one has to suffer from the iniquities of the fathers. Such a collective determinism irrespective of individual and personal faith could have no place alongside the Yahweh-faith of Israel. In short, the same faith, which makes the very basis for man's moral behavior within the family-context, serves simultaneously as guard against a «collectivism» which asserts its own will and authority over against God and deprives the individual of his/her personal resonsibility and dignity. In this respect the Old Testament is witnessing to a belief which runs through the New Testament as well and belongs to the very foundation of Christian ethical thinking.

What, then, about the critique which in Japan has often and strongly been raised against Christianity that it teaches unfilial conduct/*oyafuko*?[479] It is obvious, on the basis of what we have said above, that whether such a critique is valid or not depends on the premises upon which it is made. There is no doubt a genuinely Christian way to speak of filial piety, as we have pointed out. For this reason the critique should not be made easily, nor should it be accepted easily. If, however, the critique is made upon the old, traditional premise that filial piety implies the duty of the individual to submit to the will of the family and the ancestors as ultimate authority, the critique contains a significant element of truth. Openly and frankly to accept such a critique and to fight vigorously against the dangers of a feudalistic collectivism inherent in the traditional family-system is one of professor Sumiya's chief concerns. When Sumiya seems to pay too little attention to filial piety in genuine Christian terms, it may be explained by the fact that he was writing within the first decade after Japan's experience with feudalistic collectivism in the Second World War. His emphasis, however, that Christianity calls for nothing less than a fundamental ethical change, because a real understanding of personal dignity and basic human equality with corresponding genuine personal relationships can develop and be sustained only on the basis of a firm belief in a personal God, is an emphasis that has not lost its actual significance.[480]

At the same time, the basic aspects of Christian faith that we have developed in this chapter guard firmly against any kind of individualism which, in its busy concerns with the rights and the freedom of the individual, neglects man's God-given responsibilities vis-à-vis the primary social nexus of the family. Even though the Old Testament knows of «ein Pflicht zum Ungehorsam», it knows very well that the kind of «individualism» where «the son treats the father with contempt, the daughter rises up against her mother, the daughter-in-law against her mother-in-law; a man's enemies are the men of his own house» (Micah 7,6), is a result of man's sinfulness which makes the prophet «look to the Lord» and «wait for the God of my salvation» (7,7).[481] In the same way Jesus emphatically rejects the kind of individual piety which ignores the obligations towards father and mother using religious duties as a nice-sounding pretext, «thus making void the word of God through your tradition which you hand on» (Mk. 7,13). When both Kashiwai and Matsunaga in their articles on death and funeral, in the Old- and New Testament respectively, emphasize the danger in making a modern, individualistic value-norm the self-evident presupposition for interpreting the Scriptures, the point is well taken and should be emphasized also from our point of view in this chapter.[482]

No simple solution exists, in other words, to the tension inherent in man's existence as an individual in family context. Both a consequent individualism, on the one hand, and a consequent collectivism on the other may equally well prove to be destructive to both individual and community. When the family is seen in a Christian theological perspective, however, the faith in God as the ultimate authority above both the collective and the individual keeps the two in balance. The fundamental challenge which Christianity puts before traditional Japanese culture at this point is, therefore, how such a wholesome and constructive balance between family-individual and family-collective may be established and sustained if one rejects such a theological perspective?

The section we are now concluding has illustrated – maybe better than any of the preceding ones – what we meant when we said in chapter 3.0 that a simultaneity and dialectic of adoption and rejection has to be applied to the various aspects of ancestor worship. When ancestor worship confronts us with the problem of individual and collective in the family context, there is, however, still more to be said to the issue in the Christian perspective.

3.3.2 *Family in Eschatological Perspective*

Our discussion in the preceding section centered around the Christian belief in God as creator of man in community and sustainer of human life in and through orders of creation. To this theological dimension, however, comes the eschatological dimension of Christian faith: The new reality in Christ Jesus. We have already in section 3.2.3 focused on this in our discussion on the communion of saints as a community based on faith in Christ. Now, with the statement of faith that anyone who is in Christ is a new creation, we are once again encountered with a fundamental doctrine of the New Testament with far-reaching ramifications. Having been grafted into Christ through faith the Christian is reborn to a new existence which has its basis in the redemptive act of God. To a Christian, therefore, life has a profound dual dimension: It is life as a gift of creation in God-given institutions which are constantly exposed to sinful man's exploitation; it is life as a new creation in Christ, who is both the perfect revelation of God's will for life in community and the redemptive power for a life in accordance with the new reality. What does this dual dimension with its eschatological perspective imply with regard to our problem of the individual in the family context?[483]

3.3.2.1 *Christ and the Natural Family*

We have already made references to Jesus's acceptance of the fourth commandment, both to the fact that he characteristically sends people back home to their families, and that he rejects the kind of piety which neglects one's parents under religious pretexts. What, then about the harsh-sounding words of the Lord which apparently collide head on with filial conduct: «If any one comes to me and does not hate his own father and mother and wife and children...he cannot be my disciple» (Lk. 14,26)? Is not the meaning of these words that life as a new creation in Christ can take place only as all considerations and loyalty-ties to one's family are radically and unconditionally offered on the altar of discipleship? Consequently, that to enter into discipleship of Christ necessarily means a breakdown of family community, «for I have come to set a man against his father, and a daughter against her mother, and a daughter-in-law against her mother-in-law» (Mt. 10,35)? It is no wonder when these sayings of Jesus sound unacceptable to young and old in the Japanese family and make the impression that Christianity after all teaches *oyafuko/* unfilial conduct.[484] Obviously – as we have seen in section 3.3.1 – such an interpretation would run into great difficulties not only with others of his own sayings but with the rest of the Scriptures as well. How are they, then, to be understood?

It is commonly agreed among commentators that by the verb *misein*, to hate; to renounce, is not referred to hate in psychological categories.[485] What is meant by the term is to «utterly subordinate anything, even one's own being, to one's commitment to Jesus.»[486] Understood in this way, Matthew's rendering of this saying of Jesus proves the best exegesis of

Luke's version: «He who loves father or mother more than me is not worthy of me; and he who loves son or daughter more than me is not worthy of me». (Mt. 10,37)[487] What Jesus is aiming at, in other words, is an absolute preference in loyalty and love. To enter into discipleship is to enter into a realtionship with Christ to which any other ties of loyalty and love are subordinate. Not in every situation, therefore, does discipleship of Christ imply a breakdown in the family-community. The conflict arises when the latter inhibits the disciple of Christ in placing his ultimate loyalty in his Master. Insofar as Lk. 14,26 contains a general demand, it is a demand for «die unbedingte *Bereitschaft* zu solcher in bestimmter Situation gebotener unbedingter Entscheidung.»[488]

What we have in this startling utterence of Jesus is, in other words, no contradiction of the fourth commandment and of filial piety in Christian terms. To the contrary, it is a radical and pregnant way of underlining this commandment's subordinate position to the first, as we have observed it already in the Old Testament. When obedience to the demands and the ways of the fathers clashed with obedience to Yahweh, there was no other way than the «Pflicht zum Ungehorsam». The eschatological character of these sayings of Jesus is eminently clear in the way he equals this loyalty and love towards Yahweh with ultimate loyalty and love towards himself. Seen in such a context with the Old Testament these utterances of Jesus can be interpreted as nothing less than the words of God incarnate: Life in fellowship with God is realized through life in discipleship of Christ. In this way both the first and the fourth commandments are reemphasized and placed decisively in christological and eschatological perspective.

To the disciple as a new creation in Christ daily life is life within the God-given order of family-community on the basic premise that this «Ordnung» is subordinate to the lordship of Christ.

The perspective of the lordship of Christ is not only of principal importance, however, but of the greatest practical significnce for personal intercourse within the family. When a person is made a new creation in Christ, he/she is made partaker in a new community where «there is neither Jew nor Greek, there is neither slave nor free, there is neither male nor female» (Gal. 3,28), and made disciple of the Lord who gave himself as the unique paradigm for human behavior. «Even as the Son of man came not to be served but to serve, and to give his life as a ransom for many» (Mt. 20,28), so the same law of service and self-sacrifice is supposed to rule among his disciples:«...whoever would be great among you must be your servant, and whoever would be first among you must be your slave». (Mt.

20,26–27. Cf. Mt. 23,11; Mk. 9,34–35.) This radical reversal of the ordinary rule of «great men» (Mt. 20,25) is the decisive key to the ethical aspects of discipleship all through the New Testament. John links in with Jesus' symbolic washing of the disciples' feet (John 13), and according to Paul the mind of Christ who «emptied himself, taking the form of a servant» (Phil. 2,7) is to be reflected in his disciples. To «bear one another's burdens» may therefore be identified with fulfilling «the law of Christ.» (Gal. 6,2. Cf. 5,13b.) Just as Christ as the serving and redeeming Lord gave himself up for his disciples, so the latter in him are freed to an imitatio Christi in reciprocal service and self-sacrifice. The lordship of Christ in this respect, in other words, is decisively pictured in the perspective of theologia crucis: It is realized among his disciples in and through reciprocal «Hingabe» of the one for the other.[490]

This is the overriding perspective within which we have to understand the New Testament's advices concerning family life in the so-called Haustafeln. These are not abstract theologizing on models for a new, Christian family-system, but very concrete and relevant moral advices for Christians living within the framework of the antique patriarchal «house».[491] What were the implications of their new life in Christ with regard to their various positions in their actual family? The conscious subordination of the specific advices to the overriding perspective of reciprocal service and self-sacrifice is obvious in Ephesians 5, where Paul introduces the Haustafel with a general demand: «Be subject to one another out of reverence for Christ.» (5,21)[492] By this Paul is saying that whatever counsels are now to be given to the various partakers in the house, they are given in the overriding perspective of the «freedom» where everybody is to be «servants of one another» «through love». (Gal.5,13)[493] The following exhortations to the wives to be subject to their husbands (v. 22,24) can therefore be no simple apostolic confirmation of a patriarchal patria potestas, according to which «der Ehemann die legale unbestrittene Führungsrolle besass».[494] Nor can the expression that «the husband is the head of the wife» (v. 23) be simply a Pauline concession to the husband to stick to his actual and legal superior position. As the repeated references to Christ in these verses show, the key to a proper understanding of Paul's counsels is not the sociological pattern of the contemporary family but the family-member's new being in Christ. When Christ is used as prototype of what it means to be «head», the ideal to be imitated is not a patria potestas in terms of «die legale unbestrittene Führungsrolle», but the self-sacrificing love «as Christ loved the church and gave himself up for her». (5,25) «Die Rolle des Mannes in der Ehe hat nicht Selbstbehauptung, sondern Selbesthingabe zu sein».[495]

It seems to us, in other words, that Ephesians 5 shows that Paul in his concrete advices to actual family life is not concerned with a new, Christian «structure» in terms of systematizing a Christian hierarchy of superior and inferior positions, a Christian view of who is supposed to serve whom in hierarchical order. On the one hand, he commands the wives to be subject to their husbands, as it is repeated other places in the New Testament as well. (Col. 3,18; 1 Peter 3,1.) In this way they could and should realize their imitatio Christi in the actual social order of the family. On the other hand, he argues for this in a way which is simply incommensurable with ordinary human standards in terms of superior/inferior, master/servant. He puts the radical demand of self-sacrifice in love before the pater familias and says that the slave is to be treated no longer as «slave» but as a brother in the Lord. (Eph. 6,9. Cf. Philemon v. 15–16.)

But do not Paul's concrete demands for the subordination of the wives nevertheless imply that even the Christian family is to be shaped by a basic pyramidal structure in which the husband after all is the one who must take the lead in initiative and carry the final responsibility? Such an interpretation of the relevant scriptural material has been, and is still, widespread within the church. A typical representative of this position is Barth in his *Kirchliche Dogmatik*: «Die ordungsmässige Ungleichheit von Mann und Frau gerade in der Ehe besteht schlicht darin, dass die Verantwortung sowohl dafür, dass ihre Gemeinschaft eine Gemeinschaft in der Freiheit, wie dafür, dass ihre Freiheit eine Freiheit in der Gemeinschaft sei, bleibe und immer wieder werde, immer *zuerst* die Sache des *Mannes* ist. Sie wird und ist dann auch die Sache der Frau.... Er muss ihr darin *voran*gehen, er muss sowohl in Sachen der Freiheit wie in Sachen der Gemeinschaft die *Initiative* ergreifen.... *Er* hat die *erste* Verantwortung.»[496] Even though the primacy of man to woman is a «Primat des *Dienstes*», it has nevertheless to be affirmed with respect to marriage and family «dass die *Ordnung*, in der er der Erste, sie die Zweite ist, gerade hier zur Geltung komme und in Kraft bleibe.»[497] In other words, the Christian family will in all actual contexts have to be shaped according to some kind of patriarchal, pyramidal family structure.

It will be clear from what we have said above that we have great difficulties with Barth's systematic approach at this point.[498] Firstly, such a far-reaching differentiation between the man/husband as «der Erste» and the woman/wife as «die Zweite» seems to us problematic. May such consequences be drawn without confusing «die ordnungsmässigen Ungleichheit von Mann und Frau» with the actual, tragic result of man's broken relationship with God: «...and your desire shall be for your husband, and he shall rule over you» (Gn. 3,16)? And may such a consistent differentiation be upheld without coming into conflict with the principle New Testament statement that in Christ «there is neither male nor female»? Secondly, to find a universally applicable basis for such a patriarchal structure in the Haustafeln seems again problematic. Does a «der Erste»-«die Zweite» structure do justive to Paul's radical reinterpretation of the relationship between husband and wife «in Christ» as it is seen in Ephesians 5? And is it consistent when this particular aspect of the patriarchal structure in the Haustafeln is conserved as a divine institution, while others, like the relationship between master and slave, are not?[499] Thirdly, no matter how one emphasizes the primacy of the man as a «Primat des *Dienstes*», a basic order in terms of «der Erste» and «die Zweite» runs, as far as we can see, into an unsolvable dilemma with the overriding New Testament demand for reciprocity in service and self-sacrifice.

What we are suggesting, then, is not that a Christian family is simply without structures, something that should be clear from what we have developed in section 3.3.1. The family is fundamentally structured in the husband-wife and the parent-child relationship with the consequence that practical ethical advice to its members may well be given with due reference to the person's particular place in the family community. It is not necessarily structured, however, in a pyramidal, hierarchical order of relationships in the way that a certain model of patriarchal family once and for all is to be labelled «the Christian family». The new reality in Christ, into which the members of the family have been incorporated through faith, makes the question who is the first and who is the second simply irrelevant.

What, then is the function and meaning of the Haustafeln if it is not to give a universal blueprint of «The Christian family»? They show eminently well that the imitatio Christi is not something that has to wait for new social orders to be established before it may take place. Or in other concepts: They show how the new, eschatological reality in Christ is to be realized in the life of Christians in the midst of the old sociological context of history.[500] The Christian, whether a pater familias, a wife, a child or a slave, was – and still is – called upon not to estrange oneself from one's historical and social context, but to lead a life in discipleship within the particular situation in which one found – and finds – oneself.[501]

At the same time, however, such an imitatio Christi within the actual antique family context could not but put in motion «ein Aufbruch aus der konkreten geschichtlichen Situation», and «eine Bewegung, einen ufbruch auslösen, der die bestehende Ordnung von innen her wandelt».[502] This is an affirmation of the greatest significance. Being «eine Bewegung» put in motion by the eschatological reality of the new life in Christ, it is determined precisely by the essential nature of biblical eschatology: It has its cause in the fact that the coming age is already present; its consummation coincides with the consummation of the lordship of Christ in the age to come. This is tantamount to saying that the Christian family always represents «ein Aufbruch», «ein Aufbruch» from any actual family-system.[503] Just as the individual Christian family-member is caught in the radical tension and constant battle between the old and the new man, so is the Christian family as such involved in the same battle between the old man with his inclination towards self-assertion and exploitation, and the new man in Christ who gives himself in service and self-sacrifice. A Christian family, accordingly, is not something that may eventually be grasped and secured through structures and system, but a reality that is lived in the continuous struggles of a corporate imitatio Christi in actual discipleship.

The relevance of what has here been developed to our particular discussion should not be hard to discern. On the one hand, it implies that when we approach the problem of the individual and collective in the family context from the eschatological point of view, Christianity cannot simply be conceived of in terms of a revolutionary, ideological movement which breakes the walls of the Japanese family-structure. Christianity in Japan should not be identified as the main proponent of some kind of Western, nuclear family-system introduced as «The Christian family». Just as the New Testament Haustafeln testifies to the apostolic affirmation of the Christians' «concrete position within the process of history», Christians in the Japanese family context have to affirm their particular «finitude within the social order».[504] The new life in Christ – the discipleship's imitatio Christi in terms of service and self-sacrifice in love – is to be realized within the framework of the particular family-collective to which one belongs and within the family-structure of the social order of which one is a part. Saying this we are not contradicting or minimizing the possibility of conflict which the religious aspects of family life centered around ancestral rites may create for a Christian. This we have dealt with in sections 3.3.1 and 3.3.2.1, and we shall return to the problem once more below. Such a conflict, however, with the possibility of a painful break-down in family-relationships, does not exempt the Christian from a continuous readiness for service and «Hingabe» in and for his/her family-community.

On the other hand, also in a Japanese family-structure, Christianity brings about a motion that changes existing orders from within. The point we just made does not mean that Christianity may be employed as an effective force for the conservation of old structures, because after all – one might think – a Japanese patriarchal, extended family-system seems more akin to the structures of the Bible than does the individualistic, nuclear family of the West. As we have seen, in Christian thinking the family as such is put decisively into eschatological perspective by being subordinate to the lordship of Christ, and the individual members of the family – each in one's particular position sharing in the new creation in Christ through faith – is a disciple living the daily struggle of imitatio Christi. Thus the change that takes place from within is not a simple, once-and-for-all substitution of an old set of structures with a new one. Rather is it a process that reveals itself in changes towards an ever greater realization of a family-fellowship in reciprocal service and self-sacrifice of the one for the other under the common authority of the lordship of Christ.

3.3.2.2 *The Natural Family and Familia Dei*

Finally, what has here been said about the family in theological and eschatological perspectives has to be integrated with what we in section 3.2.3 developed with regard to communio sanctorum and communio familiae. In that chapter we saw how the relationship of individual and collective is significant not only from the point of view of man's life in natural orders of creation but from the point of view of redemption as well. Having been made a new creation through faith in Christ man is incorporated into a new community. Also within the reality of redemption, in other words, man is a social being. Due to the fact that Jesus himself at times spoke of this community in family concepts, communio sanctorum has also been called familia Dei: «And stretching out his hand toward his disciples, he said, 'Here are my mother and my brothers! For whoever does the will of my Father in heaven is my brother, and sister, and mother'» (Mt. 12, 49–50).

We emphasized in section 3.2.3 that familia Dei is a religious and spiritual community in Christ, and neither a human community in general nor a community based on blood-relationship. The basic implication of this fact is simply that any Christian is an individual who simultaneously belongs in two «families» corresponding to the dual dimension of his existence: On the one hand, to a natural family as a gift of creation, on the other, to familia Dei as a new creation in Christ. Just as we in section 3.2.3 underlined the need not to blur the distinction between communio sanctorum and communio familiae, it is necessary in this section to underline the simultaneity of the Christian's two belongings without confusing them. If, as we have seen, it is possible on the one hand to trace a certain interpretation of communio sanctorum in the direction of a vague and untenable inclusion of communio familiae, we find on the other hand a theological interpretation of man's natural family which tends to confuse it with familia Dei. This seems to us to be the result of Barth's heavy emphasis upon «Lernwilligkeit» – the readiness on part of the children to accept spiritual guidance and teaching from the parents – as the very heart of the fourth commandment.[505] Such an understanding of «der Nerv des Ganzen» in the parent-child relationship, namely, leads Barth to an interesting conclusion: When Paul in the New Testament calls his fellow Christians who are taught by him «beloved children», and himself their «father in Christ Jesus» (1 Cor. 4,14–15), and when Jesus refers to familia Dei as «those who hear the word of God and keep it» (Lk. 11,28), it is – according to Barth – «keine *metabasis eis allo genos*» as far as family concepts are concerned; i.e., it is in essence the same kind of family-relationship as the fourth commandment assumes for man's natural family.[506]

As far as we can see, the consequence of saying that the two «families» are of the same «genos» is in the end to say that there is no essential difference between natural family and familia Dei, between creation and redemption. It will be clear from what has been developed over the preceding pages of chapter 3.3, however, that we against such an interpretation have to confirm both the essential difference in «genos» between the natural family and familia Dei and the simultaneity of the two in the life of the Christian. By birth man is incorporated into the former, by faith and baptism into the latter.

This concurrent duality has to be clearly acknowledged not least when a family as a whole turns Christian. On the one hand, the household continues to be a natural, blood-related fellowship interrelated in this primary social milieu independent of faith in Christ. On the other hand – and at the same time – the family-members form a fellowship in Christ which has its basis in faith independent of consanguinity. What is the significance of a clear understanding of this duality in our particular context? Some examples may serve to clear the point. We have made repeated references above to Morioka's study of the acceptance of Christianity in rural Annaka in the latter half of the last century. One reason why Annaka has been an interesting case study is precisely the fact that from the very beginning many families turned Christian. The fact that there were households with many individual Christians proved an asset – according to Morioka – in the subsequent time of persecution.[507] However, Morioka at the same time points to a danger in this. Such a family, especially where also the house-head/*kacho* was a Christian, very soon came to be referred to by outsiders as a «Christian house». Thereby the possibility was close at hand that Christianity would step into the traditional rôle of Buddhism as an *ie*-religion, where the responsibilities for the church would lie with the house and not with the individual believer.[508] Then the conclusion could easily follow that to be a Christian was not a question of personal faith but of social belonging to a «Christian house».[509]

This point is even more directly stated in Nishiyama's study of the Fukuda Anglican Church, which we introduced in section 3.0.2.3. The Shimo Fukuda village resembles Annaka in that also here quite a number of houses turned Christian as a gathered social unit, a fact which – according to Nishiyama – may be taken as one important reason for the stabilization of Christianity in the village.[510] At the time of Nishiyama's field-work the church-members actually living in the village (79 altogether) were all members of houses that for generations had been known as «Christian houses». There was not a single so-called «individual believer».[511] Nishiyama's interesting conclusion emerges from a closer study of this group, which shows that of the about 40 % who received adult baptism (mostly in-marrying wives) 78.6 % gave the answer that «Christianity is the religion of the house», whereas only 21.4 % gave more direct personal reasons.[512] Nishiyama concludes that today the Christian faith in the village can not be said – mostly – to be an individual and conscious faith.[513] In other words, to partake in the Christian fellowship of the family tends to be removed from the realm of personal involvement in faith and simply conceived of as another aspect of sharing the traditional ways of the house. In this way Christianity runs the risk of developing into a new *ie*-religion, i.e., a new family-religion where there is no longer any essential difference between the natural communio familiae and familia Dei.

One should be careful, of course, in drawing general conclusions from Annaka and Shimo Fukuda, and one cannot simply draw theological inferences from socio-religious studies like these. Nevertheless, they seem to underscore what we have said from a theological point of view on the need for clear distinctions at this point. No matter how important it is to emphasize the significance of the family as man's primary solidarity-group, as we have done in section 3.3.1, it is necessary at the same time to distinguish clearly between one's family as a blood-related community and community in Christ through faith. There seems to be a particular need for this when a family in the Japanese context turns Christian as a gathered social unit.

If there is a danger that one's belonging to familia Dei, on the one hand, and to a natural family on the other may be confused in the direction of an untenable identification of the two when a family as a whole turns Christian, there is the opposite possibility of the two developing into serious conflict when an individual turns Christian in a non-Christian household. As we have seen above, such a conflict is not unavoidable. A person's incorporation into familia Dei does not in itself constitute a betrayal of one's communio familiae. To the contrary, faith in Christ should move a person to an imitatio Christi within one's household which ought to serve as the best proof of the Christian's gratitude, love, and loyalty. At this point Lutheran ethics with its traditional emphasis on the Christian's everyday service – «ein jeder nach seinem Beruf» – as a genuine Christian service, seems to us to have a significant contribution to make in Japan. In a household-context centering around the ancestral rites, however, the conflict in question comes to the surface as far as the family insists on the religious aspects of the household community, maintains the harmony of the house and the will of the fathers as the ultimate criteria for acceptable individual behavior, and tolerates no deviation on the part of the Christian on these principle issues of basic importance. In such a case no Christian, neither in Japan nor anywhere else in the world where similar claims are made, avoids the painful conflict between the will of one's pater familias and the will of «the Father, from whom every family in heaven and on earth is named» (Eph. 3, 14-15).

This has taken us to the end of our third chapter, and we summarize briefly our findings.

Firstly, the question of the right relationship between individual and collective in the family setting, which is a problem of major significance in the context of ancestor worship, is a central issue also to Christian faith. Man's createdness as a social being in family community is a basic order of creation out of which man cannot opt. Also at this point, however, Christian thinking has to take into account that actual man is man post lapsum. His life within the order of the family, therefore, is caught in a paradoxical tension: At the same time, the individual is involved in a God-given «Ordnung» to be affirmed and in structures which sinful man may exploit for evil purposes and which therefore involves man in an ethical struggle in the family context. When the Scriptures talk of man within the family, we have seen that they emphasize this primary social milieu both in terms of continuity from past into future and in terms of actual solidarity. They interpret the fourth commandment in a way which has affinities both to the idea of filial piety and to the reciprocal obligations within a Japanese household. The key, however, to a genuine and whole-some balance between individual and family collective lies – according to Christian faith – in a proper subjection of the fourth commandment to the first. The will of God for interpersonal life in the order of the family guards both against a collectivism which deprives the individual of his/her perso-nal dignity and responsibility and against an individualism which neglects man's God-given responsibilities vis-à-vis the family community. At this point Christian faith presents the understanding of individual and collec-tive assumed in the ancestral rites with a fundamental challenge.

Secondly, no discussion of these problems from a Christian point of view can take place without the decisive eschatological perspective: A Christian is a new creation through faith in Christ. Thereby life is given a profound dual dimension. The Christian as individual and family-member is subject to the lordship of Christ which means a very practical imitatio Christi in terms of service and self-sacrifice in the actual family context. This implies, on the one hand, that structural changes in family-system are not conditions that have to be met before an imitatio Christi can take place. On the other hand, no family-system can ever protect itself against the change from within which the new life in Christ sets in motion. What Christian faith, therefore, means with respect to the actual structures of the Japanese family should not primarily be conceived of in terms of an alternative, Christian «system» but in terms of an «Aufbruch» towards an ever greater realization of a family-fellowship in reciprocal service and self-sacrifice under the authority of the lordship of Christ.

Thirdly, we have to affirm the simultaneity of the Christian's belonging to a natural family and to familia Dei without confusing the two. If this distinction is not made properly, a false identification of the two may cause Christianity to develop into a new *ie*-religion where social belonging supplants personal faith as basis for sharing in the Christian community. On the other hand, there is the danger of open conflict between the two when the former asserts its position and function in ultimate categories in the way that a Christian is forced to choose where to place his/her final

allegiance. Also at this point the proper balance derives from the overriding, theological perspective of God who relates to man in creation and
redemption.

3.4 Conclusions

We have ended our inquiry into the theological concerns that arise from
the encounter between Japanese ancestral rites and Christian faith. In an
introductory chapter (3.0) we identified our conversation as a discussion
pertaining to the wider problem of Christianity's accomodation and
indigenization with respect to particular cultures, we presented some
important principles in the light of the history of theology, reviewed
historical and actual parallels, and put our study into the framework of
related research done in the Japanese context.

Our subsequent discussion focused on the three main issues that emerged
from our systematic analysis of ancestor worship in part 2: The community
of obligation, the community of interdependence, and the community of
cosmic continuity. Starting with the latter we saw (chapter 3.1) how the
basic Christian view of God and man as creator and creation also in this
case is of crucial importance for a relevant discussion on the relationship
between the human and the divine. The process of integration from the
realm of the former to that of the latter which the ancestral rites imply
actualizes such well known and much debated theological issues as imago
Dei, man's theopoiesis and participation «of the divine nature», the
incarnation of God in Christ, and the position of the saints. Vis-à-vis the
ultimate integration of the human and the divine which the ancestral rites
presuppose, Christianity cannot but testify to the humanness of man and
the divinity of God decisive for all further Christian thinking. In other
words, the issue of idolatry – understood the way we have made clear in
section 3.1.3 – cannot be left as non-existent but must be openly faced as
a significant aspect of this encounter. At the same time deliberate efforts
must be made lest the Christian conception of God be misunderstood in
terms of a remote and unconcerned divinity. Such a twisted idea of the
Christian view of God is not only repulsive in the context of Japanese
ancestor worship. It is a radical distortion of the basic concern of the
Scriptures which from beginning to end talk of God and man in relationship.
    Secondly, we encountered the problem of death (chapter 3.2) with the

challenge to re-think the relationship between the living and the dead presented by the ancestral rites' view of reciprocal interdependence. Again our confrontation has actualized important theological issues that are by no means settled within the church. We saw in part 2 how the ancestral rites present «afterlife» in naturalistic and anthropological perspectives which provide a meaningful modus vivendi with death. Even though Christianity should carefully avoid becoming another «funeral-religion» it belongs to its essential theological task as a religion of the living to come to terms with the ancestral rites' concern with death and the dead. In this respect it is imperative for the church to present clearly the ramifications of Christianity's view of death in theological perspective, both with regard to the dreadfulness of death as the wages of sin and man's enemy and to its conquest in Christ and its ultimate subjugation in man's resurrection on the final day. Only in such a theological perspective can death be comprehended in Christian terms, in its radical absoluteness as death of man in his totality as well as in the continuity it nevertheless contains between the man of the tomb and the man of the resurrection.

Left in this radical tension there is a meaningful way for the Christian to talk of an intermediate state. He believes both that all people are being upheld in death in an irrevocable God-relationship towards resurrection and judgment and that the dead in Christ are taken into a new being with the Lord, which means a blessed foretaste in waiting of the glory to come.

In this perspective we discussed what we called parallels in Christian context to ancestor *kuyo* and the transfer of merits/*tsuizen eko*. We found, however, that neither the idea of vicarious baptism nor the creedal affirmation of Christ's descensus ad inferos can legitimately be utilized to establish a theological basis for the living somehow to assist in a salvatory process of the dead. Man's acceptance into the presence and glory of God is not dependent upon any kind of human mediation, except for what the One Mediator once and for all did for the many. Man's hope of salvation vis-à-vis death and the life to come is built solely upon God's own redemptive acts for man in Christ. As for the dead in Christ, therefore, the bereaved – in the midst of grief and mourning – may rejoice in assurance of salvation. As for the pre-Christian departed, the living may faithfully commit them into God's righteousness and mercy. On the orther hand, even though the basic premise that God is the One who redeems precludes a Christian exploitation of the soteriological motif of the rites with their interdependence between the living and the dead, there is also in Christian faith a significant interrelatedness between the two. Within communio sanctorum the living and the dead in Christ are partaking in a community which bridges the chasm of death and is heading towards the consummation.

Finally, our encounter necessitated an examination of the relationship between individual and collective in the household context (chapter 3.3). To Christian faith man's existence as a social being in household community is a basic order of creation out of which man cannot opt. The Scriptures emphasize this primary social nexus both in terms of continuity from past into future and in terms of actual solidarity in a way which has obvious affinity to such ideas as filial piety and reciprocal obligation within the Japanese household. Also in this respect, however, man is man post lapsum which implies that this basic order of creation is constantly exposed to evil exploitation in the direction of either radical collectivism or radical individualism – both equally destructive. To Christian faith the wholesome balance between the two is again given with its basic theological perspective where the fourth commandment – «Honor your father and your mother» – acquires its proper place in clear subjection to the first – «You shall have no other gods before me».

The problem of individual and household cannot be properly considered from Christian point of view, however, without bringing in what we called the eschatological perspective – the Christian as a new being in Christ. This implies that no family system can protect itself against the change from within which the actual imitatio Christi sets in motion. The effect of Christian faith in its encounter with the traditional Japanese household is therefore neither a conservative bolstering of old structures nor a simple replacing of the old with an alternative system. It is an effect that has rather to be seen in terms of an «Aufbruch» towards ever greater realization of a household community marked by reciprocal service and self-sacrifice under the lordship of Christ.

Such a view of individual and family in the light of creation and redemption also implies the significant simultaneity of the Christian's belonging both to a natural family and to familia Dei. Proper distinction between the two must be carefully made. On the one hand, namely, an illegitimate identification may cause Christianity simply to develop into a new ie-religion. On the other hand, conflict between the two may develop if the former asserts its position in ultimate categories which force the Christian to choose where to place one's final allegiance.

This attempt at a thorough inquiry into the theological issues that arise in the encounter between ancestor worship and Christian faith seems to have verified our introductory thesis. There can be no simple Christian approach either of acceptance or of rejection of the assumptions sustaining the ancestral rites. No doubt there is conflict. It is a conflict, however, that can be responsibly and constructively dealt with only in appreciation of the legitimate concerns of the rites. In such a simultaneity of rejection and acceptance the significant motives of ancestor worship are re-interpreted into a new whole in the theological perspective of the gospel. What that implies with regard to a contextualized practice and liturgy is a question which points beyond the task we set before us and is most confidently left to competent and mature Japanese churches to answer.

Notes to Part 3

1. Agency for Cultural Affairs 1972, p. 25.
2. Reimer 1975, pp. 165–166. Reimer himself puts this bluntly as a positive statement, not as a question.
3. Hwang 1977, p. 359.
4. All quotations from the Bible are rendered according to the Revised Standard Version.
5. Voss 1943, p. 532. Cf. B. Hwang: «It [Christianity] can never accept any pagan beliefs and practices that are not compatible with the teaching of Christ handed down by the apostles.» (Hwang op.cit., p. 356.) It is quite another matter that many protestants have doubts as to whether assertions like these can be upheld in the light of the history and practices of Catholicism. The above quotation from Voss, for example, is a rebuke of A. Harnack's contention that the rapid expansion of Roman Catholicism in Europe came «as the result of syncreatistic tendencies». (Voss op.cit., p. 531.) We shall have ample opportunity to return to this problem below.
6. Kraemer 1956/1958[2], p. 390. We want to make the comment at this point that in our view H. Kraemer's works are among the ablest and most rewarding contributions to the whole problem of the relationship between Christianity and religion/religions. As will be apparent below, we have benefited a great deal from his approach, not least from his *Religion and the Christian Faith*, in which he tries both to underscore his main concerns in the much debated book *The Christian Message in a Non-Christian World*, and to remedy what he considers the latter's weaknesses.
7. Myklebust 1976, p. 116. (Translation ours.)
8. Ibid., p. 182. (Translation ours.)
9. Voss op.cit., pp. 526, 535–536. Voss's contribution to the problem of accomodation in a missionary perspective is referred to with approval in current Roman Catholic writings on mission. Cf. B. Hwang: «Fr. Gustav Voss has done substantial groundwork in developing the theology of accomodation. It is advisable to build on what he has already done». (Hwang op.cit., p. 355.)
10. Kraemer op.cit., p. 391.

11. Ibid., pp. 390–391.
12. Ibid., p. 409.
13. Myklebust op.cit., p. 116. The last expression – to make the Gospel «understandable» – is somewhat problematic. It raises the whole problem of epistemology, but the author does not deal extensively with that question. It seems to us, however, that Myklebust by this expression is only saying what he later on puts this way: «The Gospel is to be proclaimed as the authentic and unchangeable message from God, but at the same time clearly acknowledgeing the necessity of that relatedness to context which is a consequence of the fact that it is to be presented – i.e., articulated, incarnated – in a historical situation.» (Ibid., p. 181. Translation ours.)
14. Hwang op.cit., p. 356.
15. In Kraemer 1956/1958[2], part three («Theological Attempts to Deal with the Problem of Religion and Religions»), there is a good introduction to this discussion. We refer to this for a historical survey of the debate. To the debate after Kraemer, see, e.g., Hallencreutz 1970.
16. This is well-known Roman Catholic theology, clearly presented in, e.g., K. Adam's popular and widely published book from 1924: *Das Wesen des Katholizismus*, used by us in its Danish edition from 1965. See pp. 178–179, 187–189.
17. Voss op.cit., pr. 530, who quotes Adam with approval.
18. Ibid., pp. 538, 540.
19. Ibid., pp. 538, 540.
20. Hwang op.cit., pp. 355, 363.
21. Ibid., p. 356.
22. This becomes evident when Hwang says: «One thing is certain. She [the church] knows that her Divine Founder is not only living and working in those who accept her teaching but also very active in the whole world and in the entire cosmos. She believes that the redemptive grace of Christ radiates beyond her sacramental and juridical boundaries into the heart and soul of every person born into this world, redeeming and transforming all men who seek the truth and want to be saved. She does not believe the total degeneration of mankind by reason of the Fall. She knows that the divine goodness still finds a place in man and it is her job to bring to awareness this goodness and to help to bring it to full blossom by the grace of Christ.» (Ibid., pp. 356–357.) It seems to us, in other words, that what Hwang does is not so much to question the concept of «continuum», as to refuse to include Christianity in an evolutionistic view of religious development.
23. Bekenntnisschriften 1930/1959[4], p. 53.
24. As to the reformers' – especially Calvin's and Luther's – approach to religion/religions, see Kraemer op.cit., pp. 168–174.
25. Troeltsch 1905, p. 6.
26. Ibid., p. 53.
27. Ibid., p. 54.
28. Troeltsch 1925, p. 2.
29. Otto 1917/1926[15], p. 33.
30. Ibid., p. 51.

31. Ibid., pp. 48, 51.
32. Ibid., pp. 69, 71, 75.
33. Cragg 1968/1969², pp. 79–80.
34. Ibid., p. 85.
35. Ibid., p. 87.
36. It is therefore not surprising to find Cragg in vehement opposition to Kraemer's position, whereas, concerning K. Rahner's far-reaching deductions on the basis of Roman Catholic nature-grace theology, he says that this «certainly... is a theology which faces the right way». (Op.cit., p. 83.) Cragg, however, finds Rahner to give a «too tidy and systematized conclusion» (p. 83), while he himself prefers «to live with permanently unanswered questions». (p. 84) In the same connection he raises some of the questions which people, whom he calls «those of Barthian tutorship» will direct against his position (e.g., that of the perversity of man). He concedes that «there is here an important truth», but he does not really enter into a serious consideration of this «truth». (p. 84)
    We cannot go further into current Protestant trends along similar lines. It seems to us, however, that Cragg is a typical representative of ecumenical dialogue-theology in recent years, and that the basic model of complementary fulfilment in some way or other lies behind its concern for inter-religious sharing in spirituality.
37. Barth 1938, p. 327. As to Barth's position see especially § 17 in his *Kirchliche Dogmatik*, Vol. I, part 2: «Gottes Offenbarung als Aufhebung der Religion». Barth's position is further well-known from his discussion with E. Brunner in the 1930's on the «point of contact». Presentation and critique of Barth is further found in Kraemer 1956/1958², pp. 185–196, and in P. Althaus 1947/1949², pp. 47–50, 68–73, 164–165.
38. «Gerade das unsichtbare, unzugängliche Wesen Gottes, seine ewige Kraft und Gottheit, wird von der Erschaffung der Welt her in seinen Werken begriffen und geschaut (Röm. 1,20). Gerade von einer Bekanntschaft mit Gott, und zwar gerade von einer Bekanntschaft auf Grund von Offenbarung, kommen die Menschen immer schon her, in dem die Offenbarung in Christus zu ihnen kommt (Röm. 1.19).» (Barth op.cit., p. 334.)
39. «Aber irgendwelche Bedeutung bekommt diese Erkenntnis für die Theologie nicht....» (Althaus op.cit., p. 47.)
40. Kraemer op.cit., p. 193.
41. Althaus op.cit., p. 47. It is interesting to see that Kraemer shares Althaus' dissatisfaction with Barth's exegesis of Romans 1 and 2: «A deplorable feature in Barth's profound but too dogmatic approach is that he feels thereby obliged to give an exegesis of Romans 1 and 2 which does not agree with Paul's tenor of reasoning.» (Op.cit., p. 309.)
42. This is pertinently pointed out by Althaus when he distinguishes between «Gottgebundenheit» and «Gottverbundenheit»: «Diese Gottgebundenheit des Menschen hebt seine Verlorenheit so wenig auf, dass diese erst und gerade an ihr *entsteht*: das Verhältnis des Menschen zu Gott ist durch die Sünde nicht aufgehoben, sondern verkehrt; an seinen Verhältnis zu Gott ist der Mensch krank und schuldig. Der «gottlose» Mensch ist gerade nicht los von Gott,

sondern seine Gottlosigkeit hat ihren Ort in der unaufhebbaren Beziehung zu Gott, deren der Mensch sich bewusst ist.» (Op.cit., p. 70.)

43. Kraemer op.cit., p. 309. This is what Althaus calls «das ständige Getroffensein der Menschen von Gott.» (Op.cit., p. 174.)

44. The following presentation of this early encounter is based on J. Jeremias' little book *Heiligen-Gräber in Jesu Umvelt*, Göttingen 1958, which is a very interesting study of the practices referred to in Mt. 23, 29–30; Lk. 11,47, and on N. Müller's detailed investigation «Koimeterien. Veranstaltungen zum Gedächtnis der Toten in den Kirchen» in *Realencyclopädie für Protestantische Theologie und Kirche*, Leipzig 1901[3], Vol. 10, pp. 814–840.

45. Jeremias op.cit., pp. 127,141.

46. Ibid., p. 121: «Herodes' Bau [of a memorial stone at the grave of David] war ein *hilasterion mnema*, und die Bauten, die die Zeitgenossen Jesu über den Gräbern der Märtyrerpropheten errichteten, sollten die Blutschuld der Prophetenmörder sühnen. Doch war das Motiv der Sühne...nicht das einzige; etwa der mächtige Bau über den Gräbern der Patriarchen in Hebron...bezweckte lediglich die Ehrung der Toten.»

47. Ibid., pp. 129–138. Especially powerful as thaumaturge was Elisha, and the fathers Abraham, Isaac, and Jacob buried in Hebron were regarded as the most influential intercessors.

48. Ibid., pp. 142–143.

49. Ibid., p. 141.

50. Müller op.cit., p. 815.

51. Ibid., pp. 815–816. The practice of separate Christian grave sites may have started already in apostolic times. It is clearly testified to at the time of Tertullian.

52. Ibid., p. 819.

53. Ibid., p. 831. The earliest witness to this practice seems to be the annual memorial of the death of bishop Polycarp, while later on Tertullian testifies to a more widespread practice of Christian memorial services. According to Müller, the eucharist as the Christian meal of community between the living and the dead was the center in the Christian memorials and that which above anything else gave them their Christian characteristic.

54. Ibid., p. 831, where reference to the Church-fathers is given.

55. Ibid., pp. 832–834.

56. Of special interest to us at this point is the research done by two Norwegian scholars, Emil Birkeli and Reidar Th. Christiansen. Their studies do not lie in the field of missiology but within the science of religion and folklore. They nevertheless make interesting references to Christianity's confrontation with and accomodation to these religious practices. Although both are mainly concerned with Norway and the Nordic countries, they draw the lines to the wider European context.

57. Birkeli 1938, pp. 19–20. Proof of this is found, e.g., in letters from Pope Gregory III to the bishops of Bayern and Allemagne ca. 737–739, and in Pope Zachariah's letter to Boniface of May 1, 784.

58. Ibid., pp. 20, 69. (Translation ours.)

59. Ibid., p. 63. In Norway such memorials seem to have been conducted on the

seventh and the thirtieth day after death, and then at the annual death-day.

60. Ibid., p. 63. (Translation ours.)

61. Ibid., pp. 64, 70, 72. To the memorial feasts with the dead in Eastern Europe as compared to the Scandinavian countries, see Christiansen 1946, pp. 54–63. There is an interesting difference from the point of view of missiology: According to Christiansen, in Eastern Europe the Greek Orthodox church adopted the practice, «took it under its protection, and made it possible for it to survive down to recent years.... while in the West it was discarded at such an early date that very few traces remain.» (pp. 55, 61.) In the West, namely, «the Roman Catholic church monopolized the regulation of the relations between the living and the dead. The assistance given passed through the offices of the church in masses, pious gifts, donations of one kind or another, and certain days were set apart for the memory of the deceased in general». (p. 62.)

62. Birkeli op.cit., p. 63. (Translation ours.)

63. Cf. Mbiti 1967 and Mbiti 1971, especially the chapters on «The Nearness of the Spirit World», and «The Resurrection and Corporate Eschatology», pp. 127–181.

64. Cr. Fasholé-Luke 1974.

65. Cf. Mosothoane 1973.

66. Ibid., pp. 86–87.

67. Cf. Thom 1973, p. 77.

68. Daneel 1973, p. 69.

69. Kollbrunner 1975, p. 19.

70. See to this proposal by Kumbirai also Daneel, op.cit., pp. 61–62.

71. Kollbrunner op.cit., p. 26.

72. Cf. Zimmer 1949. According to an editorial remark preceding the article, the author submitted the 3-page paper with an appeal for help for the missionary to tackle the practical implications of the issue.

73. Cf. Schreiner 1972, see especially chapter VI: «Das Verhältnis von christlichem Glauben und Adat in der Ahnenverehrung und im Gräberkult.» This is a study of particular interest to us since there are obviously significant parallels between ancestor worship in Japan and Indonesia. Coming over from the African setting, we note, e.g., how the author presents the element of apotheosis in Indonesian ancestor worship, and its conflict with fundamental Christian doctrine. See, e.g., pp. 254–256.

74. Ibid., p. 243.

75. Ibid., p. 258.

76. Reimer op.cit., p. 166.

77. Ibid., p. 167.

78. Quoted from Voss 1943, pp. 542–543.

79. Ibid., p. 543. When Reimer says about the Roman Catholics that «the church did not change its official stance until Vatican II» (Reimer op.cit., p. 167, note 2), this is obviously not correct.

80. Cf. David C. E. Liao: «In Taiwan, Roman Catholics are coming back to the position held by Ricci. Yu Pin, Archbishop of Peiping (Peking) but currently the president of the Roman Catholic Fu-jen University in Taiwan, was

quoted to the effect that Taiwan Catholics are going to continue in the line of Li Matou (Matteo Ricci) in the matter of ancestor worship....'If anybody wants to prevent you from performing ceremonies to your ancestors, you come to me. I have the approval of Rome.'» (Liao 1972, p. 126.) By this reference to Rome, Yu Pin may have in mind Pius XI and Pius XII's enactment on the matter.

81. Jackson 1907, in China Centenary Missionary Conference Shanghai 1907, pp. 215–246. The records also contain a very interesting report of the discussion following the paper and the resolution it proposed. Although this conference finally adopted an unanimous resolution, it is obvious that there were widely differing views within the Protestant camp, not least on the implications of the term «worship». A paper at the conference in 1890 for example, caused heated discussion, and Jackson says about this conference that «our subject [ancestor worship] was perhaps...the one over which the Conference came nearest to losing its temper!» (p. 215.)

82. China Centenary 1907, p. 623.

83. China Christian Yearbook 1917, p. 296, quoted from Liao op.cit., p. 128.

84. Liao op.cit., p. 128.

85. Ibid., p. 129.

86. Doi 1960, pp. 42, 47.

87. The investigation revealed that among Christians belonging to Christian homes (defined as a family where the head of the family is a Christian), 60 % reported to have no *butsudan*, whereas 40 % had one. Among Christians belonging to non-Christian homes, 76 % reported that the family had a *butsudan*, 24 % that it did not. (Table 16, p. 217.) Concerning actual performance of rites 13 % reported doing this voluntarily on their own responsibility, whereas 71 % said they took part in the ancestral rites and/or festivals of the gathered family. (Table 17, pp. 218–219.)

88. Ibid., pp. 48, 220.

89. Ibid., p. 220. (Translation ours.)

90. Ibid., pp. 48–49. (Translation ours.)

91. Nishiyama 1975, p. 61.

92. Ibid., pp. 55, 61. On a national scale, accordingly, this study is very limited as far as numbers are concerned. It is difficult, therefore, to generalize on the basis of this particular case study. Nevertheless, it is a very important and interesting investigation from the point of view of mission.

93. Ibid., p. 53. (Translation ours.)

94. Ibid., pp. 67–68, where this trend is documented through statistics.

95. Ibid., p. 73. (Translation ours.)

96. It will be clear from what we have said in parts 1 and 2 that although Doerner is concerned with ancestors in «folk Shinto», the missiological aim and implications are of great interest to us.

97. Ibid., p. 151.

98. Ibid., p. 152.

99. Ibid., p. 158.

100. Ibid., p. 159.

101. Ibid., p. 173.

102. Ibid., p. 174.
103. Ibid., pp. 175–176.
104. Ibid., p. 176.
105. See to this Lee 1966 and Swyngedouw 1967 for a Reformed and a Roman Catholic presentation of the problem. Our widening of scope at this point is justified by the inherent connection between domestic and national ancestors pointed out above. This connection was demonstrated in the historical context by the fact that the Catholic instructions and stand on the matter were not restricted to the Shinto ceremonies alone but applied in general to filial piety towards the ancestors. (Swyngedouw op.cit., p. 583.)
106. Famous Protestant theologian Ebina Danjo's words in the National Christian Council's Bulletin, December 1936, have become well-known: «Let us hold the national position in regard to shrines as not religious. Let us not fight over the religious side. Do not refuse to go to the shrine». (Quoted from Lee op.cit., p. 140.)
     The same position is clearly formulated in the official Roman Catholic instruction from the Sacred Congregation for the Propagation of the Faith of May 26, 1936; «Therefore, since rites of this kind are endowed with a purely civil value, it is lawful for Catholics to join in them and act in accord with the other citizens.» (Quoted from Swyngedouw op.cit., p. 583.)
107. Voss op.cit., p. 544.
108. Thus Voss, op.cit., p. 544, who refers to the Osservatore Romano Dec. 18–19, 1939 for the same opinion.
109. So Holtom 1938, which is a weighty voice in the debate.
110. The predicament is obvious, however, already in the Roman instruction of 1936. On the one hand it says that the rites are «endowed with a purely civil value». On the other that the Catholics should make known their intentions before participating «if this be necessary for the removal of any false interpretations of their acts.» (Swyngedouw op.cit., p. 583.) It is acknowledged as a possibility, in other words, that participation may be interpreted as Christian partaking in other religious ceremonies, although the rites officially are not religious! This seems to us to be a clear indication that the Roman Catholics partly accepted the non-religious interpretation as valid, partly had to take precautions because the interpretation was not waterproof.
111. Cf. Roman Catholic B. Hwang who, with clear reference to the official Roman instructions, says: «The official decisions already made have caused more confusion and stirred up more controversy among Christians than they have served to solve the problem or transform the cult itself. Just allowing Christian converts to practice veneration is not enough.» (Hwang op.cit., p. 351.)
112. We cannot enter into a serious discussion of this vast and complex problem. One of the main contributors to the study of secularization in the Japanese context is Jan Swyngedouw, to whom we have already referred repeatedly. See Swyngedouw 1976 and Swyngedouw 1979.
113. Swyngedouw 1967, p. 662.
114. Ibid., p. 663.
115. Ibid., p. 662.

116. This perspective is not within Swyngedouw's horizon in his conclusive remarks to the Shinto problem.
117. See particularly two books published by the United Church of Christ: Hiyane 1959 and United Church of Christ 1974. The first contains a comprehensive article by Hiyane Antei («The Christian Funeral Service and Its Other-religious Soil») together with responses from various points of view. The second is a publication on death and the funeral service in biblical, historical, and actual perspective. Further is Yamauchi 1973, interesting as a Lutheran voice, and the whole series of articles by Obata Susumu in the popular magazine *Hyakumannin no fukuin*, as a conservative Reformed contribution. (Obata 1974–76.)
118. Hiyane op.cit., pp. 6, 14. As examples he mentions condolence-addresses to the dead and offerings of fruit etc. in Christian funerals. (See pp. 40–43.)
119. Ibid., pp. 62–64.
120. Ibid., e.g., p. 70 (Asano Junichi) and pp. 72–74 (Takasaki Tsuyoshi).
121. Ibid., p. 70. (Asano. Translation ours.)
122. Ibid., p. 74. (Takasaki. Translation ours.)
123. Ibid., p. 96. (Saji Ryozo. Translation ours.) According to Saji, the view of the world-to-come «is very vague among us. Thinking of this, the situation of the Catholics is envious. Right or wrong, the church at least has an established and plainly stated, consistent view of afterlife». (p. 96.) Kumano Yoshitaka, in the same book, makes a similar point when he says that clear theological understanding is a prerequisite for a proper funeral, and that the doubts about the proper funeral in Japan originates in vagueness of faith and doctrine. (p. 109)
124. Obata 1976, No. 2, p. 68. (Translation ours.)
125. Obata 1976, No. 4, p. 68. (Translation ours.) Cf. Anglican priest Kochi Tokio: «All non-Christian participants in a funeral must be given a basic understanding of the essentials in a Christian view of life–death.... The basis of a Christian funeral has to be the faith in the resurrection, and no kind of sentimentalism.» (Kochi 1969, p. 24. Translation ours.)
Cf. also the following practical instructions given in the Lutheran handbook for Christians: «Following the instructions of the pastor, the decorations after encoffinment should be arranged in a simple way and in accordance with one's faith.... Cross, flowers and the like may be used, but not offerings to the dead, and one should be careful lest the atmosphere expresses in any way worship towards the dead.» (Lutheran Church 1966/1967[2], p. 109. Translations ours.)
126. Doerner op.cit., p. 176.
127. Ibid., p. 176.
128. Dumoulin 1964, pp. 174, 177–178.
129. See, e.g., Anzai 1965 and particularly Suzuki 1974. The latter is a preliminary report – privately published – of an investigation in 1972–73 into two villages which both converted to Catholicism after the war, Ryujin-mura in Wakayama Prefecture and Saga-mura in Kyoto Prefecture. The investigation especially focuses on the rôle of ancestor worship in the villages.
130. Suzuki op.cit., p. 68. (Translation ours.)

131. Ibid., p. 72. (Translation ours.)
132. Agency for Cultural Affaris 1972, p. 79. Cf. Professor Tagita Koya who says that the *Kirishitans* «have lost the Christian idea of the Supreme Being and observe a syncretistic ritual of Christianity and ancestor worship.... It is more through their reverence and loyalty to the ancestral martyrs than anything else that the Secret Kirishitans have adhered to this persecuted religion». (Tagita 1960, pp. 445–446) Cf. also Furuno 1957, pp. 9–10.
133. Morioka has undertaken several interesting case studies concerning Christianity in the Japanese society, see Morioka 1959 A, Morioka 1959 B, Morioka 1965. The gist of these studies is given in Morioka 1976. Re the conflict Morioka says: «However, ancestor worship is not only an expression of respectful love and remembrance. It has obviously completely other-religious traits, such as the repose of the soul and prayer for its happiness.» (Morioka 1976, p. 107. Translation ours.) In the *butsudan* there is «a head-on collision between a Christian concept of God and the fundamental Japanese faith in the god of the house who bestows divine assistance to the descendants in return for their respectful worship and service». (Ibid., pp. 142–143. Translation ours.)
134. Morioka op.cit., pp. 279–280.
135. See, e.g., Saji's article in Hiyane 1959, pp. 93–94, referred to above.
136. Ito 1963, p. 119.
137. Ibid., p. 120. See also Morioka op.cit., where this danger is well portrayed (pp. 280–281).
138. Ito op.cit., p. 121. (Translation ours.)
139. Morioka op.cit., p. 281. (Translation ours.)
140. See Nakamura 1967, vol. I. pp. 126 ff: «Suzuki Shosan's Chriticism of Christianity».
141. Ibid., p. 133. The «competition» mentioned is «as if a sparrow were fighting against an eagle, or a firefly against the moon». (p. 133.)
W. Dening gives a similar account of a controversy between Tokugawa Confucianist Hayashi Razan (1683–1657) and one of the early missionaries. Razan denounced Christianity «on the ground that its cosmological teaching and its explanation of the relation of the supposed Creator of the world to the world in which we live seemed to him to be irrational and contradictory». (Dening op.cit., p. 141.)
142. Lee op.cit., p. 195. Whether Lee is correct or not in this contention, we are not in a position to judge.
143. Benz 1970[5], p. 124. The same point is made in Callaway's study *Japanese Buddhism and Christianity*, 1957, p. 24. Further, Takatori/Hashimoto 1968/1975 says that the core of the problem Christianity faces in Japan lies in its concept of an absolute, transcendent, and personal God to which there is no parallel in Japan. (p. 84) Suzuki/Spae 1968 sees the view of God as the second of three typical traits in Japanese religiosity: God does not belong to another dimension but is conceived of as an extension of the dimension of man himself. The borderline God-man is not clearcut but ambiguous and vague. (pp. 148–149) According to Buddhist Professor Bando Shojun the implications of faith in God continue to be a vital problem in ongoing Buddhist-Chri-

stian discussions: «A Buddhist finds it difficult to accept the Christian stress on God's personality, and the belief in God as Creator, which seem to be incompatible with Buddhist ideas of causality and dependent origination.» (Thelle 1979, p. 49.)

144. We believe it to be verified in chapter 2.3 that this is not far-fetched theorizing but an inevitable consequence of the implications of the rites themselves.

145. Brunner 1937, p. 79. What is developed by us at this point may be found in almost any textbook on Christian dogmatics. We want to refer especially, however, to two well-known books by E. Brunner: *Der Mensch im Widerspruch*, 1937, and *Truth as Encounter*, 1964.

146. Stauffer 1965/74[5], p. 114. Cf. Brunner 1964, p. 89, where it is pregnantly stated that «God is first», by which is meant that whereas man has his dependence in God's creative act, God has no reciprocal dependence in man.

147. In Norwegian context penetrating theological and philosophical analysis of the problems involved in pantheistic approaches to Christian faith is given in Valen-Sendstad 1970, and 1973, pp. 97–209.

148. Brunner 1964, p. 87.

149. Cf. Owen 1971, p. 40.

150. Ibid., p. 41.

151. Stauffer op.cit., p. 118. Stauffer does not give any further suggestions re the understanding of the speech.

152. Re the exegetical discussions on this controversial passage, see esp. Gasque 1975 for the main representative positions. See further Gärtner 1955; Kümmel 1974; Bruce 1976/1977; and in Norwegian, Moe 1944, and Frøvig 1944.

153. See Gasque op.cit., pp. 209–213. Kümmel regards Dibelius' interpretation completely convincing: «Denn die Areopagrede ist, wie *M. Dibelius* überzeugend nachgewiesen hat, 'eine hellenistische Rede von der wahren Gotteserkenntnis', die im Neuen Testament als ganze und in vielen ihrer einzelnen Gedanken völlig fremd dasteht und nur als Vorläufer der philosophischen Theologie der apologeten des 2. Jahrhunderts angesehen werden kann. Das stoisch-pantheistische Menschenverständnis von Apg. 17, 28 kan daher begreiflicherweise mit den übrigen neutestamentlichen Anschauungen von Menschen nicht in Einklang gebracht werden.» (Kümmel op.cit., p. 211.)

154. Gasque op.cit., p. 213.

155. Bruce, op.cit., p. 11.

156. In the same way O. Moe sees no real problems in understanding this verse in terms of Jewish-Christian faith in God's creation and sustenance. Like Gärtner, Bruce and others, he sees the perspective of missionary preparatio as hermenutical key to an adequate interpretation. (Moe op.cit., pp. 223–231.). D.A. Frøvig, however, seems to us to express himself in much more ambiguous terms: «According to Biblical thinking God is close to anybody with his life-giving spirit, and it is presupposed at this place that Paul in affinity to [i tilknytning til] stoic thought has understood this to mean that we live and move and exist in God himself as our element of life.» (Frøvig op.cit., p. 282. Our own translation.) The perspective of missionary preparatio is not prevalent in his exegesis.

157. Bruce op.cit., p. 10.

158. Ube Daimyojin, quoted after Kato 1918. See above, p. 99.
159. Cf. Brunner's talk of man's existence as a being in responsibility. The God-man relationship is characterized by God's call («Anruf») and man's response («Antwort»). (Brunner 1937, pp. 87–89.)
160. Brunner – in his dispute with Barth – said that man created in the image of God implied that man was «wortempfänglich». As far as this means that man is created for personal correspondence with God on the basis of his word/address, we think Brunner is correct and only pointing to what Luther could characterize as «an ability which is given neither trees nor animals». (See Prenter 1955[2], pp. 301–302. Translation ours.)
161. This translation of 1 Cor. 15,28 is our own rendering of the greek *panta en pasin*. The RSV has translated: «that God may be everything to every one», which may well be a correct interpretation in a wider biblical context, but scarcely a precise rendering of the actual text. Many translations have therefore kept the more pantheistic-flavored wording.
162. Kümmel op.cit., pp. 210–212. H. Windisch sees 2 Peter 1, 3–4 saturated with Hellenistic piety, a strong indication that the letter cannot be genuinely Petrine. (Windisch 1930, p. 85) Cf. also H. Köster in the article on «Fysis» in the *Theological Dictionary of the New Testament*. He refers to Windisch and sees 2 Peter 1, 3–4 out of step with New Testament teaching on redemption. (Köster 1974, p. 275.)
163. Hägglund 1956, pp. 29–32.
164. See Kraemer 1956/1958[2], pp. 151–153. There is not little affinity between the thoughts of Clemens and Origin at this point and the ultimate coalescence of the individual soul with the supra-individual ancestral spirit in ancestor worship.
165. Ibid., p. 153. According to Kraemer this represented a distortion of «the Biblical *kerygma* in a very serious manner». (p. 153.)
166. For a brief introduction to the significance of the doctrine of «theiosis» in Greek theology and mysticism, see Johannes N. Karmiris: «Abriss der Dogmatischen Lehre der Ortodoxen Katholischen Kirche», and Andreas Theodorou: «Die Mystik in der Ortodoxen Ostkirche», both in Panagiotis Bratsiotis (ed): *Die Ortodoxe Kirche in Griechischer Sicht*, Stuttgart 1959/1970[2].
167. Karmiris op.cit., p. 45.
168. Cf. Theodorou op.cit., p. 188.
169. Karmiris op.cit., p. 64.
170. Ibid., p. 66. Note that Karmiris here refers to 2 Peter 1,4. Cf. Theodorou op.cit., p. 191.
171. «Es versteht sich von selbst, dass diese Vergottung nur in ethischem und nicht in realem oder auf Pantheismus hintendierendem Sinne gedacht werden muss, da ja die menschliche Natur gewissermassen aus Gnade vergottet wird, indem sie von der göttlichen durchdrungen wird – so ungefähr wie Eisen vom Feuer durchdrungen wird – jedoch ohne dass die menschliche Natur verdrängt und in die göttliche umgekehrt wird.» (Karmiris op.cit., p. 66. Cf. Theodorou op.cit., pp. 187–189.)
172. This is pointed out by Kawada Kumataro in his short essay «On the

Fundamental Difference between Buddhism and Christianity», delivered at the ninth International Congress for History of Religion, Tokyo 1958: «The mediator between God and men [in Christianity] is, therefore, God-Man and not Man-God. He is originally God, who became a man and not a man who became God. And it is not the Man-God, but the God-Man, that Christianity does profess, defend and teach.» (Kawada 1960, p. 326.)

173. Cf. to this point A. Valen-Sendstad: «Never does God interfuse his nature wih the human, and never can a man blend himself with the divine – not to say coalesce with him or become one with his essence and nature. This is to say that in Christian faith the personal category is *never* dissolved. I am I, you are you, and God is God. The personal category is ontological constitutive in true Christianity. The personal category is therefore constitutive in the God-man relationship as well in this life as in the life to come.» (A. Valen-Sendstad 1970, p. 482. Our own translation.)

174. See, e.g., J. Schneider 1961, pp. 103–104; K.H. Schelkle 1964, pp. 186–189; and T. Fornberg 1977, pp. 85–89.

175. According to Fornberg there is good reason – on the basis of popular Hellenistic tradition – to maintain that the expression to «partake in the divine nature» is simply another way of saying that man shall participate in divine immortality: «If this [2 Peter 1,4] is seen against the background of what was described above as 'popular Greek tradition', it seems highly probable that by participation in the divine nature the author of 2 Peter meant immortality, and that his mode of expression reflects popular Greek philosophy.» (Fornberg op.cit., p. 88.)

176. Cf. Schneider: «Die Vollendung der Gotteskindschaft aber besteht in der Gottgleichheit. Das ist der kühnste Gedanke, der im Neuen Testament ausgesprochen ist.» (Ibid. p. 161) To the exegesis of 1 John 3,2 see also F.F. Bruce 1970, pp. 85–88.

177. «...et illi confidere», as it says in the Latin text, which stresses the personal pronoun more than the German. (Bekenntnisschriften op.cit., p. 507. Our own translation.)

178. Ibid., p. 563.

179. Ibid., p. 564.

180. Ibid., p. 562. As examples of «idols», Luther therefore mentions both pecuniary wealth, wisdom and power, and even the Christian saints.

181. Nakamura 1967, p. 142.

182. Bellah 1970, p. 123.

183. Ibid., p. 124. Bellah adds on his own account that they at this point were «quite right». (p. 124.)

184. As this has for many years been a burning issue among Old Testament scholars, we are aware of the danger of drawing unfouned conclusions. On the one hand, there are scholars who see ancestor cult as an important part of the religious life among early Hebrew tribes, also in pre-mosaic Israel, and who interpret – with individual differences – a lot of references in the Old Testament texts in the light of this assumption. So, e.g., Schwally 1892; Charles 1913 (reprinted 1963); Pedersen 1934; and Schmid 1962B. On the other hand, there are scholars who object to such a heavy emphasis on

ancestor cult as a significant phenomenon in early Israel and its surrounding peoples, and are reluctant in interpreting Old Testament texts as referring to such practices. So, e.g., Eichrodt 1961[4]. Also Wächter 1967 shows the difficulties in assuming a real cult of the dead based on a belief in their powerful position. Balanced presentations of the problem have been given in the Japanese context in Kashiwai 1974 and Culpepper 1975.

185. According to Pedersen it was a common view in Western Asia – adopted by the Israelites in Canaan – that the dead were thought of as divine beings. (Pedersen op.cit., p. 366.) Pedersen, however, seems to us to be very biased in his exegesis of many old Testament texts where such an affinity to old ancestral cultic practices does not seem to be the only possible interpretation.

186. Eichrodt op.cit., pp. 145, 148; Charles op.cit., pp. 24–28. Wächter's position is close to that of Eichrodt. Where Psalm 106, 28 is concerned he points to the possibility that by the reference to «the dead» at this place is meant the dead idols. (Op.cit., pp. 185–187.)

187. Charles op.cit., p. 28.

188. «Zu behaupten, dass diese Sitte nur aus der früheren Verehrung des gemeinsamen Ahnen hervorgegangen sein könne und nicht auf die Bedeutung der Familie als der ursprünglichsten sozialen Gemeinschaft sich gründe, ist die reine petitio principii». (Eichrodt op.cit., p. 150.)

189. Ibid., p. 150.

190. According to Charles, «Yahwism from the first was implicitly engaged with it in irreconcilable strife.» (Op.cit., p. 19.) In Eichrodt's view, although there were «Ansatzpunkte» in the Israelic world of ideas for a development of a real cult of the dead, it was effectively inhibited by the exclusive lordship of Yahweh (op.cit., p. 151), and Pedersen sees Yahwism in eventual fight against ideas pertaining to the ancestral cult. (Op.cit., pp. 365–366.)

191. This is the case in Psalm 106,28. As to the meaning of Dt. 26,14 the text itself may contain an ambiguity: Are all sacrifices to the dead condemned, or only the practice of using the tithe for such offerings? The problem does not seem to be too important, however. Even though the proper offering of the first fruits is in focus in this verse, the wider Old Testament context does not allow for an interpretation that sees offerings to the dead from the tithe prohibited, while otherwise offerings to them should be no problem.

192. Culpepper op.cit., p. 38.

193. In our view the proper place for dealing with the saints in Christian theology is in the context of chapter 3.2 below where we shall return to the issue. There are implications, however, concerning the general relationship God-man that have to be dealt with already at this point. As to the historical development of the veneration of saints see E. Lucius 1904 (reprinted 1966); J. N. D. Kelly 1958/1977[5]; R. Seeberg 1910 and 1913; and the two articles, K. Grüneisen 1879 and R. Klauser 1959.

194. Lucius op.cit., p. 34.

195. Ibid., pp. 25–34 re the Christian encounter with the peculiar ancestor cult, and pp. 35–48 re the interaction with the wider theological development and the significance of the martyrs. For the latter, see also Klauser op.cit., p. 171, and Kelly op.cit., pp. 490–491.

196. Lucius op.cit., pp. 33–34. See also Birkeli 1938: «It is not, however, their gods the [Christianized] Germans make into saints, but their own dead.» (p. 69. Our own translation.)
197. Lucius op.cit., p. 34.
198. Re the early belief in the protective function of the martyrs for the living church, see Lucius op.cit., pp. 127–128. This equivocal interwovenness of intercession and protection is conspicuous in Tridentinum's statement on the saints, which Klauser says gives «die heutigen Grundlagen der Heiligenverehrung»: «Die Heiligen herrschen zusammen mit Christus, sie bringen ihre Gebete für die Menschen Gott dar. Es ist gut und nutzbringend, sie um Hilfe anzurufen und zu ihren Gebeten, ihrer Macht und Hilfe Zuflucht zu nehmen, un von Gott durch seinen Sohn Jesus Christus, unseren Herrn, der allein unser Erlöser und Heiland ist, Wohltaten zu erlangen.» (Quoted from Klauser op.cit., p. 174.)
     According to Adam op.cit., the saints together with the angels are God's co-workers in the work of redemption (p. 134). They are both willing and able to assist us, not by their own power, but by the arm of God (p. 144). Thus, their powerful position to help us on our way of salvation by their providence of love and their intercessions, justifies our calling upon them. (p. 145)
199. The distinction latreia-dulia was officially introduced at the second council in Nicea 787 and later elaborated on in scholastic theology. (Klauser op.cit., p. 174, and Seeberg 1913, pp. 452–453). Cf. Adam who says that it is a main point in the preaching and theology of the Roman Catholic church that the veneration of angels and saints is in its essence different from the worship of God. (Op.cit., p. 144.)
     It should be noticed in this connection that prayer to the saints with corresponding veneration is not confined to the Roman Catholic church. A report of the Archbishops' Commission on Christian Doctrine from 1971 (*Prayer and the Departed*) makes it clear that the Anglican church is divided on the issue.
200. Our analysis of the Roman Catholic position is at this point based mainly upon booklets aimed at ordinary Catholic believers and new converts. There is no elaborate theological treatise among these. However, the content of catechetical material produced with the definite purpose of elementary guidance, may be regarded as basic.
201. Christiaens 1975B, p. 562.
202. Ibid., p. 562.
203. Ibid., p. 562. Cf. also how the traditional doctrines on the saints and the purgatory are presented as the two main points of contact with ancestor worship in Christiaens' booklet *Katorikku no sosen sukei* (Catholic Veneration of Ancestors), 1976, pp. 9–11.
204. Christiaens 1975B, pp. 562–563.
205. «Accordingly, the believer does not only venerate all these [saints], but he may ask for their protection and solicit their intermediation.» (Christiaens 1976, p. 9. Our own translation.) His distinction *suhai – sukei* is mentioned in a special note on the same page.

206. *Kirisuto to warera no misa* (Christ and our Mass), undated but in use in the 1970's, pp. 6, 52.
207. Christiaens 1976, p. 9. (Our own translation.) Re a similar calling upon both saints and ancestors of departed Christians for help and protection in an African Roman Catholic context, see the prayers in Kumbirai's controversial funeral liturgy, Daneel op.cit., p. 61.
208. Ibid., pp. 20–21. Cf. Christiaens 1975B: «Among them [the innumerable uncannonized saints] are certainly some of our ancestors, even if they did not belong to a Christian Church in their earthly lives.» (p. 563.)
209. According to the text the offering of incense is not compulsory but may be done. (*Kirisuto to warera no misa*, p. 4.)
210. «Kore wa shukyoteki sonkei no koi de aru....» (Ibid., p. 4.)
211. «Ko o tsukau no wa, seirei no shinden de aru shisha no karada ni tai suru sonkei o arawsu tame no mono desu». (*Sogi no shiori* 1971/1974, p. 4.)
212. Ibid., p. 35.
213. Ibid., p. 55.
214. See re early critique Lucius op.cit., pp. 325–336: «Gegner und Gönner des Märtyrerkultus», and Grüneisen op.cit., who refers to later voices of criticism. The best known of the early Christian critics is presbyter Vigilantius of Barcelona in the beginning of the 5th century. He objected strongly to the cult of the martyrs, contending that none of the departed Christians were related to the living in a way that justified man's calling upon them, and he rejected the popular honoring of relics as idolatry. (Lucius op.cit., pp. 328–329; Grüneisen op.cit., p. 710.)
215. In the Lutheran confessional writings at the time of the Reformation, we find the reformers dealing with the saints, e.g., *Confessio Augustana*, Article XXI and the *Apology*, Article XXI.
216. «Vom Heiligendienst wird von den Unseren also gelehret, dass man der Heiligen gedenken soll, auf dass wir unsern Glauben stärken, so wir sehen, wie ihnen Gnad widerfahren, auch wie ihnen durch Glauben geholfen ist; darzu, dass man Exempel nehme von ihren Guten werken, ein jeder nach seinem Beruf....» (Bekenntnisschriften op.cit., p. 83b.)
217. «Durch Schrift aber mag man nicht beweisen, dass man die Heiligen anrufen oder Hilf bei ihnen suchen soll.... Das ist auch der hochste Gottesdienst nach der Schrift, dass man denselbigen Jesum Christum in allen Noten und Anliegen von Herzen suche und anrufe....» (Ibid., pp. 83b–83c.)
218. «In unser Confession leugnen wir nicht, dass man die Heiligen ehren soll». (Ibid., p. 317.)
219. Ibid., p. 318.
220. «Wir reden hie noch nicht von groben Misbräuchen, ... wir reden, was ihre Gelehrten von diesem Stücke predigen, schreiben und in ihren Schulen lehren». (Ibid., pp. 319–320.)
221. This is especially pointed out in relation to the doctrine on the superfluous merits of the saints, which implies that one makes «aus den Heiligen nicht allein Fürbitter, sondern Mittler und Versühner.» (Ibid., p. 319.) However much the Confutation distinguishes between mediators who pray for us, and the one mediator who has redeemed us, «so machen sie doch aus den heiligen

Mittler....» (p. 319.)

222. Ibid., p. 319.
223. Through such a teaching «so wird doch Christus und seine Wohltat ...unterdrückt, und vertrauen da auf die Heiligen, da sie auf Christum vertrauen sollten.» (Ibid., p. 319.)
224. Ibid., p. 320.
225. Ibid., p. 324. The Anglican report *Prayer and the Departed* referred to above, gives a series of examples of how this Protestant critique of the traditional veneration of saints won wide acceptance in the Anglican church in the 16th century.
226. A short comment is necessary on the practice of bowing and offering incense to the coffin in the same way as to the altar in the funeral service, on the account that the corpse is the sanctuary of the Holy Spirit. One thing is that such a practice – in a setting where people are accustomed to dead human beings being honored like *kami* and *hotoke* – seems well-suited to give the impression that the same is the case with the dead in Christian thinking. Another thing is that the reason given seems theologically untenable. There is no scriptural basis for paying religious homage to man bacause of the Holy Spirit who dwells in him. To us the reason given for this practice sounds more like a theological attempt to justify a custom which – after all – may have been adopted because of other considerations. It is interesting in this connection to notice that Fr. Maruyama, in his little pamphlet *Katorikku no sogi to sosen suhai* (Catholic Funeral and Ancestor Worship), says that Catholics pay respect to the spirit of the departed because of its immortality. (Maruyama 1958, p. 1.)
227. No comprehensive review of Protestant churches is attempted. We focus on some representative writings from within the United Church of Christ, the Japan Evangelical Lutheran Church, and the Presbyterian Church in Japan.
228. Lutheran Church 1966/1967[2], p. 108. (Our own translation.)
229. Re the «encoffinment»: «... Cross, flowers and the like may be used, but not offerings to the dead, and one should be careful lest the atomsphere expresses in any way worship towards the dead.» (Ibid., p. 109.) Re the funeral-service: «... and when a photo is used, one may express respect and love to the dead, but one should be careful lest this develops into worship.» (p. 110.) Re the memorials: «...one may well make an altar in the home where a Bible and a cross may be put together with photos.... However, one must always take care lest it develops into idolatrous worship». (pp. 111–112. Our own translation.)
230. *Shinto hikkei* 1976, p. 105. (Our own translation.) Cf. pp. 106–107 where there are similar warnings as in the Lutheran handbook that «one should not worship».

231. Special mention should be made of the widely circulated popular magazine of the United Church of Christ, *Shinto no tomo*, which stresses this need both in the special issue on Christian ceremonial occasions, November 1971, and on death and the funeral in November 1975. The 1971 issue says that since both in Shinto and Buddhism the deceased is an object of worship in the

funeral, but not in Christianity, this may easily cause misunderstanding in Japan. (p. 19.) In the 1975 issue, dealing with the problem of how to handle offerings brought by guests in the funeral, it says that these are to be handled properly. But an offering is a dedication of sacrifice and an act of worship, and – even if it is common in Japan – Christians do not deify or worship men. (p. 11.)

232. Because of the difference in manners and customs between Japan and the West, not least when it comes to ways of courtesy, some writers contend that foreign missionaries are apt to see religious homage where only human courtesy is intended and are not really competent to understand and answer to this central problem. (So, e.g., Hiyane op.cit., pp. 52–53, and Yamauchi op.cit., pp. 149–150.) There may well be a point in this. On the other hand, the problem is not so simple that the division of opinions runs along the dividing line between nationals and expatriates. Japanese Christians are not agreed among themselves in their understanding as to where the borderline has to be drawn, and the same is probably just as true for missionaries.

233. It should be observed, however, that such a farewell ceremony of flower-offering is not inserted into the official order of the funeral in the United Church of Christ, neither in the liturgies from 1950/1953 and 1959, nor in the private proposal given in *Shi to sogi*, 1974. In the latter it says: «In principle flower-offering farewell ceremony should rather not be held.» (Tamai 1959, pp. 104–105, and United Church of Christ 1974, p. 277. Our own translation.) Instead of flower-offering some local churches have adopted the Buddhist custom of offering incense at the farewell ceremony.

234. So Takayanagi, p. 63. A similar opinion is expressed by Lutheran pastor Yamauchi Rokuro: «At the vigil and the farewell ceremony there is the offering of incense. This is a custom mainly used in Buddhism, but it should not be wrong to use it also in the Christian church». (Yamauchi op.cit., p. 149. Our own translation.) Yamauchi justifies his position by saying that the original purpose of the use of incense was to take away the smell of death.

235. So Takasaki, pp. 77–78.

236. So, with minor individual differences, Yuki pp. 85–86; Matsumura p. 90; Saji p. 96; Matsumoto p. 101; and Tamai pp. 104–105.

237. Yamamoto 1974, p. 259. The same cautious approach rather preferring the abolishment of the practice, is taken in the two issues of *Shinto no tomo* referred to above. (11/1971, p. 20; 11/1975, p. 13.)

238. Obata 1976 No. 5, pp. 71–72. Obata mentions also the offering of *sakaki*-branches to the *kami*-spirit of the dead in Shinto funerals as a predecessor after which the Christian flower-offering may have been copied (p. 72). The same is done in *Shinto no tomo*, 1971 No. 11, p. 19.

239. See above, p. 253, note 123.

240. Kochi op.cit., p. 14. A proof that Protestants have consciously attempted to improve on this is, for example, United Church of Christ 1974, as we have referred to repeatedly.

241. See above, p. 141.

242. Doerner op.cit., pp. 158, 176.

243. See above, p. 138.

244. «Afterlife» is consciously put into quotation-marks. We use the term as a translation of the Japanese *shigo no sekai* (literally: «the world after death») and equivalents, and we have not passed any judgment upon the term's suitability in Christian perspective.
245. Ooms op.cit., p. 286.
246. Hiyane op.cit., pp. 40–41.
247. Kochi op.cit., p. 14.
248. Quoted from Ōmiya 1974, p. 94. (Translation ours.) This decision of 418 is also referred to by Obata in his discussion on the meaning of death, Obata 1974, No. 10, p. 25.
249. Wächter op.cit., pp. 9, 128.
250. Ibid., p. 203. «Weder der irgendwann erfolgte Tod Adams noch die Sterblichkeit des Menschen werden als Strafe Gottes verstanden». (p. 203) This is Wächter's conclusion on his exegetical considerations over Gn. 2 and 3. He concedes that this is a conclusion that can be arrived at only «wenn man die Literarkritik zu Hilfe nimmt» (p. 202). By the use of literary criticism he manages to reduce the motif of the tree-of-life into only marginal significance not really playing any rôle in the context.
251. Althaus 1962, p. 918. This article of Althaus is very instructive on this view of death in later Protestant theology.
252. Ibid., p. 917.
253. Ibid., p. 916.
254. Ibid., pp. 915–916.
255. Ibid., p. 917.
256. Althaus seems to be more driven by a desire to come to terms with the predicament into which he feels traditional Christian theology has been put by modern science, which has proven death to be a reality in creation long before man and sin entered the scene: «Der immer wieder unternommene Versuch jener Herleitung [of death from sin] ist als Spekulation gnostischer Art abzulehnen. Er bringt die Theologie und das Christliche Denken...in einen unheilbaren Konflikt mit den klaren Erkenntnissen der Naturwissenschaft – der Tod im biologischen Sinne geht dem Auftreten des Menschen unendliche Zeiten voraus....» (Ibid., p. 917.) Althaus obviously points at an important problem. According to Gn. 1 man's dominion over creation, implying its use of it for food, seems, without further reflection, to presuppose biological death in nature as an order of creation. How such an original function of death in nature is related to that of death in the actual corrupted world of sin, of which Paul says that the whole creation is «groaning in travail» and waits for its liberation from its bondage to decay (Rom. 8, 18–21.), is a problem into which we cannot enter here. The point which is important to make in our concern with the death of man, is that we do not find scriptural evidence to maintain that even for man – created in the image of God for God-fellowship – death was an original and natural element of the order of creation.
257. Cf. Schmid 1962A, p. 912.
258. Vriezen 1956, p. 174. «Es verhält sich also nach diesem Zeugnis so, dass dem Menschen auf Grund der Sünde des Ungehorsams, der Eigenmächtigkeit, der

Hybris die Möglichkeit des Zugangs zum Lebensbaum genommen ist. Der Tod ist Strafe für die Sünde des Menschen.... Der Mensch wollte nicht als Kind bei Gott leben, sondern sich selbst ihm gegenüber behaupten. Und diese Ursünde brachte der Tod über ihn.» (pp. 174–175.)

259. Quell 1925/1967², p. 36.
260. Cf. B. Reicke in his excellent little article on death in the New Testament: «Er [Christ] hat die uralte Verbindung von Sünde und Tod gelöst, indem er beide auf sich nahm, ohne selbst von Sünde belastet zu sein». (Reicke 1962, p. 914.)
261. For such a position see O. Cullmann's chapter «The wages of sin: Death» in his little, much debated book *Immortality of the Soul or Resurrection of the Dead?*, 1958: «Death is not something natural, willed by God.... It is rather something unnatural, abnormal, opposed to God.» (p. 28) A recent contribution from the same position in Scandinavian context is A. Valen-Sendstad, 1979: «Therefore is death nothing *natural* for the Christian in the meaning that it is something *original*. On the contrary, it is the wages of sin (Rom. 6,23) and the last enemy (1 Cor. 15,26).» (p. 371. Our own translation.)
262. Althaus op.cit., p. 918.
263. Kashiwai op.cit., pp. 18–19.
264. Ibid., p. 32.
265. Matsunaga 1974, pp. 63, 68. The same emphasis on death as such as wages of sin is further found in Kochi 1969, p. 18; Obata 1974, No. 10, pp. 23–26; and in more popular terms in *Shinto no tomo* 1975, No. 11, pp. 4–5, where this dreadful aspect of death is compared to a tendency in Japan to beautify death.
266. This is strongly emphasized with particular reference to the Pauline literature in Paul Hoffmann's comprehensive study *Die Toten in Christus*, 1966/1978³. Hoffmann talks of what he calls a «Christologisierung» and « Personalisierung» in Paul of his inherited eschatological expectations (p. 311), and shows how all anthropological and apocalyptic speculations find in Paul a radical theological and christological reduction and concentration (pp. 340–341).
267. Cf. Cullmann op.cit., pp. 41–42 for this tension between the victory over death already and decisively inaugurated in Christ and yet only inaugurated. Cf. also Hoffmann who concludes his study by saying that the present history, according to Paul, is determined by two poles: the resurrection of Christ as the first among the dead, and the final destruction of death yet to come. (Hoffmann op.cit., p. 344.)
268. Kumano 1959, p. 109.
269. The same purely other-worldly-oriented perspective of salvation after death is presented in Fr. Maruyama's little pamphlet on Catholic funeral and ancestor worship. (Maruyama 1958.)
270. Horikoshi 1973. Horikoshi makes a brief sketch of what he calls «the world-view of the Bible» without mentioning the resurrection of the body. (Op.cit., pp. 8–10.)
271. Yamauchi 1973, pp. 159–164. Especially the prayer to be used at the crematory is saturated by faith in the resurrection of the body (p. 167).
272. Ibid., p. 129. (Our own translation.)
273. Ibid., p. 130. (Our own translation.)

274. *Sogi no shiori*, 1971/1974, p. 1.
275. Nemeshegyi 1972, p. 104.
276. Murakami 1972/1974[2], p. 120. (Our own translation.) Examples may be multiplied. Just as we found both Episcopalian Kochi and Presbyterian Obata to be strong in their emphasis on death as wages of sin we find both equally and emphatically stating the Christian hope over against death in eschatological terms of the resurrection. According to Obata, Christianity is assured of a world to come, not, however, in vague terms of the immortality of the soul, but in terms of resurrection of the body. (Obata 1975, No. 9, pp. 66–67. Cf. Kochi op.cit., pp. 18–20.)
277. Anyone who is to some extent familiar with Christian theology knows something about the vast amount of literature this problem has produced, both in the long history of doctrine as well as in contemporary theology. After the war a renewed, lively discussion was triggered by Cullmann's little book on immortality or resurrection already referred to, and a very interesting survey of the modern debate on death and immortality in Protestant theology – seen through Roman Catholic glasses – is given in Ahlbrecht 1964. In Japanese context we may refer again to Omiya 1974 for historical perspectives, and to Culpepper 1975, especially chapter IV: «Unresolved Issues», for an interesting contribution to the debate.
278. Maruyama op.cit., p. 1. (Our own translation.)
279. Horikoshi op.cit., p. 5. (Our own translation.)
280. Ibid., p. 7. The grouping together of these three authors does not mean that we presume they will agree on an elaborate anthropology. We bring them together only because they all – from their different positions – put heavy emphasis on a doctrine of the immortality of the soul.
281. At this point theologians of very different positions are unanimous. According to Cullmann op.cit., death is to «die in body and soul, lose life itself» (p. 26), since «both [body and soul] belong together, both are created by God.» (p. 33) H. Thielicke talks of man «als einer Personganzheit, bei der eine Aufteilung des Menschen nach Leib und Seele nicht vollziehbar ist», with the consequence that one has to talk «von dem totalen Sterben des Menschen». (Quoted from Künneth 1951, p. 235.) Künneth agrees with Thielicke as far as the basis for this idea of an intermediate state «liegt also nicht, worin wir Thielicke zustimmen, im Menschen selbst, nicht in der unsterblichen Seele, nicht in einer Ichteilung....» (Ibid., p. 236.) Cf. in Scandinavian context Valen-Sendstad 1979: «The fact that the Bible talks of an intermediate state is not a contradiction of the thought that it is *the total man* who dies. Not only *a part* of man dies (e.g. the body), while *another* continues its existence (e.g. the soul). Death comprehends man as a whole». (p. 373. Our own translation.)
282. Cf. Vriezen op.cit.: «Gn. 2f lehrt, dass nach Gottes Willen dem Menschen im Anfang die Möglichkeit des ewigen Lebens durch die Frucht des Lebensbaumes geschenkt war.... Von Diesem Lebensbaum jedoch ist der Mensch als Folge seiner Sünde entfernt werden.» (p. 174) This interpretation of the tree-of-life motif seems to us to be a more convincing exegesis of the actual text than Wächter's reduction of its significance by the use of literary

criticism.

283. This point is developed and emphasized in Valen-Sendstad 1979, pp. 373–374: «When the Bible talks of *resurrection*... it shows that God's upholding applies even to the body, not only to the soul. If the body were obliterated and annihilated, it would be meaningless to talk of resurrection.» (p. 373. Our own translation.)

284. We agree to a large extent with Culpepper in his critique of the consequences which Cullmann seems to draw of man's total death, as we shall see below. According to Culpepper «the New Testament view of the resurrection of the dead must be distinguished carefully from the Greek doctrine of the immortality of the soul...but however carefully one makes the distinction the doctrine of the resurrection of the dead alone is not enough. Some sort of view of immortality is needed to support it.» (Op.cit., p. 64) Thus far we may agree. When Culpepper, however, infers that such a sort of immortality has to be «some kind of...survival of the inner man, the soul, or the spirit...for the interim between the death of the individual and the final resurrection» (p. 64), we disagree. Such a limitation of the «view of immorality» to man's soul/spirit seems to us to be based on a common but unbiblical assumption that what may be uphold through death is man's soul and not his body. Thereby the bodily continuity between the man who dies and the man who rises is rejected. To us the only position possible seems to be to maintain the radical tension of the simultaneity between total man's mortality and «immortality» as delineated above.

285. Hoffmann op.cit., p. 334.

286. Murakami op.cit., p. 118. (Translation ours.)

287. Christiaens 1975B, p. 563. Cf. Christiaens 1976, pp. 10–11, where the purgatory-idea is used in the same way. This parallel between Japanese indigenous ideas of a growth of the soul after death and the Roman Catholic teaching on the purgatory, is further pointed to in Ooms op.cit., p. 287, and in Watanabe op.cit., pp. 107–108.

288. Althaus in the 4th edition of *Die Letzten Dinge*, quoted from Künneth op.cit., pp. 234–235.
Ahlbrecht shows how this position of Althaus is very close to that of other outstanding representatives of modern Protestant theology. Younger Barth, in his concern for the eschatological character of the here and now, showed little interest for the time-dimension and the successiveness of eschatology, and has no room for an intermediate state. (Ahlbrecht op.cit., pp. 89–90.) In this respect Bultmann carried further Barth's early position toward an «Entzeitlichung der Eschatologie». (Ibid., pp. 90–91.) Brunner, again, is very close to Althaus's conception of time-eternity, where an interval between death and resurrection is only real seen from this side of death, not from the other. (Ibid., p. 106.)

289. So Thielicke, who doubts whether Althaus's «theologische Geschlossenheit» does justice to biblical thinking: «Könnte es nicht sein, dass die Geschlossenheit [of Althaus's system] zugleich eine Verengung bedeutet gegenüber dem Reichtum und der strömenden Fülle biblischer Aussagen?» (Quoted from

Künneth op.cit., p. 235.) Künneth sees Althaus' approach «offenbar genom-
men aus den logischen Prinzipien der Philosophie und den Grundsätzen einer
Zeitlosigkeitsmetaphysik», an approach that does not come to terms with the
«Stufenfolge» in biblical eschatology. (Ibid., p. 235.)

290. Ahlbrect shows how this has already been pointed out as a weak point in
Althaus. When the universal «Vollendung» is related to the particular death
of each individual, it is not a far step to view the eschatological hope as
something «jenseits» this world. This conclusion is drawn by Althaus-disciple
H. Grass, who has no longer room for the resurrection but sees the hope in
«einem 'Jenseits' dieser Welt.» Ahlbrecht concludes that whereas Althaus
started out wanting to take resurrection and universal consummation seriously, the consequence of his approach turns out the opposite. (Ahlbrecht
op.cit., p. 108.)

291. Quoted from Ahlbrecht op.cit., p. 128, who refers to Althaus' paper
«Retraktationen zur Eschatologie», given at the »evangelischen deutschen
Theologentag» in 1950. That Althaus, after all, is not so consistent with regard
to the consequences of man's total death as presentations of his view often
give the impression of becomes clear when we notice that in the first editions
of *Die Letzten Dinge* we do not find such «eine runde Ablehnung» (Schreiner
op.cit., p. 260) of the intermediate state as in later editions. At this early stage
he may say: «Dass er [God] Wege vielleicht auch jenseits des Todes hat, sich
seine Kinder zu rufen, wird nicht bestritten.» Such a «Mittelzustand», however, «ist...unseren Blick verhüllt. Gottes Handeln mit den Abgerufenen bleibt
Geheimnis.» (Althaus op.cit. pp. 236–237.)

292. For brief introductions to the idea of the purgatory, its phenomenological
parallels, historical development, and dogmatic significance, see Hofmann
1879; Schmidt-Clausing 1958; and Adam op.cit., pp. 126–131.
We are well aware of the fact that traditionally the purgatory does not relate
to all the dead inasmuch as it is only one of the five «rooms» where the dead
are thought to be. The purgatory is for those who are destined for heaven,
and with reference to the dead in purgatory one may therefore speak of the
ecclesia patiens. This is, however, at least in Japanese context today, given an
interpretation in so wide and general terms that the purgatory-idea for all
practical purposes presents itself as the relevant Roman Catholic response
when the problem of the actual state of the dead is approached from the point
of view of ancestor worship. This will be clear in a later chapter.

293. Christiaens 1975B, p. 563.

294. See Schmidt-Clausing op.cit., p. 893, with reference to H. Schmaus.

295. Ibid., p. 893.

296. Ibid., p. 893.

297. Nemeshegyi op.cit., p. 106, in his commentary to *Katorikku nyumon* (Catholic Catechism) 1971/1975, p. 208.

298. Adam op.cit., pp. 126–127. (Translation ours.)

299. Ibid., p. 127.

300. Ibid., p. 129. (Translation ours.)

301. Whether the suffering in purgatory is to be regarded only as «satispassio» in
terms of fulfilment of penance, or also as an atonement for venial sins, seems

to us not to be quite clear. Nemeshegyi underscores that also for the daily sins (venial sins) – and not only for mortal sins – man is dependent upon God's forgiveness (op.cit., p. 75), and Ahlbrecht arrests Althaus for a «weithin übliche Misverständnis vom Purgatorium», because the latter – in Ahlbrecht's view – does not seem to know that the Catholic doctrine on the purgatory «nur von einem Aus*leiden* (satis*passio*) der Sünden*strafen*...spricht.» (Ahlbrecht op.cit., p. 111.) We purposely choose, however, to speak also of an atonement for venial sins. If this is a misunderstanding of Roman Catholic doctrine, it seems to us, namely, that the Catholic presentation of the idea is not without responsibility. In Japan the purgatory may be presented as «an intermediate state of purification for those who still have sins to atone for before going to heaven.» (Doerner op.cit., p. 158.)

302. Adam op.cit., p. 128. (Translation ours.)
303. This approach is dominating in Luther's «Widerruf vom Fegefeuer», 1530. (WA Vol. 30[II], pp. 367–390.) Here Luther treats the various scriptural texts usually given in support of the purgatory, starting out with its locus classicus in apocryphal 2 Macc. 12,41–45, and shows how the Roman Catholic interpretation cannot be maintained without either a serious twisting of the actual text, or a making of inferences that are nowhere explicitly stated.
304. Bekenntnisschriften p. 420, from the *Smalcald Articles*, part II, article 2, where it says concerning the purgatory: «Drumb ist Fegfeuer mit allem seinem Gepränge, Gottesdienst und Gewerbe fur ein lauter Teufelsgespenst zu achten; denn es ist auch wider den Häuptartikel, dass allein Christus und nicht Menschenwerk den Seelen helfen soll, ohn dass sonst auch uns nichts von den Toten befohlen noch gepoten ist....» See also the *Apology*, Article XII, pp. 252–291.
305. Althaus op.cit., p. 226.
306. Cullmann op.cit., p. 51.
307. Ibid., p. 54.
308. Culpepper op.cit., p. 65.
309. Künneth op.cit., p. 237. Such an upholding of all people for final resurrection and judgment is no new idea in the New Testament. It was present already in pre-Christian Judaism, as may be seen in the Book of Henoch, and was carried further in rabbinic writings in the first centuries A. D. This is important to keep in mind when one reads the New Testament passages just mentioned. See to this point in the Jewish background of the New Testament, Hoffmann op.cit., pp. 105–111, 170–174.
310. A thorough and convincing exegesis of this text is given in Hoffmann op.cit., pp. 286–320, where the conclusion is that even if Paul does not know the term, the Christ-fellowship he talks of here must be seen as an intermediate state. (p. 313.) The same understanding is found in Cullmann op.cit., pp. 50–51, and in Norwegian context in Kvalbein 1969, p. 192: «Paul here talks of the community with Christ immediately following death as an obvious and undisputable reality.» (Translation ours.) What concerns the other main text which has traditionally been taken as a Pauline reference to the interme-diate state – 2 Cor. 5,1–10 – the exegesis seems much more problematic. Cullmann advocates the traditional view (op.cit., pp. 52–55), whereas both

Hoffmann (op.cit., pp. 253–285) and Kvalbein conclude that Paul here is not referring to the intermediate state but to the final consummation.

311. Re such an understanding of this text as a reference to the intermediate state, see Künneth op.cit., p. 238, and Cullmann op.cit., p. 50.

312. Hoffmann has again given a very valuable contribution to the understanding of the idea of «Todesschlaf» in the New Testament, op.cit., pp. 186–206. He concludes that nowhere in the New Testament is there any indication that the concept implies anything more than simply the act of dying, or the state of being dead. It does not intend to portray in any way the character of the state of being dead, not even does it say that Paul regards death «als ein Zustand der Ruhe» (pp. 205–206).

313. At this point it is interesting to note that Roman Catholic Hoffmann says there is nothing in the text to support the exegesis that Paul expected a special fate because of his martyrdom. This interpretation eventually developed in the Church and is seen first in Tertullian. (Op.cit., p. 290)

314. Künneth op.cit., p. 238.

315. Ibid., p. 238.

316. Ibid., p. 239, note 82.

317. Ibid., p. 239, note 82.

318. «Und wiewohl die Engel im Himmel fur uns bitten (wie Christus selber auch tut), also auch die Heiligen auf Erden oder vielleicht auch im Himmel, so folget daraus nicht....» (Bekenntnisschriften, p. 425.)

319. Ibid., p. 318.

320. This aspect of waiting is generally stressed by theologians who acknowledge the idea of the intermediate state. According to Cullmann, the perspective of waiting, of yet to come, is exactly the point when the New Testament talks of the dead as «sleeping»: «... he [the dead Christian] still 'sleeps' and still awaits the resurrection of the body, which alone will give him full life....» (Op.cit., p. 55.) Cf. Künneth op.cit., p. 239, and Kvalbein op.cit., p. 192.

321. This is what Murakami seems to do in his answer to the question quoted on p. 185 above. The main point in his answer is that life everlasting starts here and now through faith in Christ and is brought to fulfilment with the parousia and final resurrection. Referring to the crucified criminal he says that «he experienced an instantaneous participation in salvation on the cross. He did not go to heaven after death, but was made a man of the heavenly kingdom while still in this world. There was no need for him to sleep for a long time after death....» (Murakami op.cit., p. 119. Translation ours.) How ever important this may be, it seems to be a dodging of the actual problem the question raises.

322. See Rissi 1962, pp. 59–66. Re the importance of prayers and good works for the sake of the dead in later Middle Eastern and European Judaism, see Zenner 1965.

323. This particular practice of the church is mentioned in Agency for Cultural Affairs 1972, p. 220. Iesu no Mitama Kyokai is an indigenous and fast-growing church, in the above-mentioned book characterized as a «sect» which «claims to restore the true church as it existed in primitive Christianity.» (p. 220.)

324. The author has a few notes from the short but very interesting interview. Our plan to record a more extensive conversation did not materialize due to great difficulties in obtaining a second interview with Murai.
325. See Rissi op.cit., pp. 6–51 for an interesting survey of its history of interpretation.
326. Ibid., pp. 7–8. A similar spiritual interpretation is found already in Tertullian and also in Augustine. (Ibid., pp. 10–11.)
327. Ibid., pp. 11–12. According to Rissi, the situation in the old Church seems to have been that gnostic wishes to help the dead have used the unclear reference in 15,29 so that vicarious baptism developed in some circles with apparent apostolic sanction. (Ibid., p. 67.) Also J. Jeremias sees the gnostic vicarious baptisms as practices which «evidently have their origin in a misinterpretation of our verse itself.» (Jeremias 1955/56, p. 155.)
328. Ibid., p. 14.
329. Ibid., p. 17.
330. For advocates of this view see, for example, Rissi op.cit., and Odeberg 1944.
331. The former position is taken by Rissi (op.cit., p. 90), the latter by Odeberg (op.cit., p. 290).
332. Beasley-Murray 1962/1972, p. 189. See re this, however, Jeremias op.cit., pp. 155–156, where Jeremias points out that in whole chapter 15 Paul consistently uses *hoi nekroi* for departed Christians, and *nekroi* for the dead in general. *hyper ton nekron* in v. 29 is therefore, says Jeremias, a reference to departed Christians.
333. For this reason Beasley-Murray rejects this position saying that even though one limits «the dead» to catechumens or family-members this objection remains valid. (Op.cit., p. 189.) Odeberg does not discuss this crucial problem at all. Rissi's position is unacceptable to us simply because he – on the other hand – does not reject only a magical understanding, but fails to come to terms with the sacramental understanding of baptism in Paul. He regards baptism as a «Bekenntnis des Gehorsamswillens». (Op.cit., p. 83) Vicarious baptism to Rissi therefore means only a vicarious confession of faith on behalf of the dead: «Der Täufer, der stellvertretende Täufling und die Gemeinde wollten mit dieser Taufe zeichenhaft bekennen: wir glauben an die Auferstehung dieses Toten, für den diese Taufe geschiet....» (Op. cit., p. 89)
334. For a thorough and well-documented presentation of this view, see Beasley-Murray op.cit., pp. 185-192.
335. Beasley-Murray op.cit., p. 187.
336. Ibid., p. 190.
337. Ibid., p. 190.
338. See Raeder 1955, pp. 258–260, and Jeremias op.cit., pp. 154-156. According to Jeremias, Raeder «has, in my opinion, solved the riddle of this crucial verse, taking up an exegesis which was propounded in the eighteenth century». (Op.cit., p. 155.)
339. Raeder op.cit., p. 259; Jeremias op.cit., p. 156.
340. Jeremias op.cit., p. 156.
341. This interpretation is rejected by Beasley-Murray because «despite Jeremias' careful presentation of the argument... it demands the insertion of too much

that has been left unexpressed.» (Op.cit., p. 186.) On the other hand we have the noted contemporary Roman Catholic authority on Pauline theology on baptism, R. Schnackenburg, who has cautiously accepted Raeder/Jeremias' arguments and changed his former position. In his dissertation *Das Heilsgeschehen bei der Taufe nach dem Apostel Paulus*, 1950, pp. 90–98, Schnackenburg sees *hyper ton nekron* as referring to a vicarious baptism. In the revised English edition from 1964 – *Baptism in the Thought of Paul* – he concedes, however, with reference to Raeder/Jeremias that «it may well be that an exegetical solution has been found which, in a simple and yet convincing way, settles an old *crux interpretum*.» (p. 102) Cf. also E. Schlink 1970, p. 718, note 83.

342. Nemeshegyi, op.cit., p. 102. Cf. *Katorikku nyumon* op. cit., pp. 202–203.

343. *Katorikku nyumon* op.cit., p. 203.

344. *Kirisuto to warera no misa*, pp. 29–30. For the occasion when the mass is offered for the sake of one particular departed person (*shisha misa*/mass for the dead) a special prayer is inserted on pp. 31–32. This conception of the Holy Mass as an offering for the dead combined with intercession on their behalf is further evident in the alternative dedication prayers listed in the back of the booklet, pp. 50–68.

345. Maruyama op.cit., p. 6. (Translation ours.) If the family so wishes, the frequency of the mourning masses may be synchronized with the traditional Buddhist pattern. (Ibid., p. 6.)

346. Suzuki 1974, pp. 70–71.

347. *Sogi no shiori* op.cit., p. 48, similar p. 78. (Translation ours.)

348. Ibid., p. 61. (Translation ours.)

349. See Rietschel 1952[2], pp. 231–258. To the development of intercession and Holy Mass for the dead in the old and medieval Church see also Dix 1945/1970, pp. 495–511.

350. Rietschel op.cit., pp. 268, 276, 280.

351. Dix op.cit., p. 507.

352. Dix. op.cit., p. 507; Rietscel op.cit., p. 327.

353. Dix op.cit., p. 499, where reference is made to a supposed discussion on the matter in Jerusalem in pre-Nicean times.

354. Rietschel op.cit., pp. 761–762.

355. Ibid., pp. 761–763.

356. For examples of old liturgical prayers for dead Christians together with the offering of the mass for their benefit, see Schierse 1975, pp. 151-158.

357. Rietschel op.cit., pp. 353, 764. We notice that the intercessions – both for living and for dead – were removed from the eucharist-liturgy already in Luther's German Mass of 1526.

358. Note that many evangelical funeral liturgies from the 17th century are introduced with a word on the meaning and purpose of the rite: It is of no use to the dead but a witness to the faith in the resurrection and the consolation coming thereof. (Rietschel op.cit., pp. 766–768.)

359. Quotation from Sundkler 1960, p. 291. Descensio Christi and/or the crucial texts in 1 Peter are brought into the missiological discussion of Christianity's approach to ancestor worship in both African and Asian contexts. Re the

African discussion see Sundkler op.cit., pp. 290–294, and Mosothoane op.cit., pp. 94–95. In his book on the significance of the old Batak «Lebensord-nungen» for the church in Indonesia, Schreiner discusses the relevancy of these aspects in two chapters on «Die Christusgemeinschaft der Vor-Christen und die Hadesvorstellung» and «Der Heilsuniversalismus». Schreiner op.cit., pp. 261–266. As for Japan an editorial article in the November issue, 1975, of *Shinto no tomo* quotes 1 Peter 3,19, saying that this text is the Bible's testimony that «Christ is still working on the unsaved souls», and that the living's duty in this regard is «personally to intercede in prayer» on their behalf. (p. 7. Our own translation.)

360. We are well aware of the fact that the doctrine of descensio Christi is not dependent only upon 1 Peter 3, 18 ff. However, since we cannot take up this problem in all its complicatedness, we will approach the descensio-idea from the point of view of its relationship to this crucial pericopee in 1 Peter 3. For an extensive introduction to the history of interpretation of 1 Peter 3, 19 and of Christ's descensus ad inferos we refer to the two monographs Reicke 1946 and Bieder 1949 respectively. A brief presentation of the three main types of interpretation of descensio Christi – Christ's victory over death and Hades, Christ's liberation of the dead, Christ's proclamation in the underworld – is given in Reicke 1957.

361. We shall not enter into the discussion as to whether 3,19 refers to an activity of Christ between his death and resurrection, or whether it is something which takes place after his resurrection and thus, rather than being referred to as «descensio Christi», should be related to his ascension.

362. See note 359.

363. For a recent and typical example see Goppelt 1978, pp. 246–254, 276–278. From a Norwegian point of view it is interesting to notice that Prof. S. Odland in his extensive article «Kristi prædiken for 'aanderne i forvaring' (1 Pet. 3,19)» advocates this understanding of the verses. (Odland 1901, pp. 116-141, 185–229.) The same interpretation is maintained in Odland 1927.

364. Goppelt op.cit., p. 254. Cf. Odland 1901, pp. 186, 217–218, for the same point of view.

365. Goppelt op.cit., p. 254.

366. Ibid., pp. 276, 278.

367. Ibid., p. 276. Cf. Odland op.cit., pp. 226–227. Now, the question whether also for the dead the gospel retains its «Verborgenheit» – as it has for the living – and thus makes a «Glaubensentscheidung» possible is, according to Goppelt, left open together with all other «Bemühen um Vorstellbarkeit.» (Ibid., pp. 277–278.)

368. Reicke 1946, p. 69. Bieder seems to accept Reicke's position that one has to think of both demonic powers and human beings under the overriding motive of the fallen angels. (Bieder op.cit., pp. 112-113.) So also Selwyn 1946, p. 199.

369. So Kelly 1969/1976, who says that there is «a growing conviction among scholars» at this point. (p. 153) Likewise France op.cit., p. 270, and Schelkle op.cit., pp. 106-107.

370. Goppelt op.cit., pp. 248–249. When Goppelt rejects the thought of the fallen angels on this account, however, his argument is based upon an understanding

of *keryssein* that is not necessarily correct, as we shall see.

371. See France op.cit., p. 271; Selwyn op.cit., p. 200; and Kelly op.cit., p. 156.

372. Reicke 1946, p. 120. Selwyn, Kelly, and France are all – with some nuances – of the same opinion. (Selwyn op. cit., p. 200; Kelly op.cit., p. 156; France op.cit., p. 271.)

373. So Bieder op.cit., pp. 122-127.

374. Reicke 1946, pp. 204–205.

375. Ibid., pp. 208–209. The «underlying principle» is «that the Gospel is to be communicated to all beings so that the judgment can be performed on the basis of everybody's attitude to the Gospel». (p. 209.) This, after all, is the same «underlying principle» as we found in Goppelt and Odland.

376. Goppelt op.cit., p. 276.

377. So Selwyn op.cit., pp. 214, 337–339; Kelly op.cit., p. 174; and France op.cit., pp. 269, 280.

378. Quotation from Künneth op.cit., p. 237. That Lutheran theologians draw different conclusions at this point is obvious if we compare this position of Künneth with that of Prenter. According to the latter, any «speculations about a particular proclamation and conversion after death is completely superfluous». (Prenter op.cit., p. 604. Our own translation.) Rom. 2,14-16 shows, according to Prenter, that the Scriptures conceive of a righteous judgment of God without having to speculate along these lines. (pp. 604–605.)

379. Cf. Luther's stand on the problem, made plain in «Ein Sendbrief über die Frage, ob auch jemand, ohne Glauben verstorben, selig werden möge», 1522: God does not save anybody except through faith; whether God may give this faith to people after death, is another problem; who would deny that he can? It can never be proved, however, that he does. (Luther 1522 in WA 10[II], pp. 318–326.) Note that this letter of Luther is translated into japanese by Suzuki Masahisa and published in Hiyane op.cit., pp. 126-134.

380. For a study of this aspect in New Testament theology, see Caird 1956, and Schlier 1958.

381. On the significance of the belief in Christ as victor in the African context see, e.g., Mbiti 1967, pp. 141-142, and Mbiti 1971, pp. 140 ff. On its significance in an Indonesian shamanistic context, see Schreiner op.cit., pp. 271–272.

382. The only passage in the New Testament «to which appeal has traditionally been made to support the practice of intercession for the dead« (*Prayer and the Departed*, op.cit., p. 27), is 2 Tim. 1,16ff: «...may the Lord grant him [Onesiphorus] to find mercy from the Lord on that day....» Such an understanding of this Pauline utterance, however, seems to us to be an overinterpretation of the text, which is to be regarded more as a pious wish of Paul mentioned in passing than as an explicit prayer to God for Onesiphorus.

383. Rietschel op.cit., p. 772.

384. Quoted after Rietschel op.cit., p. 773.

385. Ibid., p. 773. Note that the view of Luther and Calvin together with the later ambivalence in the German Lutheran churches at this point is presented in Japan in Suzuki 1959, and Kato 1974.

386. As in Matsumura op.cit., p. 90.

387. See Takasaki op.cit., p. 77, and Matsumoto Yoshimi op.cit. pp. 101-102.

388. Yamamoto op.cit., pp. 255, 260.
389. See the prayers for the coffining rite and the funeral by Fukuda and Kashiwai, pp. 281–291.
390. Murakami op.cit., p. 174.
391. Lutheran Church 1966/1976², p. 108. (Our own translation.)
392. Lutheran Church 1968, pp. 184-188. In the case of a child the prayer goes: «O God, your beloved Son received the small children and blessed them. Please keep the soul of this child in your merciful hands, and bestow upon us all....» (p. 187. Our own translation.)
393. Ibid., pp. 246–254.
394. Ibid., pp. 240, 244. (Our own translation.)
395. Lutheran pastor Yamauchi Rokuro, in his suggestions for the various funerary ceremonies, goes a far step further than the official liturgy on this point. Intercessions in terms of prayers for the protection of the soul on its voyage, and for its final repose appear repeatedly, and may be included in the funeral-service itself. (Yamauchi op.cit., pp. 130, 144, 150, 164.) In Yamauchi this creates an impossible ambiguity vis-à-vis the confident belief that the dead is already with the Lord in Heaven, which is also repeatedly expressed. (pp. 146-147.)
396. Kelly 1950/76³, p. 388. We shall not enter into the much debated problem whether «sanctorum» was originally understood in a masculine (communion of holy persons) or neuter (communion in holy things, i.e., the eucharistic elements) sense. Re this discussion see Kelly op.cit., pp. 388–397. Kelly himself advocates the first solution, an interpretation which has also been most commonly adopted in the West. Also in Japan the masculine understanding is chosen inasmuch as the clause is translated «seito (or: shoseito) no majiwari».
397. From the Lutheran funeral liturgy, Lutheran Church 1968, pp. 185-186. (Translation ours.) A similar emphasis on the fellowship with the dead is found in Fukuda's funerary prayers in United Church of Christ 1974, pp. 283, 287. Cf. also the mourning-prayer given in the Roman Catholic Sogi no shiori op.cit., p. 84.
398. Christiaens 1975B, p. 563.
399. Rietschel op.cit., p. 762. In this connection the practice occurred of having even the dead partake in the meal by placing the host in his/her mouth. (Ibid., p. 762.) Even though the church had to prohibit this practice, it is an interesting witness to the strong sense of community between the living and the dead in Christ as it is particularly expressed in the eucharist. This aspect of the eucharistic practices in the old Church is also pointed out in Kitamura 1974, p. 132.
400. Such is the text widely used in English-speaking churches, e.g. in the Anglican Book of Common Prayer (see Reindell 1955, p. 506), and in the Service Book of the American Lutheran Church. (Service Book and Hymnal 1958/1961⁵, p. 31.) It is equivalent to the Japanese text in the liturgy of the Japanese Evangelical Lutheran Church: «Yue ni watashitachi wa, tenshi to tenshi no osa, oyobi ten no gunshu to tomo ni, anata no eiko aru mina o hometatae, tsune ni Shu o agamete iimasu.» (Lutheran Church 1968, p. 18.)

401. Quoted from *An Order of Service for Worship and Communion in the Church of Norway*. In Norwegian the text goes: «Derfor lovsynger englene din herlighet, og din menighet i himmelen og på jorden priser ditt navn med samstemmig jubel. Med dem vil også vi forene våre røster....» (*Ny Høymesseliturgi*, 1977, p. 31.)
A parallel interpretation is given in post-Vatican II editions of the Roman Mass, particularly in the liturgy for All Soul's Day:
Father, all-powerful and ever-living God,
we do well always and everywhere to give you thanks.
Today we keep the festival of your holy city,
the heavenly Jerusalem, our mother.
Around your throne
the saints, our brothers and sisters,
sing you praise for ever.
Their glory fills us with joy,
and their communion with us in your Church
gives us inspiration and strength
as we hasten on our pilgrimage of faith,
eager to meet them.
With their great company and all the angels
we praise your glory
as we cry out with one voice: ....
(Roman Missal, 1974, p. 474.)

402. Reindell op.cit., p. 455.

403. As for the traditional Roman Mass see Reindell op.cit., pp. 481–488. For its Japanese text see *Kirisuto to warera no misa* op.cit., pp. 41–50. Before the present wording the Norwegian liturgy went as follows: «...The angels praise thy majesty and the Holy Seraphim join in lauding thy name. We would also join our voices....» (Alterbog 1893, p. 18. Our own translation.) H. Fæhn, in his study of the order of the worship service, points to the change in 1914 without giving any reasons for the adoption of the new wording. (Fæhn 1963/1968², p. 86.)

404. Cf. Reindell who says that at this point in the eucharist liturgy «die Anbetung nimmt die jenseitige Welt im Glauben vorweg!» (Reindell op.cit., p. 517.)

405. So the Church of Sweeden in Gudstjänstordning 1976, p. 27. (Translation ours.)

406. *Sogi no shiori* op.cit., p. 80. (Our own translation.)

407. Ibid., p. 84. (Our own translation.)

408. Lutheran Church 1968, p. 253. (Our own translation.)

409. «God created humanity as one body. Therefore there is a connection between ancestors and descendants that transcends time. For example: The people of the old covenant were saved because of the merits of Jesus Christ who came later on. Likewise, because of the merits of Jesus Christ the prayers of a Christian descendant have affects for the salvation of ancestors. Thus we may think that God, knowing beforehand of the faith and prayers of the descendant(s), bestows upon the ancestor(s) the grace that leads to salvation.» (Christiaens 1976, pp. 6–7. Our own translation.)

410. Ibid., p. 13. (Translation ours.)
411. Ibid., p. 19. (Translation ours.) This is said as an answer to the problem of whether even Catholics believe in ghosts (*muenbotoke*).
412. The same approach is found in Fr. Maruyama's pamphlet in his answer to the question whether the fate of a baptized Catholic after death will be another than that of his/her belowed non-Christian departed. No one should worry about this, says Maruyama, since the perfect communion with God after death is also a perfect and everlasting communion with one's close relatives, even if they happened to be non-Christians. (Maruyama op.cit., p. 10.)
413. Fasholé-Luke op.cit., p. 216.
414. Ibid., p. 217.
415. Ibid., p. 217.
416. Ibid., p. 220.
417. The lingering significance – with missiological ramifications – of basic principles in spite of legal and structural changes in family life is well illustrated if we look at the concept of *kacho*/househead. As stated above (p. 59) *kacho* no longer figures as a legal institution. Accordingly, in Doi 1960 the term *kazoku sekininsha* is used to denote the responsible, central person in the family. Whether this particular person is Christian or not is the criterion for whether the family is regarded as a «Christian home» or not. (Doi op.cit., pp. 47, 217.) In *Shinto no tomo* 11/1975 we still find the term *kacho* in use in the discussion on the Christian funeral (p. 8). In other words, whether the traditional concept is used or not, the idea for which it stands is still of actual importance.
418. Motoda 1928, p. 87. Motoda was at this time bishop of Tokyo in the Episcopal Church of Japan.
419. Quoted from Minear op.cit., p. 75.
420. Ibid., p. 76.
421. Sumiya 1954, especially the chapter «Nippon no kazokuseido to Kirisuto-kyo» («The Japanese Family-system and Christianity»), pp. 48–64, to which we shall return later.
422. Cf. Morioka's studies of the churches in Annaka, Shimamura, and Kusakabe, to which we have referred before. (Morioka 1976, pp. 65-194.) A brief, English presentation of these case studies is given in Morioka 1966.
423. «V. May we now ask you about the reactions of your family to your baptism or confirmation?» (LWF 1973–74, p. 42.)
424. Ibid., p. 34.
425. Ibid., p. 34.
426. Ibid., p. 35.
427. Magaki 1978, pp. 60–61. We shall return to Magaki's article below.
428. For a brief introduction to this tradition in German missiology and its critics, together with later developments in the debate, see Vicedom 1958, pp. 73–84.
429. Ibid., pp. 74–76.
430. Ibid., pp. 75–76.
431. Ibid., p. 81. «Dieses wurde aufs Neue angeregt durch die Arbeiten von MacGavran [Vicedom's spelling] und Sp. Trimmingham, welche nachweisen, dass die Kirche und die Mission nur dann in der Ausbreitung Erfolg haben können, wenn sie ihre Botschaft durch die natürlichen Kanäle wie Verwandts-

chaft und Freundschaft anbieten.... Dadurch entsteht nicht ein sozialer Bruch, der Bekehrte habe den Anschluss an seine Familie und Sippe, die Gemeinde werde von ihrer Grundung an eine soziale Grösse, die Geborgenheit vermittelt....» (p. 81.)

432. E.g., McGavran 1955, pp. 20–23.
433. See the paragraphs «People Movements» and «Kinds of People Movements and their Care» in McGavran 1980, pp. 333–372.
434. From the abundance of literature some typical and significant contributions should be mentioned. E. Brunner: *Das Gebot und die Ordnungen. Entwurf einer Protestantisch-Theologischen Ethik*, 1938. W. Elert: *Das Christliche Ethos*, 1949, especially the chapter «Die natürlichen Ordnungen», pp. 111-187. K. Barth: *Kirchliche Dogmatik III/4*, 1957, especially the chapters on «Mann und Frau» and «Eltern und Kinder», pp. 127–320, are illustrating to Barth's aversion for concepts like «Schöpfungsordnung». To the problem of «Naturrecht» and «Ordnung» with special reference to the change in family-structures in Euroupe, see H. Begemann: *Strukturwandel der Familie*, 1960/1966², especially the chapter «Das Naturrecht und die Familie in der Sicht evangelische Sozialethik», pp. 49–67. As for the particular discussion on the «Eigengesetzlichkeit» of the natural orders in modern Luther-research as well as for the importance of the problem of «Ordnungen» in modern European theology, see A. Hakamies: *«Eigengesetzlichkeit» der Natürlichen Ordnungen als Grundproblem der Neueren Lutherdeutung*, 1971.
435. «Gerade die für unseren Begriff von «Familie» so wichtige *Breite* des Geschlechtszusammenhanges hat schon im Alten Testament keinen Ton. Und noch weniger kann davon im Neuen Testament die Rede sein.... Das Geschlechtskollektiv als solches spielt schlechterdings keine Rolle mehr». (Barth 1957, p. 271.)
436. Ibid., p. 271.
437. Brunner 1932, pp. 278–279. Elert op.cit., p. 76. Cf. also Brunner 1938, pp. 165-167, where the author points to the fruitful interaction between individual and collective in Christian thinking, and says that to Christian faith really independent existence and really social existence are two sides of the same coin.
438. Barth 1957, pp. 127-128.
439. Above, p. 138. Doi op.cit., p. 49.
440. Brunner 1932, p. 195. Cf. Elert op.cit., pp. 65, 112.
441. Elert, op.cit., pp. 65, 111-114.
442. Trillhaas 1970³, pp. 316, 336.
443. Barth 1957, pp. 128, 269.
444. Ibid., pp. 156-157. Barth quotes Althaus' *Grundriss der Ethik*, 1931: «Und die Ehe ist die höchste Aufgabe persönlicher Gemeinschaft – niemand hat das Recht, sich ihr zu entziehen» (p. 157).
445. Ibid., p. 157.
446. Ibid., pp. 301, 157 for the two quotations respectively.
447. Ibid., pp. 157-158.
448. Ibid., p. 301.
449. Ibid., p. 205. Cf. p. 162.

450. To us there seems to be an unsolvable dilemma at this point in Barth's *Kirchliche Dogmatik*. On the one hand, he talks of man's «Generationsfolge» as belonging «zur Geschöpflichkeit des Menschen», on the other hand, he adopts an approach which never allows him to develop the significance and implications of this «Geschöpflichkeit».

451. Lutheran Church 1966/1967², p. 58.

452. *Shinto hikkei* 1976, p. 97. (Our own translation.)

453. Begemann op.cit., p. 112. Cf. Trillhaas who speaks of the «Elastizität der Familienordnung». On the one hand, the family may undergo sociological and structural changes. On the other hand, as «Urform des Gemeinschaftslebens» it survives somehow all changes, proving «eine unerhörte Regenerationsfähigket. Sie ist ein Ort, an dem uns Gott immer aufs Neue mit seiner Erhaltungsgnade begegnet». (Trillhaas op.cit., pp. 336–342.)

454. Cf. Brunner 1932, p. 321: «Wohl sind die unveränderlichen Grundformen dieser Ordnungen Gabe des Weltschöpfers und -erhalters; aber ihre jeweiligen wechselnden Formen; ihre jeweilige geschichtliche-konkrete Erscheinung ist Wirkung der menschlichen *Sünde*....» The same basic position is taken by Elert, who in this respect may say that «das Böse geschieht mit Hilfe des Guten». (Elert op.cit., p. 110.)

455. Brunner 1932, p. 321. We are thus in basic agreement with Brunner's conclusion in his chapter «Die natürlichen Gemeinschaften»: «Was ist denn also die richtige Stellung? ... Ein immer wachsames, kämpfendes Nein auf dem Grund – wohlverstanden: auf dem Grund! – eines dankbaren, dienstwilligen Ja.» (p. 322.)

456. Ibid., pp. 201, 322.

457. When Begemann op.cit., p. 85 says that the reason for this obviously was not because Jesus wanted «die Familie um ihrer selbst willen zu erhalten», but because he wanted the people to testify to what he had done to them, he seems to us to be operating with a false alternative, putting up against each other aspects that should rather be kept together. To this we shall return in our next section.

458. Bekenntnisschriften op.cit., pp. 586–587.

459. van Oyen 1967, p. 117. Cf. Barth who says that parenthood impresses upon man a «*character indelebilis*» which implies honor and responsibility. (Barth 1957, p. 311.)

460. Bekenntnisschriften op.cit., p. 587.

461. Barth 1957, p. 274.

462. Ibid., p. 277. Because the parents «in der Blickrichtung auf *Gott* stehen» is their authority a «von *Gott* anvertraute Autorität» (p. 282). Cf. van Oyen op.cit., p. 117: «Das Ehren der Eltern ist in die Blickrichtung auf Gott hin orientiert und daran wird die jüngere Generation immer zu denken haben....»

463. See van Oyen op.cit., pp. 117-118, where it is pointed out that the parents' oral tradition was the link to the fathers, and provided the continuity with Yahweh's revelation to them. This point is heavily emphasized by Barth who says that to honor one's parents simply means «sie sich als Lehrer und Ratgeber gewichtig sein lassen», and that «jene Lernwilligkeit» is the very nerve in the fourth commandment. (Barth 1957, pp. 273–274.)

464. Bekenntnisschriften op.cit., p. 603.
465. Ibid., p. 603.
466. When we use a term like «patriarchal extended family» we do not mean to say that the family all through the Old and the New Testament is presented as a rigid, unchanging external system. Borders between tribe, clan and family/ household are diffuse; parts of the Old Testament – as the Book of Ruth – may seem to reveal certain maternalistic traits («her mother's house», Ruth 1,8); even the fourth commandment itself with its equalling of father and mother as parents remains a crux to a purely paternalistic pattern. Nevertheless, the family as it by and large confronts us in the Scriptures is to be characterized in terms of a paternalistic, extended family. E.g., Pedersen op.cit., pp. 35–61, and Hempel 1964, pp. 67–93. For a further analysis of the patriarchal family in the Bible and in subsequent European Christianity we may refer to Begemann op.cit., pp. 68-111.
467. Cf. Pedersen op.cit., p. 14. According to Pedersen, the family in the Old Testament is «the source from which life flows, and those who are of the same family share in a community of life». (p. 37. Our own translation of the Danish text.) To the levirate law, see above, pp. 162–163.
468. Moe 1915, p. 18. (Our own translation.) The term we have rendered with «belonging» («sammenheng») might as well be translated «continuity».
469. When this has been strongly re-emphasized especially in McGavran's missiological writings over the last decades, he seems to us to be on firm biblical ground, and Magaki – in his article on individual and community referred to above – is justly asking for a renewed reflection upon this aspect in the New Testament and its significance for Christianity in Japan.
   It will be clear from what we have developed above that we strongly disagree with Barth when he says that the family – understood in a broader sense than the parent- child relationship – is of no importance either in the Old or in the New Testament. (Above, p. 222, and note 435 on p. 277.) To us Barth seems to disregard simple scriptural evidence.
470. See Rienecker 1960[10] who, with reference to H. von Soden, translates *amoibe* in plural: «Leistungen in Wiedervergeltung für Selbstempfangenes» (p. 495).
471. Wolff 1973, p. 264. This derivative nature of parental authority in Christianity as compared to its ultimate nature in Confucianism, is pertinently pointed out in Bellah 1970, pp. 76–99: «Father and Son in Christianity and Confucianism», and in Sumiya op.cit., pp. 50–56: «Kazoku seido no honshitsu to hihan» («Essence and Critique of the Family System»).
472. Wolff op.cit., p. 264.
473. When Barth, in his eagerness to underline the parents' function as God's representatives vis-à-vis their children, says that in the Old Testament – different from the New – honor to God and honor to parents coincide in practice to the extent that «eine Begrenzung des fünften durch das erste Gebot kann praktisch nicht stattfinden» (Barth 1957, p. 278), he again disregards significant scriptural evidence. At this point the Old and the New Testament cannot be put up against each other. Acts 5, 29 has its clear parallel in Ez. 20, 18–20.
474. E.g., Robinson 1913/1959[2], pp. 87–91: «The Relation of the Individual to the

Society».

475. Ibid., p. 90. Robinson does not overlook the merits of the first stage. It was, however, an «error», although it contributed to «the new truth» (pp. 90–91).

476. E.g., Rowley 1956/1965, pp. 99-123; Eichrodt op.cit., pp. 157-183; Hempel op.cit., pp. 32–67; van Oyen op.cit., pp. 159-164; and Seierstad 1971, pp. 23–40.

477. Hempel op.cit., p. 45. Cf. Eichrodt op.cit., pp. 162-163: «Hier [i.e., in der Gottesgemeinschaft] gibt also die Solidarität freien Raum für eine durchaus personale Gottesbeziehung.... Die kollektive Verbundenheit erweist sich als Stärkung der individuellen Lebensgestaltung.» Cf. also van Oyen op.cit., p. 164.

478. See Seierstad op.cit., which is an excellent study to this problem in Ex. 20, 5b.

479. E.g., Sumiya op.cit., pp. 48–50, 56–57.

480. Sumiya is severe in his critique of what he regards as Christian compromise with the basic values of the traditional family-system: «...Whether the Christians will be able to accomplish their mission towards the Japanese society today or not, depends on to what extent Japanese Christians are able to subjugate the former compromise and negate the traditional social relationships.» (Ibid., p. 60. Our own translation.)

481. Cf. Wolff's comment on this text in Micah 7: «Diese chaotische Not scheint unabweisbar, wo Menschen – sei es als die alte oder als die junge Generation – sich selbst als letzte Instanz ansehen und sich an Gottes Stelle setzen, anstatt mit seinem guten Wort zu leben». (Wolff op.cit., p. 269.)

482. Kashiwai op.cit., p. 40; Matsunaga op.cit., p. 62.

483. Re the implications of the eschatological dimension for Christian ethics in general, see e.g., Brunner 1932, «Zweites Buch, zweiter Abschnitt: Der neue Mensch», pp. 136-171, and Elert op.cit., «Zweiter Teil: Ethos unter der Gnade», particularly chapter five: «Begegnung mit Christus», and chapter six: «Die neue Kreatur». As for its particular implications with respect to man in the family, see Begemann op.cit., pp. 82-104: «Das Verhältnis von Oikos und Gemeinde im Neuen Testament.»

484. It is interesting to notice that when Murakami answers the question «What is the Christian teaching on filial piety?», he finds it necessary to quote and comment on the words of Jesus in Mt. 10,35, which he says are «apparently contradictory to filial piety». (Murakami op.cit., p. 173. Our own translation.)

485. Schmid 1955/1960⁴, p. 247: «Nicht Hass im psychologischen Sinn wird verlangt....» Cf. Barth 1957 p. 293: «Es ist also zunächst festzustellen, dass das Luk. 14,26 nicht als Abneigung und Feindschaft, Verachtung und Abscheu im Sinne eines Affektes, überhaupt nicht psychologisch zu verstehen ist....»

486. Ellis 1966/1974², p. 195.

487. Cf. Schmid op.cit., p. 247: «Der von Jesus hier geforderte Hass ist bei Matthäus treffend umschrieben.»

488. Barth 1957, p. 294.

489. Cf. Schmid op.cit., p. 248: «Jesus hebt das vierte Gebot nicht auf, sondern erkennt es an (vgl. 18,20=Mk 10,19; Mk 7,10-12). Aber das Gebot des

Anschlusses an ihn ist wichtiger und vordert vom Jünger, im Konfliktsfall selbst Vater und Mutter als Feinde der Sache Gottes anzusehen (vgl. Deut 33,9).»

490. Cf. Elert op.cit., 262–264. «Die Dienstbarkeit unter dem Herrn ist das von uns gelebte Erlöstsein.» (p. 264.)

491. This is clear already from the fact that the Haustafeln are structured in a way which corresponds to the structure of the contemporary family-system: «In einem dreifachen Querschnitt wird die christliche Familie angesprochen, der der Struktur der antiken Familie entspricht: zunächst die Ehefrauen und ihre Ehemänner, dann die Kinder und ihre Väter, schliesslich die Sklaven und ihre Herren.» (Gnilka 1971, p. 272.)

492. We shall not enter into a discussion on whether this sentence is to be understood as the end of the preceding pericope or as the introductory «Themasatz» to the following. With most newer commentators we prefer the latter reading of the text. E.g., Gnilka op.cit., pp. 263, 273, and Schlier 1957/1968⁶, pp. 250–252.

493. Cf. Gnilka op.cit., p. 275: «V 21 ist analog 1 Peter 5,5b; Phil 2,3b; Gal 5,13b zu verstehen, dass sich die Christen in gegenseitiger Hochschätzung begegnen sollen.»

494. Ibid., p. 275.

495. Ibid., p. 279. Cf. Begemann op.cit., p. 94: «Das hat zur Volge, dass die Haustafeln den Oikos nicht mehr als den alleinigen Vervügungsbereich des Mannes anerkennen.»

496. Barth 1957, pp. 216–217.

497. Ibid., pp. 190, 216 respectively.

498. It is impossible for us to enter into a full discussion of this problem, which involves intricate hermeneutical questions with regard to the interpretation of the concrete parenetic material in the New Testament. For an extensive introduction to the vast ammount of literature on the Haustafeln we refer to Crouch 1972. Fully realizing the intricacy of the problems involved at this point our own position is taken as a step in an ongoing struggle towards deeper insight.

499. Cf. Crouch who comments on «the approaches which either affirm the 'eternal truth' of the Haustafel requirements or interpret them in such a manner that they conform to modern social sensitivities.... Both approaches fail to deal with the various elements of the Haustafel consistently, for no one today suggests treating slavery as a divinely ordained institution. Within the context of the Haustafel, however, the obedience of slaves receives the same approval as the submission of wives. If one statement involves 'eternal truth', then all statements must be accorded the same authority.» (Op.cit., pp. 155-156.)

500. Cf. Crouch op.cit., p. 158: «Ultimately...both 1 Cor. 7 and the Haustafel call the believer to an affirmation of his finitude within the social order and, in larger sense, of his concrete position within the process of history.»

501. Cf. Elert op.cit., p. 330: «Die autorität Christi verlangt daher zuvorderst, dass wir in Wahrheit sind, wozu uns das kreatorische und gubernatorische Tun Gottes gemacht hat, ein rechter Vater, ein rechter Gatte, ein rechter Arbeiter,

ein Mensch dieses unseres Jahrhunderts. So versteht sich der Satz der lutheri-
schen Bekenntnisse, dass die Christen der neuen Gehorsam, die guten Werke
zu leisten haben 'ein jeder nach seinem Beruf'».

502. Begemann op.cit., p. 94.
503. This is well expressed by Begemann: «Aber mehr als ein Aufbruch kann eine
     Neuordnung sozialer Verhältnisse angesichts der in Christus verwirklichten
     eschatologischen Gemeinschaft aller nicht sein; denn die Verwandlung der
     Welt, die das Neue Testament verkündigt, ist keine soziale, sondern eine
     eshatologische.» (Op.cit., p. 94.)
504. Crouch op.cit., p. 158.
505. Barth 1957, p. 274. Above, note 463, p. 278.
506. Ibid., p. 273. «Man sieht von hier aus, dass es im biblischen Denkzusammen-
     hang gerade kein uneigentliches, sondern ein eigentliches Reden bedeutet,
     wenn Paulus 1. Kor. 4,15,17 die korinthischen Christen seine 'geliebten
     Kinder' nennt....» (p. 274.)
507. Morioka 1976, p. 101.
508. Ibid., p. 102.
509. That this to a certain degree happened in Annaka is pointed out by Shimpo
     Mitsuru: «In conclusion, Christians moved from unsatisfactory social rela-
     tions in the social system caused by their different religious aspiration toward
     a state of new equilibrium in the social system by two means: a high rate of
     socially approved activities and compromise with traditional group-oriented-
     ness. The Christians did this at the cost of individual-orientation in their
     Christian faith.» (Shimpo 1968, p. 72.)
510. Nishiyama op.cit., p. 60.
511. Ibid., p. 61.
512. Ibid., p. 64.
513. Ibid., pp. 64–66. This conclusion is said to be supported by statistics on
     worship-participation, Bible-reading, and family-devotion, which all show a
     low rate of active involvement. (pp. 64–66.)

BIBLIOGRAPHY

The following bibliography consists of books and articles quoted or referred to in the text and notes. For works in the Japanese language the original title is given with English translation in parenthesis. In some cases this translation is found in the actual book/article or in published bibliographies, in other cases it is our own translation.

Adam, Karl 1924/1965: Katolicismens inderste væsen, København 1965.
Agency for Cultural Affairs 1972: Japanese Religion, Tokyo 1972.
Ahlbrecht, Ansgar 1964: Tod und Unsterblichkeit in der evangelischen Theologie der Gegenwart, Paderborn 1964.
Alterbog 1893: Alterbog for Den norske kirke, Kristiania 1893.
Althaus, Paul 1926³: Die letzten Dinge, Gütersloh 1926³.
Althaus, Paul 1947/1949²: Die Christliche Wahrheit I, Gütersloh 1947/1949².
Althaus, Paul 1962: Tod. IV Dogmatisch. In: RGG Vol.VI, Tübingen 1962, pp. 914–918.
An Order of Service 1977: An Order of Service for Worship and Communion in the Church of Norway, Oslo 1977.
Anesaki, Masaharu 1930/1966: History of Japanese Religion, London 1930/1966.
Anzai, Shin 1964: Gendai Nihon shakai to Kirisutokyo to (Moderne Japanese Society and the Christians), Tokyo 1964.
Anzai, Shin 1965: Hekichi shakai to Katorikku no juyo. (Acceptance of Catholicism in a Remote Village.) In: Okada: Nihon no fudo to Kirisutokyo. (Japan's Natural Features and Christianity.) Tokyo 1965.
Anzai, Shin 1968: Catholicism in an Isolated Village. In: Morioka/Newell: The Sociology of Japanese Religion, Leiden 1968.
Ariga, Kizaemon 1969: Nippon ni okeru senzo to ujigami. (Ancestors and Clan-gods in Japan.) In: Ariga Kizaemon chosakushu (The Collected Works of Ariga Kizaemon), Vol. VIII, Tokyo 1969.

Ashikaga, Ensho 1950: The Festival of the Spirits of the Dead in Japan. In: Western Folklore, Vol. 9, No. 3, 1950, pp. 217–228.

Aston, W.G. 1905: Shinto. The Way of the Gods, London 1905.

Baber, Ray E. 1958: Youth Looks at Marriage and the Family. A Study of Changing Japanese Attitudes, Tokyo 1958.

Barth, Karl 1938: Kirchliche Dogmatik I/2, Zollikon 1938.

Barth, Karl 1957: Kirchliche Dogmatik III/4, Zollikon 1957.

Basabe, Fernando M. 1968: Religious Attitudes of Japanese Men. A Sociological Survey, Tokyo 1968.

Beardsley R.K./Hall J.W./Ward R.E. 1959: Village Japan, Chicago 1959.

Beasley-Murray, G.R. 1962/1972: Baptism in the New Testament, Exeter 1962/1972.

Befu, Harumi 1962/1963: Corporate Emphasis and Patterns of Descent in the Japanese Family. In: Smith/Beardsley: Japanese Culture: Its Development and Characteristics, Chicago 1962/London 1963, pp. 34–41.

Begemann, H. 1960/1966²: Strukturwandel der Familie, Witten 1960/ 1966².

Bekenntnisschriften 1930/1959⁴: Die Bekenntnisschriften der evangelisch-lutherischen Kirche, Gøttingen 1930/1959⁴.

Bellah, Robert N. 1957/1969: Tokugawa Religion. The Values of Pre-industrial Japan, Glencoe 1957/1969.

Bellah, Robert N. 1970: Beyond Belief. Essays on Religion in a Post-traditional World, New York 1970.

Benedict, Ruth 1946/1974: The Chrysanthemum and the Sword. Patterns of Japanese Culture, Boston 1946/Tokyo 1974.

Benz, Ernst 1970⁵: On Understanding Non-Christian Religions. In: Eliade/Kitagawa: The History of Religions. Essays in Methodology, Chicago 1970⁵.

Bernier, Bernhard 1970: The Popular Religion of a Japanese Village and its Transformation. Unpublished doctoral dissertation, Cornell University 1970.

Bieder, Werner 1949: Die Vorstellung von der Höllenfahrt Jesu Christi, Zürich 1949.

Birkeli, Emil 1938: Fedrekult i Norge, Oslo 1938.

Birkeli, Emil 1944: Huskult og hinsidighetstro, Oslo 1944.

Boyer, Martha 1966/1967: Ancestor Worship in Contemporary Japan. In: Folk, Vol. 8–9, 1966/1967, pp. 37–54.

Bratsiotis, Panagiotis 1959/1970²: Die Orthodoxe Kirche in Griechischer Sicht, Stuttgart 1959/1970².

Brown, Delmer M. 1968: Kami, Death and Ancestral Kami. In: Proceedings of the Second International Conference for Shinto Studies. The-me: Continuity and Change, Tokyo 1968.

Brown, Keith 1964: Dozoku. A Study of Descent Groups in rural Japan. Unpublished doctoral dissertation, University of Chicago 1964.

Bruce, F.F. 1970: The Epistles of John, London 1970.

Bruce, F.F. 1976/1977: Paul and the Athenians. In: Expository Times, Vol. 88, 1976/1977, pp. 8–12.

Brunner, Emil 1932: Das Gebot und die Ordnungen, Tübingen 1932.

Brunner, Emil 1937: Der Mensch im Widerspruch, Berlin 1937.

Brunner, Emil 1938: The Christian Understanding of Man. In: Church, Community and State, Vol. II, 1938, pp. 139–178.

Brunner, Emil 1964: Truth as Encounter, London 1964.

Caird, G.B 1956: Principalities and Powers, Oxford 1956.

Callaway, T.N. 1957: Japanese Buddhism and Christianity, Tokyo 1957.

Charles, R.H. 1913: Eschatology, London 1913. (Reprinted New York 1963.)

China Centenary 1907: China Centenary Missionary Conference, Shang-hai 1907.

Christiaens, M. 1975A: Sosen suhai o meguru shikyo-jo no mondaiten. (Pastoral Problems concerning Ancestor Worship.) In: The Japan Mis-sionary Bulletin, Vol. XXIX, No. 10, 1975, pp. 579–581.

Christiaens, M. 1975B: Catholic Veneration of the Ancestors. In: The Japan Missionary Bulletin, Vol. XXIX, No. 10, 1975, pp. 561–564.

Christiaens, M. 1976: Katorikku no sosen sukei. (Catholic Veneration of Ancestors.) Tokyo 1976.

Christiansen, Reidar Th. 1946: The Dead and the Living, Oslo 1946.

Cragg, Kenneth 1968/1969^2: Christianity in World Perspective, London 1968/1969^2.

Crouch, James E. 1972: The Origin and Intention of the Colossian Haustafel, Göttingen 1972.

Cullmann, Oscar 1958: Immortality of the Soul or Resurrection of the Dead? The Witness of the New Testament, New York 1958.

Culpepper, Robert N. 1975: Biblical Perspectives on Death. In: Hayama Missionary Seminar 1975: Christian Perspectives on Death, pp. 30–82.

Daneel, M.L. 1973: The Christian Gospel and the Ancestor Cult. In: Missionalia, Vol. 1, No. 2, 1973, pp. 46–73.

Dening, Walter 1908: Confucian Philosophy in Japan. Reviews of dr. Inoue Tetsujiro's three Volumes on this Philosophy. In: Transactions of the Asiatic Society of Japan, Vol. 36, 1908, pp. 101–152.

Dix, Dom Gregory 1945/1970: The Shape of the Liturgy, London 1945/ 1970.

Doerner, David L. 1977: Comparative Analysis of Life after Death in Folk Shinto and Christianity. In: Japanese Journal of Religious Studies, Vol. 4, No. 2–3, 1977, pp. 151–182.

Doi, Masatoshi 1960: Nihon ni okeru Kirisutokyo to shoshukyo to no sesshoku no mondai. (The Christian Church in Japan and the Problem of Contact with other Religions.) Tokyo 1960.

Dore, R.P. 1958: City Life in Japan, London 1958.

Dore, R.P. 1967: Aspects of Social Change in Modern Japan, Princeton, New Jersey 1967.

Dorson, Richard M. 1963: Studies in Japanese Folklore, Indiana 1963.

Dumoulin, Heinrich 1964: Nihon no shukyoteki dento to Kirisutosha. (Japan's Religious Traditions and the Christian.) In: Anzai: Gendai Nihon shakai to Kirisutokyo to, Tokyo 1964, pp. 169–181.

Eder, Matthias 1956: Totenseelen und Ahnengeister in Japan. In: Anthropos. Vol. 51, No. 1–2, 1956, pp. 97–112.

Eder, Matthias 1957: Familie, Sippe, Clan und Ahnenverehrung in Japan. In: Anthropos, Vol. 52, No. 5–6, 1957, pp. 813–840.

Eder, Matthias 1958: Shamanismus in Japan. In: Paideuma, Vol. 6, No. 7, 1958, pp. 367–380.

Eichrodt, Walter 1961[4]: Theologie des Alten Testaments. Teil 2/3, Stuttgart 1961[4].

Elert, Werner 1949: Das Christliche Ethos, Tübingen 1949.

Eliade, M./Kitagawa, J. 1970[5]: The History of Religions. Essays in Methodology, Chicago 1970[5].

Ellis, E. Earle 1966/1974[2]: The Gospel of Luke, London 1966/1974[2].

Fähn, Helge 1963/1968[2]: Høymessen igår og idag, Oslo 1963/1968[2].

Fairchild, William P. 1962: Shamanism in Japan. In: Folklore Studies, Vol. 21, 1962, pp. 1–122.

Fasholé-Luke, Edward W. 1974: Ancestor Veneration and the Communion of Saints. In: Glasswell/Fasholé-Luke: New Testament Christianity for Africa and the World. Essays in Honor of Harry Sawyerr, London 1974, pp. 209–221.

Ferguson, DeLancy 1966: Hearn Lafcadio. In: Encyclopedia Americana, Vol. 14, 1966, p. 35b.

Fisher, Galen M. 1908: Nakae Toju, The Sage of Omi. In: Transactions of the Asiatic Society of Japan, Vol. 36, 1908, pp. 25–96.

Fornberg, Tord 1977: An Early Church in a Pluralistic Society. A Study of 2 Peter, Lund 1977.

France, R.T. 1977: Exegesis in Practice: Two Examples. In: Marshall: New Testament Interpretation, Exeter 1977, pp. 252–281.

Frøvig, D.A. 1944: Kommentar til Apostlenes Gjerninger, Oslo 1944.

Fujii, Masao 1974: Gendaijin no shinko kozo. Shukyo no fudo jinko no kodo to shiso. (The Structure of Faith of Modern Man. The Conduct and Thoughts of the Religiously Fluctuating Population.) Tokyo 1974.

Fukuda, Masatoshi 1974: Nokanshiki no inori. (Prayers for the Coffining Rite.) In: United Church of Christ: Shi to sogi, Tokyo 1974, pp. 281–288.

Furukawa, Tesshi 1967/1973: The Individual in Japanese Ethics. In: Moore: The Japanese Mind, Honolulu 1967/Tokyo 1973, pp. 228–244.

Furuno, Kiyoto 1957: Ikezuki no Kirishitan buraku: Tokuni saishi soshiki ni tsuite. (Kirishitan Villages in the Ikezuki Islands: Their Organization for Rites.) In: Kyushu bunkashi kenkyu kiyo, Kyushu University, Vol. 5, 1957, pp. 1–44.

Gabriel, Theodor 1938: Das Buddhistische Begräbnis in Japan. In: Anthropos, Vol. 33, 1938, pp. 568–583.

Gärtner, Bertil 1955: The Areopagus Speach and Natural Revelation, Uppsala 1955.

Gasque, W. Ward 1975: A History of the Criticism of the Acts of the Apostles, Grand Rapids 1975.

Glasswell, M.E./Fasholé-Luke, E.W. 1974: New Testament Christianity for Africa and the World. Essays in Honor of Harry Sawyerr, London 1974.

Goppelt, L. 1978: Der Erste Petrusbrief, Göttingen 1978.

Gnilka, Joachim 1971: Der Epheserbrief, Freiburg 1971.

Grüneisen, K. 1879: Heilige, deren Anrufung und Verehrung. In: Realencyclopedie für Protestantische Theologie, Vol. 5, Leipzig 1879, pp. 708–713.

Gubbins, John, H. 1877/1878: Review of the Introduction of Christianity into China and Japan. In: Transactions of the Asiatic Society of Japan, Vol. VI, 1877/1878, pp. 1–62.

Gudstjänstordning 1976: Gudstjänstordning för Svenska Kyrkan, Lund 1976.

Haga, Noboru 1974: Sogi no rekishi. (The History of the Funeral Rites), Kyoto 1974.

Hägglund, Bengt 1956: Theologins Historia. En teologisk översikt, Malmø 1956.

Hakamies, Ahti 1971: 'Eigengesetzlichkeit' der Natürlichen Ordnungen als Grundproblem der neueren Lutherdeutung, Witten 1971.

Hall, J. Carey 1915: Teijo's Family Instruction: A Samurai's Ethical

Bequest to his Posterity. In: Transactions and Proceedings of the Japan Society, London, Vol. 14, 1915, pp. 128–156.

Hall, R.K./Gauntlett, J.O. 1949: Kokutai no hongi: Cardinal Principles of the National Entity of Japan, Cambridge, Mass. 1949.

Hallencreutz, Carl F. 1970: New Approaches to Men of other Faiths, Geneva 1970.

Hanayama, Shoyu 1969: Buddhist Handbook for Shin-shu Followers, Tokyo 1969.

Hastings, James 1917: Encyclopedia of Religion and Ethics, New York 1917.

Hearn, Lafcadio 1904/1917: Japan, an Attempt at Interpretation, London 1904/1917.

Hempel, Johannes 1964: Das Ethos des Alten Testaments, Berlin 1964.

Herbert, Jean 1967: Shinto, London 1967.

Hirai, Atsuko 1968: Ancestor Worship in Yatsuka Hozumi's State and Constitutional Theory. In: Skrypczak: Japan's Modern Century, Tokyo 1968, pp. 41–50.

Hiyane, Antei et al. 1959: Kirisutokyoshiki sogi to sono ikyo jiban. (The Christian Funeral and its Other-religious Soil.) Tokyo 1959.

Hoffmann, Paul 1966/1978³: Die Toten in Christus, Münster 1966/1978³.

Hofmann, R. 1879: Fegfeuer. In: Realencyclopädie für Protestantische Theologie, Vol. IV, Leipzig 1879, pp. 514–517.

Holtom, D.C. 1938: State Shinto and Religion. In: International Review of Missions, Vol. 27, 1938, pp. 158–174.

Holtom, D.C. 1940/1941: The Meaning of Kami. In: Monumenta Nipponica, Vol. III. No. 1, pp. 1–22, No. 2, pp. 392–413, 1940; Vol. IV, No. 2, pp. 351–394, 1941.

Hori, Ichiro 1951: Minkan shinko (Folk Beliefs), Tokyo 1951.

Hori, Ichiro 1953: Wagakuni minkan shinkoshi no kenkyu. (Studies in the History of Japanese Folk Religion.) Tokyo 1953.

Hori, Ichiro 1962: Nihon shukyo no shakaiteki yakuwari. (The Social Role of Japanese Religion.) Tokyo 1962.

Hori, Ichiro 1967/1973: The Appearance of Individual Self-consciousness in Japanese Religion and its Historical Transformations. In: Moore: The Japanese Mind, Honolulu 1967/Tokyo 1973, pp. 201–227.

Hori, Ichiro 1968: Folk Religion in Japan, Chicago 1968.

Hori, Ichiro 1975: Shamanism in Japan. In: Japanese Journal of Religious Studies, Vol. 2, No. 4, 1975, pp. 231–287.

Horikoshi, Nobuji 1973: Kirisuto ni aru shi oyobi shigo no mondai. (Death in Christ and the Problem of Afterlife.) Tokyo 1973.

Hozumi, Nobushige 1901/1943: Ancestor Worship and the Japanese Law, Tokyo 1901/1943.

Hwang, Bernhard 1977: Ancestor Cult Today. In: Missiology, Vol. 5, No. 3, 1977, pp. 339–365.

Inoguchi, Shoji 1965: Nippon no soshiki. (The Japanese Funeral.) Tokyo 1965.

Ito, Kyoji 1963:. Fukuin no dochakuka. (The Indigenization of the Gospel.) In: Nihon Kirisuto Kyodan: Fukuin wa dochaku dekiru ka. (Can the Gospel be Indigenized?) Tokyo 1963, pp. 71–125.

Jackson, James 1907: Ancestral Worship. In: China Centenary Missionary Conference, Shanghai 1907, pp. 215–246.

Jeremias, Joachim 1955/1956: 'Flesh and Blood cannot Inherit the Kingdom of God'. In: New Testament Studies, Vol. II, 1955/1956, pp. 151–159.

Jeremias, Joachim 1958: Heiligen-Gräber in Jesu Umwelt, Göttingen 1958.

Joya, Mock: Things Japanese, Tokyo News Service, Tokyo. (Undated)

Karmiris, Johannes N. 1959/1970[2]: Abriss der Dogmatischen Lehre der Orthodoxen Katholischen Kirche. In: Bratsiotis: Die Orthodoxe Kirche in Griechischer Sicht, Stuttgart 1959/1970[2], pp. 15–120.

Kashiwai, Norio 1974: Kyuyaku ni okeru shi to sogi. (Death and Funeral in the Old Testament.) In: United Church of Christ: Shi to sogi, Tokyo 1974, pp. 7–47.

Kashiwai, Tadao 1974: Sogi no inori. (Prayers for the Funeral.) In: United Church of Christ: Shi to sogi, Tokyo 1974, pp. 289–291.

Kataoka, Nizaemon 1974/1975: Wasurerarete iru senzo no kuyo. (The Forgotten Masses for Ancestors.) Tokyo 1974/1975.

Kato, Genchi 1918: The Warongo or Japanese Analects. In: Transactions of the Asiatic Society of Japan, Vol. 45, 1918, pp. 1–138.

Kato, Tsuneaki 1974: Doitsu fukuinshugi kyokai ni okeru sogi. (The Funeral in German Evangelical Churches.) In: United Church of Christ: Shi to sogi, Tokyo 1974, pp. 172–203.

Katorikku Nyumon 1971/1975[4]: Katorikku nyumon (Catholic Catechism). Tokyo 1971/1975[4].

Kawada, Kumataro 1960: On the Fundamental Difference between Buddhism and Christianity. In: Proceedings of the Ninth International Congress for History of Religion, Tokyo 1958. Tokyo 1960, pp. 325–329.

Kawakoshi, Junji 1957: Kazoku ni okeru dentoteki kihan to sono hokai.

(The Family: Its Traditional Norms and their Collapse.) In: Aichi Daigaku Bungaku-bu, Tenth Anniversary Issue, 1957, pp. 95–122.

Kawashima, Takeyoshi 1950: Nihon shakai no kazokuteki kosei. (The Familistic Structure of Japanese Society.) Tokyo 1950.

Kawashima, Takeyoshi 1957/1959: Ideorogi to shite no kazoku seido. (The Family System as Ideology.) Tokyo 1957/1959.

Kawashima, Takeyoshi 1967/1973: The Status of the Individual in the Notion of Law, Right, and Social Order in Japan. In: Moore: The Japanese Mind, Honolulu 1967/Tokyo 1973, pp. 262–287.

Kelly, J.N.D. 1950/1976³: Early Christian Creeds, London 1950/1976³.

Kelly, J.N.D. 1958/1977⁵: Early Christian Doctrines, London 1958/1977⁵.

Kelly, J.N.D. 1969/1976: A Commentary on the Epistles of Peter and Jude, London 1969/1976.

Kerner, Karen 1976: The Malevolent Ancestor: Ancestral Influence in a Japanese Religious Sect. In: Newell: Ancestors, The Hague 1976, pp. 205–217.

Kirby, R.J. 1910: Ancestral Worship in Japan. In: Transactions of the Asiatic Society of Japan, Vol. 38, 1910, pp. 233–267.

Kirisuto to warera no misa. (Christ and our Mass.) Osaka undated.

Kishimoto, Hideo 1967/1973: Some Japanese Cultural Traits and Religions. In: Moore: The Japanese Mind, Honolulu 1967/Tokyo 1973, pp. 110–121.

Kitamura, Soji 1974: Kirisutokyo sogi no dento to eigoken ni okeru sogi. (The Traditions of the Christian Funeral and the Funeral in the English-speaking Context.) In: United Church of Christ: Shi to sogi, Tokyo 1974, pp. 123–172.

Kitano, Seiichi 1962/1963: 'Dozoku' and 'ie' in Japan: The Meaning of Family Genealogical Relationships. In: Smith/ Beardsley: Japanese Culture: Its Development and Characteristics, Chicago 1962/London 1963, pp. 42–46.

Klauser, R. 1959: Christliche Heiligenverehrung. In: RGG, Vol. 3, Tübingen 1959, pp. 171–175.

Kochi, Tokio 1969: Kirisutokyo no shigokan to shisha girei. (Christian View of Afterlife and Ceremonies for the Dead.) In: Deai, Vol. 2, No. 4, 1969, pp. 14–25.

Kojien 1955/1975: Kojien, Tokyo 1955/1975.

Kollbrunner, Fritz 1975: Auf dem Weg zu einer Christlichen Ahnenverehrung? In: Neue Zeitschrift für Missionswissenschaft, Vol. 31, No. 1, 1975, pp. 110–133.

Kosaka, Masaaki 1967/1973: The Status and Rôle of the Individual in

Japanese Society. In: Moore: The Japanese Mind, Honolulu 1967/ Tokyo 1973, pp. 245–261.

Köster, Helmut 1974: Fysis. In: Theological Dictionary of the New Testament, Vol. IX, Michigan 1974, pp. 251–277.

Koyama, Takashi 1960/1972: Gendai no kazoku no kenkyu. (An Investigation of the Contemporary Family.) Tokyo 1960/1972.

Koyama, Takashi 1962/1963: Changing Family Structure in Japan. In: Smith/Beardsley: Japanese Culture: Its Development and Characteristics, Chicago 1962/London 1963, pp. 47–54.

Kraemer, Hendrik 1938: The Christian Message in a non-Christian World, New York 1938.

Kraemer, Hendrik 1956/1958²: Religion and the Christian Faith, London 1956/1968².

Kumano, Yoshitaka 1959: Shiken no ni-san. (Some Points in a Personal Opinion.) In: Hiyane et al.: Kirisutokyoshiki sogi to sono ikyo jiban, Tokyo 1959, pp. 108–110.

Kümmel, Werner Georg 1974: Römer 7 und das Bild des Menschen in Neuen Testament, München 1974.

Künneth, Walter 1951: Theologie der Auferstehung, München 1951.

Kvalbein, Hans 1969: 2 Kor. 5,1–10 og spørsmålet om «mellomtilstanden» hos Paulus. In: Tidsskrift for Teologi og Kirke, 1969, No. 3, pp. 179–195.

Lee, Kun Sam 1966: The Christian Confrontation with Shinto Nationalism, Philadelphia 1966.

Liao, David C.E. 1972: The Unresponsive. Resistant or Neglected? Chicago 1972.

Lucius, E. 1904: Die Anfänge des Heiligenkultus in der Christlichen Kirche, Tübingen 1904. (Reprinted 1966)

Luther, Martin 1522: Ein Sendbrief über die Frage, ob auch jemand, ohne glauben verstorben, selig werden möge. WA 10/II, pp. 318–326.

Lutheran Church 1966/1967²: Ruteru kyokai shinto hikkei. (Handbook for Believers of the Lutheran Church.) Tokyo 1966/1967².

Lutheran Church 1968: Kyokai shikibun. (The Liturgy of the Church.) Tokyo 1968.

Lutheran World Federation 1973/1974: How Japanese Become Christians, Tokyo 1973/1974.

Lutheran World Federation 1976: LWF Information No. 38/76, pp. 10–11.

Maeda, Takashi 1965: Sosen suhai no kenkyu. (A Study of Ancestor Worship.) Tokyo 1965.

Magaki, Yosuke 1978: Seisho ni okeru ko to kyodotai – Nippon no jokyo no naka de. (Individual and Community – in the Bible and in Japan.) In: Shingaku Zasshi. Vol. 11, 1978, pp. 58–61.

Malalasekera, G.P. 1965: Encyclopedia of Buddhism. Vol. I, Fascicle 4, Colombo 1965.

Marshall, I.H. 1977: New Testament Interpretation, Exeter 1977.

Maruyama, Yoshitaka 1958: Katorikku no sogi to sosen suhai. (Catholic Funeral and Ancestor Worship.) Kyoto 1958.

Mason, James W.T. 1935: The Meaning of Shinto, New York 1935.

Masuoka E.C./Masuoka J./Kawamura N. 1962: Role Conflicts in the Modern Japanese Family. In: Social Forces, Vol. 42, No. 1, 1962, pp. 1–6.

Masutani, Fumio 1957: A Comparative Study of Buddhism and Christianity, Tokyo 1957.

Matsudaira, Narimitsu 1963: The Concept of Tamashii in Japan. In: Dorson: Studies in Japanese Folklore, Indiana 1963.

Matsumoto, Yoshimi 1959: Bokkaisha no hitori to shite. (From the Pastoral Point of View.) In: Hiyane et al.: Krisutokyoshiki sogi to sono ikyo jiban, Tokyo 1959, pp. 97–102.

Matsumoto, Y. Scott 1960: Contemporary Japan: The Individual and the Group. In: Transactions of the American Philosophical Society, New Series 50, Part 1, Philadelphia 1969, pp. 5–75.

Matsumura, Katsumi 1959: Kirirsutokyoshiki sogi no kento. (An Examination of the Christian Funeral.) In: Hiyane et al.: Kirisutokyoshiki sogi to sono ikyo jiban, Tokyo 1959, pp. 87–91.

Matsunaga, Kikuo 1974: Shinyaku ni okeru shi to sogi. (Death and Funeral in the New Testament.) In: United Church of Christ: Shi to sogi, Tokyo 1974, pp. 49–87.

Mbiti, John S. 1967: Afrikanisches Verständnis der Geister im Lichte des Neuten Testamentes. In: Theologische Stimmen, Vol. II, 1967, pp. 130–147.

Mbiti, John S. 1971: New Testament Eschatology in an African Background, Oxford 1971.

McGavran, Donald A. 1955: The Bridges of God, London/New York 1955.

McGavran, Donald A. 1970/1980[2]: Understanding Church Growth, Grand Rapids 1970/1980[2].

Minakawa, Kogi 1972: Sosai ni tai suru hitobito no ishiki. (People's Attitude towards Funerals and Subsequent Masses.) Komazawa University 1972.

Minear, Richard H. 1970: Japanese Tradition and Western Law. Emperor, State and Law in the Thought of Hozumi Yatsuka, Cambridge, Mass. 1970.

Miyagi, Shizuka 1969: Bukkyo no shigokan to shishagirei. (Buddhist View of Death and Ceremonies for the Dead.) In: Deai, Vol. 2, No. 4, 1969, pp. 62–69.

Moe, Olaf 1915: Kristendom og slegtskap, Kristiania 1915.

Moe, Olaf 1944: Apostelen Paulus. Hans liv og gjerning, Oslo 1944.

Mogami, Takayoshi 1963: The Double-Grave System. In: Dorson: Studies in Japanese Folklore, Indiana 1963, pp. 167–180.

Moore, Charles A. 1967/1973: The Japanese Mind, Honolulu 1967/Tokyo 1973.

Morioka, Kiyomi 1959A: Nihon noson ni okeru Kirisutokyo no juyo. (Acceptance of Christianity in the Japanese Rural Community.) In: Kindai shiso no keisei, Tokyo 1959, pp. 193–260.

Morioka, Kiyomi 1959B: Chiho shotoshi ni okeru Kirisutokyo kyokai no keisei. Joshu Annaka kyokai no kozo bunseki. (Formation of Christian Churches in Small Local Cities. Analysis of the Structure of Annaka Church in Japan.) Tokyo 1959.

Morioka, Kiyomi 1965: Nihon noson ni okeru Kirisutokyo no dochakuka. Yamanashi-ken Kusakabe kyokai no baai. (Indigenization of Christianity in Japanese Rural Community. The Case of Kusakabe Church in Yamanashi Pref.) In: Shakai kagaku ronshu, Tokyo University of Education, No. 12, 1965, pp. 1–82.

Morioka, Kiyomi 1966: Christianity in the Japanese Rural Community: Acceptance and Rejection. In: The Sociological Review, Monograph No. 10, 1966, pp. 183–197.

Morioka, Kiyomi 1975: Religion in Changing Japanese Society, Tokyo 1975.

Morioka, Kiyomi 1976: Nihon no kindai shakai to Kirisutokyo (Modern Japanese Society and the Christian Church.) Tokyo 1976.

Morioka, Kiyomi 1977: The Appearance of «Ancestor Religion» in Modern Japan: The Years of Transition from the Meiji to the Taisho Periods. In: Japanese Journal of Religious Studies, Vol. 4, No. 2–3, 1977, pp. 183–212.

Morioka, K./Newell, W. 1968: The Sociology of Japanese Religion, Leiden 1968.

Mosothoane, Ephraim K. 1973: Communio Sanctorum in Africa. In: Missionalia, Vol. 1, No. 2, 1973, pp. 86–95.

Motoda, J.S. 1928: Opportunities of the Japanese Church. I: General. In: Stauffer: Japan Speaks for herself, London 1928.

Müller, Nikolaus 1901[3]: Koimeterien. Veranstaltungen zum Gedächtnis der Toten in den Kirchen. In: Realenzyklopädie für Protestantische Theologie und Kirche, Vol. 10, Leipzig 1901, pp. 794–877.

Murakami, Osamu1972/1974[2]: Kirisutokyo e no gimon ni kotaeru. (Answering Questions to the Christian Church.) Tokyo 1972/1974[2].

Myklebust, Olav G. 1976: Misjonskunnskap, Oslo 1976.

Nagai M./Bennett J.W. 1953: A Summary and Analysis of «the Familial Structure of Japanese Society» by Takeyoshi Kawashima. In: South-West Journal of Anthropology, Vol. 9, No. 2, 1953, pp. 239–250.

Nakamura, H./Wiener, P.P. 1964: The Ways of Thinking of Eastern Peoples, Honolulu 1964.

Nakamura, Hajime 1967: A History of the Development of Japanese Thought, Vols. I-II, Tokyo 1967.

Nakane, Chie 1970/1974: Japanese Society, Harmondsworth 1970/1974.

Naoe, Hiroji 1963: A Study of Yashiki-gami, the Deity of House and Grounds. In: Dorson: Studies in Japanese Folklore, Indiana 1963, pp. 198–214.

Nemeshegyi, Peter 1972: A Commentary to the New Japanese Catechism, Tokyo 1972.

Newell, William H. 1976A: Ancestors, The Hague 1976.

Newell, William H. 1976B: Good and Bad Ancestors. In: Newell: Ancestors, The Hague 1976, pp. 17–29.

Nishiyama, Shigeru 1975: Nihon sonraku ni okeru Kirisutokyo no teichaku to henyo. (The Fixation and Change of Christianity in a Japanese Village.) In: Shakaigaku hyoron, Vol. 26, No. 101, 1975, pp. 53–74.

Norbeck, Edward 1954: Takashima, a Japanese Fishing Community, Salt Lake City 1954.

Norbeck, Edward 1970: Religion and Society in Modern Japan: Continuity and Change, Houston 1970.

Ny høymesseliturgi 1977: Ny høymesseliturgi. Tillegg til Alterboken, Oslo 1977.

Obata, Susumu 1974–1976: Kirisutokyo kaichogaku jiten. (A Guide to Christian Festivals and Funeral.) In: Hyakumannin no fukuin, No. 9–12, 1974, No. 8–12, 1975, No. 1–7, 1976.

Odeberg, Hugo 1944: Pauli brev til Korintierna, Lund 1944.

Odland, Sigurd 1901: Kristi Prædiken for «aanderne i forvaring» (1. Petr. 3,19). In: Norsk Teologisk Tidsskrift, Vol. II, 1901, pp. 116–144, 185–229.

Odland, Sigurd 1927: Fortolkning av Jakobs, Peters, Judas' og Johannes' brever, Oslo 1927.

Offner, C.B. 1963: Modern Japanese Religions, Leiden 1963.

Okada, Junichi 1965: Nihon no fudo to Kirisutokyo. (Japan's Natural Feature and Christianity.) Tokyo 1965.

Omiya, Hiroshi 1974: Kyorishi ni okeru shi to sogi. (Death and Funeral in the History of Doctrine.) In: United Church of Christ: Shi to sogi, Tokyo 1974, pp. 89–121.

Ono, Sokyo 1968: The Concept of Kami in Shinto. In: Proceedings of the Second International Conference for Shinto Studies, Tokyo 1968, pp. 11–15.

Ooms, Herman 1967: The Religion of the Household: A Case Study of Ancestor Worship in Japan. In: Contemporary Religions in Japan, Vol. 8, No. 3–4, 1967, pp. 201–333.

Otto, Rudolf 1917/1926[15]: Das Heilige, Gotha 1917/1926[15].

Owen, H.P. 1971: Concepts of Deity, London 1971.

Oyen, Hendrik van 1967: Ethik des Alten Testaments, Gütersloh 1967.

Pedersen, Johannes 1920/1934[2]: Israel I-II, København 1920/1934[2].

Pedersen, Johannes 1934: Israel III-IV, København 1934.

Plath, David W. 1964: Where the Family of Gods is the Family. The Rôle of the Dead in Japanese Households. In: American Anthropologist, Vol. 66, No. 2, 1964, pp. 300–317.

Prayer and the Departed 1971: A Report of the Archbishops' Commission on Christian Doctrine, London 1971.

Prenter, Regin 1955[2]: Skabelse og genløsning, København 1955[2].

Proceedings 1968: Proceedings of the Second International Conference for Shinto Studies. Theme: Continuity and Change, Tokyo 1968.

Quell, Gottfried 1925/1967: Die Auffassung des Todes in Israel, Darmstadt 1925/1967.

Raeder, Maria 1955: Vikariatstaufe in 1. Cor. 15,29? In: Zeitschrift für die Neutestamentliche Wissenschaft, Vol. 46, 1955, No. 3–4, pp. 258–260.

Reicke, Bo 1946: The Disobediant Spirits and Christian Baptism, Lund 1946.

Reicke, Bo 1957: Höllenfahrt Christi. In: RGG, Vol. III, Tübingen 1957, pp. 408–410.

Reicke, Bo 1962: Tod im NT. In: RGG, Vol. VI, Tübingen 1962, pp. 913–914.

Reimer, Reginald E. 1975: The Religious Dimension of the Vietnamese Cult of the Ancestors. In: Missiology, Vol. III. No. 2, 1975, pp. 155–168.

Reindell, Walter 1955: Die Präfation. In: Leiturgia, Vol. II, Kassel 1955, pp. 453–522.

Reitz, Karl 1939: Totenriten des Shinto. In: Annali Lateranensi, Vol. 3, 1939, pp. 61–89.

Revon, Michel 1917: Ancestor Worship and Cult of the Dead (Japanese). In: Hastings: Encyclopedia of Religion and Ethics, New York 1917.

Rienecker, Fritz 1960[10]: Sprachlicher Schlüssel zum Griechischen Neuen Testament, Gessen 1960[10].

Rietschel, Georg 1951: Lehrbuch der Liturgik, Göttingen 1951.

Rissho Kosei-kai 1972: Rissho Kosei-kai. For our New Members, Tokyo 1972.

Rissi, Mathis 1962: Die Taufe für die Toten, Zürich/Stuttgart 1962.

Robinson, H. Wheeler 1913/1959[2]: The Religious Ideas of the Old Testament, London 1913/1959[2].

Rowley, H.H. 1956/1965: The Faith of Israel, London 1956/1965.

Roman Missal 1974: The Roman Missal Revised by Decree of the Second Vatican Council and Published by Authority of Pope Paul VI. Official English Text, Dublin 1974.

Røkkum, Arne K. 1975: Possession and Structural Harmony, Shamanism in Two Japanese Island Communities. Unpublished dissertation, Bergen University 1975.

Saeki, Ariyoshi 1937: Shinto daijiten. (Shinto Encyclopedia.) Tokyo 1937.

Saji, Ryozo 1959: Shu to shite noson dendo to no kanren kara. (From the Point of View of Rural Evangelism.) In: Hiyane et al.: Kirisutokyoshiki sogi to sono ikyo jiban, Tokyo 1959, pp. 92–96.

Sano, Chiye 1958: Changing Values of the Japanese Family, Washington 1958.

Sansom, George B. 1951: The Western World and Japan, New York 1951.

Schelkle, Karl Hermann 1964: Die Petrusbriefe. Der Judasbrief, Freiburg 1964.

Schierse, Franz Joseph 1975: Altchristliche Gebete, Düsseldorf 1975.

Schlier, Heinrich 1957/1968[6]: Der Brief an die Epheser, Düsseldorf 1957/1968[6].

Schlier, Heinrich 1958: Mächte und Gewalten im NT, Freiburg 1958.

Schlink, Edmund 1970: Die Lehre von der Taufe. In: Leiturgia, Vol. V, Kassel 1970, pp. 641–808.

Schmid, H. 1962A: Tod und Totenreich im AT. In: RGG, Vol. VI, Tübingen 1962, pp. 912–913.

Schmid, H. 1962B: Totenverehrung im AT. In: RGG, Vol. VI, Tübingen 1962, pp. 961–962.

Schmid, Josef 1955/1960[4]: Das Evangelium nach Lukas, Regensburg 1955/1960[4].

Schmidt-Clausing, F. 1958: Fegfeuer. In: RGG, Vol. II, Tübingen 1958, pp. 892–894.

Schnackenburg, Rudolf 1950: Das Heilsgeschehen bei der Taufe nach dem Apostel Paulus, München 1950.

Schnackenburg, Rudolf 1964: Baptism in the Thought of St. Paul, Oxford 1964.

Schneider, Johannes 1961: Die Kirchenbriefe, Göttingen 1961.

Schreiner, Lothar 1972: Adat und Evangelium. Zur Bedeutung der Alt-Völkerischen Lebensordnungen für Kirche und Mission unter den Batak in Nord-Sumatra, Gütersloh 1972.

Schwally, Fr. 1892: Das Leben nach dem Tode nach der Vorstellungen des Alten Israel und des Judentums, Giessen 1892.

Seeberg, R. 1910: Lehrbuch der Dogmengeschichte. Bd. II, Leipzig 1910.

Seeberg, R. 1913: Lehrbuch der Dogmengeschichte. Bd. III, Leipzig 1913.

Seierstad, Ivar P. 1971: Enkeltmannen og ansvarsgruppen i 2. Mos. 20,5b. In: Seierstad: Budskapet, Oslo 1971, pp. 23–40.

Selwyn, E.G. 1946: The First Epistle of St. Peter, London 1946.

Service Book and Hymnal 1958/1961[5]: Service Book and Hymnal Authorized by the Lutheran Churches Cooperating in the Commission on the Liturgy and Hymnal, Minneapolis 1958/1961[5].

Shibata, Chizuo 1978: Nippon bunka no ichi keitai to shite no sosen suhai to Kirisutokyo. (Christianity and Japanese Ancestor Worship – Considered as a Basic Cultural Form.) In: Shingaku Zasshi, Vol. 11, 1978, pp. 45–57.

Shimpo, Mitsuru 1968: Impact, Congruence and New Equilibrium: A Case-Study of Annaka Church, Gumma Prefecture. In: Morioka/Newell: The Sociology of Japanese Religion, 1968, pp. 54–72.

Shinto hikkei 1976: Shinto hikkei. (Handbook for Believers.) United Church of Christ, Tokyo 1976.

Shinto no tomo: Vol. 11, Tokyo 1971. Vol. 11, Tokyo 1975.

Skrypczak, Edmund 1968: Japan's Modern Century, Tokyo 1968.

Smith, Robert J. 1974: Ancestor Worship in Contemporary Japan, Stanford 1974.

Smith, R.J./Beardsley, R.K. 1962/1963: Japanese Culture: Its Development and Characteristics, Chicago 1962/London 1963.

Sogi no shiori 1971/1974: Sogi no shiori. (A Funeral Guide.) The Roman Catholic Church in Japan, Tokyo 1971/1974.

Spae, Joseph J. 1965: Christian Corridors to Japan, Tokyo 1965.

Stauffer, Ethelbert 1965/1974[5]: – The Personal Being of God. – The Transcendence of God. In: Theological Dictionary of the New Testament. Vol. III. Michigan 1965/1974[5]. pp. 109–119.

Stauffer, Milton 1928: Japan Speaks for herself, London 1928.

Steiner, Kurt 1950: Revisions of the Civil Code of Japan: Provisions Affecting the Family. In: Far Eastern Quarterly, Vol. 9, No. 2, 1950, pp. 169–184.

Stoetzel, Jean 1955: Without the Chrysanthemum and the Sword. A Study of the Attitude of Youth in Post-War Japan, New York 1955.

Sumiya, Mikio 1954: Nippon shakai to Kirisutokyo (Japanese Society and Christianity.)Tokyo 1954.

Sundkler, Bengt 1960: The Christian Ministry in Africa, Uppsala 1960.

Suzuki, Daisetz 1948/1973: The Essence of Buddhism, Kyoto 1948/1973.

Suzuki, Masahisa 1959: Iesu no jidai no hakasuhai to kyokaishi ni okeru soshiki no mondai. (Grave-worship at the Time of Jesus and the Funeral-problem in Church-history.) In: Hiyane et al.: Kirisutokyos-hiki sogi to sono ikyo jiban, Tokyo 1959, pp. 113–134.

Suzuki, Norihisa 1974: Nihon no Katorikku mura. (Catholic Villages in Japan.) Privately published 1974.

Swyngedouw, Jan 1967: The Catholic Church and Shrine Shinto. In: Japan Missionary Bulletin, Vol. XXI, No. 10, pp. 579–584, No. 11, pp. 659–664, 1967.

Swyngedouw, Jan 1976: Secularization in a Japanese Context. In: Japanese Journal of Religious Studies, Vol. 3, No. 4, 1976, pp. 283–306.

Swyngedouw, Jan 1979: Reflections on the Secularization Thesis in the Sociology of Religion in Japan. In: Japanese Journal of Religious Studies, Vol. 6, No. 1–2, 1979, pp. 65–88.

Suzuki, N./Spae, J. 1968: Nihonjin no mita Kirisutokyo. (A Japanese View of Christianity.) Tokyo 1968.

Tagita, Koya 1960: Some Aspects of Japanese-Christian Acculturation. In: Proceedings of the Ninth International Congress for History of Religion Tokyo 1958. Tokyo 1960, pp. 444–448.

Takahashi, Hiroko 1975: Kazoku keitai to senzo saishi. (Family Type and Ancestor Worship.) In: Kazoku kenkyu nenpo, No. 1, 1975, pp. 37–52.

Takakusu, Junjiro 1947: The Essentials of Buddhist Philosophy, Honolulu 1947.

Takasaki, Tsuyoshi 1959: Kirisutokyo sogi no motifu to katachi. (The Form and Motive of the Christian Funeral.) In: Hiyane et al.: Kirisuto-kyoshiki sogi to sono ikyo jiban, Tokyo 1959, pp. 71–79.

Takayanagi, Isaburo 1959: Shu to shite shinyaku no men kara. (From a New Testament Point of View.) In: Hiyane et al.: Kirisutokyoshiki sogi to sono ikyo jiban, Tokyo 1959, pp. 59–65.

Takatori, M./Hashimoto, M. 1968/1975: Shukyo izen. (Before Religion.) Tokyo 1968/1975.

Takeda, Choshu 1957/1975: Sosen suhai. Sono minzoku to rekishi. (Ancestor Worship: Its Folklore and History.) Kyoto 1957/1975.

Takeda, Choshu 1965: Ancestor Worhip III: Japan. In: Malalasekera: Encyclopedia of Buddhism, Colombo 1965, pp. 593–600.

Takeda, Choshu 1976: «Family Religion» in Japan: IE and its Religious Faith. In: Newell: Ancestors, The Hague 1976, pp. 119–128.

Tamai, Yoshiharu 1959: Tadashii yoshiki o motomeru. (In Search of a Right Form.) In: Hiyane et al.: Kirisutokyoshiki sogi to sono ikyo jiban, Tokyo 1959, pp. 103–107.

Tamamuro, Taijo 1971/1974: Soshiki Bukkyo. (Funeral Buddhism.) Tokyo 1971/1974.

Thelle, Notto R. 1979: Buddhist Views on Interfaith Dialogue. In: Japanese Religions, Vol. 10, No. 4, 1979, pp. 46–50.

Theodorou, Andreas 1959/1970[2]: Die Mystik in der Orthodoxen Ostkirche. In: Bratsiotis: Die Orthodoxe Kirche in Griechischer Sicht, Stuttgart 1959/1970[2], pp. 176–209.

Thom, Gideon A. 1973: A Reformed Perspective on African Belief in Ancestors. In: Missionalia, Vol. 1, No. 2, 1973, pp. 73–85.

Thomsen, Harry 1963: The New Religions of Japan, Tokyo 1963.

Trillhaas, Wolfgang 1970[3]: Ethik, Berlin 1970[3].

Troeltsch, Ernst 1905: Psychologie und Erkenntnistheorie in der Religionswissenschaft, Tübingen 1905.

Troeltsch, Ernst 1925: Glaubenslehre, München/Leipzig 1925.

Tsuboi, Hirobumi 1970: Nipponjin no seishikan. (The Japanese View of Life and Death.) In: Minzokugaku kara mita Nippon, Tokyo 1970, pp. 7–34.

Tsurumi, Kazuko 1970: Social Change and the Individual, Princeton 1970.

United Church of Christ 1963: Fukuin wa dochaku dekiru ka. (Can the Gospel be Indigenized?) Tokyo 1963.

United Church of Christ 1974: Shi to sogi. (Death and Funeral.) Tokyo 1974.

Valen-Sendstad, Aksel 1970: Panteismen og vår virkelighetsforståelse. In: Kirke og Kultur, Vol. 75. 1970, pp. 477–484.

Valen-Sendstad, Aksel 1973: Filosofi til kristentroen, Stavanger 1973.

Valen-Sendstad, Aksel 1979: Kristen dogmatikk, Oslo 1979.

Vicedom, Georg F. 1958: Missio Dei, München 1958.

Vogel, Ezra F. 1963: Japan's New Middle Class: The Salary Man and his Family in a Tokyo Suburb, Berkeley 1963.

Vogel, Ezra F. 1967: Kinship Structure, Migration to the City, and Modernization. In: Dore: Aspects of Social Change in Modern Japan, Princeton, New Jersey, 1967, pp. 91–111.

Voss, Gustav 1943: Missionary Accomodation and Ancestral Rites in the Far East. In: Theological Studies, Vol. 43, 1943, pp. 525–560.

Vriezen, Th. C. 1956: Theologie des Alten Testaments in Grundzügen, Wageningen 1956.

Wächter, Ludwig 1967: Der Tod im Alten Testament, Stuttgart 1967.

Wagatsuma, Sakae 1950: Democratization of the Family Relations in Japan. In: Washington Law Review, Vol. XXV, 1950, pp. 405–426.

Watanabe, Shoko 1959/1975: Shigo no sekai (The World of Afterlife.) Tokyo 1959/1975.

Watanabe, Shoko 1964: Japanese Buddhism. A Critical Appraisal, Tokyo 1964.

Wimberley, Howard 1969: Self-realization and the Ancestors: An Analysis of Two Japanese Ritual Procedures for Achieving Domestic Harmony. In: Anthropological Quarterly, Vol. 42, No. 1, 1969, pp. 37–51.

Wimberley, Howard 1972: The Knights of the Golden Lothus. In: Ethnology, Vol. 11, No. 2, 1972, pp. 173–186.

Windisch, Hans 1930: Die Katholischen Briefe, Tübingen 1930.

Wolff, Hans Walter 1973: Anthropolgie des Alten Testaments, München 1973.

Yamamoto, Naotada 1974: Kyo no Nihon ni okeru sogi no shomondai. (Problems concerning Funerals in Contemporary Japan.) In: United Church of Christ: Shi to sogi, Tokyo 1974, pp. 253–272.

Yamauchi, Rokuro 1973: Kirisutokyo kankon sosai nyumon. (Introduction to the Christian Ceremonial Occasions.) Tokyo 1973.

Yanagida, Kunio 1970: About our Ancestors, Tokyo 1970. (This book is a translation of Senzo no hanashi, Tokyo 1946.)

Yonemura, Shoji 1976: Dozoku and Ancestor Worship in Japan. In: Newell: Ancestors, The Hague 1976, pp. 177–203.

Yuki, Yasushi 1959: Kirisutokyoshiki sogi no kaizen ni tsuite. (On the Improvement of the Christian Funeral.) In: Hiyane et al.: Kirisutokyoshiki sogi to sono ikyo jiban, Tokyo 1959, pp. 80–86.

Zenner, Walter P. 1965: Memorialism – Some Jewish Examples. In: American Anthropologist, Vol. 67, 1965, pp. 481–483.

Zimmer, W. 1949: Totenehrung und Totenverehrung in der Christlichen Gemeinde. In: Evangelisches Missionsmagazin, Vol. 93, 1949, pp. 148–151.

INDEX OF AUTHORS AND PERSONAL NAMES